AF684281

The Econometrics of Energy Systems

The Econometrics of Energy Systems

Edited by

Jan Horst Keppler
Régis Bourbonnais
and
Jacques Girod

With an Introduction by

Jean-Marie Chevalier

palgrave
macmillan

Selection and editorial matter © Régis Bourbonnais, Jacques Girod and Jan Horst Keppler 2007
Introduction © Jean-Marie Chevalier 2007
Individual chapters © contributors 2007

All rights reserved. No reproduction, copy or transmission of this publication may be made without written permission.

No paragraph of this publication may be reproduced, copied or transmitted save with written permission or in accordance with the provisions of the Copyright, Designs and Patents Act 1988, or under the terms of any licence permitting limited copying issued by the Copyright Licensing Agency, 90 Tottenham Court Road, London W1T 4LP.

Any person who does any unauthorized act in relation to this publication may be liable to criminal prosecution and civil claims for damages.

The authors have asserted their rights to be identified as the authors of this work in accordance with the Copyright, Designs and Patents Act 1988.

First published 2007 by
PALGRAVE MACMILLAN
Houndmills, Basingstoke, Hampshire RG21 6XS and
175 Fifth Avenue, New York, N.Y. 10010
Companies and representatives throughout the world.

PALGRAVE MACMILLAN is the global academic imprint of the Palgrave Macmillan division of St. Martin's Press, LLC and of Palgrave Macmillan Ltd. Macmillan® is a registered trademark in the United States, United Kingdom and other countries. Palgrave is a registered trademark in the European Union and other countries.

ISBN-13: 978–1–4039–8748–8
ISBN-10: 1–4039–8748–3

This book is printed on paper suitable for recycling and made from fully managed and sustained forest sources.

A catalogue record for this book is available from the British Library.

Library of Congress Cataloging-in-Publication Data
The econometrics of energy systems / edited by Jan Horst Keppler, Régis Bourbonnais and Jacques Girod.
p. cm.
Includes bibliographical references and index.
ISBN 1–4039–8748–3
1. Energy industries. 2. Energy policy. 3. Econometrics. I. Keppler, Jan Horst, 1961 – II. Bourbonnais, Régis. III. Girod, Jacques.
HD9502.A2E248 2007
333.7901′5195—dc22 2006048296

10 9 8 7 6 5 4 3 2 1
16 15 14 13 12 11 10 09 08 07

Transferred to Digital Printing 2009

Contents

List of Tables vii

List of Figures ix

Notes on the Contributors xi

Introduction: Energy Economics and Energy Econometrics xiii
Jean-Marie Chevalier

1 Energy Quantity and Price Data: Collection, Processing and Methods of Analysis 1
Nathalie Desbrosses and Jacques Girod

2 Dynamic Demand Analysis and the Process of Adjustment 27
Jacques Girod

3 Electricity Spot Price Modelling: Univariate Time Series Approach 51
Régis Bourbonnais and Sophie Méritet

4 Causality and Cointegration between Energy Consumption and Economic Growth in Developing Countries 75
Jan Horst Keppler

5 Economic Development and Energy Intensity: A Panel Data Analysis 98
Ghislaine Destais, Julien Fouquau and Christophe Hurlin

6 The Causality Link between Energy Prices, Technology and Energy Intensity 121
Marie Bessec and Sophie Méritet

7 Energy Substitution Modelling 146
Patricia Renou-Maissant

8 Delineation of Energy Markets with Cointegration Techniques 168
Régis Bourbonnais and Patrice Geoffron

9 The Relationship between Spot and Forward Prices in Electricity Markets — 186
Carlo Pozzi

10 The Price of Oil over the Very Long Term — 207
Sophie Chardon

11 The Impact of Vertical Integration and Horizontal Diversification on the Value of Energy Firms — 225
Carlo Pozzi and Philippe Vassilopoulos

Index — 255

List of Tables

1.1	Industrial energy consumption in France: 1978–2004	11
1.2	Quantity and price indices	18
1.3	Decomposition of energy intensity changes	22
3.1	The different types of stochastic processes	57
3.2	Data sources	69
4.1	Key indicators for selected developing countries	76
4.2	Comparison of empirical results from causality tests for developing countries	82
4.3	Testing for non-stationarity	86
4.4	Testing for non-stationarity – first differences	87
4.5	Results of Granger causality tests	89
4.6	Unrestricted cointegration rank test	91
4.7	Estimating the error correction model	92
5.1	LM_f tests for remaining nonlinearity	111
5.2	Determination of the number of location parameters	112
5.3	Parameter estimates for the final PSTR models	112
5.4	Individual estimated income elasticities	113
5.5	Quadratic energy demand function, fixed effects model	118
6.1	Measured rebound effect on various devices	126
6.2	Part of road transport in the total consumption of oil products in 2002	128
6.3A	ADF unit root tests – oil intensity	130
6.3B	ADF unit root tests – oil price	131
6.3C	ADF unit root tests – fuel rate	131
6.4A	Unit root tests with a structural break in 1973 – oil intensity	132
6.4B	Unit root tests with a structural break in 1973 – oil price	133
6.4C	Unit root tests with a structural break in 1973 – fuel rate	134
6.5	Cointegration tests based on the Johansen ML procedure	135
6.6	Results of the causality tests	138
7.1	Market shares of fuels in France and the United Kingdom	152
7.2	Long-run mean price elasticities for a four-fuels model for the period 1978–2002	159
7.3	Long run mean price elasticities for a three-fuels model for the period 1978–2002	160
7.4	Long-run mean price elasticities for a four-fuels model for the period 1960–88	161
8.1	Dickey–Fuller and Phillips–Perron unit root tests (model with constant)	177

8.2	Synthesis of Johansen–Juselius cointegration test results	178
8.3	Synthesis of the Johansen–Juselius cointegration tests (period 1991–8)	179
8.4	Synthesis of Johansen–Juselius cointegration tests (period 1999–2005)	180
8.5	Number of VAR lags	180
8.6	Estimation of the France–Germany VECM (1992–2005)	181
9.1	OLS statistics for single business day estimations	197
9.2	ARMA estimation statistics	198
9.3	GMM estimation statistics	200
9.4	EGARCH estimation statistics	202
9.5	Residual distribution statistics	203
10.1	Quadratic trend estimated on the sample (1865; 2004)	209
10.2	Results of unit root tests	213
10.3	Perron test's equation	215
10.4	Critical values of the asymptotic distribution of t_α when $\lambda = 0.4 - 0.6$ according to Perron's simulations	216
10.5	OLS initialization of the Kalman filter	222
10.6	Kalman filter estimation	222
11.1	Basic portfolios	229
11.2	Basic and integrated portfolios	230
11.3	Equation (11.1): OLS statistics, full dataset – basic and integrated portfolios	237
11.4	Equation (11.1): OLS statistics, entire dataset – aggregated portfolios	243
11.5	Equation (11.2): OLS statistics, entire dataset – aggregated portfolios	245
11.6	Rolling regressions: estimation statistics, equation (11.2)	246

List of Figures

1.1	Comparison between the Törnqvist aggregate index and the toe-aggregate index	12
1.2	Decomposition of energy intensity changes	23
2.1	Industrial energy consumption, average price and value added/GDP: France 1978–2002	40
3.1	Simplified strategy for unit root tests	61
3.2	Evolution of the spot price of electricity expressed in logarithms (LPRIX)	62
5.1	Commercial energy intensity in selected countries	99
5.2	Transition Function with $m = 1$ and $c = 0$ (analysis of sensitivity to the slope Parameter)	107
5.3	Individual PSTR and FEM income elasticities (1950–99)	117
7.1	Energy cost shares in French and British industrial sectors in per cent	153
8.1	Gas network and interconnection map of Europe	173
8.2	Biannual evolution of the price of gas for industrial use	176
9.1	Adjusted basis vs. residual load	196
9.2	Adjusted basis vs. ARMA modelled residual load	198
9.3	Adjusted basis vs. EGARCH modelled residual load	202
10.1	Log price of crude oil in 2005 dollars (1865–2004)	210
10.2	Log oil price forecasts	223
11.1	Portfolio positioning and value in the mean-return/market beta space	236
11.2	Vertically integrated vs. non-integrated oil portfolios: risk-adjusted returns	238
11.3	Vertically integrated vs. non-integrated natural gas portfolios: risk-adjusted returns	239
11.4	Vertically integrated vs. non-integrated power portfolios: portfolio values and risk-adjusted returns I	240
11.5	Vertically integrated vs. non-integrated power portfolios: portfolio values and risk-adjusted returns II	240
11.6	Horizontal diversification between oil and natural gas: absolute and risk-adjusted returns I	242
11.7	Horizontal diversification between oil and natural gas: absolute and risk-adjusted returns II	242
11.8	Horizontal diversification between natural gas and power: portfolio values and risk-adjusted returns I	243

11.9 Horizontal diversification between natural gas and power: portfolio values and risk-adjusted returns II 243
11.10 Horizontal diversification: all fuels, aggregated portfolios 244
11.11 Horizontal diversification: mean rolling regressions results 247
11.12 Market risk dynamics 248
11.13 Cumulated excess returns 249

Notes on the Contributors

Marie Bessec is Assistant Professor in Economics and member of the EURIsCO research centre at Dauphine University in Paris. She has published several articles on econometric modelling in macroeconomics.

Régis Bourbonnais is Assistant Professor at Dauphine University and specializes in econometrics. He is the author of several books on econometrics and sales forecasting (*Prévisions des ventes* with J. C. Usinier, 2001, *Econométrie*, 2003, *Analyses des séries temporelles en Economie*, 2004). He also is the co-director of the Master in Logistics at Dauphine University.

Sophie Chardon works at Natexis Banques Populaires, the financing and investment bank of the Banque Populaire Group, where she specializes in fixed income quantitative analysis. She holds an advanced degree in energy and environment economics from Toulouse University and a MSc in Statistics and Economics from ENSAE, the French 'Grande Ecole' for Statistics and Economic Administration.

Jean-Marie Chevalier is Professor of Economics at Dauphine University in Paris and Director of the Centre de Géopolitique de l'Energie et des Matières Premières (CGEMP). He is also a senior associate with the Cambridge Energy Research Associates (CERA). He has published a number of books and articles on industrial organization and energy. His latest book is *Les grandes batailles de l'énergie*.

Nathalie Desbrosses works at ENERDATA, an independent company specializing in the energy and environment sectors, where she specializes in energy demand forecasting. She holds an advanced degree in energy economics and modelling from the Institut Français du Pétrole.

Ghislaine Destais is Assistant Professor in Economics at Pierre Mendès France University in Grenoble and a member of the Energy and Environment Policy Department(LEPII-EPE). Her principal area of expertise is energy and economic modelling. She is also an engineer of the Ecole Centrale de Lille and the author of a software package which measures the profitability of firms in relation to their global productivity.

Julien Fouquau is a PhD student in Economics at the University of Orléans. His work deals with Panel Threshold Regression models. The aim of his dissertation is to apply this methodology to various economic problems, with a special FOCUS on threshold effects in data dynamics.

Patrice Geoffron is Professor of Economics at Dauphine University in Paris and vice-president for International Relations. He is senior researcher at the

Centre de Géopolitique de l'Energie et des Matières Premières (CGEMP). His main area of research is the industrial organization of network industries.

Jacques Girod is Director of Research (CNRS) at the Energy and Environmental Policy Group, LEPII Laboratory Grenoble, France. His areas of research are energy in developing countries and energy planning and modelling. He is also the author of several books on these topics.

Christophe Hurlin is Professor of Economics at the University of Orleans. He teaches econometrics in the Master of Econometrics and Applied Statistics of the University of Orleans and at Dauphine University, Paris. His principal areas of research are econometrics of panel data models and time series models.

Jan Horst Keppler is Professor of Economics at Dauphine University in Paris and Senior Researcher at the Centre de Géopolitique de l'Energie et des Matières Premières (CGEMP). He held previous appointments with the International Energy Agency (IEA) and the Organisation for Economic Co-operation and Development (OECD). His main areas of research are electricity markets and energy and development.

Sophie Méritet is Assistant Professor in Economics at Dauphine University and is a member of the Centre de Géopolitique de l'Energie et des Matières Premières (CGEMP). After completing her PhD in Economics at Dauphine University, she worked for two years in Houston, Texas, in the energy industry. She published several articles on the deregulation process in the electricity and natural gas industries in the US, Europe and Brazil.

Carlo Pozzi is Associate Researcher with the Centre de Géopolitique de l'Energie et des Matières Premières (CGEMP) at Dauphine University Paris and a Lecturer at the Department of Finance of ESSEC Graduate School of Business in Paris. A graduate of Bocconi University, he holds a doctorate and a master in International Relations with a specialization in International Finance from the Fletcher School at Tufts University.

Patricia Renou-Maissant is Associate Professor at the University of Caen and member of the Centre for Research in Economics and Management (CREM). Her research deals with applied econometrics in the fields of energy and money demands. Published works concern interfuel and monetary assets substitution modelling and analysis of convergence of money demands in Europe.

Philippe Vassilopoulos is a PhD student in Economics at the Centre de Géopolitique de l'Energie et des Matières Premières (CGEMP) of Dauphine University and cooperates closely with the French Energy Regulatory Commission (CRE). His research focuses on price signals and incentives for investments in electricity markets.

Introduction: Energy Economics and Energy Econometrics

Jean-Marie Chevalier

Energy is today, more than ever, at the core of the world economy and its evolution. One of the major challenges of the century is to generate more energy, to facilitate access to energy and economic development of the poor, but also to manage climate change properly in a perspective of sustainable development. The growing importance of energy matters in the daily functioning of the world economy reinforces the need for a stronger relationship between energy economics and econometrics. Econometrics is expected to improve the understanding of the numerous, interconnected, energy markets and to provide quantitative arguments that facilitate the decision-making process for energy companies, energy consumers, governments, regulators and international organizations. Econometrics is a tool for meeting the energy and environmental challenges of the twenty-first century.

The academic field of energy economics has been completely transformed in the last twenty years. Market liberalization and globalization have accelerated for the oil industry, but also, more dramatically, for the natural gas and power industries. New economic issues that emerge in energy economics are combining macro-economics, investment decisions, economy policy, but also industrial organization and the economics of regulation. In addition, the approach to energy economics has to be multi-energy because the growing complexity of markets open new opportunities for inter-fuel substitution and fuel arbitrages. Another factor is rapidly emerging: the concern for protecting the environment by reducing greenhouse gas emissions. All these changes have to be explained and analysed, with the econometric instruments that have been developed recently. Historically, the energy sector has always had very good data infrastructure – even if these data are sometimes in dire need of interpretation. This data base and the growing complexity of energy markets allow the extensive use of econometric techniques.

The development of econometric methods has accelerated considerably in the last twenty years, in parallel with the development of the new technologies of information and communication. Research work on non-stationary time series, unit root testing and co-integration opened the door for a renewed analysis of time series. Autoregressive conditional heteroskedasticity offers new modelling opportunities for analysing volatility. Nobel Prize winners Daniel McFadden and James Heckman (2000), Robert Engle and Clive Granger (2003) symbolize this recent development and the importance of econometrics in modern economic analysis. For energy economists, facing an increasing number of data, the use of sophisticated econometric tools is becoming essential and can be easily achieved by simple web browsing. Through the net, they can access data and initiate the implementation of advanced econometric software algorithms, rapidly producing graphics and other results.

All these arguments show that energy economics and econometrics are interlocked. A new research programme has to be launched. However, there is no single manual on the use of econometric techniques in the energy sector currently available. The work currently done on energy econometrics is widely dispersed in specialized journals and company research departments that often have limited circulation. This book, written and edited jointly by energy economists and econometricians, offers to the practitioner an introduction to the state of the art in econometric techniques, while showing some of the most pertinent applications to the daily issues arising in energy markets. Not all energy issues that call for econometric analysis are covered in this book. The field is virtually unlimited. A great number of other applications could be surveyed but the book should, nevertheless, provide a referential framework.

Using econometric methods in the field of energy economics implies having a global vision of the world energy sector at the beginning of the twenty-first century. The purpose of this introduction is, therefore, to avoid the 'pure' economic and econometric approach without losing track of energy realities and associated challenges.

Our global energy consumption comes from oil (37 per cent) coal (23 per cent) and natural gas (21 per cent). This means that more than 80 per cent of final energy consumption is produced through fossil resources that are, by nature, exhaustible. However, one should keep in mind that energy consumption is not a target *per se*. Energy production and transformation are directly related to human needs for: heating, cooling, lighting, transportation, power and high temperature heat for industrial processes, specific needs for electricity for running computers and all the other electrical appliances and devices. A large part of the world population is consuming energy to meet these needs, although more than 1.5 billion people still do not have access to modern energy sources (petroleum products and electricity) and therefore to economic development. Energy consumption must be seen in its relation to economic growth and economic development (Chapter 4).

In less than a century, commercial energy has become the engine of economic activity and, in our energy final consumption, electricity is now considered as an essential product. Every blackout demonstrates how the extent to which affluent societies are dependant on electricity. The energy industry is a large field for empirical research in applied economics. Energy data invite econometric testing and research. The evolution of the price of oil is one of the most popular time series and has been investigated thousands of times. It raises Hotelling's old question of pricing exhaustible resources.

Even if this book does not cover the whole field of energy economics, it is nevertheless useful to have a general introduction which raises key questions investigated today by energy economists. These questions concern: i) industrial organization; ii) markets and prices; iii) the relationship between energy and economic activity; iv) corporate strategies; v) regulation and public policy.

The ongoing revolution in the organization of the world energy industry: toward competitive markets

The original question of industrial organization stems from Alfred Marshall's pioneering work and the birth of antitrust economics in the United States. The question, for a given industry, is to know what the best type of organization for ensuring efficiency is. Competition is the answer given for many industries, the oil industry in particular, even if reality doesn't correspond to theory. Regulated monopoly is the answer given for industries in which there are elements of natural monopoly.

In the energy industry, a number of different industrial dynamics can be identified. The oil industry provides a cyclical example where competition alternates with monopoly. Rockefeller established the first oil monopoly in the US market at the end of the nineteenth century. At that time a few international oil companies competed for access to oil resources. In 1928 the Seven Sisters decided to stabilize the market by establishing the International Oil Cartel. After World War II, a number of European state-owned companies tried to break Major's dominance, bringing in new competition. Then, at the first oil shock in 1973, OPEC took the lead in establishing oil prices. Today, OPEC still has market power, especially to oppose lowering prices.

For natural gas and electricity, the situation is very different, since certain segments of these industries are considered natural monopolies, which means that competition doesn't work. A wind of market liberalization began to blow in the gas and power industries in the early 1980s, bringing an incredible number of radical changes to two industries which had been static for decades in terms of industrial organization. The changes that are occurring in the power industry illustrate an organizational revolution that no other industry has experienced in the past. The old model was vertically integrated, monopolistic, often state owned, with no competition and no risk. In the new model, value chains are deconstructed, competition is introduced almost everywhere with new forms of market mechanisms, private investors, overwhelming risks. The simple and comfortable world of monopoly, managed through long-term planning, was purring with satisfaction. The new competitive players are harassed by risks, complexity and the uncertainties of the future.

The key idea of the new model of organization is to break up vertical integration and to introduce competition wherever it is possible. Competitive pressures are expected to bring innovation, lower costs and efficiency. Vertically integrated structures are called into question through the implementation of three basic principles: unbundling, third party access, and regulation. In Europe, these principles are the key elements of the European directives for gas and power markets.

Unbundling

The concept of unbundling is directly derived from the theory of contestable markets. In order to introduce more competition in vertically integrated organizations, it was considered highly desirable to identify clearly each segment of the integrated value chain in order to make a clear separation between the competitive segments, on the one hand, and the regulated segments on the other hand. Regulated segments are those in which natural monopoly is justified and, therefore, must be regulated in order to avoid the negative effects of monopoly. Competitive segments are those where competition can work. When decentralized decision-making is possible for competitive markets, the role of econometrics becomes important.

In the case of electricity, the primary energy fuels (coal, fuel oil, natural gas, nuclear fuels) are sold in markets. Electricity produced through various generating units can be sold in markets, but power transmission represents a natural monopoly that has to be separated and regulated. The final delivery to customers can be organized on a competitive basis. Behind the idea of breaking up the total value chain into its component parts was the object of replacing a cost internal approach by a market price approach for some segments of the chain: a market for fuel inputs, a market for kilowatt-hours, a regulated tariff for transmission, a wholesale market for large users and traders and a retail market for small end-users.

Third party access and the recognition of essential facilities

Third party access was the second building block in the liberalization process of network industries. In the power and natural gas industries, some segments of activity cannot be open to competition. They remain as natural monopolies and they have to be considered as essential facilities, meaning that they have to be open to any qualified person, provided that he pays a fee which reflects the cost of the service plus a fair rate of return on the invested capital. To avoid the payment of monopoly rents, discrimination and cross subsidies, the level of the fee has to be controlled by an independent authority.

Regulation

Regulation is the last piece of the institutional framework which is required by the directives. The word 'regulation' stems from the old American distinction between regulated and non-regulated industries. Industries that need to be regulated are those in which there is a natural monopoly. In the United States such industries, considered as a whole (from upstream to downstream), were regulated through state and federal commissions. The theory of contestable markets resulted in the introduction of competition in certain segments of the industry, segments which were then 'deregulated'. Deregulation is by no means the withdrawal of regulation but, rather, its limitation to monopoly segments. In Europe the liberalization process implies the implementation of regulation. The setting up of regulatory authorities is something new for many European countries and most of them are committed to a learning process that implies dialogue, discussion, cooperation and harmonization among member states.

At the very beginning of the liberalization process, two major actions are expected from the regulatory agencies: (i) effective and efficient control over the conditions of access, including a proper unbundling and appropriate tariffs and (ii) the introduction of competition wherever possible, at a rhythm which is socially and politically acceptable. Social and political considerations tend to slow liberalization, so that it is not an event but a long process of evolution. It is generally slower than was initially expected, except in the case of the United Kingdom.

In parallel with the liberalization process, there has been a rapid consolidation of the energy industry. Through mergers and acquisitions, companies are searching for economies of scale, scope and synergies. New business models are emerging. Industrial organization enables a wide range of econometric tests and analyses that are not presented in this book but which could be further developed.

Markets and prices

The evolution of the world energy system in the last twenty years has been characterized by the development of a great number of markets that provide a broad set of time series to which the most recent econometric instruments need to be applied (Chapter 1). These applications are needed by energy companies, governments, national and international agencies, and, more and more, by the financial community, which plays an increasing role in the daily functioning of energy markets. The use of econometric tools is expected to provide ideas about the expected evolution of energy prices, but also to provide strategic tools in order to benefit from all of the arbitrage opportunities, not only for a given form of energy but also among a range of energy sources that can be seen as substitutable or competitive. The main categories of markets are oil, natural gas, coal and electricity, with their physical and financial components, but the picture is complicated by the actual structure of the industry. A refinery, for example, can be seen as a 'fuel arbitrager' where the fuels concerned are crude oil (with various characteristics of crude) and petroleum products, but also, possibly, natural gas, the electricity bought or sold by the refineries and heat that can also be produced and sold. The operation of the plant is based upon permanent arbitrages among various fuels. Econometric techniques are useful for taking account of prices and markets.

Most of the energy markets that have emerged in the last twenty years have followed a sequential evolution that can be summarized as follows. First, there is the appearance of spot pricing. Then, by nature, volatility develops with all of its associated risks. Then, financial instruments and derivatives are developed in order to mitigate risks. The process is significantly different for storable goods (oil products, natural gas) and non-storable goods such as electricity. Clearly, the whole process contains an enormous number of arbitrage opportunities, not only within each fuel but also among fuels.

Oil markets were the first to develop sophistication with a volume of financial transactions that now represents more than four times the physical transactions. There is extensive diversity in crude oils, from a heavy, high sulfur content crude (such as Dubai) to a very light low sulfur content crude (such as Algerian or Libyan). Price differentials depend on the quantitative and qualitative balance between crude oil production, the demand for petroleum products, the level of inventories and the availability of shipping facilities. Transactions are spot sales and OTC sales through formulas that are market related. Data on oil prices make possible a huge variety of econometric applications. Oil prices can be analyzed in a very long-term perspective with a long memory process and the integration of shock analyses (Chapter 10). The analysis of oil price evolution in the long term can be extremely sophisticated if one takes into account the amount of recoverable oil reserves. This is a highly controversial question which raises a number of important issues: accuracy of reserves data, strategies of the players (companies, oil rich countries), influence of prices and technology, investments in exploration and development (drilling activity), threats to oil demand due to climate change concerns. Associated with all these elements, there is the question of the peak in oil production. When will the decline in oil production or in oil demand begin?

Natural gas markets are very similar in nature but, for the time being, they still reflect their historical regional development. The United States has a regional competitive gas market which is strongly influenced by spot pricing at several gas hubs, the most important being Henry Hub. In this market, the correlation between gas prices and the prices of oil products may be disrupted by unexpected events such hurricanes Katrina and Rita in 2005. In Europe the British market has been entirely liberalized with a spot-pricing mechanism at Bacton. In continental Europe the situation is much more complex. The price of spot sales, which represents a small share of gas supply, is influenced by British spot prices, while most of the gas used is still affected by long-term contractual conditions between the European gas utilities and their major suppliers, such as the Russian and Algerian state-owned monopolies Gazprom and Sonatrach. In these long-term 'Take or Pay' contracts, the price of gas is closely related to the price of petroleum products, through specific formulas of indexation, which are supposed to reflect the competitiveness of natural gas at the burner tip (that is, at the end-user's location). Contractual pricing is also dominant in Asia's gas markets where Japan, South Korea and Taiwan import large volumes of liquefied natural gas (LNG) from the Middle East and Southern Asia. The current transformation of the world gas markets is today strongly influenced by the growing need for imported gas in the United States. The development of the LNG business strengthens the interconnections between the three large regional markets and opens a range of new opportunities for arbitrages between markets.

Since the early 1990s, markets for electricity have been developed in many countries in order to liberalize their power sector. Electricity is a non-storable product and the physical laws governing power transmission prevent the identification of the path followed by electrons. The first question raised in the implementation of power markets is the question of 'market design', a question that underlines the very specific nature of electricity. Power markets are certainly the most complex and sophisticated markets from the point of view of applied economics and economic theory. The first question is the question of price volatility, which is closely related to the non-storability of electricity. Observed volatility is much higher for electricity than for any other product. Electricity price spikes raise issues that are highly political since electricity has become an essential product in our industrial societies. A number of recent crises and blackouts show that the changing structure of the power industry, from a vertically integrated monopoly – with no market – to competition and multiple markets, is not easy to monitor (Chapter 3). In these markets, one serious question concerns the exercise of market power, its identification and measurement, and the need for econometric tests.

The relationship between spot prices and forward prices is at the core of power market problematic efficiency (Chapter 9) and there are also interesting cross-sectional comparisons between regional markets. Power markets also offer a number of opportunities for modeling and forecasting electricity prices in wholesale markets (Chapter 3). Coal markets used to be more simple competitive markets, escaping the sophistication of other energy markets. However, since the establishment of power markets and the surge of oil prices in 2004 and 2005, coal markets seem to be joining the dance by offering new opportunities for arbitrages, especially because power generators sometimes have the possibility of shifting between coal, oil products and natural gas, or of drawing more on hydro capacity. The spikes in gas prices have reinforced coal competitiveness in power generation. The consolidation of the world coal industry for exports brings a new element into coal price determination.

A new market that is emerging in parallel with energy commodities markets is the CO_2 market. The European Emission Trading Scheme (ETS) was implemented in January 2005 in Europe and a market for CO_2 has emerged with average 2005 prices well above what was expected by energy experts. The development of CO_2 trading opens new opportunities for arbitrages, econometric tests and correlation studies. The relationship between the price of CO_2 and the price of electricity in wholesale markets is a complex story which might reveal some sort of cyclical reversibility in causality between the two prices. Behind CO_2 trading is the crucial question of the competitiveness of the industry since CO_2 prices tend to be passed on, at least partly, through electricity prices.

The multiplication of physical and financial energy markets, some of them global, some of them regional or local, is leading to a radical transformation in the field of energy economics. Time series and cross-sections, volatility, price spikes, risks and risk-mitigation instruments, enlarge the possibilities for econometric analysis in order to provide a better comprehension of the industry's dynamics. However, economic theory is seriously put into question. Market imperfections and market failures could again reinforce political interference in the energy business.

Energy, energy intensity and economic growth

Since the first oil shock, energy intensity and its evolution have been extensively studied through time series and cross-sections (Chapter 1). A number of important questions have been raised about the relationship between energy intensity and energy efficiency. With stronger current environmental constraints and higher prices, there has been a renewal of interest in the relationships between energy prices, energy intensity and energy efficiency, including the important influence of technological progress and the analysis of causality among the three elements, while not forgetting the rebound effect. Econometric tests facilitate a better understanding of causality (Chapter 6). Energy intensity also reflects the degree to which a given country depends on energy, which can either be imported or produced locally. It leads to the question of energy vulnerability, both in terms of physical supply and in terms of price shocks.

When the second oil shock occurred (1979–1980) countries were much more oil intensive than they are today. The very high price shock (more than $80 per barrel in 2005 dollars) strongly hurt economic growth. In 2005–06, most countries became much less oil intensive, but it appears to be much more difficult to identify the oil price impact on economic growth in industrialized countries. Apparently, the existing trends of economic growth in the United States, Europe and Japan were not broken or even slowed by high oil prices. Quantification difficulties call for further research and investigation, using the most modern techniques. There is still progress to be made in order to fully understand the impact of a large increase in oil prices on the economic growth in various countries or regions.

Another key question is the relationship between energy demand and economic growth. This problem is important for defining energy policy. Consider, for instance, that a government would like to introduce measures to control energy demand (say, an energy tax) in order to improve its environmental performance and to reduce its dependence on foreign imports. If energy consumption precedes or causes economic growth, such policies could hamper further economic development (Chapter 4).

Energy intensity, energy demand, price elasticity and economic growth are key entries for modeling energy systems and their evolution in the short, medium and long term. Macro-energy models are expected to give some insight into the energy future. Even if medium- and long-term forecasting has to be considered with caution, it may help in the understanding of possible energy futures. Some of these models also include an environmental dimension, with concerns for the volume of greenhouse gas emissions that are associated with evolution. These approaches are providing interesting information that can be included in energy policy recommendations. However, energy systems modeling is not part of this book, although some contributions lead in this direction.

The analysis of energy demand raises the very important question of inter-fuel substitution (Chapters 2 and 7). Inter-fuel substitutions are at the crossroads of micro-decisions and macro-decisions. Some energy end users are in a position which enables them to compare permanently the prices of competing fuels (for instance coal versus natural gas versus fuel oil) provided that they have the flexibility to switch from one fuel to another, either through technical flexibility or because they have a diversified portfolio of generating capacities. Energy switching capability has a cost, but it is a strategic instrument which helps to mitigate risks and future uncertainties. At the macro level, the level of prices (taxes included) is an important factor in influencing the choice of energy investments and it can bring structural change to the national energy fuel mix. The history of European energy can be seen as an on going competitive battle between coal, fuel oil, natural gas and nuclear, for the production of electricity as well as for heating and even transport. National governments may use taxes for monitoring the change and to build a better fuel mix between domestic production and energy imports.

Corporate strategies

The global energy industry is made up of various categories of firms. There are still vertically state-owned monopolies but the share of private corporations under competitive pressure is increasing. Corporate strategies have now to be developed in a new organizational environment which is full of risks and uncertainties. Many corporate decisions are founded upon a thorough risk analysis which tries to identify each category of risks – project risks, market risks, country risks – in order to find the most efficient instruments for risk mitigation. Corporate strategy provides an enormous field for research in applied economics but, in energy economics, a few elements are essential: corporate positioning on the energy value chains, mergers and acquisitions, choice of fuel mix.

With the liberalization of energy markets, energy value chains are deconstructed vertically and horizontally. The first strategic question for an energy company is to choose its positioning with respect to value chains: upstream versus downstream, regulated activities versus competitive activities, mono-energy choice versus multi-energy choice. Behind these choices, with the associated risks, there are various corporate models, ranging from an upstream oil and gas company to a multi-utility company selling households not only gas and electricity but also water, telecommunications, internet and other services. There is no optimal model and the successful corporate models of the future will depend on technological evolution and generalization of the new technologies of information and communication, as well as on a number of factors that need to be identified and appreciated. Any corporate model, in the energy business, also reflects a choice between physical assets (oil and gas fields, power plants, refineries, pipe lines) and skills (trading, arbitrage, commercial and financial expertise). The bankruptcy of Enron put an end to the Enron model but technological evolution may provide new opportunities for skill-based virtual companies of the future. Testing business models, with the influence of horizontal diversification and vertical integration, is an important step for building the strategies of the future (Chapter 11). All these elements tend to show that corporate choices in the energy business are now more difficult than they were in the good old days of comfortable local monopolies.

Globalization of the energy industry provides an invitation for industry concentration, mergers and acquisitions. Recent concentrations in the oil, gas and power industries tend to corroborate the idea that size has become a competitive advantage *per se*. Large size enables companies to act rapidly when new opportunities are offered on the market. Mergers and acquisitions in the energy industry raise the question of synergies, a question that has been extensively studied and which needs more research. Is it possible to evaluate *ex-ante* economies of scale, the economies of scope and other synergies that can be expected from a merger? Is it possible to measure *ex-post* the effect of a merger and its influence on financial markets? Mergers and acquisitions also provide some elements that could help to better understand barriers to entry and the dynamics of entry.

One of the most important decisions for a power company is the choice of fuel for new generating capacity to be installed. The cost per kilowatt-hour is made up of several components: capital cost (which represents the cost for building the plant), fuel cost and operating cost. The *ex-ante* economic feasibility of the plant depends on a great number of hypotheses: the actual capital expenditure, the duration of the construction, the expected life of the plant, the anticipated prices of fuels and of electricity to be sold. What is new today, compared with the past, is the extent of the uncertainties about the future because, when a company decides to build a power plant, the output (electricity) will have to compete with electricity produced by competing generators. The economic choice is therefore more difficult and companies may turn to portfolio theory and real option value in order to simplify their strategic choices.

Energy policy and regulation

Problems concerning energy policy and regulation are also much more complicated now than they were twenty years ago. In the 'good old days', energy policy was a matter of national sovereignty and, in many cases the energy policy of a country (France, United Kingdom, Italy) was decided at governmental level and executed by state controlled companies in the oil, gas and electricity sectors. Today, energy policy is still an important matter which is less centralized and less national. In Europe, the long process of market liberalization has produced a new European regulatory framework for the gas and power industries. Besides gas and power directives, some other European directives have indicated a number of non-binding targets for energy efficiency and the development of renewable energies. In addition, European countries have signed the Kyoto Protocol and set up in 2005 the first Emission Trading Scheme for CO_2. In this context, the role of national governments in defining their own energy policy is limited by the European framework but, within this framework, member states can use subsidiarity if they want to develop – or to refuse – nuclear energy, to accelerate the development of renewable energies beyond the common targets. Within this global vision, energy policy, at least in Europe, is focused on three elements: public choices, regulation and antitrust policy.

In the energy sector, public choices are related to the public goods that are used in the present energy systems but they are also related to a vision of the energy future. One of the first questions to consider is a precise definition of *public service, universal service* or public service obligations. If one takes the example of electricity, a recent French law has established a 'right to electricity' because electricity is now considered as an essential product. In addition, *service public de l'électricité* has been precisely defined by law, with its associated cost and financing. The *service public de l'électricité* covers some tariff principles but also the diversification of generating capacity with subsidies given for combined heat and power production (cogeneration) and for the development of renewable sources (mostly wind turbines). Public choices are also confronted with the externalities of the energy systems: local and global pollution, gas emissions and all the social costs associated with the production and consumption of energy. The idea of measuring externalities and internalizing their costs is gaining wider acceptance and now constitutes an important element of the energy and environmental challenges of the twenty-first century.

The economics of regulation constitutes, in many countries, a new issue which opens the door for a number of renewed analyses. Starting from the basic model of industrial organization (structure – behaviour – performance) the economics of regulation aims to set up *ex-ante* the conditions for good performance within monopolistic structures. More precisely, regulation of natural monopolies is expected to ensure that third party access is well organized, that tariffs are cost reflecting, that grids are appropriately developed, that technical progress and productivity improvements are assured. The efficiency of regulation is a research field *per se*, which needs to be explored, with all the benchmarking studies that can be undertaken in a region like Europe for identifying the best practices and also the causes of non-performing mechanisms. Regulation has a cost and key questions remain concerning the independence and accountability of the regulator and the financing of regulation.

Antitrust economics deals with the parts of the energy system that are supposed to be ruled by competition. Antitrust economics is basically focused on structure and behaviour with an *ex-post* evaluation of the degree of competition. Competition authorities do not expect a situation of pure and perfect competition but, at least, a situation of 'workable competition'. Competitive structures are related to industrial concentration, as measured by various indices, and the control of mergers and acquisitions. In Europe the whole process of concentration is supposed to be controlled at national levels and also at the European level. A number of tests have been – and have to be – established to reinforce the methodological basis of antitrust enforcement. The control of behaviour concerns all practices that are deemed to be uncompetitive: price manipulation, collusion, discrimination, market foreclosure.

The identification of market power and the abuse of dominant positions is essential to antitrust economics, especially in the energy industry, because of the extreme sophistication of power and gas markets and the great difficulty in identifying and prosecuting excessive market power. Another important question concerns vertical integration, not in terms of structure, but in relation to long-term contracts signed for oil, gas and electricity supply. Long-term contracts are frequently associated with market foreclosure but they can also be considered as a form of risk mitigation which reinforces security of energy supply.

Finally, energy economics has a growing international dimension which defines a strong linkage between energy consumption, economic development and the protection of the environment. The link between these three elements tells us that in some countries an increase in energy consumption is needed to enhance economic development, while the global environment has to be protected to ensure our long-run survival. Any research programme in energy economics has to include this perspective of sustainable development.

1

Energy Quantity and Price Data: Collection, Processing and Methods of Analysis

Nathalie Desbrosses and Jacques Girod

Energy data and summary accounts

This chapter is devoted to data on the quantity and price of energy, as well as the various methods used to analyse, aggregate or decompose these data. Collection and processing of the data, energy aggregates, quantity and price indices and decomposition of energy intensity are considered in turn.

Before presenting the econometric formalizations employed in energy economy, it seemed worthwhile to spell out the detailed nature of the variables included in the models. These are often the result of complex processing of the elementary data observed and are defined in the framework of hypotheses and conventions that are probably worth reviewing. Often a preliminary step to modeling, the calculation of aggregates, indicators and indices also requires special methods, several of which are applications to the energy sector of more general economic methods. Decomposition methods applied to energy intensity are, however, more specific.

Definitions of the data, the conditions under which they are measured, the rules and conventions introduced and the calculation methods, are found scattered in numerous documents and review articles. Their collection within this chapter aims to facilitate their access and we hope that the details provided and the references cited will make it a useful working instrument, particularly for readers who are not familiar with energy questions.

Each of the subjects examined could certainly be developed more extensively if we were to consider all of the questions they raise and discuss all of the work that has been devoted to them. A selection of the most important aspects had to be made. The methods used for indices, aggregates and energy intensity more closely related to econometric techniques are, therefore, presented in greater detail than data collection and processing.

The classification plan for energy statistics reproduces quite faithfully the steps followed by energy flow, from the primary energy supply to transformation operations to secondary or derived fuels, and the final consumption by the user sectors.

The energy system considered is, however, implicitly limited:

- *Upstream*: primary production includes only the quantities of energy that can be put to advantage in commercial form, that is to say that the operations of extraction, of first processing the raw materials in the field and the enrichment of fissile materials are all excluded here, all of these operations being considered as conditioning of the resources and not as energy transformations.
- *Downstream*: the limit is the energy delivered to the consumer, referred to as apparent energy which means that the modalities of use of the energy in industrial or domestic installations are not, in principle, recorded by the statistics. The consumption data are a measure of the quantities of energy arriving at the consumer's door or at the terminals of the electricity or gas meters.

Another limitation is that there is only consumption in economic terms if the energy is used and degraded in an energy device, which excludes many energy flows available naturally ('natural' and free solar or wind energy) or if produced spontaneously or artificially (human energy, explosives, fertilizers). Although a clothesline is not an energy device, nevertheless, a 'three stone fire' is one. In other words, the consumption of energy goods or inputs is necessarily associated with the existence of capital equipment (even very rudimentary). In this context, human energy (and animal energy) are much better quantified in terms of quantity of work (or reduction in the quantity of work) than in terms of a quantity of energy.

This reference to economic concepts is not fortuitous. It is largely because of the overlap of the energy system space with that of economic accounting that common concepts can be defined and methods of analysis can be harmonized.

Within these limits (which some find much too narrow; see below) the transit of energy flow is decomposed into three major stages which make up the *blocks* of the energy balance. In the first, the various sources of supply of primary energy are recorded, as well as the imports, exports (including marine bunkers) of secondary energies, assimilated with the primary sources of supply in the framework of national energy accounting. The transformation part inventories the inputs and outputs of the conversion units of primary (or secondary) energy as secondary energy. The last step is that of final consumption.

Classification of energy sources

Besides the distinction between primary and secondary (or derived) energy, the nature of energy sources determines other categories. Next to the major distinctions between fossil and fission energy, the distinction between renewable and non-renewable energies is the most frequently referred to. Together they are sufficient, within the framework of energy accounting, to define a first level of classification.

For each of the energy sources, this time taken separately, important distinctions are made as a function of their physicochemical characteristics. Above all, at the level of primary production, these sources are far from homogeneous. There are many varieties of coal and the same goes for the physical and chemical properties of oil and gas which vary from deposit to deposit. National and international classifications have been established to characterize the varieties of these products and to unify the nomenclature (American Society for Testing and Materials – ASTM; International Organization for Standardization – ISO). Aside from their technical interest, these classifications are also essential for the execution of commercial transactions.

Recording the elementary data

Energy flows are recorded at each of the steps in their transit and twice in the transformation processes, at the input and the output. For supply and transformation, the data are furnished by the energy producers. The data for final consumption are obtained either from sales made by energy distributors, by inquiry, or from the balance of the transiting quantities in the two preceding steps.

At this stage, the units of measure are units of mass and volume for combustibles, plus specific units for electricity (kWh and its multiples) and for heat (Joules, calories and their multiples). In addition to the international metric units, other units remain for countries that have not gone metric (short and long ton, cubic foot, gallon, Btu, and so on) or certain units associated with specific energies and sanctioned by usage, such as the barrel for oil and petroleum products or the stere for wood. Conversion tables between these various units are readily available.

In addition, it is necessary to establish a set of rules and conventions specifying either the nature of the operation which is to be measured or the place or level of this measurement. For example, for primary production it is good to distinguish between the gross production and the net production according to whether or not one accounts for the quantity of energy consumed in order to produce this energy. The same goes for imports and exports, the transit between countries being the object of special rules.

First reconstitution of the elementary data

A central question for energy data is that of aggregation, which goes much further than that of counting and adding. It presents methodological problems which will be taken up later in this chapter. Successive reconstitutions of the elementary data are necessary before one can construct an accounting framework for synthesis. By reducing the process to just two steps, the first reconstitution can be performed on the data in their original unit of measure (adding), while the second (aggregation) implies the initial conversion to the same unit of measure.

In the first step, the principal regrouping depends on the energy sources, since it is not, in practice, possible to take account of all their diversity. The sources which have sufficiently similar characteristics – their calorific value in particular – are assembled into a single category. The directories and the data bases do not generally include more than about 30 different energy sources.

The second regrouping concerns energy operations. In the supply part, all of the primary production of a given energy coming from a country's various deposits is added to a single value. The same is true for imports and exports. In the transformation part, the regroupings are established as a function of the equipment used (refineries, coking plants, power stations, and so forth) independent of their individual characteristics. In the consumption part, it is the nomenclature of the national accounting procedure which provides the key to the regrouping: industry and its industrial sub-sectors (decomposed by two, three or four digits) the services sector, households and agriculture. The only exception is the transportation sector which collects together the energy consumption of all the transportation activities, whatever the category or commercial status of the users. Most often, 20 or so consumption categories are retained.

All of these regroupings, imposed for practical reasons, inevitably introduce a loss of information. Most of the characteristics of the energy sources and equipment are erased, including their spatial characteristics, since the territorial dimension is lost.

At this point, several synthesis tables are generally constructed:

- *Commodity balances or commodity energy flows* present, in the columns reserved for each energy source, a balance sheet of supplies, transformation inputs, distribution losses, uses of the energy sector and final consumption. The distinction between primary and secondary energy is not made at this time, all of the energies produced being included in the same plan and accounted for on the same line (production). As direct transpositions of the accounting methods for recording availability and employment, these tables are designed as an intermediate stage, before the establishment of the energy balance. They are also often accompanied by energy flow charts giving a graphical representation of the main flows.
- *The sectorial accounts regroup,* for a given consumption sector, data decomposed according to various reconstitution types. The decomposition of consumption by usage is the most frequent.
- *The regional accounts* proceed to a territorial decomposition of the data.

The second data reconstitution and aggregation procedures

This second phase in the data processing is intended to get around the constraint that energies cannot be added when they are measured in their different specific units. For aggregation, it is first necessary to agree on a common energy unit, then to define the conversion factors of the physical units into the energy unit chosen.

Referring to thermodynamic principles, energy can be arbitrarily evaluated in the form of work in Joules (J) or as heat measured in calories (cal), the equivalence between the two units being defined as:

$$1 \text{ calorie} = 4.186 \text{ Joules}$$

For the kWh, another unit derived from the International System, the equivalence is:

$$1 \text{ kWh} = 860 \text{ kcal} = 3600 \text{ kJoules} \tag{1.1}$$

A different unit of measure is the British thermal unit (Btu), defined by the equivalence:

$$1 \text{ Btu} = 1055.06 \text{ Joules}$$

Although the various energy sources have multiple physicochemical characteristics, the only common denominator retained for energy accounting aggregation procedures is the quantity of heat produced by the complete combustion of a unit of each energy, called energy content or calorific value.[1] The calorific values of fuels are used as conversion factors. For electricity, the thermodynamic equivalence is retained (except when other provisions are made).

Standard lists have been established by national and international statistics organizations for primary and secondary energies. Thus, if oil from a given source has a calorific value (net) of 10.25 Gcal per tonne, this value will be used to evaluate the quantity of heat from each tonne of oil. If, in addition, we define 10 Gcal as an accounting unit, this tonne of oil will be evaluated as 1.025 units. These 10 Gcal define, in fact, the tonne of oil equivalent (toe), which is the quantity of heat liberated by a fictional reference tonne of oil. It is a purely conventional accounting unit, as was the case when the promoters of the metric system aligned the kilogramme to the mass of a litre of water, and is only useful to convert all values measured to an oil equivalent, the dominant energy. The unit tonne of coal equivalent (tce), defined as 1 tce = 7 Gcal, has a similar interpretation. In the official unit, the Joule, by virtue of the equivalences (1.1), these 10.25 Gcal are evaluated by $10.25 \times 3600/860 = 42.91$ GJ.[2]

This form of aggregation, called toe-aggregation or btu-aggregation, is the most often used, particularly on energy balance sheets. The method is simple and easy to use. It is also a consequence of energy history of decades past when the sources of energy used were, for the most part, intended to produce heat. With the progression of electricity and mechanical applications, this aggregation is no longer as pertinent as it was.

For derived energy, like thermal electricity, there is another accounting method. Rather than measure the amount of heat produced, it consists of accounting for the amounts of primary energy (oil, gas, coal) or secondary energy (diesel-oil, fuel-oil and so forth) *entering* into the generating plants. For example, if 500 g of coal, with a net calorific value of 6.5 kcal/g are necessary to produce 1 kWh, this kWh can be measured, not as 860 kcal, but as 3250 kcal. This method can be generalized to all forms of secondary energy. This system is either called primary equivalence accounting or else partial substitution, to the extent that it is only really applied 'partially', in this case for energy coming from low efficiency transformations, particularly thermal electricity (30–50 per cent) and charcoal (15–25 per cent).

For aggregation and evaluation procedures, it is necessary to define hypotheses and establish accounting mechanisms which make it possible to conciliate contradictory requirements as well as possible, knowing that no accounting system can totally assure thermodynamic coherence over the entire energy flow. A result of compromise between various organizations (IEA, Eurostat and so on), the new system of accounting for primary and secondary energy benefits from extensive international recognition.[3] It leads to a mixed system, combining, by appropriate hypotheses, primary equivalence evaluation for production and final equivalence evaluation for consumption (IEA-OECD-Eurostat, 2004).

The energy balance sheet

After having completed this second phase of conversion of all quantities of energy to a common unit of measure, it is possible to construct an energy balance sheet which, within the limits of the energy system established above, presents for a country or region and for a year the decomposition of the energy flow produced, transformed, consumed and lost, as well as their respective sums.

Several types of balance sheet can be constructed as a function of the accounting method chosen for the quantities of primary and secondary energy. Rules of internal coherence must also be specified in order to assure a compatibility with the commodity balances, without double counting the primary energies with the secondary energies derived from these primary energies. Rules for + and – signs can be set up to better distinguish between input and output flows. Certain accounting mechanisms have been introduced in order to more easily balance the balance sheet when the origin or destination of the flows cannot be clearly determined in a fixed framework (United Nations, 1982; Eurostat, 1982).

It remains true that the energy balance is only recapitulative of a given energy situation and its potential for analysis is rather limited. Its construction requires the use of complex methods and very detailed rules in order to assure a balance of availability and employment. It is significant that commodity balances which are not subject to a large number of rules and which contain the same information are becoming the accounting instruments of choice. Understanding their elements is much easier.

Energy aggregates

The calculation of aggregates is a continuous process in energy accounting. Although the methods are simple in the case of elementary data, they become more and more complex when the aggregates include disparate elements. We come up against the classical problem in economy to aggregate heterogeneous goods, with the additional particularity for energy that there are many quantities to measure (heat, work, useful work, useful energy, free energy and so forth) and that the qualitative attributes of the various energy sources (heat density, capacity to do work, ease of use and so on) are very important in their allocation to different uses. In addition, the definitions depend on the energy system considered. The present tendency is always to push back these limits to include a maximum number of components (embodied energy, waste, emissions, externalities, totality of material and so on) and to extend aggregates to the dimensions of the biosphere.

The most common energy aggregates are:

- the aggregates of the energy balance which directly use the calorific values as weights
- the 'economic' aggregates which transfer to energy the methods habitually used in economy, notably the functions of cost and index number.[4]

The aggregates of the energy balance sheet

As with all balance sheets, the successive summations of the rows and columns determine intermediate aggregates and overall aggregates. The regroupings most often performed are done, either for each of the three blocks of the balance sheet (supply, transformation, consumption), or for each of the categories of energy products (coal, oil, gas, electricity, renewable energies). The three aggregates that are supposed to best characterize energy systems are:

- the production of primary energy
- the consumption of primary energy and equivalent sources (imports and exports of secondary energy), also called internal supply
- the final consumption of energy.

They can be calculated by energy, by energy category, and for all energies. Their principal usefulness resides in the comparisons that they permit: comparison of the value in one year with the values of previous years, comparisons between countries, comparisons between aggregates themselves.

Many other aggregates can be calculated as needed. In their analysis, we must not forget the hypotheses and conventions adopted for energy accounting, nor the simplifications introduced. It is certain that the desire to assemble into a single quantity fossil fuels, electricity and renewable energies presents evident theoretical and methodological problems which call for less radical solutions.

Among these, an aggregation mode frequently encountered is the decomposition of final consumption into three components:

- fossil fuels for thermal use
- fuels used for transportation
- electricity for all of its uses.

Without pretending to resolve all of the problems of aggregation, this method has the advantage of distinguishing among more homogeneous ensembles than those of the balance sheet and can, for this reason, show more significant evolutions.

For practical applications, the aggregates of the balance sheet are the most commonly used. They are universally adopted and, despite their imperfections, they have the advantage of providing a common basis of evaluation for all countries. The economic aggregates are less common and their definitions are more varied. These aggregates try to overcome the difficulties encountered in the construction of aggregates of the energy balance sheet. Trying to agree on common conventions is secondary to the requirement to establish them on solid theoretical bases.

Economic-energy aggregates

The qualitative attributes and prices are explicitly incorporated as supplementary properties in order to provide to aggregates an economic significance that the accounting rules eliminate by aggregating energies on the unique basis of their quantity of heat. The functions of cost and index numbers are used to determine the appropriate weighting. Crossing quantities of energy and price, expenditures and cost of energy inputs in the production function is basic to the definition of these aggregates.

To the extent that economic activities become more and more complex, the development of an energy source becomes increasingly tied to its capacity to produce useful work rather than heat and recourse to more and more efficient energies appears indispensable. The successive transitions from wood to coal, then to oil, gas and electricity show very well the direction of past evolution.

However, there is no strict concordance between calorific value, work content and economic value.

For heat content- or toe-aggregates, the energy flows are counted in the form of the lowest quality and most easily degraded energy. The implicit calculation hypotheses are:

1) that all of the energy sources are perfect substitutes;
2) that the quantity of heat is the common denominator for all energies, and that their capacity to raise temperature is as important as their capacity to do work;
3) that there is no difference, from an economic point of view, between a coal toe of heat and a electricity toe of heat.

For Adelman and Watkins (2004), these aggregates 'lack economic meaning'. Even if this coal toe has the same calorific value as the electricity toe (10 Gcal), the difference in price between them clearly contradicts these hypotheses. Innate characteristics (power density, ease of use and distribution, possibilities for fine adjustment, environmental impact and so forth) predispose each energy to certain uses and, in many cases, disallow substitutions. Zarnikau *et al.* (1996) call them 'form value attributes' to show that they confer specific economic value to each energy source.

These quality attributes are not generally directly measurable. To evaluate them, Cleveland *et al.* (1984) and Kaufmann (1994, 2004) use the bias that economic production value corresponds to energy use value and emphasize that 'a heat unit of energy that generates US$ 2 of economic value does more useful work than a heat unit that generates US$ 1 of economic value'. Previously, Adams and Miovic (1968), in the same vein, had used a regression model of industrial production as a function of the energy inputs and had found, for the countries considered, that oil was 1.6–2.7 times and electricity 2.7–14.3 times more productive than coal. Turvey and Nobay (1965) preferred to use marginal reasoning: 'The relevant conversion factors for different fuels are either their marginal rates of transformation or their rates of substitution in consumption' (p. 788).

Following in this direction, Cleveland and Kaufmann define Value Marginal Products (VMP) as the change in economic output, given a change in the use of a heat unit of an individual fuel. The VMP are associated with energy characteristics; the energies which have more sought-after characteristics benefit from a higher VMP and higher market prices. At equilibrium, for a rational consumer and in a perfectly competitive market, the respective ratios of VMP correspond to price ratios.[5]

Relative prices are acceptable approximations for relative marginal products, which are indicators of the respective qualities of energies. It is, therefore, legitimate to retain them as weighting factors in aggregates in order to establish a concordance between thermodynamic value and economic value.

At the micro-economic level, Zarnikau show that this economic aggregate can be calculated by optimizing the production function $Y = f(K, L, M, g(x))$ where K, L and M are classical production factors and where $g(x)$ represents the aggregate in relation to energy inputs $(x_i) = x$ whose prices are $(p_i) = p$. By proceeding in two steps and by supposing, in the second, that the firm chooses the x_i so as to maximize the marginal products with respect to the x_i under the budget constraint m, so that max $g(x)$, s.t. $m = \sum p_i x_i = p'.x$, the aggregate can, alternatively, be written under the continuous form of the Divisia index or under the discrete Törnqvist form:

$$d\ln\, g(x) = \sum_i \left(\frac{p_i x_i}{\sum_i p_i x_i} \right) d\ln\, x_i \tag{1.2}$$

$$\ln\, X_t - \ln\, X_{t-1} = \sum_i 0.5\, (s_{it} + s_{it-1})\, (\ln\, x_{it} - \ln\, x_{it-1})$$

$$s_{it} = \frac{p_{it} x_{it}}{\sum_i p_{it} x_{it}} \tag{1.3}$$

The rate of growth of the aggregate X_t is the average of the rates of growth of the energies x_{it}weighted by the average of the parts s_{it} of the costs which express the relative economic values of the energies i. This aggregate is defined as a 'true' index resulting from an optimizing behaviour by the firm on the basis of its production function and under the hypothesis that the choice of the x_i within $g(x)$ is independent of K, L and M. If the parts s_{it} remain constant in time, which is rather improbable, the Törnqvist index becomes the Cobb-Douglas index $E_t^\bullet = \prod E_t^{s_i}$ with $\sum_i s_i = 1$.

An application of the Törnqvist index, given by (1.3), is presented for the energy consumption of French industry over the period 1978–2004. The values of the variables x_{it} and $p_{it}(i$ = petroleum products, gas, coal, electricity) and those of the index X_t (based on 100 for 1990) are shown in Table 1.1. Figure 1.1 shows its evolution over the period, as well as that of the toe-aggregate. The relative spread between the two aggregates increases progressively because of the increasing place of electricity in the total consumption and because of its price, which is higher than that of other energies. The weighting of electricity in the toe-aggregate passes from 17.7 per cent in 1978 to 33.2 per cent in 2004, and, respectively, from 41 to 52 per cent for the Törnqvist-aggregate.

Table 1.1 Industrial energy consumption in France: 1978–2004

	Energy consumption				Energy prices				
	Petroleum products	Gas	Coal and lignite	Electricity	Petroleum products	Gas	Coal and lignite	Electricity	Divisia aggregate
Unit	ktoe	ktoe	ktoe	ktoe	E95/toe	E95/toe	E95/toe	E95/toe	Index
1978	20281	7226	9172	7878	227	176	197	674	122
1985	8646	8783	9733	8353	465	324	205	715	97
1990	6581	9117	8519	9861	226	146	157	616	100
1991	6911	9706	8240	10057	199	142	154	590	102
1992	6753	9743	7948	10410	174	132	152	572	104
1993	7365	9609	6854	10376	185	129	144	572	103
1994	6838	9536	6975	10399	174	122	137	534	102
1995	6818	10248	6959	10630	172	123	133	533	104
1996	7328	10768	6891	10710	193	124	132	505	107
1997	6694	11131	6939	10982	190	132	129	488	107
1998	5931	11718	6861	11351	158	126	125	470	109
1999	5186	12006	6411	11404	182	121	123	455	107
2000	5520	12122	6288	11622	286	171	129	424	109
2001	6951	12079	5968	11581	247	193	149	417	112
2002	5787	13399	5913	11468	234	165	142	409	112
2003	5548	12670	5771	11860	241	181	139	410	111
2004	5478	12903	5732	12000	263	175	137	409	112

Source: Enerdata-World Energy Database.

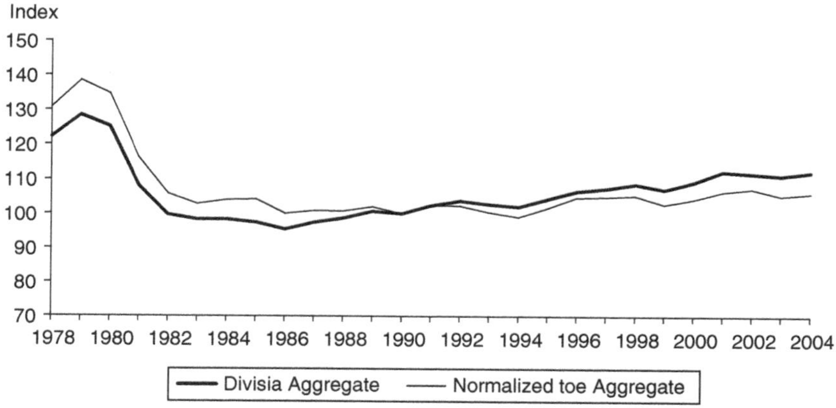

Figure 1.1 Comparison between the Törnqvist aggregate index and the toe-aggregate index (based on 100 in 1990)

Energy prices

As is the case for energy quantities, price statistics published by specialized organizations and used in analyses and modeling are the result of processing individual prices and their measurement is based on a set of rules and computing methods. Except in a few cases, these prices are averages established over a range of energy products, for various producing deposits, diverse quotation centres and markets on a set of transactions, or over a period of time going from a day to a year. Each of the values obtained makes sense only with respect to the others and, here again, the analyses mostly involve variations in time or differences in place. As opposed to quantity data, however, there are no standard aggregation procedures nor summary accounts which make it possible to verify the coherence of the collected data. We have has to limit ourselves to supplying a few details on prices of primary resources, energy prices to final consumption and some methodological points related to econometric modeling.

The prices of primary energy resources

Methods of establishing international prices of oil have often varied. After the period of domination by major companies when they controlled the entire petroleum market, the producing countries progressively took control of petroleum at the source and OPEC was able from 1973 to unilaterally fix the official selling price. At the time of the second oil shock, because of strong supply restrictions, major volumes which had up to then been sold under long-term contracts, found their way to the spot markets. Spot transactions deal with cargos for short-term delivery, whereas the delay for forward transactions may extend to between one and three months.

During the 1990s, the spot oil markets established themselves as the price barometers. Certain crude oils, such as the Brent (London), the West Texas Intermediate (New York) or the Dubaï (Singapore) are markers on which the prices of other qualities of oil are indexed. The actual prices are known *a priori* only to the contracting parties. By questioning the buyers and sellers about the prices of transactions conducted during the day, various publications such as *PLATT'S Oilgram Journal* in New York, the *Petroleum Argus* or the *London Oil Report*, manage to estimate the prices of the reference crudes and publish, daily, the preceding day's prices.

There are also several markets for the exchange of refined petroleum products. The principal markets, usually located near large exporting refineries, are New York (East Coast), Northwest Europe (Amsterdam–Rotterdam–Antwerp), the Mediterranean (Genoa–Lavera), the Persian Gulf, Southeast Asia (Singapore) and the Gulf of Mexico. About fourteen products are quoted daily and the prices published are also obtained by questioning dealers.

The operation mode of the petroleum markets has been progressively extended to other energy sources and the quoting methods and price publication systems have become similar. Gas and oil prices are published by the same organizations. For coal, we find long-term contracts, spot markets and organizations that collect transaction information such as McCloskey Coal Information Services in Europe. Electricity has been the last energy source to join the common regime with the creation of physical spot markets, power exchanges and financial markets.

Final consumption prices of energy

Prices at final consumption include five components: the cost of production, the cost of transportation, the cost of transformation, trade margins and taxes. The prices of petroleum products and coal are strongly influenced by the nature and quality of the product, while the prices of gas, electricity and heat depend more on the type of consumer, the time of the transaction and the geographical situation. For coal and domestic fuel, decomposition into two or three consumer classes is sufficient (industry, electrical sector, residential sector). For other energies, tariffs vary as a function of the quantity consumed, the place and time of delivery.

Three methods are used to measure prices. The first is to select a reference price among the range of products to be consumed. Thus, the IEA does not distinguish between various coal qualities and lists for each country the price of the quality that is most commonly consumed. The second method is to determine a weighted average of prices. The national prices of energy, established by Eurostat, are calculated on the basis of regional prices or individual localities. The third method is to calculate an average unit price based on the ratio between the incomes of energy suppliers and the quantities of energy sold, which is the method used by the IEA for the price of gas and electricity for industry and households. The use of one or another of these methods in different countries explains the variations that are sometimes observed between the statistics published by the various national or international organizations.

Prices of energy in econometric models

In econometric models, prices enter as variables in the production functions (prices of inputs) and in demand functions (prices of consumer goods). Except for supply–demand models and models determining prices based on resource volume, prices are most often exogenous explicative variables (sometimes lagged) of the volume of energy consumption. In demand models, the exogeneity of prices, generally accepted, is not verified when their level depends on quantities consumed, a frequent case for electricity where there are degressive or progressive tariffs. Instead of average prices, it is theoretically helpful to use marginal prices, a recommendation, however, rarely put into practice.

Another methodological problem raised by several authors (Bacon, 1991) is the asymmetry of price effects in case of rising or falling prices. In fact, we observe imperfect reversibility in the reactions of producers and consumers to variations in price, particularly those of oil and petroleum products. The amplitude of the variable part of the price elasticity has consequences for the evaluation of income elasticity and for the presence or absence of rebound effects.

Gately and Huntington (2003) argue that a convenient way to incorporate asymmetric effects into the models is to decompose prices into three components representing, respectively, the maximum historic price over the interval $[0, t]$, the cumulative series of price decreases and the cumulative series of price increases so that $P_t = P_{\max,t} + P_{\text{cut},t} + P_{\text{rec},t}$:

$$P_{\max,t} \equiv \max(P_0, \ldots, P_t)$$

positive and non-decreasing series

$$P_{\text{cut},t} \equiv \sum_{i=0}^{t} \min[0, (P_{\max,i-1} - P_{i-1}) - (P_{\max,i} - P_i)]$$

non-positive and non-increasing series

$$P_{\text{rec},t} \equiv \sum_{i=0}^{t} \max[0, (P_{\max,i-1} - P_{i-1}) - (P_{\max,i} - P_i)]$$

non-negative and non-decreasing series

Quantity and price indices

The basic index number problem is the same as for the aggregation problem. It is to find weighting factors for prices and quantities that make it possible to summarize or synthesize into a few significant indices the individual measurements, which are often very numerous. An energy price index (or quantity index) is a weighted mean of the change in the relative prices (or quantities) of energy sources from one situation 0 to another situation 1. Diewert (2001) formally defines the problem in these terms: 'How to determine the weights and ... what formula or type of mean should be used to average the selected item relative to prices [and quantities]' (p. 6).

Multiple solutions have been proposed over more than a century for a definition of the indices by a number of statisticians and economists (Jevons, Edgeworth, Paasche, Laspeyre, Walsh, Marshall, Fisher, Divisia). In an axiomatic approach, Diewert starts from expenditures and costs, the most natural aggregate combining prices and quantities, and deduces the indices of price and quantity from the variations V^1/V^0 of this aggregate between the dates 0 and 1 (or 0 and T). Let $V^0 = \sum_i P_i^0 Q_i^0$ and $V^1 = \sum_i P_i^1 Q_i^1$ be the values of the aggregates on dates 0 and 1 for n products i. The price index and the quantity index are defined as two functions $\boldsymbol{P}$ and $\boldsymbol{Q}$ that satisfy the following equation:

$$V^1/V^0 = \boldsymbol{P}(P^0, P^1, Q^0, Q^1) \,.\, \boldsymbol{Q}(P^0, P^1, Q^0, Q^1) \quad \text{where}$$
$$P^0 = \left(P_i^0\right), P^1 = \left(P_i^1\right), Q^0 = \left(Q_i^0\right), Q^1 = \left(Q_i^1\right) \tag{1.4}$$

The definition of the indices changes to a problem of decomposing an aggregate; the change in the value aggregate V^1/V^0 is decomposed into the product of two parts that are due to price change and to quantity change. The functions $\boldsymbol{P}$ and $\boldsymbol{Q}$ are duals in the sense that, V^1/V^0 being given, $\boldsymbol{Q}$ is completely determined if $\boldsymbol{P}$ is known. Box 1.1 shows the formal developments concerning the index Divisia and the relations of the indices to utility and cost functions.

The indices of Laspeyre and Paasche are the simplest. Both adopt for $\boldsymbol{P}$ and $\boldsymbol{Q}$ the arithmetic means, but the first keeps time 0 as reference, whereas the second uses time 1. Fisher's index is the geometric mean of the two preceding indices. It benefits from a number of formal properties and, for this reason, is often called Fisher's ideal index (Boyd and Roop, 2004). It provides a perfect decomposition of V^1/V^0 (a property which will later be used with respect to the decomposition of energy intensity). The indices of Laspeyre and Paasche do not verify the time reversal test and do not, therefore, lead to this perfect decomposition. Although the Törnqvist index only satisfies a limited number of tests, it approximates the Fisher index quite closely.

Box 1.1 Continuous form of the index and properties of the indices

Continuous form of index and Divisia index

By reducing the elementary intervals $[t-1, t]$ of the chain index to an infinitesimal increase dt, we arrive at the continuous form of the index introduced by Divisia. We assume that the aggregate is a continuous and differentiable function of time, or $V(t) = \sum_i P_i(t)Q_i(t)$. After formal calculation, Divisia obtains the two equivalent expressions:

$$V'(t)/V(t) = [P'(t)/P(t)] + [Q'(t)/Q(t)]$$

$$d \ln V(t) = d \ln P(t) + d \ln Q(t) \quad \text{where}$$

$$P'(t)/P(t) = d \ln P(t) = \sum_i s_i(t) \left[P'_i(t)/P_i(t)\right]$$

$$Q'(t)/Q(t) = d \ln Q(t) = \sum_i s_i(t) \left[Q'_i(t)/Q_i(t)\right]$$

$$s_i(t) = \frac{P_i(t)Q_i(t)}{\sum_i P_i(t)Q_i(t)}$$

By retaining as a discrete approximation of $dP(t)$, either $\Delta P = P(1) - P(0)$, or $\Delta P = P(0) - P(1)$, the Divisia index can be alternatively transformed to either a Laspeyre or a Paasche index. The discrete approximation of $P'(t)/P(t)$ leads to the Törnqvist index given in (1.3):

$$\ln P^T(P^0, P^1, Q^0, Q^1) = \sum_i (1/2) \left(s_i^0 + s_i^1\right) \ln \left(P_i^1/P_i^0\right)$$

Index and economic approach

Diewert shows that the Törnqvist index is equal to the ratio $C(P^1)/C(P^0)$ of a translog cost function evaluated at times 1 and 0. With a utility function of the form $f(Q_1, \ldots, Q_n) = [\sum_i \sum_k a_{ik} Q_i Q_k]^{1/2}$ and under the hypothesis of cost minimization, the Fisher quantity index corresponds to the ratio of the utility function, the 'true' quantity index in the economic sense: $\boldsymbol{Q}^F(P^0, P^1, Q^0, Q^1) = f(Q^1)/f(Q^0)$ and the price index to the ratio of the cost function $\boldsymbol{P}^F(P^0, P^1, Q^0, Q^1) = C(P^1)/C(P^0)$. The product of these two indices exactly restores the ratio V^1/V^0 of expenditures:

$$\boldsymbol{Q}^F(P^0, P^1, Q^0, Q^1)\boldsymbol{P}^F(P^0, P^1, Q^0, Q^1) = f(Q^1).C(P^1)/f(Q^0).C(P^0)$$
$$= \frac{\sum_i P_i^1 Q_i^1}{\sum_i P_i^0 Q_i^0}$$

These indices are called 'Superlative indices' because they are identical to the Fisher ideal index.

Rather than calculate the indices between two dates 0 and T, it is preferable to calculate them over the elementary periods $[t-1, t]$ and to accumulate the annual rates to find the index over [0, T]. That comes down to adopting a method where the base is changed each period. They are chain indices as opposed to fixed base indices. The advantage is to avoid too large deviations in the composition of goods and price levels if important changes occur between 0 and T. For the resulting index, the starting value is conventionally fixed at 1 (or 100).

Table 1.2 provides formal expressions for the most commonly used indices and the corresponding values for the example presented in Table 1.1. In order to conserve the same notation for all of the indices, these expressions are given for the time interval [0, T] and not for [0, 1]. Because of the regular evolution of consumption and the relatively slight price variations during the period 1990–2003, the values of the four quantity and price indices (Laspeyre, Paasche, Fisher, Törnqvist-Divisia) differ only slightly. The spreads between the two last indices are the smallest and the products of their quantity and price indices are equal to the expenditure index (no residual term), which is $P_{0T} = \sum_{i=1}^n P_i^T Q_i^T / \sum_{i=1}^n P_i^0 Q_i^0 = 0.908$.

Energy intensity and its decomposition

Energy intensity belongs to the general category of energy indicators which establish the ratios either between the energy system magnitudes or between these and the demographic, geographic or economic magnitudes. The consumption per inhabitant, the density of transportation and energy distribution networks (length per km^2) and the part of the energy sector in the GDP are examples. They are constructed, for the most part, for analysis purposes and present no particular problems. Among them we only deal here with energy intensity because of its importance as an indicator of performance in energy use and because of the methodological questions

Table 1.2 Quantity and price indices (values for industrial energy consumption in France between 1990 and 2003)

	Quantity index		Price index	
	Expression	Value	Expression	Value
Laspeyre	$\boldsymbol{Q}_{0T}^{L} = \frac{\sum_{i=1}^{n} P_i^0 Q_i^T}{\sum_{i=1}^{n} P_i^0 Q_i^0}$	1.106	$\boldsymbol{P}_{0T}^{L} = \frac{\sum_{i=1}^{n} P_i^T Q_i^0}{\sum_{i=1}^{n} P_i^0 Q_i^0}$	0.827
Paasche	$\boldsymbol{Q}_{0T}^{P} = \frac{\sum_{i=1}^{n} P_i^T Q_i^T}{\sum_{i=1}^{n} P_i^T Q_i^0}$	1.098	$\boldsymbol{P}_{0T}^{P} = \frac{\sum_{i=1}^{n} P_i^T Q_i^T}{\sum_{i=1}^{n} P_i^0 Q_i^T}$	0.821
Fisher	$\boldsymbol{Q}_{0T}^{F} = \left(\boldsymbol{Q}_{0T}^{L} \cdot \boldsymbol{Q}_{0T}^{P}\right)^{1/2}$	1.102	$\boldsymbol{P}_{0T}^{F} = \left(\boldsymbol{P}_{0T}^{L} \cdot \boldsymbol{P}_{0T}^{P}\right)^{1/2}$	0.824
Törnqvist-Divisia	$\boldsymbol{Q}_{0T}^{T} = \frac{\sum_{i=1}^{n} P_i^T Q_i^T}{P_{0T}^{T} \cdot \sum_{i=1}^{n} P_i^0 Q_i^0}$	1.100	$\ln \boldsymbol{P}_{0T}^{T} = 1/2 \sum_{i=1}^{n} \left[\frac{P_i^0 Q_i^0}{\sum_{i=1}^{n} P_i^0 Q_i^0} + \frac{P_i^T Q_i^T}{\sum_{i=1}^{n} P_i^T Q_i^T} \right] \ln \left(P_i^T / P_i^0\right)$	0.826

raised, in particular about its decomposition into structure and intensity effects.

Definition and measurement of energy intensity

The energy intensity of a commodity, a service or a use is the quantity of energy necessary, aggregated or for a given source of energy, to produce or satisfy this commodity, service or use. It compares, in appropriate units, the energy input with the result of an activity (output). Its value is expressed in toe per tonne of steel, in litres of petrol per passenger-km, or in kWh per m^2 for lighting. By successive aggregations, the elementary intensities become sectorial intensities and then global intensities, for which the energy intensity of the GDP is a prototype.

In fact, the measurements of energy intensity are the inverse of the energy efficiency defined as the useful output of a process divided by the energy input. However, general usage is to retain intensity indicators rather than efficiency indicators, which normally causes no problems. Thus at the global level the energy intensity of the GDP is the inverse of energy productivity.

Except for the thermodynamic indicators, most of the intensity indicators used are mixed indicators where the inputs and the outputs are in different units. We often distinguish between:

- *physico-energetic indicators*, where the denominator is expressed in a physical unit (tonne, m^3); the most common are:
  - *indicators of unit consumption*, where the output refers to a level of activity (tonnage of industrial products, number of passenger-kilometres, surface of premises and so on)
  - *indicators of specific consumption*, where the quantity of energy is measured under standard conditions (number of litres of fuel per 100 km for new vehicles and so on)
- *economico-energetic indicators*, where the denominator is measured in monetary units; when the level of aggregation rises, the monetary value becomes the only common unit of measure (value added, GDP and so on).

By combining the number of points of measurement with the level of observation, a multitude of indicators can be defined. If they are well chosen, between 5 and 10 indicators per economic sector already provide a great deal of information on the energy intensity. For purposes of analysis, less aggregated indicators can be used.

The methods of decomposition of energy intensity

When trying to estimate efficiency improvements using energy intensity indicators, it is useful to isolate as much as possible what really corresponds to improvements by neutralizing other effects which have contributed to increasing or decreasing this intensity. Above all, when intensity measurements are made at a global or an intermediate level, many factors affect the variations observed, whether they have an economic nature (activity effect, structure effect, substitution effect, price effect, and so on.) or a behavioural, climatic, technical or energetic nature. Some of them can be eliminated by adjusting the initial data: for example, by calibrating the annual energy consumption using reference temperatures to eliminate the effect of climate.[6] However, structure effects associated with the respective weights of various economic activities within a sector are more easily quantified. The intensity can thus simply decrease because energy-intensive industries occupy less space in the production cycle.

In its standard form, decomposition of intensity comes down to factoring the two effects of structure and energy intensity. The methods used are spelled out in the Index of Decomposition Analysis (IDA). Along with methodological studies, whose development has accelerated since 1990 (*Energy Policy*, 1997, Boyd and Roop, 2004, Ang, 2005, Liu *et al.*, 1992) application work is extensive, in both industrialized and developing countries. Ang and Zhang (2000) provide an inventory. Initially limited to energy intensity, work on the intensity of CO_2 emissions is now on the increase.

If $E_t = \sum_{i=1}^{n} E_{it}$ is the total energy consumption of the n sectors i and $Y_t = \sum_{i=1}^{n} Y_{it}$ is the total production, the energy intensity is defined by:

$$\boldsymbol{I}_t = \frac{E_t}{Y_t} = \sum_{i=1}^{n} \frac{Y_{it}}{Y_t}\frac{E_{it}}{Y_{it}}$$

$$= \sum_{i=1}^{n} S_{it}.I_{it} \quad \text{where} \quad S_{it} = \frac{Y_{it}}{Y_t} \text{ and } I_{it} = \frac{E_{it}}{Y_{it}}$$

S_{it} represents the part of the sector i in total production and I_{it} the energy intensity of i.[7] It should be noted that the values of S_{it} and I_{it} must be measured over a common partition for the n sectors. Since this can hardly be envisioned for households and transportation, the method is reserved, in practice, for the industrial sector.

The decomposition method is formally identical to that of the calculation of price and quantity indices. Just as the indices $\boldsymbol{P}$ and $\boldsymbol{Q}$ are determined from the variations in expenditures V^1/V^0, the two synthetic index factorials $\boldsymbol{I}_{\text{str}}$ (structure) and $\boldsymbol{I}_{\text{int}}$ (intensity) are determined from the ratio of intensities $\boldsymbol{I}_T/\boldsymbol{I}_0$ on the dates 0 and T, so that:

$$\boldsymbol{I}_T/\boldsymbol{I}_0 = \boldsymbol{I}_{\text{str}}(S_0, S_T, I_0, I_T) \,.\, \boldsymbol{I}_{\text{int}}(S_0, S_T, I_0, I_T)$$

where S_0, S_T, I_0, I_T represent the vectors of quantities $S_{i0}, S_{iT}, I_{i0}, I_{iT}$. Depending on the nature of the functional forms adopted for $\boldsymbol{I}_{str}$ and $\boldsymbol{I}_{int}$, we find, for these indices, definitions analogous to those found in Table 1.2, and with the same names (Laspeyre, Paasche, Fisher, Törnqvist, Divisia). The formal expressions are shown in Table 1.3.

The structure effect I_{str} is calculated as the change in aggregated energy intensity I_T/I_0, which would appear if the intensity of each industry remained constant over the period considered (E_{i0}/Y_{i0}) even though the respective parts (Y_{iT}/Y_T) in the production had changed over the same period. The intensity effect I_{int} is calculated as the change in aggregated energy intensity I_T/I_0 which would appear if the parts in the sectorial production were the same as at the beginning of the period (Y_{i0}/Y_0), while the energy intensity of each sub-sector had, in fact, changed (E_{iT}/Y_{iT}).

The decomposition schema so far adopted is the multiplicative schema where I_T/I_0 is the product of the two effects $I_T/I_0 = I_{str} \cdot I_{int}$. In the additive schema, the effects add according to the decomposition $I_T - I_0 = I_{str} + I_{int}$. The choice between the two schemas is linked more closely to the domain of application than to methodological differences. The advantage of the additive decomposition is to conserve, for the effects, the units of measure of intensities, whereas these effects are without units in the multiplicative decomposition.[8]

It is generally not verified whether or not the decomposition is complete or perfect, that is to say that the product or the sum of the effects integrally reproduce the variation of energy intensity between the dates 0 and T. A residual term comes in, multiplying or adding, to yield the values of I_T/I_0 or $I_T - I_0$. This residual represents a certain proportion of change in energy intensity which remains unexplained and which cannot be attributed to either the structure index or the intensity index.

The methods of Laspeyre, of Paasche, and the Arithmetic-Mean Divisia method include such a residual. The Fisher ideal index and the Log-Mean Divisia, on the other hand, benefit from a perfect or complete decomposition. This property is equivalent to that of the reversal factor in index number theory. Törnqvist's index gives a decomposition that is often quite close to Fisher's.

The existence of this residual can also be interpreted mathematically by calculating the integral $\ln(I_t/I_0) = \int_0^T [\sum_i w_i(d\ln S_i/dt)]\,dt + \int_0^T [\sum_i w_i (d\ln I_i/dt)]\,dt$ where $w_i = E_i/E$ is the part of the consumption of the sector i in the total.[9] Since the integrals defining I_{str} and I_{int} are calculated by a discrete approximation between two dates, there normally remains a spread corresponding to the integration path chosen between 0 and T. The approximation obtained from the arithmetic mean of the weights w_i between 0 and T, as defined in Törnqvist's index, allows an integration residual to remain. Ang arrives at a complete decomposition by using, instead of w_i, logarithmic mean weights (called LMD1 method) defined by $L(w_{i0}, w_{iT}) = (w_{i0} - w_{iT})/\ln(w_{i0}/w_{iT})$.[10] In order to make sure that the sum of the weights is equal to 1, we can also use the normalized weights method (LMD2 method): $w_i^{\bullet} = L(w_{i0}, w_{iT})/\sum_i L(w_{i0}, w_{iT})$.

Table 1.3 Decomposition of energy intensity changes (applications to industrial energy consumption in France between 1990 and 2003)

	Structural effect		Intensity effect		
	Expression	**Value**	**Expression**	**Value**	**Residual term**
Laspeyre	$\boldsymbol{I}^{L}_{\mathrm{str}} = \sum_i S_{iT}.I_{i0}/\sum_i S_{i0}.I_{i0}$	0.916	$\boldsymbol{I}^{L}_{\mathrm{int}} = \sum_i S_{i0}.I_{iT}/\sum_i S_{i0}.I_{i0}$	0.925	0.971
Paasche	$\boldsymbol{I}^{P}_{\mathrm{strt}} = \sum_i S_{iT}.I_{iT}/\sum_i S_{i0}.I_{iT}$	0.890	$\boldsymbol{I}^{P}_{\mathrm{strt}} = \sum_i S_{iT}.I_{iT}/\sum_i S_{iT}.I_{i0}$	0.898	1.029
Fisher	$\boldsymbol{I}^{F}_{str} = (\boldsymbol{I}^{L}_{\mathrm{str}} \cdot \boldsymbol{I}^{P}_{\mathrm{str}})^{1/2}$	0.903	$\boldsymbol{I}^{F}_{\mathrm{int}} = (\boldsymbol{I}^{L}_{\mathrm{int}} \cdot \boldsymbol{I}^{P}_{\mathrm{int}})^{1/2}$	0.911	1.000
Törnqvist or Arithmetic Mean Divisia (AMD)	$\boldsymbol{I}^{\mathrm{AMD}}_{\mathrm{str}} = \exp\left[\sum_i \frac{(w_{iT}+w_{i0})}{2} \ln(S_{iT}/S_{i0})\right]$ $w_{it} = E_{it}/E_t$	0.902	$\boldsymbol{I}^{\mathrm{AMD}}_{\mathrm{int}} = \exp\left[\sum_i \frac{(w_{iT}+w_{i0})}{2} \ln(I_{iT}/I_{i0})\right]$ $w_{it} = E_{it}/E_t$	0.914	0.998
Chained LOG Mean Divisia (LMD)	$\boldsymbol{I}^{\mathrm{LMD}}_{\mathrm{str}} = \exp\left[\sum_{t=1}^{t=T} \sum_i w^{\bullet}_{it} \ln(S_{it}/S_{it-1})\right]$ $w^{\bullet}_{it} = (w_{it} - w_{it-1})/\ln(w_{it}/w_{it-1})$	0.895	$\boldsymbol{I}^{\mathrm{LMD}}_{\mathrm{int}} = \exp\left[\sum_{t=1}^{t=T} \sum_i w^{\bullet}_{it} \ln(I_{it}/I_{it-1})\right]$ $w^{\bullet}_{it} = (w_{it} - w_{it-1})/\ln(w_{it}/w_{it-1})$	0.920	1.000

As with price and quantity indices, the decomposition methods resort, preferentially, to chain indices (or rolling base year indices). Their advantage is to better display, year by year, the evolution of the components of energy intensity. Weights are assigned to the present year and to the preceding year. Because of smaller variations between two consecutive years, the size of the residual is reduced with respect to the case of two more separated reference years.

The French industrial sector is once more used to illustrate the methods presented. The values of the indices $\boldsymbol{I}_{\mathrm{str}}$ and $\boldsymbol{I}_{\mathrm{int}}$ for the five calculation methods (Laspeyre, Paasche, Fisher and Törnqvist (arithmetic-mean Divisia) and chained log-mean Divisia (LMD) are shown in Table 1.3 with the residual term of the decomposition. The multiplicative schema is adopted. Between 1990 (reference year) and 2003, the intensity index passed from 1.000 to 0.823, for an average rate of decrease of 1.4 per cent per year, shared in approximately equal proportions between the effect of structural changes (decrease in the weight of the energy-intensive branches) and gains in energy efficiency. The values of the two indices are close for all of the methods; the LMD chained index, however, amplifies the intensity effect.

In Figure 1.2 (left), where the variations of this index are shown, we see the operation of compensations between 1990 and 1996 between the effects of structure and intensity, both then combining to accentuate the reduction of total intensity. In this same figure (right), the representation of the decomposition is given for the other indices in the additive form.[11] Very close values for the two effects are seen, each around −0.70 per cent per year. The residual term is negative for the Laspeyre index and positive for the Paasche index. It is zero for the other indices.

Although generally used, these decomposition methods have at least two disadvantages. First, they can be applied only to the industrial sector for

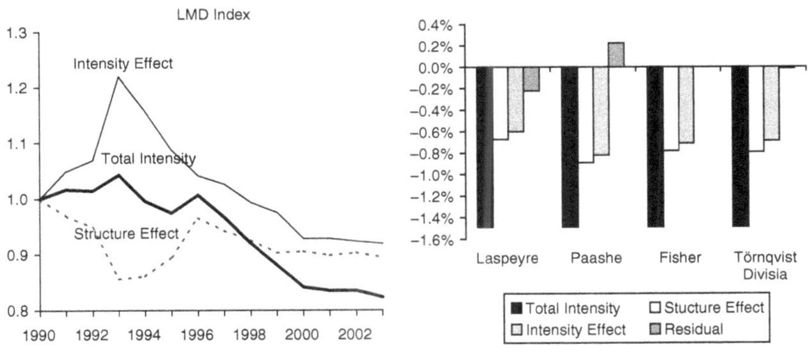

Figure 1.2 Decomposition of energy intensity changes (industrial energy consumption in France between 1990 and 2003)

Source: Enerdata, calculated using data from Table 1.1.

which the decomposition of energy consumption by sub-sectors tallies with the decomposition of the value added or of production. Secondly, they lack precious information on the unitary consumption of the energy-intensive branches, which have decisive weight in total intensity. To better eliminate certain parasitic effects, it is preferable to stay close to the physical quantities and to reconstruct the aggregated indicators from the observed unitary consumption. The ODEX-indicators (Bosseboeuf *et al.*, 2005, World Energy Council, 2004) are constructed on this basis from the ODYSSEE data.[12] This bottom-up reconstruction method for energy efficiency indices has the advantage of being adaptable to all sectors whenever the preponderant uses have been identified (Ang, 2006).

Notes

1 The gross calorific value (GCV) is the maximum theoretical quantity of heat produced by combustion, whereas the net calorific value (NCV) is the quantity of heat that can be recuperated after deduction of the heat of vaporization of the water vapour produced in combustion. The ratio between the two varies from 90 to 95 per cent for fossil fuels. The international accounting systems use NCV for coal and oil, but GCV for gas.

2 These same equivalences and the definition of the toe equal to 10 Gcal or 10^7 kcal lead to the classical equivalence of 1 GWh = 10^6 kWh = 86 toe.

3 For electricity, the production, exchange and final consumption are evaluated as a function of the energy content (1 GWh = 86 toe). The primary production of hydraulic electricity is evaluated with this same coefficient. For the production of nuclear and geothermic electricity, the coefficients are, respectively, 260 toe/GWh and 860 toe/GWh, as a result of average transformation efficiencies of 33 and 10 per cent.

4 The 'thermodynamic' aggregates, where the accounting methods are based on the physical properties of the energy, are not developed here.

5 These hypotheses have been tested a number of times by the authors on a sample of industrialized countries by proceeding to regressions between GDP (Y), primary consumption of coal (C), of oil (O), of gas and electricity, plus other explicative variables. The VMP are calculated by the differentials $\partial Y/\partial C$, $\partial Y/\partial O \dots$. The evolution of the relative VMP $(\partial Y/\partial C)/(\partial Y/\partial O)\dots$ is generally concordant with that of relative prices. For the case of the United States in 1992, the VMP of oil is 3 times that of coal (marginally, 0.33 units of oil are needed to replace one unit of coal) and the VMP of electricity is 4 times that of coal.

6 The temperature correction transforms the final total observed consumption QE into the final normalized consumption QE_n, defined for a reference annual climate. Its computation is based on the ratio between the number DD of real degree-days recorded in a year (sum of the differences between daily temperature and 18°C) and the number DD_n of degree-days in a normal year. This correction only takes account of the part K of the space heating or air conditioning in the consumption QE_n. It is expressed by one or the other of the two relations: $QE = QE_n.(1 - K) + QE_n.K.(DD/DD_n)$ and $QE_n = QE.1/(1 - K.(1 - DD/DD_n))$.

7 In certain formalizations, the decomposition into factors is applied directly at E_t and leads to the expression $E_t = \sum_{i=1}^{n} Y_t \cdot Y_{it}/Y_t \cdot E_{it}/Y_{it}$ where the variable Y_t represents an activity effect which adds to the two other effects.

8 The two types of index also verify the relation $\Delta \boldsymbol{I}_T = \boldsymbol{I}_T - \boldsymbol{I}_0 = (\boldsymbol{I}_T/\boldsymbol{I}_0 - 1) . \boldsymbol{I}_0$

9 Before they were based on index number theory, the methods made use of a decomposition at the first order of changes in intensity $\Delta \boldsymbol{I}_t = \Delta[\sum_{i=1}^{n} Y_{it}/Y_t \cdot E_{it}/Y_{it}]$ (Medina (1975), Darmstadter *et al.* 1978). The passage from first differences to differential form takes place in reference to Divisia's equation cited in Box 1.1.

10 The logarithmic-mean of two variables x and y is

$$L(x, y) = (x - y)/(\ln x - \ln y) \quad \text{if} \quad x \neq y \quad \text{and} \quad L(x, x) = x$$

11 To pass from the multiplicative form to the additive form, we use the logarithmic approximation: $\ln(I_{\text{tot}}) = \ln(1 + \bar{I}_{\text{tot}}) = \bar{I}_{\text{tot}}$ if $\bar{I}_{\text{tot}}$ is close to 0. $\bar{I}_{\text{tot}}$ ($\bar{I}_{\text{str}}$ and $\bar{I}_{\text{int}}$ respectively) are the indices of the additive form.

12 If A_t represents the production of a sub-sector, E_t the annual consumption and UC_t the unit consumption, the unit consumption effect (EFCU) is defined by $EFCU_t = A_t \cdot (UC_t - UC_0)$. The energy efficiency index is $I_t = Et/(Et - EFCUt) \cdot 100$ and the weighted index is $\boldsymbol{I}_{t-1}/\boldsymbol{I}_t = \sum_i EC_{i,t} \cdot (UC_{i,t}/UC_{i,t-1})$ where EC_{it} is the share of sub-sector i in total consumption.

References

Adams, F.G. and Miovic, P. (1968) 'On Relative Fuel Efficiency and the Output Elasticity of Energy Consumption in Western Europe', *Journal of Industrial Economics*, vol. XVII.

Adelman, M.A. and Watkins, G.C. (2004) 'Costs of Aggregate Hydrocarbon Additions', *Energy Journal*, vol. 25, no. 3.

ADEME-Danish Energy Authority-UE (2004) *Cross-Country Comparisons of Energy Efficiency Trends and Performance in Central and Eastern European Countries*. Synthesis Report.

Ang, B.W. (2005) 'The LMDI Approach to Decomposition Analysis: A Practical Guide', *Energy Policy*, vol. 33.

Ang, B.W. (2006) 'Monitoring Changes in Economy-Wide Energy Efficiency: From Energy-GDP Ratio to Composite Efficiency Index', *Energy Policy* , vol. 34, no. 5.

Ang, B.W. and Zhang, F.Q. (2000) 'A Survey of Index Decomposition Analysis in Energy and Environmental Studies', *Energy*, vol. 25, no. 12.

Ang, B.W., Liu, F.L., Chung, H. (2004) 'A Generalized Fisher Index Approach to Energy Decomposition Analysis', *Energy Economics*, vol. 26.

Bacon, R.W. (1991) 'Rockets and Feathers: The Asymmetric Speed of Adjustment of UK Retail Gasoline Prices to Cost Changes', *Energy Economics*, July.

Bosseboeuf, D., Lapillonne, B. and Eichhammer, W. (2005) 'Measuring Energy Efficiency Progress in the EU: The Energy Efficiency Index ODEX', *European Council for an Energy Efficient Economy*, EU, Brussels.

Boyd, G.A. and Roop, J.M. (2004) 'A Note on the Fisher Ideal Index Decomposition for Structural Change in Energy Intensity', *Energy Journal*, vol. 25, no. 1.

Cleveland, C.J., Costanza, R., Hall, C.A.S., Kaufmann, R.K. (1984) 'Energy and the US Economy: A Biophysical Perspective', *Science*, vol. 225.

Darmstadter, J. (1978) *How Industrial Countries Use Energy*, Johns Hopkins University Press, New York.

Diewert, W.E. (2001) *The Consumer Price Index and Index Number Theory: A Survey*, Department of Economics, The University of British Columbia, Discussion Paper no. 01–02.

Energy Policy – Special Issue (1997) 'Cross-Country Comparisons of Indicators of Energy Use, Energy Efficiency and CO_2 Emissions', *Energy Policy*, vol. 25, no. 7–9.

Eurostat (1982) *Principles and Methods of the Energy Balance Sheets*, Statistical Office of the European Communities, Luxembourg.

Gately, D. and Huntington, H.G. (2002) 'The Asymmetric Effects of Changes in Price and Income on Energy and Oil Demand', *Energy Journal*, vol. 23, no. 1.

IEA–OECD, *Energy Balances of OECD countries*, Paris (various issues).

IEA–OECD-Eurostat (2004) *Energy Statistics Manual*, Paris, Luxembourg.

Kaufmann, R.K. (1994) 'The Relation between Marginal Product and Price in US Energy Markets: Implications for Climate Change Policy', *Energy Economics*, vol. 16.

Kaufmann, R.K. (2004) 'The Mechanisms for Autonomous Energy Efficiency Increases: A Cointegration Analysis of the US energy/GDP ratio', *Energy Journal*, vol. 25.

Liu, X.Q., Ang, B.W. and Ong, H.L. (1992) 'The Application of the Divisia Index to the Decomposition of the Changes in Industrial Consumption', *Energy Journal*, vol. 13, no. 4.

Medina, E. (1975) 'Consommations d'énergie, essai de comparaisons internationales', *Economie et Statistiques*, INSEE, Paris, no. 66.

Turvey, R. and Nobay, A.R. (1965) 'On Measuring Energy Consumption', *The Economic Journal*, vol. LXXV, no. 300.

United Nations (1982) *Concepts and Methods in Energy Statistics, with Special Reference to Energy Accounts and Balances: A Technical Report*, Statistical Office, New York.

World Energy Council (2004) *Energy Efficiency: A Worldwide Review,* in collaboration with ADEME, London.

Zarnikau, J., Guermouche, S. and Schmidt, P. (1996) 'Can Different Energy Sources Be Added or Compared?', *Energy*, vol. 21, no. 6.

2
Dynamic Demand Analysis and the Process of Adjustment

Jacques Girod

Introduction

It is generally necessary to introduce dynamic components into the modelling of energy consumption because the effects of explicative factors are not totally instantaneous and lagged effects continue to act over more or less long periods of time. In other words, consumption observed at time t depends on the values of exogenous variables recorded at t, $t-1$, $t-2$ and so on, or, perhaps, this consumption is itself related to consumption observed during previous years.

Alternatively, but with a reversed perspective, the short-run behaviour of users is not independent of what they expect over the long run. The decisions they take in order to increase (or reduce), over time, their energy consumption cannot take effect instantly because of present constraints, notably those imposed by the existent stock of equipment at their disposal for their energy needs. The changes envisaged take place within a framework of internal rigidity and inertia.

It would theoretically be possible to have recourse to two types of modeling, one for the short term, the other for the long term, each calling upon different explicative variables. In fact, in order to avoid installing too evident a cut-off between the short and long term and to preserve a structural permanence in the evolution of energy consumption, we admit the existence of an adjustment between these two 'terms' and try to formalize the underlying process of the passage from the present to the future or, alternatively, from the past to the present. The simplest type of prototype of this formalization is the partial adjustment model where the consumption Y_t depends on Y_{t-1} and on various exogenous variables X_t. This is the starting point for many econometric studies intended to improve the representation of the adjustment mechanism.

Thus, in practical terms the improvement of static formalizations by the insertion of dynamic components in energy modelling comes down to defining an adjustment process for the energy consumption between the short term and the long term, and it is the lagged, exogenous and endogenous, variables that make this possible.[1] It is this process which creates the dynamics and illustrates the relation between adjustment and dynamics.

In the energy sector the presence of equipment for use and the expectation of prices and other economic variables are two characteristics that explain the interest in partial adjustment models. With appropriate hypotheses and formalizations it is possible to overcome one of the major problems concerning stocks of equipment, which is that of being obliged to enumerate them in order to be able to evaluate the corresponding demand. Except in special cases (power stations, large industrial steam generators or transport vehicles) an exhaustive inventory is practically out of the question. One can, however, reasonably assume that part of the energy consumption Y_t depends very closely on the existing stock S_{t-1}, an unobservable variable which can, however, be approximated by the observable variable Y_{t-1}. The 'adjustable' consumption between $t-1$ and t will then be a function of the current level of prices and the long-term demand will depend on expectations formulated.

The energy issues in the analysis of energy consumption

A constant objective of econometric modelling in the energy sector has been to define the appropriate methods of dealing with problems encountered by decision-makers at a given time. When the innovations were first introduced and without excluding the subsequent theoretical concerns, the objectives of the models were often to facilitate decision-making. It can be said that the problems posed have implicitly led to a selection of the nature of the data considered and have, as a result, configured the methodology. A bottom line appears, however, showing that data are assembled to an ever finer degree and the methods process data that are more and more fragmented. The focal length in the analysis of energy problems has considerably shortened since the early modelling work.

During the 1960s the questions posed by economic actors about the dynamics of energy demand remained essentially highly consolidated: national demand, sectorial demand, and demand by energy source. The expected elasticity values of the GNP, of industrial production and of the population were primordial. They have been the subject of intense debates in the annals of numerous international publications (D.H. Meadows *et al.* (1974); Goldemberg *et al.* (1988); Commission of the European Communities, 1984).

Forecasting energy consumption over the mean and long term was clearly the main objective of the first energy models used. A fundamental problem was to determine the level of investment for which to plan in order to satisfy future demand (refineries, power stations) and the volume of energy supplies to find within the nation or to be imported. The accent was put, therefore, on the aggregates of the energy balance sheet rather than on the elementary data.

In this context, the statistical extrapolation models or the trend models used up until then were too simplistic. Following the work begun during the 1930s by (Fisher, Stone, Wold and so on) on the demand functions, it was clear that more solid formulations were indispensable to incorporate the true explicative factors of demand such as the GNP, incomes and prices. In order to anticipate more correctly the rate of growth expected, it appeared necessary to proceed to an initial decomposition of the aggregated data in order to further strengthen the usual forecasting methods.

Energy demand is, in fact, a derived demand since the needs expressed for the various energy sources result from the operation of a plant or of an appliance. It is, therefore, also a conditional demand, a function of equipment stocks. Because of these characteristics, it can be said that the demand is doubly dated: 1) by the date t_1 of acquisition of the equipment to be used, and 2) by the date t_2 when this demand is fulfilled, and this distinction, by itself engages the dynamic properties. The interval of time between t_1 and t_2 determines how we distinguish between captive demand and substitutable demand and between short-run and long-run demand.

Captive demand, substitutable demand and short-run and long-run demands

The demand Y_i of a given consumer (or a supposedly homogeneous ensemble of consumers) is the product of the stock of the k equipments available S_{ik} and of the utilization rates U_{ik}, or

$$Y_i = \sum_k S_{ik} U_{ik} \tag{2.1}$$

Given that the date of acquisition t_1 is often far from the date of use t_2, an important part of Y_i is said to be captive or specific, indicating that the only possibility of modulation is to make the utilization rate U_{ik} vary. The remaining part of Y_i is said to be substitutable and corresponds to equipment acquired between $t_2 - 1$ and t_2. By omitting the indices i and k, this substitutable part YS_{t_2} breaks down in the following fashion:

$$YS_{t_2} = r\, S_{t_2-1}U_{t_2-1} + \Delta S_{t_2}U_{t_2} + S_{t_2-1}\Delta U_{t_2}$$

where the three terms on the right represent (Khazzoom, 1973):

- the demand for replacement, as a result of obsolescence of equipment at the rate r
- the demand for expansion corresponding to an increase of the stock

$$\Delta S_{t_2} = S_{t_2} - S_{t_2-1}$$

- the supplementary demand corresponding to an increase in the rate of use.

If we assume that the use rate remains ($\Delta U_{t_2} = 0$), the substitutable demand can be written:

$$YS_{t_2} = Y_{t_2} - (1 - r)Y_{t_2 - 1}$$

and, in an equivalent manner:

$$Y_{t_2} = (1 - r)Y_{t_2 - 1} + YS_{t_2} \tag{2.2}$$

In very simple form, this relation well translates the dynamics of energy consumption, one part being captive or quasi-fixed, the other being variable and flexible. The time dependence is derived from the two successive dates t_2 and $t_2 - 1$. If we assume that the use rate is variable, the dynamics of the consumption is then the result of the dynamics of the stocks and the dynamics of the use rate.

A first consequence of the decomposition introduced is to show that the forecast quality, its plausibility and reliability, imply realistic hypotheses on the extent of the substitutions between energy sources. It is equally easy to see that equation (2.2) structures the demand in time if we agree to assimilate the captive demand with the short-run demand, strongly subordinated to the use of the existing stock, and the substitutable or flexible demand to the long-run demand or, more exactly, according to the terminology used with adjustment models, to the desired, planned or targeted demand if it were made possible to instantly choose equipment or another energy source in order to profit, for example, from new price conditions appearing at t_2. The adjustment process, therefore, becomes part of optimizing behaviour by minimizing the costs of adjustment, including those associated with energy and those associated with other factors of production, notably capital.

Revision of the energy issues after the price increase of petroleum products in 1973 and 1981

It is useless to expand on the considerable impact of the rise in the price of petroleum and petroleum products and next sequent rise of all energy prices. After 1973 it became essential to know to what extent this price increase would modify the conditions of consumption adjustment that had already taken place, but an entirely new problem arose, which was to determine what would also be the repercussions on the progression of the GNP. In a complete reversal of the problem, the costs of adjustment to be retained overstepped by far the sectorial level to encompass the entire macro-economic field. The first models of energy/economy coupling date back to 1974 (Hudson, Jorgenson, Just, Nordhaus, Verleger and so on) and have led, over almost 15 years, to a number of other models for evaluating the repercussions of the energy price increase on economic growth.

If we consider only demand models, the answers to these questions could not be correctly examined in the framework of the rudimentary mechanism of adjustment between the short and the long term as described by the partial adjustment model. To restore the connections between energy adjustments and economic adjustments, more complex formalizations become necessary. We will discuss several ideas about this below.

An increased need for detailed data on the energy system

In a retrospective of questions on the determinants of energy demand and its dynamics, a constant trend is increasingly observed, that of progressively neglecting the overall level of aggregated demand in order to stress the particular dynamics of certain consumers or sectors. The questions of public administration and energy enterprises have become more direct with the object of targeting their intervention modalities on one or another consumer category.

The measures to be studied and undertaken depend on the commercial policies of energy enterprises, tariff policies, fiscal policies, various policies directed towards incitation of energy savings, replacement of poorly performing equipment or of the reduction of polluting emissions. The particular characteristics of the consumers targeted and those of their modes of energy consumption should, therefore, be collected in considerable detail in order that the planned mechanisms lead to significant results. National services and enterprises are continually involved in preliminary studies of this kind.

Recent econometric studies, for example, examine the substitutions between energy sources in the thermal power plants in Sweden (Brännlund and Lundgren, 2004), the influence of the characteristics of industrial enterprises in Denmark on their consumption of electricity (Bjorner *et al.*, 2001), the sensitivity of various household categories in the Netherlands to the Regulating Energy tax (Berkhout *et al.*, 2004), the response of Japanese households to the 'time-of-day' electricity tariff as a function of their equipment level (Matsukawa, 2001). In these models, noting the annual series of consumption, income and prices is obviously insufficient to perform the necessary analyses. The data obtained in the course of surveys or panel data lead us to process doubly indexed data, Y_{it} and X_{it}, the index i representing particular entities (enterprises, industrial branches, household categories, and so forth).

The econometric methods used for analysing the dynamics and the adjustments of energy consumption

A convenient starting point for econometric modelling is to adopt equation (2.1) which expresses energy consumption Y_i as the accumulated product of the equipment stock S_{ik} and the use rate U_{ik}. This equation defines the structural model of energy consumption as a function of two endogenous variables S_{ik} and U_{ik}, which are supposed to depend on several exogenous factors

(Bohi and Zimmerman, 1984). If we introduce the index t representing time (and if we omit k), these variables can be written:

$$S_{it} = f(X_t, Z_t, P_{it}, P_{jt}) \tag{2.3}$$

$$U_{it} = g(X_t, Z_t, P_{it}) \tag{2.4}$$

The variable X_t can represent an economic quantity (GNP, industrial production, income), Z_t one or several specific variables, P_{it} the price of energy i and P_{jt} the price of an alternative energy j. In practice, given that information on stock S_{it} is rarely available and that the decisions influencing S_{it} and U_{it} take place at two different times t_1 and t_2 respectively, the expressions (2.3) and (2.4) are combined into a single relation called the reduced form, where lagged variables are added to restore the dynamic behaviour of the decision process:

$$Y_{it} = h\,(X_t, X_{t-1} \ldots X_{t-n}, Z_t, Z_{t-1} \ldots Z_{t-n}, P_{it} \ldots P_{it-n}, P_{jt} \ldots P_{jt-n}) \tag{2.5}$$

The separate effects of the variables X_t, Z_t, P_{it}, P_{jt} on the stock and on the use rate are no longer distinguished here. Equation (2.5) shows that the formal framework of the dynamic models is that of distributed lag models where the impacts of the explicative variables on the dependent variable are gradual and distributed over a variable period of time. In its linear form and limiting ourselves to the single X_t (or considering X_t as a vector of explicative variables), the generic expression of this model is:

$$\begin{aligned} Y_t &= a + b_0 X_t + b_1 X_{t-1} + \cdots + u_t \\ &= a + \sum_{i=0}^{\infty} b_i X_{t-i} + u_t \quad \text{with} \quad \lim b_i = 0 \quad \textit{and} \quad \sum_{i=0}^{\infty} b_i = b < \infty \end{aligned} \tag{2.6}$$

where a and b_i are parameters assumed to be invariant and u_t is an error term, generally assumed to be independent of X_t, non-autocorrelated and normally distributed (n.i.d. for short). The coefficients b_i are reaction coefficients, usually decreasing in time with a zero asymptotic effect when t is sufficiently long. Their sum, the coefficient b, represents the long-run effect of a continuous change of X_t over Y_t, while b_0 represents the short-run effect.

If we define a geometric decrease (Koyck distributed lag) as a particular time structure for these lags:

$$b_i = \lambda\, b_{i-1} = \ldots \lambda^i\, b_0 \quad 0 < \lambda < 1$$

we can show by simple transformation that Y_t can be written as an autoregressive model including, on the right, the endogenous lagged variable Y_{t-1} and the exogenous variable X_t:

$$Y_t = \lambda\, Y_{t-1} + b_0 X_t + a(1 - \lambda) + (u_t - \lambda u_{t-1}) \tag{2.7}$$

This variable Y_{t-1}, also a linear combination of $X_{t-1}, X_{t-2}, \ldots$, 'summarizes' the effect on Y_t of the successive lags of the exogenous variable and is a synthetic measure of the consumption modes as they existed at the beginning of the period t. The difference $1 - \lambda$ represents the speed of adjustment of the process.

The partial adjustment model

A result of a particular specification of the lags, the energy demand Y_t expressed in the form of equation (2.7) can also be obtained starting from a hypothesis on the nature of the adjustment between the short run and the long run, an adjustment precisely called partial because it comes to pass every year in a given proportion, the complete adjustment taking place formally, and by convention, at infinity.

The demand, effective or expressed at time t, is Y_t, while the desired, planned or targeted demand, or the demand optimized in the environment of t, is the non-observable variable Y_t^*, assumed to be a function of the exogenous variables X_t. In the linear case, and with a single exogenous variable, this function is:[2]

$$Y_t^* = a + bX_t \tag{2.8}$$

The adjustment process then describes the route by which Y_t gradually approaches Y_t^*, namely:

$$Y_t - Y_{t-1} = \delta(Y_t^* - Y_{t-1}) + u_t \quad 0 < \delta \leq 1 \tag{2.9}$$

That is to say that the effective demand variation between $t - 1$ and t partially responds, by the intermediary of the parameter δ and with a stochastic disturbance term u_t, to the spread between the desired level Y_t^* and the value observed at $t - 1$. Y_t^* can thus be interpreted as a long-run equilibrium level that consumers consider to be adapted to the values of X_t observed at the time when they take their consumption decision. In fact, it is the energy YS_t of equation (2.2) that consumers have, or should have, planned to substitute in t in the absence of rigidities due the existing equipment stock. The preceding expression can, alternatively, be written in two forms:

$$Y_t = \delta Y_t^* + (1 - \delta)Y_{t-1} + u_t \tag{2.10}$$

$$Y_t^* = \frac{1}{\delta} Y_t + \frac{1 - \delta}{\delta} Y_{t-1} + u_t \tag{2.11}$$

In (2.10), Y_t appears as a weighted average of Y_t^* and Y_{t-1} (exclusive of u_t), the same property applying to Yt^* in (2.11). The parameter δ is the speed of adjustment, equal to $1 - \lambda$ in equation (2.7). Equation (2.10) means that δ% of the demand at t corresponds to the long-run optimum (2.8) and $(1 - \delta)$% to the level of demand expressed at $t - 1$. If $\delta = 1$, the adjustment to the desired demand is instantaneous, signifying complete flexibility of the stock. The closer δ is to 1, the closer the effective demand at t reflects the desired demand rather than that of former years. If δ is close to 0, the conclusions are reversed.

By the same transformation as that controlling the passage of (2.6) to (2.7), and after the elimination of Y_t^*, the partial adjustment model of the demand can be written in three equivalent forms:

$$Y_t = a\delta + (1-\delta)Y_{t-1} + b\delta X_t + u_t \tag{2.12a}$$

$$Y_t = a + b\delta \sum_{i=0}^{\infty} (1-\delta)^i X_{t-i} + \sum_{i=0}^{\infty} (1-\delta)^i u_{t-i} \tag{2.12b}$$

$$Y_t = \delta \sum_{i=0}^{\infty} (1-\delta)^i Y_{t-i}^* + \sum_{i=0}^{\infty} (1-\delta)^i u_{t-i} \tag{2.12c}$$

In (2.12a), Y_{t-1} again synthesizes the influence of all the lagged variables X_{t-i}. It is the form generally used to estimate the parameters a, b, δ. In (2.12b), the deterministic part of Y_t introduces the weighted geometric mean of the X_{t-i} and in (2.12c) that of the Y_{t-i}^*.

The adaptive expectations model

If the partial adjustment model aims to find a response to the existence of rigidities in behaviours by connecting the value of Y_t to the value of the preceding Y_{t-1}, the adaptive expectations model relates to the uncertainty affecting the explicative variable X_t. While the notions of desired value or target applied, previously, to the variable Y_t, they concern here the level of X_t and its expected level X_t^* that we assume to be linked by the expression:

$$X_t^* - X_{t-1}^* = \gamma\,(X_t - X_{t-1}^*) \tag{2.13}$$

from which:

$$X_t^* = \gamma X_t + (1-\gamma)\, X_{t-1}^* \tag{2.14}$$

$$= \gamma \sum_{i=0}^{\infty} (1-\gamma)^i X_{t-i} \qquad 0 < \gamma < 1 \tag{2.15}$$

In addition, we assume that this variable X_t^* stochastically determines Y_t by the linear relation:

$$Y_t = a' + b'X_t^* + u_t \tag{2.16}$$

By substituting (2.16) into (2.13), we arrive at the reduced form of the model of expectations:

$$Y_t = a'\gamma + (1-\gamma)Y_{t-1} + b'\gamma X_t + u_t + (1-\gamma)u_{t-1} \tag{2.17}$$

where appear on the right the lagged variable Y_{t-1} and the present value X_t, as in the partial adjustment model, the essential difference being the form of the residual which now follows a Markov process.

An extension of these two models of partial adjustment and adaptive expectations, more theoretical and hard to apply because of interpretation difficulties, is their combination in a unique formalization. By transformation of the variables X^* and Y^* and their substitution as functions of X and Y, the resulting model is:

$$Y_t = A + B\,Y_{t-1} + C\,Y_{t-2} + D\,X_t + u_t + \rho\,u_{t-1}$$

where the parameters A, B, C, D are functions of the parameters a, b, c, δ of the first model and a', b', γ of the second. We note that the endogenous variable Y appears on the right with two time lags Y_{t-1} and Y_{t-2}.

The generalization of these various formulations is the autoregressive distributed lag model (ARDL):

$$A(L)\,Y_t = B(L)\,X_t + u_t$$

where L is the lag operator ($LY_t = Y_t - Y_{t-1}$) and where A and B are polynomials in L defining the effect of the lags on the variables X and Y. If $A(L)$ is a polynomial of degree p and $B(L)$ a polynomial of degree q, the model is called ARDL(p,q).

A retrospective on the econometric models dealing with the dynamics and adjustments of the energy demand

Two pioneering studies of the dynamics of energy demand

In the econometric research conducted in the years 1950–60 on demand functions (final consumer goods and production inputs) an important place was given to replacement of static specifications by dynamic specifications. Notably, it was to evaluate the impact of the income of preceding years on household aggregated consumption that the first dynamic models were constructed (Fisher, Frisch, Tinbergen, Allais, Koyck, and so forth). Various time structures of response must be incorporated into the formalizations to restore the dynamics of the demand. These same considerations apply to the energy sector, with, however, specific difficulties that early work tried to resolve.

In a pioneering study, Fisher and Kaysen (1962) carried out a detailed study of household and industrial energy consumption in the United States. The stock S_{it} of equipment i is assumed to be fixed in the short run and the demand $Y_t = \sum_i U_{it}\,S_{it}$ is a function of this stock and the intensity of use U_{it}. In the long run, Y_t evolves in proportion to the changes occurring in this stock and in this intensity. Referring to Stone and Rowe (1957), Fisher and Kaysen initially adopt a stock adjustment mechanism that conforms to the classic expression: $S_{it} - S_{it-1} = \rho_i(S^e_{it} - S_{it-1})$ where S^e_{it} is the desired stock. Beside the difficulties in the determination of S^e_{it}, the authors, in fact, judge this mechanism to be inappropriate because it estimates that the decisions of individual consumers apply to the decision to buy or not to buy new equipment and not on the adjustment of a given stock. They prefer to have recourse to a 'disease model' defined initially by the ratio S_{it}/S_{it-1} representing the rate of growth of the 'infection', that is to say the rhythm of acquisition of the equipment *i*.

The approach adopted by Balestra and Nerlove (1966), illustrated by the example of the consumption of petrol by vehicles in the United States (Nerlove (1971)), is a direct result of the schema of decomposition of demand described by the relations (2.1) and (2.2). The total demand is the product of the capital stock S_t by the rate of use U_t measured in gallons per mile, and the substitutable demand corresponds to the demand for new vehicles I_t, so that $YS_t = U_t \cdot I_t$. If ρ is the depreciation rate of the stock, the stock at time t can be written (by removing the index *i* indicating the type of vehicle):

$$S_t = (1 - \rho)\, S_{t-1} + I_t$$

If the rate U_t remains constant between $t - 1$ and t, the total demand is:

$$Y_t = (1 - \rho)\, Y_{t-1} + YS_t$$

The second hypothesis is that the substitutable demand is a linear function of the income X_t and the price P_t:

$$YS_t = \alpha + \beta X_t + \gamma P_t + u_t$$

The total demand is then deduced as:

$$Y_t = \alpha + \beta X_t + \gamma P_t + (1 - \rho) Y_{t-1} + u_t \tag{2.18}$$

an expression which corresponds to equation (2.12a) of the partial adjustment model and in which neither the stock S_t, nor the rate of use U_t is found.[3]

The demand dynamics are implicitly related to those of the equipment stock, which makes it possible to transform a stock adjustment model of the type $S_t - S_{t-1} = \eta(S^*_t - S_{t-1})$ to a flow adjustment model for which data are more easily accessible.[4]

More complex formalizations of the adjustment process

An important criticism of a number of dynamic models is the *ad hoc* character, both of the adjustment mechanism superimposed on the static formalization and stock accumulation process itself. The dynamics introduced are not really based on an optimization process and, moreover, the demand functions obtained do not necessarily verify the required theoretical properties.

The improvements sought applied mainly to the input demand functions in the production sectors, to the extent that the traditional distinction between fixed and variable inputs could clearly appear as similar to the distinction between stock and flow. Moreover, it became possible to adopt the differentiated adjustment costs for the various inputs considered and to base the dynamic adjustment process on a really economic criterion of cost minimization. The theoretical work of Nadiri and Rosen (1969), Treadway (1969) and Keenan (1979) corresponds to these new directions and has given rise in energy econometrics to richer formalizations.

When describing a production function with two stock variables (capital and work) and two flow variables (capital service and the quantity of work) and by defining for each of the four variables a spread between the long-run equilibrium level Y_{it}^* and the effective level Y_{it}, Nadiri and Rosen generalize the input adjustment process by defining a square matrix Λ whose element Λ_{ij} characterizes the respective interactions between the inputs i and j in the path towards equilibrium. The approach of Treadway is similar, but the starting point of the adjustment mechanism is the flexible capital accelerator model for which he proposes a generalization in the case of N quasi-fixed inputs.

Another direction in the definition of the optimization process is the minimization of the various adjustment costs. In effect, these include, on the one hand, the costs induced by the disequilibrium $Y_t - Y_t^*$ between the observed and desired levels (or the short-run inefficiency costs for Hogan, 1989) and, on the other hand, by the costs corresponding to the permanent adjustments operating between the situations Y_{t-1} and Y_t (increase in rates of use, new investments, and so forth).

In the simplest case, if we adopt a quadratic loss function combining these two types of cost:

$$C(Y_t) = a(Y_t - Y_t^*)^2 + b(Y_t - Y_{t-1})^2$$

the minimization of $C(Y_t)$ with respect to Y_t leads to the relation (2.9) of the standard partial adjustment (except the error term).

Keenan (1979) extends this decision criterion over an infinite time period and shows the connection between adjustment and rational expectation. In the presence of adjustment lags between the desired stock S_t^* and the real stock S_t, all decisions to get closer to the equilibrium value, in an optimal way, imply expectations of the variables concerned. The decision rule adopted corresponds to the partial adjustment rule $S_t = (1 - \lambda)\, d_t + \lambda\, S_{t-1} + \varepsilon_t$ where d_t is a function of the target S_t^* and ε_t is a stochastic residual.

The last theoretical line of investigation considered here is more econometric in nature than economic. It was first studied by Anderson and Blundell (1982) who define the adjustment mechanism in terms of error correction models. In an extension of this work, Allen and Urga (1999) and Urga and Walters (2003) retain a dynamic autoregressive distributed lag of order 1 applied to the parts of the effective factors S_t and the desired factors S_t^*, not only at time t, but also at $t-1$:

$$S_t = D_1 S_t^* + D_2 S_{t-1}^* + D_3 S_{t-1} + \eta_t$$

where D_1, D_2, D_3 are matrices of coefficients and η_t is n.i.d. fluctuation. They deduce a generalized error correction model:

$$\Delta S_t = G \Delta S_t^* + K(S_{t-1}^* - S_{t-1}) + \eta_t \qquad (\Delta \text{ is the first difference})$$

The matrices G and K are functions of D_1, D_2, D_3.

Flexibility of the demand functions and theoretical properties of these functions

Theoretical, economic and econometric developments during the years 1970–90 have been quite rapidly incorporated into the energy models. To the extent that they integrate interaction matrices between the variables (Λ, D_1, D_2, D_3 in the preceding examples), and do not only make a unique adjustment (λ or δ), the formalizations retained apply particularly well to adjustments of the share-costs of various energies deduced from translog or logit demand functions.

Concerning the translog specifications, a large number of energy applications have been performed as a result of their introduction by Christensen, Jorgenson and Lau (1975). Setting out to base dynamic modeling on a theory of behaviour optimization, Hogan (1988, 1989) again uses, with respect to the energy input demand, the considerations habitually retained in the larger framework of production factors, which are those relating to the substitution *ex-ante* between these factors and to the absence of *ex-post* flexibility.

In similar directions, several studies set out to describe the adjustment process between the short run and the long run, either by simultaneously processing stock and flow variables (Pindyck and Rotemberg, 1983; Manning, 1988) or by incorporating equipment characteristics into the AIDS (Almost Ideal Demand System) demand functions (Deaton and Müllbauer, 1980; Berkhout *et al.*, 2004). For the older work, the various approaches followed are recapitulated in the syntheses of Bohi and Zimmerman (1984) and Dahl and Sterner (1991).

On the logit model side, the concern of Considine (1984, 1989), who developed the theoretical aspects, was to define a dynamic structure which also makes it possible to conserve the theoretical properties of the input demand functions Q_{it}, demands that are conditional with respect to the price P_{it} and to the level of production Y_t. He arrives at the adjustment model:

$$f_{it} = a_i + \sum_{i=1}^{N} c_{ij} \, Ln \, P_{jt} + g_i \, Ln \, Y_t + \mu \, Ln \, Q_{it-1} + \varepsilon_{it}$$

where f_{it} is defined by $w_{it} = e^{f_{it}}/\sum e^{f_{it}}$ with $w_{it} = P_{it}.Q_{it}/\sum_i P_{it}.Q_{it}$. In the logit model, all of the properties of the demand functions are verified.

The return of the standard formalizations of adjustment dynamics

The great wave of theoretical investigations on short-run/long-run dynamics in the energy sector during the years 1970–90 has considerably slackened. It is true that the energy policy context has also changed (generalization of energy markets, new forms of regulation, modification of actors' strategies, and so on) and the determination of a long-run optimum, and of an optimal way to get there, no longer take on the same importance, in large measure because the uncertainties about prices and sources of supply are such that these trajectories appear largely impossible to define. We have come back to much simpler formalizations.

For this reason, the relations of the partial adjustment model have assumed their classical form around which particular variants have been introduced: decomposition of price and income variables with respect to rising and falling years (Gately, 1992; Gately and Huntington, 2002; Haas and Schipper, 1998), replacing energy consumption by energy intensity (Horowitz, 2004), introduction of discrete choices (Storchman, 2005). Other procedures more frequently used for processing adjustment dynamics are the error correction models and the VAR models (Holtedall and Joutz, 2004).

Dynamics and adjustment of industrial energy consumption in France

An application of the partial adjustment model concerns final energy consumption (excluding non-energy uses) of French industry between 1978 and 2002. In many industrialized countries this consumption has undergone very rapid changes as a result of the price rise of petroleum and energy products in 1973. The reduction of energy intensity per unit of value added, particularly in the energy-intensive branches, has also been amplified by industrial restructuring which has modified the weighting of the branches in the value added of the sector. This double movement justifies an examination of the way in which adjustments of energy consumption have taken place over the period considered and an effort to point out the most significant factors of the observed trend.

The data for energy consumption in the industrial sector are shown in Table 1.1 (Chapter 1) and in Figure 2.1 for the years 1978–2002. After a short period of increase, the decrease of consumption accelerates considerably, passing from 47,200 ktoe in 1979 to 35,050 ktoe in 1983 and stabilizes around 34,000–36,000 ktoe during subsequent years.

Of the various explanations for this adjustment, we consider the most important to be the evolution of the average price of energy which, between 1978 and 1983, experienced a considerable increase (+48 per cent) and did

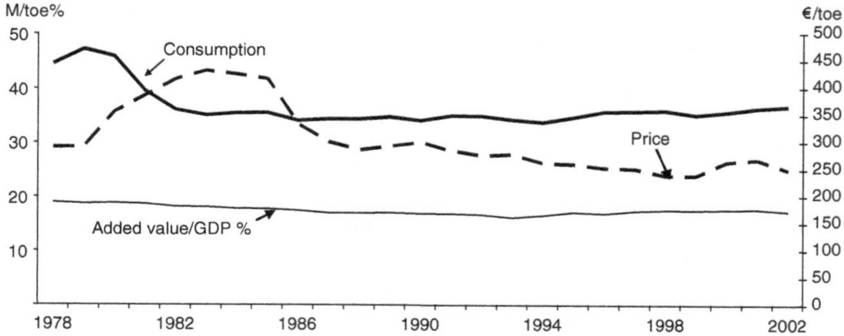

Figure 2.1 Industrial energy consumption, average price and value added/GDP: France 1978–2002

not begin to decrease until 1984. Another important factor is the value added of the industry. The trend observed in 1978 is, then, much more regular and weakly increases over the entire period considered. This factor thus enters in a direction opposite to that habitually observed in demand functions; that is to say that the average elasticity of energy consumption Y_t with respect to the value added VA_t is negative.[5] For this reason, it is preferable to retain, as an explicative factor, the part VI_t of the value added by industry in the GNP. This part decreases over the period, passing from 18.95 per cent in 1978 to 17.20 per cent in 2002. The hypothesis to be tested is whether the regular decrease of the VI_t and the effect of the average price of energy contribute to explaining the evolution of energy consumption between 1978 and 2002.

The partial adjustment model with autocorrelation of residuals

The econometric formalization retained is that of the partial adjustment model where it is assumed that there are two relations between the variables (all expressed as logarithms):

- A long-run linear relation between the consumption desired $Y_t^\bullet$, the part of the value added VI_t and the price PR_t,

$$LY_t^\bullet = a + b\,LVI_t + c\,LPR_t \tag{2.19}$$

- A stochastic relation between the desired consumption $Y_t^\bullet$ and the real consumption Y_t.

$$LY_t - LY_{t-1} = \delta(LY_t^* - LY_{t-1}) + u_t \tag{2.20}$$

The substitution of (2.19) in (2.20) leads to the expression:

$$LY_t = (1-\delta)LY_{t-1} + \delta a + \delta b\,LVI_t + \delta c\,LPR_t + u_t \tag{2.21}$$

The estimation by ordinary least squares is (t-Student in brackets below the coefficients):

$$\begin{aligned} LY_t &= \underset{(5.132)}{0.693\,LY_{t-1}} + \underset{(2.607)}{2.075} + \underset{(1.881)}{0.647\,LVI_t} - \underset{(-2.896)}{0.124\,LPR_t} + u_t \\ R^2 &= 0.882 \\ DW &= 1.367 \end{aligned} \tag{2.22}$$

The Durbin–Watson test clearly indicates the presence of autocorrelation of the residuals. These residuals show the influence of the factors which are not explicitly taken into account in the model and which most often persist from one year to the next, which leads us to admit a positive correlation between the error u_{t-1} and u_t (Malinvaud, 1970). In equation (2.22), we assume that u_t follows a first order autoregressive process leading to a new adjustment model where ε_t is n.i.d.:

$$\begin{cases} LY_t = (1-\delta)LY_{t-1} + \delta a + \delta b\,LVI_t + \delta c\,LPR_t + u_t \\ u_t = \rho u_{t-1} + \varepsilon_t \end{cases} \tag{2.23}$$

which can be written in the expanded form:

$$\begin{aligned} LY_t - \rho LY_{t-1} = {} & (1-\delta)(LY_{t-1} - \rho LY_{t-2}) + \delta a(1-\rho) \\ & + \delta b(LVI_t - \rho LVI_{t-1}) + \delta c(LPR_t - \rho LPR_{t-1}) + \varepsilon_t \end{aligned} \tag{2.24}$$

The estimation of the parameters of (2.24) by the generalized least squares method consists of performing the change of variables $Z_t = (LY_t - \rho\, LY_{t-1})$, $X_{1t} = (LVI_t - \rho\, LVI_{t-1})$, $X_{2t} = (LPR_t - \rho\, LPR_{t-1})$, and to apply OLS to the new variables Z_t, X_{1t}, X_{2t} Starting with a first evaluation of $\hat{\rho} = 0.3$, the estimation of (2.24) leads, after eight iterations, to a new value $\tilde{\rho} = 0.38$ and to the following results:

$$\begin{aligned} LY_t - 0.38\,LY_{t-1} = {} & 0.6004\,(LY_{t-1} - 0.38\,LY_{t-2}) + 0.6075\,(LVI_t - 0.38\,LVI_{t-1}) \\ & - 0.1055\,(LPR_t - 0.38\,LPR_{t-1}) + 1.8935 + \varepsilon_t \end{aligned}$$

or,

$$\begin{cases} LY_t = \underset{(2.281)}{0.6004\;LY_{t-1}} + \underset{(1.259)}{0.6075\;LVI_t} - \underset{(-1.677)}{0.1055\,LPR_t} + \underset{(1.536)}{3.054} + u_t \\ u_t = 0.38\,u_{t-1} + \varepsilon_t \end{cases}$$

$$\begin{aligned} R^2 &= 0.873 \\ DW &= 1.655 \end{aligned} \tag{2.25}$$

Interpretation of results and elasticities

Along with the statistical analysis of the model parameters, economic analysis of the results makes use of structural analysis indicators. The most commonly used are elasticities. Their definitions are given in Box 2.1 (Intriligator, 1978; Gouriéroux and Monfort, 1990).With the values of the parameters obtained in (2.25), the short-term elasticities e_{ST} and the long-term elasticities e_{LT}, with respect to the two variables VI_t and PR_t, are:

$$
\begin{aligned}
e_{ST/VI} &= 0.607 \qquad & e_{LT/VI} &= 1.520 \\
e_{ST/PR} &= -0.106 \qquad & e_{LT/PR} &= -0.264
\end{aligned}
$$

which leads to the long-term demand or desired demand:

$$LY_t^{\bullet} = 7.642 + 1.520\, LVI_t - 0.264\, LPR_t \tag{2.26}$$

and to the stochastic equation defining the adjustment process:

$$LY_t - LY_{t-1} = 0.4\,(LY_t^{\bullet} - LY_{t-1}) + u_t$$

The speed of adjustment, measured by $\delta = 0.4$, is slow, showing that the transition in the energy sector took place progressively between 1978 and 2002, and at a rather slow rhythm. The values of the short and long-run price elasticities (–0.106 and –0.264) conform with those obtained in the analogue models for the industrial sector (Bohi and Zimmerman, 1984; Fouquet *et al.*, 1997). The elasticities with respect to the part of the value VI_t are, in absolute value, considerably higher (0.607 and 1.520), but these parameters are only significant with a risk of 80 per cent. It is likely that the speed of adjustment of consumption to variations in VI_t is not the same as it is to variations of price PR_t. A model with two speeds of adjustment instead of one, as proposed by Gately and Huntington (2002) could be used.

All of these results confirm that there was an adjustment of the total energy consumption of the industrial sector, initially provoked by the rise in average prices between 1979 and 1983, and then strengthened by a regular decrease of the contribution of this sector to the GDP. These results are, nevertheless, insufficient because they block an extremely important phenomenon occurring during this period, that of substitutions between energy sources within this total consumption. Between 1978 and 2002, the part of petroleum products had, in fact, decreased from 46 per cent to 16 per cent, whereas that of natural gas passed from 16 per cent to 37 per cent and that of electricity from 18 per cent to 32 per cent. There were, therefore, in parallel, other massive adjustments which profoundly modified the initial structure of energy consumption.

Box 2.1 Elasticities

1. DEFINITIONS OF ELASTICITIES

The elasticity of the variable y with respect to the variable x is:

$$E_{y/x} = \frac{\text{percent change in } y}{\text{percent change in } x} = \frac{\Delta y}{y} \Big/ \frac{\Delta x}{x}$$

It measures the percentage of change in the variable y corresponding to a change of 1 per cent in the variable x.

A. Arc elasticity

For two pairs of values (x_0, y_0) and (x_1, y_1), with $\Delta x = x_1 - x_0$ and $\Delta y = y_1 - y_0$, the elasticity over the arc (y_0, y_1) can be measured to the points (x_0, y_0) or (x_1, y_1) yielding, in general, two distinct values. In practice, the elasticity is calculated at the mean point $E_{y/x} = \frac{\Delta y}{\Delta x} \frac{(x_1+x_0)}{(y_1+y_0)}$

B. Function elasticity

When the increases Δx and Δy tend towards 0, the elasticity can be expressed using the differentials dy and dx, yielding $e_{y/x} = \frac{dy}{y} / \frac{dx}{x}$. If the relation $y = f(x)$ between x and y is known, $e_{y/x}$ can be calculated at all points (x, y). When the relation f contains other variables, $e_{y/x}$ is measured keeping all variables constant. If the increase of other variables is not kept constant, for example, if the variations of income x have been accompanied by variations of price z, the preceding definition must be modified to take account of this complementary effect by expressing the differential of y with respect to x and z:

$$e_{y/x} = \frac{dy}{dx} \frac{x}{y} = \frac{\partial y}{\partial x} \frac{x}{y} + \frac{\partial y}{\partial z} dz \frac{1}{dx} \frac{x}{y} + \cdots$$

2. THE ELASTICITIES OF THE DEMAND FUNCTIONS. STATIC MODEL

For two products for which the quantities consumed and the prices are, (y_1, p_1) and (y_2, p_2), and for the demand functions $y_i = y_i(p_1, p_2, I)$ $i = 1, 2$ including the price and the usable income I, the definitions of the elasticities are:

income elasticity of demand for i $\quad \eta_i = \frac{\partial y_i(p_1, p_2, I)}{\partial I} \frac{I}{y_i} = \frac{\partial \ln y_i}{\partial \ln I}$

own price elasticity of demand for i $\quad \varepsilon_i = \frac{\partial y_i(p_1, p_2, I)}{\partial p_i} \frac{p_i}{y_i} = \frac{\partial \ln y_i}{\partial \ln p_i}$

cross price elasticity of demand for i $\varepsilon_{ij} = \dfrac{\partial y_i(p_1, p_2, I)}{\partial p_j}\dfrac{p_j}{y_i} = \dfrac{\partial \ln y_i}{\partial \ln p_j}$

Under the hypothesis of maximization of a utility function $U(y_1, y_2)$ and of the budget constraint $p_1y_1 + p_2y_2 = I$, the demand functions must satisfy several formal restrictions: homogeneity, non-negativity, symmetry and aggregation.

The demand function $y_i^\bullet = D_i(p_1, p_2, I)$ which maximizes the function U is called a Marshall demand function or a solution of the primal problem. The dual problem is the minimization of the total expenditure under the condition of a constant utility level. Its solution is the Hicks demand function or the *compensated demand function* $y_i^\bullet = H_i(p_1, p_2, I)$ deduced from the indirect utility function $U^*(p_1, p_2, I)$. The elasticities calculated from the functions D_i are called *non-compensated* and those calculated from the functions H_i are called *compensated.*

By Shephard's lemma and Roy's identity, the equality at equilibrium between the functions D_i and H_i leads, after differentiation, to the Slutsky equation: $\frac{\partial H_i}{\partial p_j} = \frac{\partial D_i}{\partial p_j} + y_j\frac{\partial D_i}{\partial I}$ which can also be written in terms of compensated or non-compensated elasticities $\varepsilon_{ij}^h = \varepsilon_{ij}^d + s_j\,\eta_{iI}$ where $s_j = p_jy_j/I$ is the budget-share of the goods j. The compensated price elasticity ε_{ij}^h is the sum of a substitution effect ε_{ij}^d and of an income effect $s_j\eta_{iI}$.

3. SHORT AND LONG TERM ELASTICITIES. DYNAMIC MODEL

Let the partial adjustment model be written in **reduced form,** including the endogenous variable y_t and two exogenous variables x_t and z_t.

The multiplicative form is: $y_t = k \,.\, y_{t-1}^a \,.\, x_t^b \,.\, z_t^c \,.\, v_t$

The additive form is: $Y_t = aY_{t-1} + bX_t + cZ_t + d + u_t$

(capital letters represent logarithms of the variables)

The short term elasticity of y_t with respect to x_t:

$$e_{ST} = \frac{\partial y_t}{\partial x_t}.\frac{x_t}{y_t} = \frac{\partial \ln y_t}{\partial \ln x_t} = \frac{\partial Y_t}{\partial X_t} = b$$

The long term elasticity of y_t with respect to x_t:

$$e_{LT} = \sum_{i=0}^{\infty} \frac{\partial y_t}{\partial x_{t-i}}\,\frac{y_t}{x_{t-i}} = \sum_{i=0}^{\infty} \frac{\partial \ln y_t}{\partial \ln x_{t-i}} = \sum_{i=0}^{\infty} \frac{\partial Y_t}{\partial X_{t-i}}$$

The elasticity e_{LT} measures the total rate of growth of y_t corresponding to a unitary rate of change of all the values of x_{t-i}; that is to say that it accumulates all of the short-term elasticities. Similar expressions are obtained for the elasticities of y_t with respect to z_t. The elasticities e_{ST} and e_{LT} can be calculated directly from the expression in **final form**:

$$y_t = y_0 \,.\, a^t \,.\, k^{\frac{1-a^t}{1-a}} \,.\, \left(x_t^b . x_{t-1}^{ba} \ldots x_1^{ba^{t-1}}\right) \,.\, \left(z_t^c . z_{t-1}^{ca} \ldots z_1^{ca^{t-1}}\right)$$
$$. \left(v_t . v_{t-1}^a \ldots v_1^{a^{t-1}}\right)$$

$$e_{ST/X} = b \qquad e_{LT/X} = \frac{b}{1-a}$$

$$e_{ST/Z} = c \qquad e_{LT/Z} = \frac{c}{1-a}$$

4. THE ELASTICITIES OF PRODUCTION FUNCTIONS

For a production function $y = f(y_1, y_2)$ limited to two inputs, the factor or input demand functions are: $y_i = y_i(p_1, p_2, p)$ where p is the price of production y. The calculation of price elasticities is the same as before. The cost of production is $C = \sum p_i y_i$. The optimal level of the factors, or compensated demand, is obtained by Shephard's lemma $y_i^\bullet = \partial C/\partial p_i = C_i$. The *elasticity of substitution* between the two factors is defined by $\sigma = d\ln(y_1/y_2)/d\ln(dy_1/dy_2)$ where dy_1/dy_2 is the opposite of the marginal rate of substitution. Cross-price Allen–Uzawa elasticity of substitution is defined as $\sigma_{ij} = C_{ij}\ C/C_i\ C_j$ where $C_{ij} = \partial^2 C/\partial p_i \partial p_j$. Other definitions of elasticity of substitution have been proposed by Hicks, Morishima and Sato and Koizumi.

Forecasting calculations

To complete the analysis of results, the forecasts in 2003 and 2004 of industrial consumption are calculated on the basis of estimations (2.25) of the model. For the reduced form $Y_t = aY_{t-1} + bX_t + cZ_t + d + u_t$, written without showing the logarithms of the variables, the forecast at $T + h$ is given by the expression:

$$\hat{Y}_{T+h} = \hat{a}^h Y_T + \hat{b} \sum_{j=0}^{h-1} \hat{a}^j\, \hat{X}_{T+h-j}$$
$$+ \hat{c} \sum_{j=0}^{h-1} \hat{a}^j\, \hat{Z}_{T+h-j} + \hat{d} \sum_{j=0}^{h-1} \hat{a}^j + \sum_{j=0}^{h-1} \hat{a}^j\, \hat{u}_{T+h-j} \qquad (2.27)$$

It is a conditional forecast with respect to the value Y_T, which is, in general, the last known value of the endogenous variable, assuming that the previsions $\hat{X}_{T+h-j}$ and $\hat{Z}_{T+h-j}$ of the exogenous variables are known, as well as the estimated values of the coefficients $\hat{a}$, $\hat{b}$, $\hat{c}$ *and* $\hat{d}$ and the forecast of the error terms $\hat{u}_{T+h-j}$.

For h equal, respectively, to (1.1) and (2.2), (2.27) can be written:

$$\hat{Y}_{T+1} = \hat{a}\, Y_T + \hat{b}\, \hat{X}_{T+1} + \hat{c}\, \hat{Z}_{T+1} + \hat{d} + \hat{u}_{T+1} \tag{2.28}$$

$$\hat{Y}_{T+2} = \hat{a}^2\, Y_T + \hat{b}\, (\hat{X}_{T+2} + \hat{a}\, \hat{X}_{T+1}) + \hat{c}\, (\hat{Z}_{T+2} + \hat{a}\, \hat{Z}_{T+1}) + \hat{d}(1+\hat{a}) + (\hat{u}_{T+2} + \hat{a}\, \hat{u}_{T+1}) \tag{2.29}$$

Based on the previous estimates of $\hat{a}$, $\hat{b}$, $\hat{c}$ *and* $\hat{d}$, of the value $Y_{2002} =$ 36, 567 ktoe, and of the *estimations* of the exogenous variables

$$\hat{X}_{2003} = \hat{VI}_{2003} = 17.2 \qquad \hat{X}_{2004} = \hat{VI}_{2004} = 17.0$$

$$\hat{Z}_{2003} = \hat{PR}_{2003} = 245.0 \qquad \hat{Z}_{2004} = \hat{PR}_{2004} = 270.0$$

the forecasts are:

$$\hat{Y}_{2003} = 36,672 \text{ ktoe} \qquad \hat{Y}_{2004} = 36,104 \text{ ktoe}$$

assuming $\hat{u}_{T+2} = \hat{u}_{T+1} = 0$.

The real values are:

$$Y_{2003} = 35,849 \text{ ktoe} \qquad Y_{2004} = 36,113 \text{ ktoe}$$

The long-term deduced values of the expression (2.26) are:

$$Y^*_{2003} = 36,831 \text{ ktoe} \qquad Y^*_{2004} = 35,266 \text{ ktoe}$$

The comparison between the forecasts and the real values is not very instructive here because the values of the variables VI and PR in 2003 and 2004 are estimations. If they had been available, it would have been possible to make *ex-ante* forecasts for 2003 and 2004 in order to better appreciate the conformity of the adopted model to reality.

Conclusion

The nature of the results obtained for the French industrial sector faithfully define the scope of the positive contributions of the adjustment models to the analysis of the dynamics of energy consumption and also underline some inadequacies in the application of the conclusions derived.

The process of permanently adjusting the real demand to the long-term desired demand leads us to connect the demand at time t to that observed at

$t-1$, implying the hypotheses of a 'memory' in the modes of consumption because of users' habits and of the rigidity of their equipment stock. It has been previously underlined that this process also succeeds in minimizing the quadratic sum of the disequilibrium and adjustment costs, which is another way of saying that the lags installed between the short and long term, as well as lags introduced between t and $t-1$ ... are by nature costly.

Between the initial model of Fisher and Kaysen in 1962 and the sophisticated formalizations of Manning or Hogan at the end of the 1980s, important refinements have been made in the understanding of the dynamics of energy consumption and in their formal translation. The methodological innovations have been permanent and have given rise to a large number of studies, the most important of which have been summarized above. The generalizations and extensions introduced show that it would be possible to extend to cross-sectional or panel data the econometric formalizations which, initially, were only designed in the framework of time series. In this way, the field of application of adjustment models can be enlarged to include particular categories of consumers.

Largely overshadowing the alternative of temporal or individual observations is the question of determining the pertinent level for the analysis of the dynamics of energy consumption. When we consider the total consumption of a country or a particular sectorial consumption the adjustment mechanism that comes to the fore is, in fact, the result of multiple internal adjustments and mainly those caused by substitutions among energy sources. Their shares rarely remain constant and the substitutions which take place over a given period have their own dynamics, where the evolution of relative prices plays an essential role. Similarly, what could be interpreted as a decrease in average energy intensity under the effect of a rise in average price, could simply be explained by the increased consumption of a more efficient energy at the expense of another less efficient. Certain suggestions, derived from modeling studies, have been to deal simultaneously with these internal dynamics by defining interaction matrices between them. The advantage is the possibility of a global approach and methodological coherence.

Other simpler responses are to design analyses of aggregated consumption as a first step in a much larger modeling effort whose subsequent steps influence the dynamics of substitution between energy sources. In this sense, the results of this step are only indicative of global trends and need to be enriched by recourse to different econometric techniques. That is the option adopted in this chapter and in the illustration presented. The following chapters will propose other methods and examples that will allow us to undertake these complementary analyses.

Notes

1 It is appropriate, nevertheless, to state that the adjective 'long' has no real meaning as opposed to that of 'short'. It would be more correct, in the present case, to speak

of 'mean' term when we can hardly envisage specifying the process beyond the horizon of 5–10 years. By convention, the long term only means the time corresponding to the complete renewal of a user's stock of equipment and its substantial variability is enough to invalidate any excessively strict definition.

2 Most of the authors suppose that this function is deterministic, but some hypothesize a random function by adding to (2.8) an uncertainty ξ_t (Malinvaud, 1970).

3 It should be noted that an identical result would be obtained by assuming that the renewal of the stock corresponds to the downgrading of the optimal stock, so that $I_t = \rho S_t^*$, which will lead to the two expressions:

$$S_t - S_{t-1} = \rho(S_t^* - S_{t-1}) \text{ and } Y_t - Y_{t-1} = \rho(Y_t^\bullet - Y_{t-1})$$

4 Houthakker and Taylor (1970) define the volume of the stock of equipment as a state variable S_t and the dynamics of the model are conferred by a 'state adjustment' from S_{t-1} to S_t.

5 This elasticity estimated by logarithmic regression (symbol L) $LY_t = -1.384 + 0.623\, LY_{t-1} + 0.544\, LVA_t - 0.192\, LPR_t - 0.0147\, t$ becomes positive (0.544) only if we add a time trend $\mu.t(\mu = 1.47\%)$ called autonomous energy efficiency increase whose interpretation is the object of several criticisms (Kaufmann, 2004; Hunt *et al.*, 2003).

References

Allen, C. and Urga, G. (1999) 'Interrelated Factor Demands from a Dynamic Cost Function: An Application to the Non-Energy Business Sector of the UK Economy', *Economica*, vol. 66, pp. 403–13.

Anderson, G. and Blundell, R. (1982) 'Estimation and Hypothesis Testing in dynamic Singular Equation Systems ', *Econometrica*, vol. 50, pp. 1559–71.

Balestra, P. and Nerlove, M. (1966) 'Pooling Cross Section and Time Series Data in the Estimation of a Dynamic Model: The Demand for Natural Gas', *Econometrica*, vol. 34, July, pp. 585–612.

Berkhout, P.H.G., Ferrer-i-Carbonell, A. and Muskens, J.C. (2004) 'The *ex post* Impact of an Energy Tax on Household Energy Demand', *Energy Economics*, vol. 26, pp. 297–317.

Bjorner, T.B., Togeby, M. and Jensen, H.H. (2001) 'Industrial Companies' Demand for Electricity: Evidence from a Micropanel', *Energy Economics*, vol. 23, pp. 595–617.

Bohi, D.R. and Zimmerman, M.B. (1984) 'An Update on Econometric Studies of Energy Demand Behavior', *Annual Review of Energy*, pp. 105–54.

Bourbonnais, R. (2003) *Econométrie. Manuel et exercices corrigés*, 5th ed. (Paris: Dunod).

Brännlund, R. and Lundgren, T. (2004) 'A Dynamic Analysis of Interfuel Substitution for Swedish Heating Plants', *Energy Economics*, vol. 26, pp. 961–76.

Christensen, L.R., Jorgenson, D.W. and Lau, L.J. (1975) 'Transcendental Logarithmic Utility Functions', *American Economic Review*, vol. 65, no. 3, pp. 367–83.

Commission of the European Communities (1984) *Energy and Development: What Challenges? Which Methods?* (Boston: Lavoisier Publishing Inc.).

Considine, T.J. and Mount, T.D. (1984) 'The Use of Linear Logit Models for Dynamic Input Demand Systems', *Review of Economics and Statistics*, vol. 66, pp. 434–43.

Considine, T. J. (1989) 'Separability, Functional Form and Regulatory Policy in Models of Interfuel Substitution', *Energy Economics*, vol. 11, no. 2, pp. 82–94.

Dahl, C. and Sterner, T. (1991) 'Analysing Gasoline Demand Elasticities: A Survey', *Energy Economics,* July, pp. 203–10.

Deaton, A. and Müllbauer, J. (1980) 'An Almost Ideal Demand System', *American Economic Review*, vol. 70, pp. 312–26.

Fisher, F.M. and Kaysen, C. (1962) *A Study in Econometrics: The Demand for Electricity in the United States* (Amsterdam: North-Holland Publishing Company).

Fouquet, R., Pearson, P., Hawdon, D., Robinson, C. and Stevens, P. (1997) 'The Future of UK Final User Energy Demand', *Energy Policy*, vol. 25, no. 2, pp. 231–40.

Gately, D. (1992) 'Imperfect Price-reversibility of US Gasoline Demand: Asymmetric Responses to Price Increases and Declines', *Energy Journal*, vol. 13, no. 4, pp. 179–207.

Gately, D. and Huntington, H.G. (2002) 'The Asymmetric Effects of Changes in Price and Income on Energy and Oil Demand', *Energy Journal*, vol. 23 no. 1.

Goldemberg, J., Johansson, T.B., Reddy, A.K.N. and Williams, R.H. (1988) *Energy for a Sustainable World* (New Delhi: Wiley Eastern).

Gouriéroux, C. and Monfort, A. (1990) *Séries temporelles et modèles dynamiques*, col. Economie et statistiques avancées (Paris: Economica).

Haas, R. and Schipper, L. (1998) 'Residential Energy Demand in OECD-Countries and the Role of Irreversible Efficiency Improvements', *Energy Economics*, vol. 20, pp. 421–42.

Hogan, W.W. (1988) 'Patterns of Energy Revisited', Discussion Paper Series, E-88-01, Energy and Environment Policy Centre, Harvard University, Cambridge.

Hogan, W.W. (1989) 'A Dynamic Putty-Semi-Putty Model of Aggregate Energy Demand', *Energy Economics*, January, pp. 53–63.

Holtedahl, P. and Joutz, F.L. (2004) 'Residential Electricity Demand in Taiwan', *Energy Economics,* vol. 26, pp. 201–24.

Horowitz, M.J. (2004) 'Electricity Intensity in the Commercial Sector: Market and Public Program Effects', *Energy Journal*, vol. 25, no. 2.

Houthakker, H.S. and Taylor, L.D. (1970) *Consumer Demand in the United States* (Cambridge, MA: Harvard University Press).

Hunt, L.C., Judge, G. and Ninomiya, Y. (2003) 'Underlying Trends and Seasonality in UK Energy Demand: A Sectoral Analysis', *Energy Economics*, vol. 25.

Intriligator, M.D. (1978) *Econometric Models, Techniques and Applications* (Englewood Cliffs, NJ: Prentice-Hall).

Kaufman, R. (2004) 'The Mechanisms for Autonomous Energy Efficiency Increases: A Cointegration Analysis of the US Energy/GDP Ratio', *Energy Journal*, vol. 25, no. 1, pp. 63–86.

Keenan, J. (1979) 'The Estimation of Partial Adjustment Models with Rational Expectations', *Econometrica*, vol. 47, no. 6, pp. 1441–55.

Khazzoom, J.D. (1973) 'An Econometric Model of the Demand for Energy in Canada', In *Energy: Demand, Conservation and Institutional Problems* (Toronto: Macrakis).

Malinvaud, E. (1970) *Statistical Methods of Econometrics* (Amsterdam: North-Holland Publishing Company).

Manning, N.D. (1988) 'Household Demand for Energy in the UK', *Energy Economics*, January, pp. 59–78.

Matsukawa, I. (2001) 'Household Response to Optional Peak-load Pricing of Electricity', *Journal of Regulatory Economics*, vol. 20, no. 3, pp. 249–67.

Meadows, D.H., Meadows, D.L., Randers, J. and Behrens, W.W.III (1974) *The Limits to Growth: A Report for the Club of Rome's Project on the Predicament of Mankind* (New York: Universe Books).

Nadiri, M.I. and Rosen, S. (1969) 'Interrelated Factor Demand Functions', *American Economic Review*, vol. 59, pp. 457–71.

Nerlove, M. (1971) 'Further Evidence on the Estimation of a Dynamic Relations from a Time Series of Cross Section', *Econometrica*, vol. 39, no. 2, pp. 359–82.

Pindyck, R.S. and Rotemberg, J. (1983) 'Dynamic Factor Demands and the Effects of Energy Price Shocks', *American Economic Review*, vol. 73, pp. 1066–79.

Stone, J.R. and Rowe, D.A. (1957) 'The Market Demand for Durable Goods', *Econometrica*, vol. 25, no. 3.

Storchmann, K. (2005) 'Long-run Gasoline Demand for Passengers Cars: The Role of Income Distribution', *Energy Economics*, vol. 27, pp. 25–58.

Treadway, A.B. (1969) 'On Entrepreneurial Behaviour and the Demand for Investment', *Review of Economic Studies*, vol. 36, pp. 226–39.

Urga, G. and Walters, C. (2003) 'Dynamic Translog and Linear Logit Models: A Factor Demand Analysis of Interfuel Substitution in US Industrial Energy Demand', *Energy Economics*, vol. 25, pp. 1–21.

3

Electricity Spot Price Modelling: Univariate Time Series Approach

Régis Bourbonnais and Sophie Méritet

Introduction: presentation of the energy issue

As a result of deregulation reforms, modelling and forecasting of electricity prices have become of fundamental importance to participants in electricity markets. Having an appropriate representation of the electricity price is important to the actors in this new industry which is now open to competition, quite risky and characterized by uncertainties. Modelling the price of electricity is a challenging task, considering its specific features: electricity is not storable, supply needs to be balanced continuously against demand, and there is a good deal of volatility, inelasticity, seasonality and so forth. The objective of this chapter is to model and forecast the behaviour of spot prices for two wholesale electricity markets: the Elspot of the Nord Pool in Europe and PJM spot prices in the North East region in the US (based on daily data from 29 April 2004 to 30 April 2005).

Until recently, electric power industries were organized as monopolies in most countries, often owned by government, and if not, then highly regulated by authorities. As a result, electricity prices reflected the government's social and industrial policy. In such a regulated industry, price forecasts were not critical for energy actors. Price variation was minimal, electricity prices were controlled by authorities and tended to be constant over the long term and based on costs that took into account fuel prices, technological innovation and generation efficiency. Risks taken by energy participants were limited in this regulated environment, which remained very stable for decades; there was little uncertainty in prices and there was little need for hedging electricity price risks because of the deterministic nature of prices (very predictable).

This situation changed dramatically with the deregulation reforms which, over the past several years, have spread virtually worldwide; energy network industries are undergoing a transition from regulated, vertically integrated, industries to competitive market industries. Deregulatory initiatives have been taken in the electric power industry to eliminate traditional constraints and protectionism; in some segments of the value chain, electric monopoly activities are now open to competition. Transmission and distribution segments are still considered as natural monopolies and are, therefore, regulated. Generation and retail sales activities are progressively exposed, at least to some extent, to the influence of market forces. The retail sector has been opened in many countries, but often quite slowly, and in some cases not at all. Some initiatives have been taken in power generation; wholesale competitive markets have been created in various regions and some power exchanges are taking place. In spite of electric power shortages in various countries, authorities are continuing to open up to competition, and are paying considerable attention to the new rules as well as to industry reorganization (market power of participants, incentives to investment, and development of transactions). Deregulation does not mean there is no more regulation but rather that there is new, more efficient, regulation (re-regulation) (see for example the synthesis of Newbery, 2003, and Joskow, 2006).

Electricity markets are becoming more sophisticated after several years of restructuring and market competition. What authorities had previously controlled by fixing prices as a function of supply costs has now become a market mechanism with competitive interaction of complex supply and demand functions, resulting in dynamic and uncertain electricity prices. In these new electric power markets, generators compete to sell electricity in the wholesale market while the customers purchase electricity from a pool at equilibrium prices set by the intersection of demand and supply, usually on an hourly basis.

One of the many consequences of these deregulatory changes has been an increase in the importance of modelling and forecasting electricity prices. Energy actors have always needed information about electricity prices to take their decisions. In this new competitive environment, this need becomes vital. The new rules in the electric power industry are changing the behaviour of all the actors. Forecasting prices in electric power markets is now critical for consumers and producers, in order to plan their operations and investments and manage their price risks. They also require a thorough understanding of the uncertainty (a representation of the underlying price process). Since the majority of new wholesale markets are imperfect and emerging power exchanges are incomplete and insufficiently liquid, the need for careful and detailed modelling of prices becomes an essential aspect of business in the industry for effective risk management.

Capturing electricity price evolution represents a challenging task because of its special characteristics. The crucial feature of price formation in wholesale spot markets is the instantaneous nature of the product; electricity cannot be stored once generated and supply has to be continuously balanced to demand. Across the grid, production and consumption are perfectly synchronized, without any capability for storage and, in addition, there are transmission losses. Since supply and demand shocks cannot be smoothed by inventories, electricity spot prices are characterized by a high volatility.

Electricity prices appear to be local and differ among regions or countries because of the lack of storability and constraints in transmission. As opposed to the case of storable commodities, arbitrages across time in the electricity industry are eliminated.

Electricity prices are dramatically different from other prices. The main features, linked to the instantaneous nature of the product, that make electricity so specific are:

- Electricity demand is highly inelastic because it is a necessary product. Prices are strongly dependent on the demand which is, itself, dependent on various unforeseeable factors such as weather conditions. This feature exacerbates the impact of supply and demand shocks.
- Electricity is a known as a commodity that displays one of the most pronounced *seasonal* patterns in response to cyclical fluctuations in demand. The level of electricity demand depends on economic activity and on weather conditions. It is characterized by seasonality at different levels: intra-hour, intra-day, weekend/weekday and monthly seasonality. With such a time pattern, prices are far from uniform.
- Electricity prices are marked by volatility. As a result, deregulated prices in these new markets are characterized by a volatility that varies over time and occasionally reaches extremely high levels. This phenomenon is usually explained by the non-storability of electricity, the need to have supply continuously equal to demand and by limited transmission capacity. This effect depends also on the speed of a producer's response to demand spikes. It is not unusual to notice annualized volatility of more than 1000 per cent in hourly spot prices. A rare situation, but one that occurs occasionally, is the example of June 1998 daily prices in the Midwestern region in the US where prices moved from $30 to $2500 in a few weeks.

All these characteristics of electricity spot prices influence all attempts at modelling electricity prices. Each of these features makes it more difficult to forecast spot prices. The purpose of this chapter is to model spot prices in order to improve our ability to forecast their behaviour. This subject is currently of crucial concern, given the importance of new wholesale markets and power exchanges all over the world. The discussion is stimulated by recent electricity shortages which have impacted prices.

We have decided to focus on two wholesale markets: the Elspot on the Nord Pool in Europe and PJM spot prices in the North East region in the US. They are two excellent examples as they are the largest competitive markets for wholesale electricity in the world.

Technically, we will use univariate time series models. This class of model is the most often used to model spot electricity prices, and is now the basis, in practice, for short and medium term forecasts. A general description of the assumptions used in time series models as applied to electricity markets is provided in Nogales *et al.* (2002).[1] In a univariate time series approach, the modelling of spot prices follows the following steps:

- Step 1: stationarity and unit root tests
- Step 2: ARMA models: spot prices to be forecasted are expressed as a function of previous values of the series and previous error terms
- Step 3: GARCH to capture the volatility of spot prices.

The organization of the chapter is as follows. Section 2 indicates the links between electricity price characteristics and econometric tools. Econometrically speaking, we will describe stationarity tests with an application to PJM spot prices and ARMA models. Section 3 presents an overview of the literature on electricity spot price modelling. Section 4 describes GARCH models and presents an example of forecasting of electricity spot prices using these models. Results are presented in Section 5. The chapter focuses on the econometric presentations of various models and how they can be applied to electricity spot price forecasts.

Motivation of the econometric technique and its methodological aspects

Various econometric tools are used with time series to manage electricity characteristics in order to model and forecast the behaviour of electricity prices. After the presentation of the two main features of electricity prices, this section presents stationarity and unit root tests, followed by an application to PJM spot prices. At the end of this section, ARMA models are presented.

Seasonality and price spikes

Mean reversion models linked to seasonality of electricity prices

Electricity demand is mainly influenced by economic activities and by weather conditions. These two factors explain the seasonal behaviour of electricity prices. When there are low levels of demand, generators supply electricity using base-load units with low marginal costs. During summer and winter months, certain days of the week, and even within the day itself (on-peak versus off-peak hours), larger quantities are needed and generators with higher marginal costs are used.

With this seasonal effect, it seems natural to expect some degree of mean reversion in the evolution of electricity prices; prices tend to fluctuate around the mean, although the value of this mean may slowly drift over time. Electricity prices tend to fluctuate around the values determined by market fundamentals such as the level of demand, the supply (cost of generation) and the competitive structure of the market. When spot prices are low, the supply tends to decrease, thus stimulating an upward price trend. Shifts in demand tend to push prices up, which act as an incentive for more expensive suppliers to enter the market. This, then, leads to a shift in supply. The 'merit order' approach gives support to the assumption of mean reversion of electricity prices; the less efficient power plants with the highest marginal cost respond last to the demand. Another reason is stressed by Knittel and Roberts (2001); weather, a dominant factor in prices, is also a cyclical and mean reverting process.

It has been well documented that an important property of electricity spot prices is mean-reversion (see Johnson and Barz, 1999). To model and forecast electricity prices, it is necessary to incorporate mean reverting processes to capture some of the autocorrelation present in the price series. However, these models have their limitations; they usually ignore cycles present in the series, they assumes that the volatility is constant over time and they cannot always reproduce the extreme spikes found in the data.

The jump-diffusion process to manage electricity price spikes

Another characteristic of electricity prices to consider when modelling spot prices is the presence of extreme values. The most common approach is the addition of a jump-diffusion process to a mean reverting process. Jump-diffusion models allow for sudden extreme returns and are quite successful in stock markets. They consider large variations of the underlying variable and thus might be appropriate for modelling electricity spot prices. Prices can go to extremely high or low levels, mainly due to network congestion, unexpected high demand, weather influences, generator maintenance, and so on. The more mature a market becomes (and thus the more liquid and transparent) the lower is the frequency of spikes. Even then, however, prices are relatively spiky and spikes never disappear entirely.

Technically, electricity prices 'do not jump', but 'spike'; they do not jump to a new level and stay there, but rather quickly revert to their previous levels. Unfortunately, most of the models do not incorporate another important feature of electricity, the fact that spikes are relatively short in duration. A natural way to integrate rapid variations is to introduce one or several Poisson processes. The jump-diffusion models link the price changes to arrival of information. There are two types of information: the 'normal news' with smooth variations in prices (modelled by a mean-reversion continuous time process) and the 'abnormal news' with jumps in prices (modelled with a Poisson discrete time process).

Stationarity and unit root tests

Stationarity

Economic and financial time series, and particularly price series, rarely result from stationary stochastic processes (see Box 3.1).

Box 3.1 Review of stationary processes

a) Stationary process

Let $x_t,\ t \in T$ be a real stochastic process. A stochastic process is strictly stationary if all of its characteristics, that is to say *all of its moments,* are invariant for any change in the time origin. In the case where a process $x_t,\ t \in T$ is such that $T = R, Z$ or N we can then verify that if x_t is a strictly stationary process:

$$\begin{array}{ll} E[x_t] = m & \forall t \in T \\ V[x_t] = \sigma^2 & \forall t \in T \\ \mathrm{cov}[x_t,\ x_s] = \gamma[|t - s|] & \forall t \in T, \forall s \in T, t \neq s \end{array}$$

Or again: $\mathrm{cov}(x_1, x_{1+k}) = \mathrm{cov}(x_2, x_{2+k}) = \ldots = \mathrm{cov}(x_t, x_{t-k})$. The covariance depends only on the difference in time and not on the time itself. $\mathrm{cov}[x_t, x_s]$ exists if $E[x_t^2] < \infty$ and $E[x_s^2] < \infty$ (according to the Schwarz inequality).

We are dealing, therefore, with a family of stochastic, real, homoskedastic and correlated variables.

b) The White Noise process

Let the process be $x_t,\ t \in T$. If, for all values of $t_1 < t_2 < \ \ldots \ < t_n$, the following real stochastic variables (first differences) are independent, it is then an independent growth process.

The process $x_t,\ t \in T$ is said to be a stationary independent growth process if, in addition, the probability $(x_{t+h} - x_t) \quad \forall h \in T$ does not depend on t.

A White Noise process[2] is a stochastic process with non-correlated increases. It is called 'strong' White Noise if the increases are independent. It is then a question of stochastic real homoskedastic independent variables. It is also called an *i.i.d.* process (a discrete process made up of mutually *i*ndependent and *i*dentically *d*istributed variables). If the probability law of x_t is normal, then the White Noise (or *i.i.d.* process) is called Gaussian White Noise and is then noted as *n.i.d.* (*n*ormally and *i*dentically *d*istributed). For White Noise, then:

$$\begin{array}{ll} E[x_t] = m & \forall t \in T \\ V[x_t] = \sigma^2 & \forall t \in T \\ \mathrm{cov}[x_t,\ x_{t+\theta}] = \gamma_x(\theta) = 0 & \forall t \in T, \forall \theta \in T \end{array}$$

If $E[x_t] = 0$, the White Noise is centred.

An *i.i.d.* or *n.i.d.* process is necessarily stationary, but all stationary processes are not necessarily *i.i.d.* or *n.i.d.*; in this latter case, the stationary process is called a memory process, that is to say that the process has an internal reproduction law which can, therefore, be modelled.

Table 3.1 The different types of stochastic processes

Non-stationary process	Stationary process White Noise process Gaussian White Noise process

The above table illustrates the different types of processes.

The non-stationarity of the processes can involve the first order moment (mathematical expectation) as well as the second order moment (variance and covariance of the process). Before the 1980s, rigorous analysis and tests to recognize this non-stationarity did not exist. Under those conditions, it frequently occurred that the transformation was badly adapted to the non-stationarity characteristics, which had the effect of introducing parasitic movements into the time series. Following the work of Nelson and Plosser (1982), the most common cases of non-stationarity are analysed using two types of processes:

- the TS (*Trend-Stationary*) processes which represent a deterministic type of non-stationarity;[3]
- the DS (*Difference-Stationary*) processes for stochastic non-stationary processes They constitute, for seasonal or non-seasonal time series, the models of reference for the construction of unit root tests in the absence of heteroskedasticity.

The TS processes. A TS process is expressed as: $x_t = f_t + \varepsilon_t$ where f_t is a linear or non-linear polynomial function of time and ε_t is a stationary process. The simplest TS process (and the most widely used) is represented by a polynomial function of degree 1. The TS process is then called linear and is written: $x_t = a_0 + a_1 t + \varepsilon_t$.

This TS process is non-stationary because $E[x_t]$ is a function of time. Knowing $\hat{a}_0$ and $\hat{a}_1$, the x_t process can be stationarised by removing, from the value of x_t in t, the estimated value $\hat{a}_0 + \hat{a}_1 t$. In this type of modelling, the effect produced by a shock (or by several stochastic shocks) at a time t is transitory. The model being deterministic, the time series resumes its long-term movement on the trend line. It is possible to generalize this example to polynomial functions of any degree.

The DS processes. The DS processes are processes which can be made stationary by the use of a difference filter:

$$(1 - D)^d x_t = \beta + \varepsilon_t$$

where ε_t is a stationary process β is a real constant, D is the lag operator and d is the order of the difference filter.

These processes are often represented using the first order difference filter ($d = 1$). The process is then said to be a first order process and is written:

$$(1 - D)x_t = \beta + \varepsilon_t \Leftrightarrow x_t = x_{t-1} + \beta + \varepsilon_t$$

The introduction of the constant β in the DS process makes it possible to define two different processes:

- $\beta = 0$: the DS process is said to be without trend.
  It is written: $x_t = x_{t-1} + \varepsilon_t$. Since ε_t is white noise, this process is called a Random Walk Model. It is very often used to analyze the efficiency of many markets such as raw material or financial markets.
  To stationarize the random walk, it is only necessary to apply the first order difference filter to the process: $x_t = x_{t-1} + \varepsilon_t \Leftrightarrow (1 - D)x_t = \varepsilon_t$.
- $\beta \neq 0$: the process is then called a DS process with trend. It is written:

  $$x_t = x_{t-1} + \beta + \varepsilon_t$$

  This process can be stationarized using the first order difference filter:

  $$x_t = x_{t-1} + \beta + \varepsilon_t \Leftrightarrow (1 - D)x_t = \beta + \varepsilon_t$$

In DS type processes, a shock at a given time affects, to infinity, the future value of the series; the effect of the shock is therefore permanent and decreasing.

To sum up, to stationarize a TS process, the preferred method is that of ordinary least squares; for a DS process, it is necessary to employ the difference filter. The choice of a DS or TS process for the structure of the time series is, therefore, not without consequence.

Stationarity tests: Dickey–Fuller and augmented Dickey–Fuller tests

The Dickey–Fuller test (1979). The Dickey–Fuller (DF) test makes it possible to display the stationary or non-stationary character of a time series by the determination of a deterministic or stochastic trend.

The models serving as bases for the construction of these tests are three in number. The principle of the tests is simple: if the hypothesis is $H_0 : \phi_1 = 1$ is retained, the process is then non-stationary.

$$x_t = \phi_1 x_{t-1} + \varepsilon_t \quad \text{Autoregressive model of order 1.} \tag{3.1}$$

$$x_t = \phi_1 x_{t-1} + \beta + \varepsilon_t \quad \text{Autoregressive model with a constant.} \tag{3.2}$$

$$x_t = \phi_1 x_{t-1} + bt + c + \varepsilon_t \quad \text{Autoregressive model with a trend.} \tag{3.3}$$

If the hypothesis H_0 is confirmed, the time series x_t is not stationary, whatever the model chosen.

The augmented Dickey and Fuller tests. In the preceding models, used for the simple Dickey–Fuller tests, the process ε_t is, by hypothesis, white noise. However, there is no reason, *a priori*, for the error to be non-correlated; tests that take into account this hypothesis are called Augmented Dickey–Fuller tests (Dickey and Fuller, 1981).

The ADF tests are based, under the alternative hypothesis $|\phi_1| < 1$, on the estimation by OLS of the three models:

$$\Delta x_t = \rho\, x_{t-1} - \sum_{j=2}^{p} \phi_j \Delta x_{t-j+1} + \varepsilon_t \tag{3.4}$$

$$\Delta x_t = \rho x_{t-1} - \sum_{j=2}^{p} \phi_j \Delta x_{t-j+1} + c + \varepsilon_t \tag{3.5}$$

$$\Delta x_t = \rho\, x_{t-1} - \sum_{j=2}^{p} \phi_j \Delta x_{t-j+1} + c + b\, t + \varepsilon_t \tag{3.6}$$

with $\varepsilon_t \to$ *i.i.d.*

The test is performed in a manner similar to that of the simple DF tests; only the statistical tables are different.

Extensions of the Dickey–Fuller tests: The Phillips and Perron test and the KPSS test

The Phillips and Perron (1988) test. This test is built on a non-parametric correction of the Dickey–Fuller statistics to take into account the heteroskedastic errors. Calculation of the statistics of *PP* : $t^*_{\hat{\phi}_1}$ These statistics are to be compared with the critical values in the MacKinnon table.

The KPSS (1992) test. Kwiatkowski *et al.* (1992) propose the use of a Lagrange multiplier test (*LM*) based on the null hypothesis of stationarity. After estimation of the models (3.2) or (3.3), we calculate the partial sum of the residuals: $S_t = \sum_{i=1}^{t} e_i$ and we estimate the long-term variance (s_t^2) as for the Phillips and Perron test.

The statistics then are $LM = \frac{1}{s_t^2} \frac{\sum_{t=1}^{n} S_t^2}{n^2}$. We reject the hypothesis of stationarity if these statistics are greater than the critical values found in a table assembled by the authors.

The testing strategy. We observe that, when we conduct a unit root test, the results may be different, according to the use of one or the other of the three models as process generator of the initial time series. The conclusions at which we arrive are, therefore, different and can lead to erroneous transformations. This is the reason why Dickey and Fuller, and other authors after them, have developed other test strategies. We present a simplified example (Figure 3.1) of a test strategy. The critical values of $t_{\hat{c}}$ and $t_{\hat{b}}$ that allow testing the nullity of the coefficients c and b of the models (3.2) and (3.3) are given at the end of the chapter (Table 3.7).

Example of the application of unit root tests and testing strategy

In the following, we provide an application of the unit root testing strategy to the PJM spot price of electricity from 19 April 2004 to 30 April 2005 on the basis of 366 observations (see graph below).

We start with a model with a constant and 10 lags (therefore, 10 days) in the framework of the DFA test and we decrease the number of lags to 0. We retain the lag which minimizes the Akaike information criterion. If the lag 0 is retained, we use the simple DF test. We can then apply the test strategy (Figure 3.1) and calculate all of the statistics. Let the estimation of model (3.3) be:

Null Hypothesis: LPRIX has a unit root
Exogenous: Constant, Linear Trend
Lag length: 0 (Automatic based on AIC, MAXLAG = 10)

	t-**Statistic**	**Prob.***
Augmented Dickey–Fuller test statistic	−12.61118	0.0000

We reject the null hypothesis for the coefficient of the trend (@TREND) and we reject the H_0 hypothesis of the existence of a unit root. The LPRIX process is, therefore, a non-stationary process of the type TS. See the interpretation below.

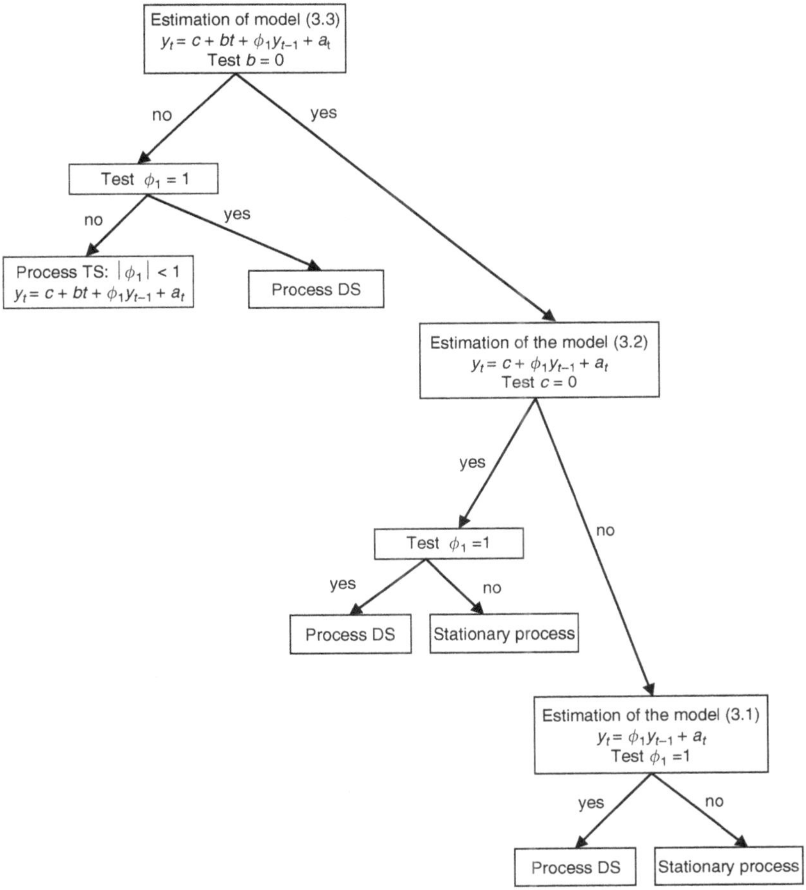

Figure 3.1 Simplified strategy for unit root tests

The Phillips–Perron test. We now proceed to the Phillips–Perron test with truncation $l = 6$. The estimation result for model (3.3) is the following:

Null Hypothesis: LPRIX has a unit root
Exogenous: Constant, Linear Trend
Bandwidth: 6 (Fixed using Bartlett kernel)

	Adj. *t*-Statistic	**Prob.***
Phillips–Perron test statistic	−12.81202	0.0000

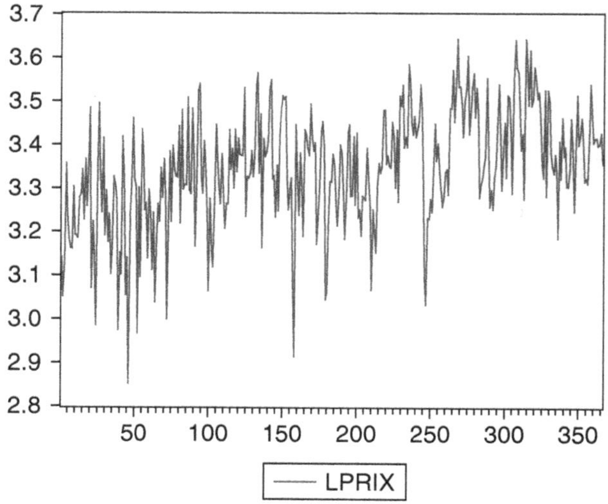

Figure 3.2 Evolution of the spot price of electricity expressed in logarithms (LPRIX)

As in the framework of the DFA test, we reject the null hypothesis for the trend coefficient (@TREND) and we reject the H_0 hypothesis for the existence of a unit root. The LPRIX process is, therefore, a non-stationary process of the TS type.

The KPSS test. Finally, we proceed to the KPSS tests.

Null Hypothesis: LPRIX is stationary
Exogenous: Constant, Linear Trend
Bandwidth: 6 (Fixed using Bartlett kernel)

		***LM*-Stat.**
Kwiatkowski–Phillips–Schmidt–Shin test statistic		0.092647
Asymptotic critical values*:	1% level	0.216000
	5% level	0.146000
	10% level	0.119000

We reject the null hypothesis for the trend coefficient (@TREND) and we accept the H_0 hypothesis for the absence of a unit root (the statistic *LM* is less than the critical value whatever the threshold).

All of the results are convergent; we can, therefore, conclude that the LPRIX process is a non-stationary process with a deterministic trend.

Interpretation: The spot price being a TS process, a price shock at time t has an instantaneous and provisional effect; there is, therefore, no persistence effect. *PJM spot prices are non-stationary prices. Electricity prices tend to fluctuate around values determined by market fundamentals. A shock in a price will have no long-term effect. Spikes in electricity prices are usually short-term. Prices can go to extremely high or low levels (network, congestion, weather, and so on) but they will then come back to a more normal level.*

The Box and Jenkins methodology: The ARMA modelization

It is not difficult to take the next step and use the classical approach of modelling a random phenomenon via time series, such as the Auto Regressive Moving Average (ARMA). The spot prices to be forecast are expressed as a function of previous values of the series (autoregressive terms) and previous error terms (the moving average terms).

ARMA models have been applied to forecast commodity prices, such as oil or natural gas (Weiss, 2000). With the deregulation process, simple ARMA models are also used to predict weekly electricity prices. A high correlation is usually present between the current price and the price of the previous hour and the current price and the price of the previous day. In Contreras *et al.* (2003), the authors focus on the day-ahead price forecast of a daily electric market, applied to the Spanish and Californian markets, using ARMA models.

The ARMA process only allows modelling of stationary series (without trend). The unit root tests (*cf.* III) make it possible to determine if the series is stationary and, in the case of non-stationarity, to determine which type: TS (*'Trend Stationary'*) which represents a deterministic type of non-stationarity or DS (*'Difference Stationary'*) for non-stationary stochastic processes. If the series studied is the TS type, it is appropriate to stationarize it by trend regression; the estimation residual is then studied according to the Box–Jenkins methodology. This makes it possible to determine the orders p and q of the parts AR and MA of the residual. The model is always, in this case, an ARIMA (p, q).

If the series studied is of the DS type, it is appropriate to stationarize it by passing to differences according to the order of integration $I = d$ (d is the number of times it is necessary to differentiate the series in order to make it stationary). The differentiated series is then studied according to the Box–Jenkins methodology which makes it possible to determine the orders p and q of the parts AR and MA. This type of model is noted ARIMA (p, d, q).

In the case where the first terms of the correlogram are different from zero, it is appropriate to model the residual term, that is to say to find the reproduction law of the phenomenon. Several more or less complex endogenous models exist. Only the Box–Jenkins method, which has been extensively applied to the forecasting domain, is presented here. Box and Jenkins (1976) have developed a solid methodology of systematic search for a suitable model for the study of empirical correlograms. They refer to two types of model: average mobile processes, autoregressive models, or a combination of both.

Literature review

The literature on electricity spot price modelling is vast and relatively new. Before the reorganization of the industry, electricity prices did not attract much attention because they were predictable. Many of the early research papers were inspired by studies of finance and of other commodities. However, all the research papers point out the current difficulties in electricity price forecasting because of the unique features of electricity. Research indicates that the models need to be relatively complex in order to model seasonality, mean reversion, high and time varying volatility, and spikes all at the same time.

Mean or non-mean reverting model

Traditional unit root tests are powerful against most mean-reverting alternatives if the errors are homoskedastic and there is no jump in the data. Pindyck (1999) deals successfully with the issue of unit root tests in the context of energy commodities (oil, gas, coal). The mean reverting specificity is also frequently applied to electricity markets but it does not perform well there because of the spikes inherent in electricity prices. Partly because Pindyck (1999) focuses on the long-run evolution of energy prices, he does not take into account the possibility of jumps or non-constant volatility in his unit root tests.

In the energy literature where the univariate time series approach is used, the majority of papers employ mean-reverting models as, for example, Deng (2000), Robinson (2000). This literature shows that there are interesting interactions of the degree of mean-reversion in the price process with other characteristics such as time varying conditional volatility and price spikes. In parallel, there are also some papers that characterize electricity prices as non-mean reverting. Escribano *et al.* (2002) offer an interesting discussion of this topic of mean or non-mean reverting models, the limits in their research work being based on international comparisons of spot electricity price modelling.

Jump-diffusion models

Working with the US power market, Kaminski (1997) points out the need for introducing jumps for fast reverting spikes and stochastic volatility in modelling electricity prices. With the model of Merton (1976), the author incorporates spiky characteristics through a random walk jump-diffusion model. However the model proposed ignores another feature of electricity prices, mean reversion.

In forecasting electricity prices, most of the research papers integrate mean reversion processes and jump-diffusion models to take into account the autocorrelation in series and the spikes in the data. In that vein, Johnson and Barz (1999) analysed the fit of mean-reverting and non-mean reverting models with and without jumps to a set of deregulated markets. They evaluated the effectiveness of four different stochastic models in describing the evolution of spot prices (Brownian motion, mean reversion, geometric Brownian motion, and geometric mean reversion). The objective was to try to reproduce electricity price behaviour in several different markets (California, Scandinavia, England and Wales, and Victoria). The authors concluded that the geometric mean reverting model gave the best performance, and that adding jumps to each of the models improved its performance. They also concluded that all models without jumps are inappropriate for modelling electricity prices.

However, their paper shows one important limit of volatility. They assume deterministic price volatility which is contradicted by empirical evolution. They do not consider the possibility of stochastic volatility. Another limit of the Johnson and Barz (1999) model is the slow speed of mean reversion after a price jump. This has later been resolved by adding downward jumps, allowing time varying parameters. Karakstani and Bunn (2004) present a jump-diffusion process for modelling electricity prices with all their limits. Their jump-diffusion model assumes that all shocks affecting price series die out at the same rate. The jump-diffusion model appears to be convenient for simulating the distribution of prices over several periods of time but is restrictive for short-term predictions at a particular time.

Volatility, ARCH and GARCH Models

While volatility has been studied in a number of papers for various commodities, electricity price volatility is the most difficult characteristic to deal with, in efforts to model prices, because of the instantaneous nature of the product. The relative insensitivity of demand to price fluctuations and the binding constraints on supply at peak times make short-term prices for electricity extremely volatile. Stoft (2002) underlines the consequences of electricity demand inelasticity on spot prices; volatility in spot prices varies over time with weather and other demand and supply forces and it is likely to be mean-reverting itself. Understanding the volatility process is critically important to actors as it influences their risks.

The most popular approach for modelling volatility in time series are GARCH family models used in the assessment of uncertainty. Auto Regressive Conditional Heteroskedasticity (ARCH) models were introduced by Engle (1982) and Generalized Auto Regressive Conditional Heteroskedasticity (GARCH) models were introduced by Bollerslev (1986). These models are presented in the next section.

It is also observed and expected that positive price shocks increase volatility more than negative shocks of the same magnitude. This is an inverse leverage effect. This terminology is derived from Black's (1976) 'leverage effect' and describes the asymmetric response of volatility to positive and negative shocks.

How factors influence the volatility process of spot prices is complex and still represents a research challenge in spite of numerous studies that have been devoted to the question. Spot volatility is transmitted to the forward curve (Longstaff and Wang, 2004) which explains all the interest in this feature for hedging risks. Robinson and Baniak (2002) employ nonparametric techniques to test for changes in volatility of the key supply driven events in the electricity markets in the UK. They show that generators may have strategic incentives to induce volatility in spot prices so as to create hedging pressure. The deregulation process has spurred a demand for realistic price models, which are needed for tasks such as production planning, portfolio optimization, derivatives pricing and risk management. The solutions to these problems do not depend only on expectations of future prices.

With respect to the volatility of spot prices alone, Karakstani and Bunn (2004) tested four approaches to explain the stochastic dynamics of spot volatility and to understand agent reactions to shocks (intra-day UK electricity prices). The limitations of GARCH models due to extreme values were resolved with a regression model with the assumption of an implicit jump component for prices. A similar approach was used by Worthington *et al.* (2003) on five regional market in Australia, and by Mugele *et al.* (2005) on three European spot prices.

As explained above, a major difficulty in modelling and forecasting electricity spot prices is taking into account all of the various features of electricity with a single method. Because deregulation is still young, there have been few empirical studies entirely devoted to modelling electricity prices. Deng (2000) is among the first research paper to try to incorporate the various features of electricity. The author studies three models of mean-reverting jump-diffusion models with volatility (with deterministic volatility, with regime switching and with stochastic volatility) to create a real option approach. Deng introduces an affine jump-diffusion process: it is flexible enough to allow capturing the features of electricity such as mean reverting, seasonality and spikes. Generalizing the previous modelling, Bystrom (2001) offers an accurate description of electricity prices including seasonality.

In a key reference paper, Knittel and Roberts (2001) offer one of the first discussions of several models of spot prices: mean-reverting processes, time varying mean, jump-diffusion processes, ARMA and E GARCH. They compare the forecasting ability of different statistical methods on California prices (from 1998–2000). In Escribano *et al.* (2002) the authors present a general model that simultaneously takes into account: seasonality, mean reversion, GARCH behaviour and time dependent jumps. They apply their model to Argentina, Australia, New Zealand, Nordpool and Spain. They show that electricity prices are mean-reverting with strong volatility and jumps of time-dependent intensity even after adjusting for seasonality. They also provide a detailed unit root analysis of electricity prices against mean reversion, in the presence of jumps and GARCH errors.

Most recent research papers take into account several features of electricity and usually model and forecast spot prices in different wholesale markets. Goto and Karolyi (2004) analyse how electricity price volatility evolves over time for various trading hubs in several world wholesale markets (US, Nord Pool and Australia). They offer a good literature review of daily spot price volatility processes related to seasonality, mean reversion, conditionally autoregressive heteroskedasticity and possible time dependent jumps.

ARCH models

The classical forecasting models, based on the ARMA models assume constant variance time series (homoskedasticity hypothesis). This modelling neglects, therefore, the information that might be contained in the residual factor of the time series. The ARCH type (*Autoregressive Conditional Heteroskedasticity*) models make it possible to model the time series (for the most part financial)[4] which have an instantaneous volatility (or variance or variability) that depends on the past. It is thus possible to create a dynamic forecast of the time series in terms of its mean and its variance.

Initially presented by Engle (1982), these models were the object of very important developments and applications during the decade. In this chapter, we will take up the various classes of ARCH, GARCH (Generalized Autoregressive Conditional Heteroskedasticity) and ARCH–M (Autoregressive Conditional Heteroskedasticity–Mean) models, the statistical tests making it possible to recognize them, and then we will consider the methods of estimation and forecast.

The study of financial time series then comes up against two types of problem:

- the non-stationarity of the series
- the leptokurtic character of the data distribution.

Specification of the model. Let AR(p) be a model: $\phi_p(B)x_t = \varepsilon_t$ (or a regression model $y = Xa+\varepsilon$). With $\varepsilon_t = u_t \times h_t$ where $u_t \longrightarrow N(0,1)$ (we replace z_{t-1} by h_t in the preceding expression) and $h_t^2 = \alpha_0 + \sum_{i=1}^{p} \alpha_i \varepsilon_{t-i}^2 = \alpha_0 + \alpha(B)\varepsilon_t^2$ where $\alpha_0 > 0,\ \alpha_i \geq 0\ \forall i$ and $\alpha(B) = \alpha_1 B + \alpha_2 B^2 + \cdots + \alpha_p B^p$; h_t^2 is called an ARCH process of order p and is noted ARCH(p).

The model AR (regression model) is called an AR error model ARCH(p).

The GARCH type process

The GARCH[4] model is a generalization (*Generalized*), due to Bollerslev (1986) of the ARCH type models. Its specifications are as follows:

$y = Xa + \varepsilon$ with $\varepsilon_t = u_t \times h_t$, $u_t \longrightarrow N(0;1)$ and $h_t^2 = \alpha_0 + \alpha(D)\varepsilon_t^2 + \beta(D)h_t^2$

$h_t^2 = \alpha_0 + \sum_{i=1}^{p} \alpha_i \varepsilon_{t-i}^2 + \sum_{j=1}^{q} \beta_j h_{t-j}^2$ which is the expression for a GARCH (p,q).

Remarks:

- If $q = 0$ we have a GARCH (p,q) = GARCH $(p,0)$ = ARCH (p) and if $q = 0$ and $p = 0$ then $\varepsilon_t \rightarrow n.i.d.$
- A GARCH (p, q) type process is equivalent to an ARCH(∞) type process, which can be demonstrated by recurrence (by replacing h_t^2 by h_{t-1}^2 etc.). This equivalence allows us to determine the stationarity conditions of a GARCH type process: $\alpha(1) + \beta(1) < 1$

The GARCH processes are similar to the usual ARMA processes in the sense that the degree q appears as the degree of the mobile part of the mean and p appears as the degree of the autoregressivity; that allows the introduction of the effects of innovation. The conditional variance is determined by the square of the p preceding errors and of the q past conditional variances.

Example of the ARMA model

As pointed out, electricity prices present unusual time series characteristics which can be explained by the special features of electricity; these include mean-reversion, multi-level seasonality, extreme behaviour with fast-reverting spikes and non-normality, manifested as positive skewness and leptokurtosis.

Using time series, our data are day-ahead wholesale electricity prices for one market in the United States, the PJM, and one in the European Union, the Nord Pool. These two wholesale markets are among the largest competitive markets for wholesale electricity power in the world (the most liquid and transparent). They provide two basic types of markets in which participants may trade electricity. The first is a spot market and is referred to as the real time market. Participants can enter sale offers and purchase bids for electricity on a real time basis. The second market is a forward market referred to as the day ahead market,[5] in which participants can hedge against price risks by entering into forward purchases or sales of electricity. As an example, each day, there are 24 distinct prices reported for both the spot and forward markets in the PJM market.

In North America, the Pennsylvania–New Jersey–Maryland (PJM) system oversees the electricity production, transmission and trading functions of

300,000 GW each year. Created in 1997, PJM is an integrated power pool which operates as a single system within the Mid-Atlantic area. It administers the largest competitive wholesale electricity market in the world; its territory is 12 states and the District of Columbia (about 45 million people). As a pool, it also ensures the reliability of the grid (peak load in MW of 131,330), provides real-time information, plans transmission and generation expansion, and operates independently of any market participant. PJM, the first fully functioning American regional transmission organization, currently coordinates a pooled generating capacity of more than 134,250 megawatts. About 53 per cent of the electricity traded on the PJM grid is through bilateral agreements between member companies, and 38 per cent is through real-time spot market trading.

In Europe, the Nord Pool spot market organizes the physical day-ahead market, Elspot, in the Nordic countries (Norway, Finland, Denmark and Sweden, which represent 24 million customers). It also operates the intra-day market (Elbas in Finland, in Sweden and in Eastern Denmark). There is no centralized dispatch (generators and loads self-dispatch). Created in 1996, the Nord Pool spot market provides a marketplace for participants in which they can buy or sell physical power. It is the central counter-party in all trades, guaranteeing settlement for trade and anonymity to participants. The Elspot price is the reference price for the Nordic financial power market as well as for the bilateral wholesale power market covering this region. During 2004 about 167 TWh, which represents over 43 per cent of the Nordic consumption, was traded in Elspot.

We work with daily averages of electricity spot prices (over peak and off-peak hours), so we have a single price for each day. All the series are expressed in the local currency of the market. Data have been obtained from each of the pools directly on their websites.

We have shown previously that the logarithm of the spot price of electricity is a TS process. To model it, therefore, we incorporate as explicative variable a deterministic trend (@TREND). A first attempt, using only a trend, is not conclusive because the residual of the estimation is not white noise. We then incorporate an AR(1) component, with the following estimation result:

Table 3.2 Data sources

Market	Data	Frequency	Years	Sources
PJM (USA)	Daily real time prices	Hourly ⇒ daily	1998-2005	*www.pjm.org*
Elspot (Nord Pool)	Daily system price	Daily	1998-2005	*www.nordpool.no*

Dependent variable: LPRIX
Sample (adjusted): 2 366
Included observations: 365 after adjustments

Variable	Coefficient	Std. error	*t*-Statistic	Prob.
C	3.242029	0.018768	172.7413	0.0000
@TREND	0.000568	8.86E-05	6.410396	0.0000
AR(1)	0.389587	0.048403	8.048898	0.0000

The coefficients all being significantly different from 0, we conduct tests on the estimation residual. However, is the result white noise? An ARCH test shows a critical probability of 0.03; we are, therefore, led to refuse the H_0 hypothesis of a zero coefficient for the lagged residual.

ARCH Test:			
F-statistic	4.425370	Prob. *F*(1,362)	0.036098
Obs* *R*-squared	4.396078	Prob. Chi-Square(1)	0.036022

It is, therefore an ARCH error model; a first estimation of an ARCH(1) does not permit us to completely whiten the residual. We estimate, therefore, a GARCH(1, 1) model:

Dependent variable: LPRIX
Sample (adjusted): 2 366
Included observations: 365 after adjustments

	Coefficient	Std. error	Z-Statistic	Prob.
C	3.270038	0.008008	408.3245	0.0000
@TREND	0.000449	4.51E-05	9.951705	0.0000
AR(1)	0.404072	0.038148	10.59223	0.0000
	Variance equation			
C	−7.50E-05	1.25E-06	−59.79359	0.0000
RESID(−1)^2	−0.003179	5.13E-05	−61.95966	0.0000
GARCH(−1)	1.008602	0.000111	9064.971	0.0000

The coefficients are all significantly 0; the autocorrelation function of the assorted residual of the Ljung-Box(Q-Stat.) statistic, as well as the critical probability of the test, are as follows:

The critical probabilities of the *Q*-Stat. are all greater than 0.05 whatever the lag; we are, therefore, led to accept the H_0 hypothesis of zero for all of the autocorrelation coefficients. The residual is, therefore, white noise. However, is the residual a Gaussian white noise? The Jarque and Bera statistic, making it possible to test the hypothesis of normality (J B = 4.44), is matched with a critical probability of 11 per cent. We are, therefore, led to accept the H_0 hypothesis; the residual is, therefore, Gaussian.

This specification, is, therefore, totally validated from a statistical point of view. The model can be written:

$$\text{Log(price)} = 3,27 + 0.000449\ t + \varepsilon_t + 0,4 \times \varepsilon_{t-1}$$

$$\varepsilon_t = u_t \times h_t; h_t^2 = -0,000075 - 0,0031 \times \varepsilon_{t-i}^2 + 1,008 \times h_{t-j}^2$$

Results and comments

The goal of this chapter was to model and forecast electricity spot prices. Taking into account the features of electricity prices presented and the literature on this subject, we followed three steps.

- Step 1: we tested the stationarity of our electricity price series with unit root tests.
- Step 2: spot prices to be forecasted are expressed as a function of previous values of the series and previous error terms. We used ARMA models to forecast spot prices assuming constant variance time series.
- Step 3: We used GARCH models to capture the volatility of spot prices. These models make it possible to forecast spot prices with an instantaneous volatility that depends on the past.

The results are the following:

- *On seasonality*: In North America, the PJM market appears to be a non-seasonal market, as opposed to the Scandinavian wholesale market, which is affected by weekly seasonality.

  The explanation could lie in the different sources of the electricity supplied. In PJM, hydroelectricity accounts for less than 2 per cent of the load, and imports/exports are less than 0.1 per cent of the load on average; 60 per cent of the electricity generated in PJM is from fossil fuels with the remainder being supplied by nuclear power. In the Nord Pool, almost all of the electricity is from hydropower. In that case, we can consider electricity to be a storable commodity. Hydro reservoirs play the role of indirect storage of electricity. Weekly seasonality comes from differences in industrial activity between working days and weekends. The consumption clearly shows a weekly path. Seasonality in prices is due to the strong dependence of electricity demand on weather conditions, but also on social and economic activity. We did not consider monthly seasonality because we worked with short term data over a year.

- *On stationarity*: Spot prices from the PJM market and Nord Pool are both non-stationary processes. The choice of a DS or a TS process for the structure series is not without consequence. On PJM, a shock at time t has an instantaneous effect with persistence (TS type), as opposed to the Nord Pool market where a shock at time t has an instantaneous effect (DS type). Most of the electricity traded on the Nord Pool market is produced by hydropower and, therefore, is dependent on long-run weather conditions. Mean reversion in electricity prices exists since weather is a dominant factor. A shock in prices will have a persistent effect in a market depending on hydroelectricity. The reservoir levels seem to exhibit long-term memory.
- *In terms of forecasting*: The objective of this chapter is to model and forecast the behaviour of spot prices for two wholesale electricity markets: the Elspot of the Nord Pool in Europe and PJM spot prices in the North East region in the US. Modelling the price of electricity is a challenging task, considering its specific features: electricity is not storable, supply needs to be balanced continuously against demand, and there is a good deal of volatility, inelasticity and seasonality.

  In both markets, it is possible to model the spot prices and therefore to make forecasts. Two GARCH models of process can be written with coefficients that are significant. As PJM spot price series can be considered to be a TS process, an explicative variable, a deterministic trend, has been incorporated.

The most surprising result of our work is the possibility, in theory, to forecast prices. The direct consequence is the possibility of making money thanks to the forecast of electricity prices. Having an appropriate representation of the electricity price is important to the actors in this new industry which is now open to competition, quite risky and characterized by uncertainties. Some analysts would be in a position to know the prices of electricity tomorrow on the two biggest wholesale markets in the world. Therefore, the two markets we studied can be seen as non-efficient because it appears possible to forecast electricity spot prices.

Notes

1 Another part of the economic research literature, focused on ex ante economic modeling of electricity markets, uses game theory or simulation methods.

2 Name given by engineers in reference to the spectrum of white light.
3 By definition, a process is stochastic so that the term deterministic process is ambiguous.
4 T. Bollerslev (1988).
5 Local Marginal Prices reflect the value of energy at the specific location and at the time it is delivered. The real time market is a spot market where current LMPs are calculated every five minutes. A day-ahead market is a market in which hourly LMPs are calculated for the next operating day.

References

Black, F. (1976) 'Studies of Stock Market Volatility Changes', Proceedings of the American Statistical Association, *Business and Economic Statistics Section*, pp. 177–181.

Bollerslev, T. (1986) 'Generalized Autoregressive Conditional Heteroskedasticity', *Journal of Econometrics*, vol. 31, pp. 307–27.

Bollerslev, T. (1988) 'On the Correlation Structure for the Generalized Autoregressive Conditional Heteroscedastic Process', *Journal of Time Series Analysis*, vol. 9.

Box, G. and Jenkins, G. (1976) *Time Series Analysis, Forecasting and Control* (San Francisco: Holden-Day).

Bystrom, H. (2001) 'Extreme Value Theory and Extremely Large Electricity Price Changes', Lund University, Working paper.

Contreras, J., Conejo, A., Nogales, F. and Espinola, R. (2002) 'Forecasting Next-Day Electricity Prices by Time Series Models', *IEEE Trans Power System*, vol. 17(2), pp. 342–8.

Contreras, J., Conejo, A., Nogales, F. and Espinola, R. (2003) 'ARIMA Models to Predict Next Day Electricity Prices', *IEEE Trans Power System*, vol. 18(3), pp. 1014–20.

Deng, S. (2000) 'Stochastic Models of Energy Commodity Prices and their Applications: Mean-Reversion with Jumps and Spikes', University of California, Energy Institute, Working Paper.

Dickey, D. and Fuller, W. (1979) 'Distribution of the Estimators for Autoregressive Time Series with Unit Root', *Journal of the American Statistical Association*, vol. 74, p. 366.

Dickey, D. and Fuller, W. (1981) 'Likelihood Ratio Statistics for Autoregressive Time Series with Unit Root', *Econometrica*, vol. 49, no. 4.

Engle, R. (1982) 'Autoregressive Conditional Heteroskedasticity with Estimates of the Variance of UK Inflation', *Econometrica*, vol. 50, pp. 987–1008.

Engle, R.F., Lilien, D.M. and Robbin, R.P. (1987) 'Estimating Time Varying Risk Premia in the Term Structure : the ARCH-Model', *Econometrica*, vol. 55.

Escribano, A., Pena, J. and Villaplana, P. (2002) 'Modelling Electricity Prices: International Evidence', Universidad Carlos III de Madrid, Working Paper.

Goto, M. and Karolyi, G. (2004) 'Understanding Electricity Price Volatility Within and Across Markets', Ohio University, Working Paper.

Guirguis, H. and Felder, F. (2004) 'Further Advances in Forecasting Day-Ahead Electricity Prices Using Times Series Model', *KIEE International Transactions on PE*, vol. 4–A(3), pp. 159–66.

Johnson, B. and Barz, G. (1999) *Selecting Stochastic Processes for Modelling Electricity Prices, Energy Modelling and the Management of Uncertainty*, London: Risk Publications.

Joskow, P. (2006) 'Markets for Power in the United States: An Interim Assessment', *Energy Journal*, January, vol. 27, no. 1, pp. 1–36.

Kaminski, V. (1997) 'The Challenge of Pricing and Risk Managing Electricity Derivatives', *The U.S. Power Market*, November, pp. 149–71.

Karakatsani, N. and Bunn, D. (2004) 'Modelling the Volatility of Spot Electricity Prices', London Business School, EMG Working Paper.

Knittel, C. and Roberts, M. (2001) 'An Empirical Examination of Deregulated Electricity Prices', University of California, Energy Institute, Working Paper, October, PWP 087.

Kwiatkowski, D., Phillips, P., Schmidt, P., Shin, Y. (1992) 'Testing the Null Hypothesis of Stationarity Against the Alternative of a Unit Root', *Journal of Econometrics*, vol. 54, 159–78.

Longstaff, F. and Wang, A. (2004) 'Electricity Forward Prices: A High-Frequency Empirical Analysis', *Journal of Finance*, vol. 59, no. 4, pp. 1877–900.

Merton, R. (1976) 'Option Pricing when Underlying Stock Returns are Discontinuous', *Journal of Financial Economics*, vol. 3, pp. 125–44.

Mugele, C., Rachev, S. and Trück, S. (2005) 'Stable Modelling of Different European Power Markets', *Investment Management and Financial Innovations*, vol. 3.

Nelson, C.R. and Plosser, C. (1982) 'Trends and Random Walks in Macroeconomics Time Series: Some Evidence And Applications', *Journal of Monetary Economics*, vol. 10.

Nelson, D. (1991) 'Stationarity and Persistence in the GARCH Model', *Econometric Theory*, vol. 6, pp. 318–44.

Newbery, D.M. (2003) 'Regulatory Challenges to European Electricity Liberalisation', *Swedish Economic Policy Review*, vol. 9, no. 2, Fall, 9–44.

Nogales, F., Contreras, J., Conejo, A. and Espínola, R. (2002) 'Forecasting Next-Day Electricity Prices by Time Series Models,' *IEEE Transactions on Power Systems*, vol. 17, no. 2, pp. 342–8.

Phillips, P. and Perron, P. (1988) 'Testing for Unit Root in Time Series Regression', *Biometrika*, vol. 75.

Pindyck, R. (1999) 'The Long Run Evolution of Prices', *Energy Journal*, vol. 20, no. 2, pp. 1–27.

Robinson, T. and Baniak, A. (2002) 'The Volatility of Prices in the English and Welsh Electricity Pool,' *Applied Economics*, vol. 34, no. 12, August.

Robinson, T. (2000) 'Electricity Pool Prices: A Case Study in Non-Linear Time-Series Modelling', *Applied Economics*, vol. 32, pp. 527–32.

Stoft, S. (2002) *Power System Economics* (New York: John Wiley).

Weiss, E. (2000) 'Forecasting Commodity Prices Using ARIMA,' *Technical Analysis of Stocks and Commodities*, vol. 18, no. 1, pp. 18–19.

Worthington, A., Kay-Spratley, A. and Higgs, H. (2003) 'Transmission of Prices and Price Volatility in Australian Electricity Spot Markets: A Multivariate GARCH Analysis', *Energy Economics*. vol. 27, no. 2, pp. 337-50.

4

Causality and Cointegration between Energy Consumption and Economic Growth in Developing Countries[1]

Jan Horst Keppler

Presentation of the energy issue

Estimating the relation between energy demand (or of any of its components such as electricity) and economic growth (GDP) is one of the classic applications of econometrics in the energy sector (see Bohi and Zimmerman, 1984; Dahl, 1994; or Table 4.2 for surveys). It is also an issue of high relevance for development and energy policies. Consider, for instance, that a government would like to introduce measures to control energy demand (say, an energy tax) to improve its environmental performance and to reduce its dependence on foreign imports. If energy consumption precedes or causes economic growth, such policies would hamper further economic development.

Until the 1990s, the prevailing view was that economic growth caused increased energy consumption. The essential parameter was the income elasticity of energy consumption (see also Chapter 5). Following the seminal work of Engle and Granger, the increasing use of causality tests threw some doubt on the direction of the link between income and energy consumption (Engle and Granger, 1987, 1991). Several authors, as will be discussed later, showed that causal relations could run from energy consumption to economic growth, from economic growth to energy consumption or in both directions at once.

The hypothesis that energy consumption causes economic growth has great intuitive appeal and can be rationalized by the existence of positive externalities. Energy and, in particular, electricity consumption are often associated with positive impacts on health (decreasing indoor biomass burning, refrigeration) and education (reading after dark, television, radio) and thus can contribute to higher economic growth (Keppler and Lesourne, 2002). Motive power, lighting and air-conditioning instead are preconditions for local enterprise and economic activity.

The questions raised by the link between energy consumption, energy prices and economic growth are far from theoretical. In a period when oil prices are above USD 50 per barrel, the question is whether higher energy prices imply only a one-off wealth transfer from importers to exporters or whether the reduced energy consumption imposes an added second-round penalty on economic development. On the other hand, global efforts under the UNFCCC to reduce energy-related greenhouse gas emissions offer a bonus for the reduced consumption of hydrocarbons. Again, the question is whether such efforts could constitute a brake on economic growth.

This study considers the GDP-energy relationship in ten developing countries at different stages of development over the thirty-two-year period 1971–2002: Argentina, Brazil, Chile, China, Egypt, India, Indonesia, Kenya, South Africa and Thailand (three from Latin America, three from Africa and four from Asia). The three Latin American Countries and South Africa have comparable levels of income and are characterized by relatively stable levels of *per capita* energy consumption and *per capita* GDP (although South Africa has a much higher level of energy intensity). The four Asian countries and Egypt have all experienced fast growth from low levels in both *per capita* income and *per capita* energy consumption during the last three decades, although to different degrees. Finally, *per capita* income in Kenya has been more or less stable, while *per capita* energy consumption has been *reduced* over the period of analysis.[2]

The ten countries were selected according to two criteria: (1) no 'small' countries and (2) no *major* energy exporters. Concerning the first condition, countries with less than 10 million inhabitants were excluded because in

Table 4.1 Key indicators for selected developing countries[3] (*per capita* values 1971 and 2002)

	ELEC 1971 (kwh)	ELEC 2002 (kwh)	OIL 1971 (toe)	OIL 2002 (toe)	ENRGY 1971 (toe)	ENRGY 2002 (toe)	GDP (USD 1995)	GDP (USD 1995)
Argentina	870	2082	1,02	0,55	1,38	1,54	7088	6842
Brazil	456	1843	0,28	0,5	0,71	1,09	2601	4642
Chile	783	2745	0,53	0,61	0,92	1,59	2526	5432
China	151	1184	0,05	0,19	0,47	0,96	114	944
Egypt	214	1120	0,19	0,41	0,23	0,79	485	1250
India	99	421	0,04	0,11	0,33	0,51	212	493
Indonesia	16	428	0,07	0,27	0,29	0,74	310	1060
Kenya	68	121	0,11	0,08	0,65	0,49	266	322
South Africa	2246	4542	0,38	0,25	2,01	2,50	4226	4020
Thailand	124	1682	0,17	0,62	0,38	1,35	765	3000

Source: IEA (2004b).

such countries a single project (one dam, one pipeline connection) can make an enormous difference in the availability and the real cost of energy. Modelling such structural breaks would have enormously complicated the data requirements of this study.

Concerning the second condition, countries in which energy exports make up a major portion of GDP often maintain arbitrarily low domestic price levels that do not reflect the full opportunity cost of consumption (Keppler and Birol, 1999). Modelling the policy decisions that go into such implicit subsidization would again have gone beyond the boundaries of this study. Countries in which energy exports exceed 50 per cent of TPES were thus excluded. An exception was made for Indonesia to analyse the impact of its fast growing electricity consumption.

Further, for the obvious reason of availability of information, the study only considers so-called 'commercial energies' and does not consider the use of energies such as biomass for which no internationally comparable market data exist. This omission is justified by the fact that such consumption of non-commercial energy has little impact on measurable GDP. Finally, the study models price impacts by using the real world oil price.

Motivation of the econometric technique and methodological aspects

Non-stationarity and cointegration: two major features of time series testing

Historically, the great problem for applied econometric work was that standard techniques, such as Ordinary Least Squares, were developed for stationary time series (that is, time series whose mean, variance and auto-covariance were constant over time; thus any equation such as $y_t = \alpha x_t + \beta y_{t-1} + \varepsilon_t$ would be considered stationary as long as $|\beta| < 1$.). However, in economics, and the domain of energy is no exception, non-stationarity of time series is to be expected, the most important reason being constant legislative or technical change that *continuously* introduces structural breaks in economic relationships (while structural breaks can also occur with stationary variables, the relationships between them are stable before and after breaks). The irregularity of economic growth, which if regular and predictable could be modelled as a stable trend, equally plays a role. Non-stationarity thus also holds for most energy-related variables. Such non-stationarity can create spurious results for standard OLS regressions and requires more sophisticated econometric techniques.

Non-stationarity presents perhaps the most fundamental and most common complicating issue econometricians are confronted with. A second complicating feature is cointegration between non-stationary variables, the primary reason for the problem of spurious regressions. For instance, an

OLS-regression of two variables growing over time will yield high R^2-values but reveal little about their true underlying relationship. Often, cointegration happens because the two variables under consideration depend on a third variable. For example, higher economic growth might drive up energy prices as well as energy consumption but it would be wrong to assume on the basis of an OLS-regression that higher prices cause higher consumption.

Formally, two non-stationary series, x_t and y_t, are cointegrated if they can produce a linear combination such as $x_t - \beta y_t$ that will yield a new series, z_t, which is stationary. The cointegration vector $[1, -\beta]$ yielding a stationary series may or may not exist, so two non-stationary series may or may not be cointegrated. To account for the presence of cointegration, the Error-Correction Model (ECM), developed by Engle and Granger (1987) and refined by Johansen (1988) needs to be employed. Masih and Masih (1996b) Cheng (1996) Asafu-Adjaye (2000) Yang (2000) Bourbonnais (2006) Holtedahl and Joutz (2004) Narayan and Smyth (2005) all provide guidance on applying cointegration techniques to estimate energy demand.

The Error Correction Model (ECM) exploits the fact that an appropriate linear combination of cointegrated variables yields a stationary series to correct for temporary (common) deviations from the long-term relationships between two variables. With the ECM, cointegration is transformed from a source of error into an added tool for uncovering information; wherever cointegration is present an appropriate ECM can be constructed.

The modelling strategy employed

We employ the following modelling strategy to test the relationships (causality, long-run elasticities and short-run elasticities) between energy demand (energy, oil and electricity consumption), income (GDP) and energy prices. First, we search for Granger causality between energy demand and income. This requires testing for stationarity of the time series and taking first differences in case of non-stationarity, before applying the Granger test. In a second step, we will test for the long-term elasticities between the different variables, choosing as the independent variables those that have been shown to have relatively higher explanatory power in the Granger tests. Finally, we will test formally for cointegration of the time series and set up the appropriate Error Correction Model. These procedures raise several methodological issues that are treated individually in the following.[4]

Issue 1: The Granger causality test

The first step is testing for non-stationarity. Chapter 3 discusses theoretical motivation and practical implications. Such stationarity tests need, in principle, to be performed as part of complete testing strategies that account for the possible existence of fixed terms and autonomous constant trends in the data. In practice, economic (non-financial) data usually do not have a zero mean nor are they subject to autonomous trends (this clearly is not true in other areas where mathematical statistics can be applied, such as mechanics or finance). For economic time series the most likely constellation is thus the existence of an intercept and the absence of an autonomous trend.

Once stationarity has been confirmed or non-stationary variables have been normalized by taking first differences, the Granger causality test looks at 'causality' in the sense of 'precedence' between time series. It is named after the first causality tests performed by Clive Granger in 1969. It analyses the extent to which the past variations of one variable explain (or precede) subsequent variations of the other. Granger causality tests habitually come in pairs, testing whether variable x_t Granger-causes variable y_t and *vice versa*. All permutations are possible: univariate Granger causality from x_t to y_t or from y_t to x_t, bivariate causality or absence of causality. In all cases, the two series need to be rendered stationary. Applying the Granger causality test to non-stationary data can lead to spurious causality relationships (Cheng, 1996).

Granger causality does not imply 'causality' in the colloquial sense of an unavoidable logical link but in the sense of an intertemporal correlation. Formally, the Granger causality test analyses whether the unrestricted equation:

$$y_t = \alpha_0 + \sum_{i=1}^{T} \alpha_{1i} y_{t-i} + \sum_{j=1}^{T} \alpha_{2j} x_{t-j} + \varepsilon_t \quad \text{with } 0 \leq i, j \leq T$$

yields better results than the restricted equation:

$$y_t = \beta_0 + \sum_{i=1}^{T} \beta_{1i} y_{t-i} + \varepsilon_t \text{ with } \sum_{j=1}^{T} \alpha_{2j} x_{t-j} = 0 \text{ (the null hypothesis)}$$

In other words, if $H0$, in which $\alpha_{21} = \alpha_{22} = \cdots = \alpha_{2T} = 0$, is rejected then one can state 'variable x_t Granger-causes variable y_t'. The results of the Granger causality test are sensitive to the number of lags specified. In principle, one should include the maximum number of lags over which an economically meaningful relationship between two variables may exist. In this chapter, we work with three-year lags. Eviews always tests for the null-hypothesis that variable X *does not* Granger-cause variable Y. Eviews will calculate the F-statistic of the regression under the null hypothesis that $\alpha_{21} = \alpha_{22} = \cdots = \alpha_{2j} = 0$.[5] This statistic then needs to be compared to the tabulated critical values. The critical level of certainty for not falsely rejecting the null hypothesis is again the 5 per cent level.

Once the direction of causality between income and energy consumption has been established, we will formulate the equation for the OLS estimation of the long-run relationship between income and energy consumption. The result of the Granger causality test will decide our choice of dependent and independent variable.

Issue 2: Testing for cointegration and the error correction model

To know when to use the ECM, one needs to test for the presence of cointegration. According to Hendry and Juselius (2000) there are many techniques, among them the vector autoregressive representation (VAR) presented in Johansen (1988). The VAR needs to be employed if there is multiple cointegration, that is to say cointegration between more than two variables (see also Chapter 6 of this volume). The point is always the same; one tries to find a linear combination of two non-stationary series that will yield a stationary series. If no such linear combination can be found, the variables are not cointegrated and there is no use (and no need) to apply the Error Correction Model. Absence of cointegration implies the existence of a stable long-term relationship between the two variables that can be estimated without further ado by an OLS regression.

Engle and Granger (1987) establish that cointegration is present if the residual of the OLS equation, $\hat{u}_t$, contains a unit root. If '*a*' and '*b*' are the estimated parameters of the true parameters α and β in the regression equation:

$$y_t = \alpha + \beta x_t + u_t$$

then

$$\hat{u}_t = y_t - a - bx_t$$

When testing for cointegration between y_t and x_t, the null hypothesis H_0 is that $\varphi = 1$ for $\hat{u}_t = \varphi \hat{u}_{t-1} + \varepsilon_t$. If the residual follows a random walk then the two variables are cointegrated (Hendry and Juselius, 2000, p. 24).[6] An alternative is to employ the pre-programmed Johansen cointegration test provided by Eviews. This is handy, since the unit root test of the estimated residuals of the OLS equation no longer allows using the widely available tabulated values provided by Dickey and Fuller that are also reported in programmes such as Eviews. The specially calculated values for testing for unit roots in estimated data can only be found in specific papers such as McKinnon (1991).

Once cointegration has been established, the Error Correction Model (Engle and Granger, 1987) allows estimating the short-run relationship between variables. Specified in first differences, the ECM corrects for shocks that drive the variables away from the long-run trend, exploiting the fact that for co-integrated non-stationary series, a suitable linear combination makes the series stationary. As Hendry and Juselius point out, what Engle and Granger did was to prove that cointegration and the existence of a meaningful Error Correction Model is the same; one mechanically implies the other (Hendrik and Juselius, 2000, p. 16). If the original OLS regression is based on the equation:

$$y_{t-1} = \beta_0 + \beta_1 x_{t-1} + \varepsilon_t$$

then the corresponding Error Correction Model needs to be specified as

$$\Delta y_t = \alpha_0 + \alpha_1 \Delta x_t + \alpha_2 (y_{t-1} - \beta_1 x_{t-1} - \beta_0) + \varepsilon_t$$

The term $\alpha_2(y_{t-1} - \beta_1 x_{t-1} - \beta_0)$ is the error correction term, in which α_2 is always < 0. The error correction term indicates the strength of the 'pull-back' to the stable long-run relationship in the face of transitory short-run deviations. It can be interpreted as an adjustment coefficient for the speed of adjustment of the system (example: if $\alpha_2 = 0.2$ and the data are annual, then it will take five years for the system to recover from a shock and to return to the long-run stable relationship). In the absence of co-integration β_1 and β_0 indicate the true long-term structural relationship.

Literature review

The literature on the relationship between energy consumption and GDP in developing countries is extensive but paints a slightly confusing picture. Different papers imply widely differing and even contradictory results, allowing for few policy conclusions. Lee (2005) presents a broad survey of the studies that have tried to find out the causal relationship between energy and economic growth during the past twenty years (see Table 4.2 overleaf). He points out that currently there is no consensus, neither on the long-run nor on the short-run relationships, and states that 'to date, the causality may run in either direction' (pp. 415–16) and that 'results have been mixed and conflicting'.

The example of Taiwan illustrates the lack of convergence between study results well. Yang (2000) concluded there is bidirectional causality between total energy consumption and income as well as between coal and electricity consumption. He also found unidirectional causality running from GDP to oil consumption and from gas consumption to GDP. Five years later, Lee and Chang (2005) agree with Yang only on the bidirectional link between income and total energy and coal consumption. They reject his other results, concluding that unidirectional causality runs from both electricity and oil consumption to economic growth and that gas consumption produces a stationary variable.

To add to the confusion we anticipate the results of our own Granger causality tests. Working with *per capita* figures, we have not – with the important exceptions of China and India – found Granger causality between

Table 4.2 Comparison of empirical results from causality tests for developing countries

Author	Countries and period	Causal relation
Yu and Choi (1985)	South Korea, Philippines (1954–76)	GDP → Energy
Masih and Masih (1996)	Malaysia, Singapore, Philippines, India, Indonesia, Pakistan (1955–90)	Mixed
Glasure and Lee (1997)	South Korea and Singapore (1961–90)	Energy ↔ GDP
Masih and Masih (1998)	Sri Lanka and Thailand (1955–91)	Energy → GDP
Asafy-Adjaye (2000)	India, Indonesia and Turkey (1973–95), Thailand, and Philippines (1973–95)	Energy → GDP Energy ↔ GDP
Yang (2000)	Taiwan (1954–97)	Energy ↔ GDP
Soytas and Sari (2003)	Argentina, South Korea, Turkey, Indonesia, Poland (1950–92)	Mixed
Fatai *et al.* (2004)	India, Indonesia (1960–99), Thailand and Philippines (1960–99)	Energy → GDP Energy ↔ GDP
Jumbe (2004)	Malawi (1970–99)	GDP → Energy
Morimoto and Hope (2004)	Sri Lanka (1960–98)	Energy ↔ GDP
Oh and Lee (2004)	South Korea (1970–99)	Energy ↔ GDP
Paul and Bhattacharya (2004)	India (1950–96)	Energy ↔ GDP
Lee (2005)	18 countries (1975–2001)	Energy → GDP
Ambapour and Massamba (2005)	Congo (1960–99)	GDP → Energy
Keppler (2006)	China (1971–2002) India (1971–2002)	Energy → GDP GDP → Energy

Source: Adapted from Lee (2005) p. 417.

energy consumption and economic growth in eight of the ten countries under consideration. This holds for total energy consumption as much as for oil or electricity consumption. It also holds regardless of the direction, that is, whether we look at economic growth causing energy consumption or energy consumption driving economic growth. Of course both are non-stationary variables that grow over time. However, as soon as we stationarize, as required, most causality relationships disappear at the 5 per cent level of significance. India and China, however, form two important exceptions. The relationships, however, point toward different directions of Granger causality. We identified a link between electricity consumption and economic growth in China and between economic growth and oil consumption in India.[7]

One of the differences between the present study and several previously published papers is that this study worked only with *per capita* figures whereas many studies, for instance Cheng (1996) Yang (2000) or Lee (2005) work with absolute figures of energy consumption and economic (income) growth. This is not formally wrong. However, the common development over time (the co-integration captured by the Granger causality method) is stronger with data that is *not* normalized by population growth. Without normalizing, population growth will simultaneously drive national energy consumption and national income, thus overestimating the link between the two. In addition, including small countries such as Singapore, Malawi gives undue weight to single projects that can distort results.

A further source of divergence between different studies is the nature of GDP data, an important issue about which most studies are coy. When working with developing countries, the question of whether to work with international exchange rates or purchasing power parities arises. This study used the dollar value of nominal income (provided by the IEA statistics) and (de-)inflated by the US GDP deflator to arrive at a measure for real income in constant 1995 US dollars. The alternative, working with local currencies, would have introduced additional bias through the arbitrary nature of currency regimes in many developing countries.

Clearly such a procedure can underestimate the income-relevant utility of non-exchangeable goods such as perishable food-stocks or housing. This is a well-known bias that needs to be considered by the reader. Working with Purchasing Power Parities, however, introduces the specific bias of the individual researcher or research institution that developed them. This second bias is much more difficult to assess. Contrary to the first issue (*per capita* vs. total values) however, the choice between the various GDP measures does not introduce a systematic bias when assessing the energy-income relationship.

Data used

Data for total energy consumption, electricity consumption, oil consumption, population and GDP have been sourced from *IEA Energy Statistics of OECD Countries 1960–2002* (2004) and *IEA Energy Statistics of non-OECD Countries 1960–2002* (2004). Since data were not available for all ten countries from 1960 onwards, the exercise was restricted to the period 1971–2002 (32 years). The information about nominal oil prices resulted from the US Department of Energy's Energy Information Administration (DOE-EIA) at http://www.eia.doe.gov/emeu/CHRONOLOGIES/chron_aug2005.xls. For the years 1974–2002, the Refiner Acquisition Cost of Imported Crude was taken and for the years 1971–73, the Official Price of Saudi Light. Subsequently, prices have been normalized to 1995 levels by taking the US GDP deflator.

As Masih and Masih (1996b) point out, cointegration techniques such as the Error Correction Model work best with large-sample, high frequency data. In the case of empirical work, in particular on developing countries, such data are, however, very difficult to come by. Data over long time spans or over several countries might also be inconsistent and thus useless for econometric analysis. Relying on homogenized data sets from international organizations such as the International Energy Agency is thus the prudent choice.

Presentation and specification of the model and its equations

Once the Granger causality test shows a causal relationship between two variables, the choice between exogenous and endogenous variables can be specified. In addition we will test for the influence of the oil price. In the case that energy (total *per capita* consumption, *per capita* electricity consumption or *per capita* oil consumption) is the explanatory variable, the following equation is tested:

$$gdp_t = \alpha_0 + \alpha_1\ energy_t + \alpha_2\ oil\ price_t + \varepsilon_t \tag{4.1}$$

where α_1 and α_2 mark the long-term elasticities of GDP with respect to energy consumption and the energy price.

In the case that *gdp* (*per capita* income in 1995 USD) is the explanatory variable, the following equation is tested:

$$energy_t = \alpha_0 + \alpha_1\ gdp_t + \alpha_2\ oil\ price_t + \varepsilon_t \tag{4.2}$$

where α_1 and α_2 mark the long-term elasticities of energy consumption with respect to GDP and the energy price.

After testing for cointegration of the different variables, the Error Correction Model can be set up. In the case that energy (total *per capita* consumption, *per capita* electricity consumption or *per capita* oil consumption) is the explanatory variable together with the oil price, equation (4.1) will yield the following error correction term (ecm):

$$ecm = e_{t-1} = gdp_{t-1} - \alpha_0 - \alpha_1\ energy_{t-1} - \alpha_2\ oil\ price_{t-1} \tag{4.3}$$

To set up the full Error Correction Model, the original model needs to be rewritten in linear dynamic form, replacing ε_t with the error correction term:

$$\begin{aligned} gdp_t = {} & \beta_0 + \beta_1\ energy_t + \beta_2\ oil\ price_t + \beta_3\ gdp_{t-1} + \beta_4\ energy_{t-1} \\ & + \beta_5\ oil\ price_{t-1} + \upsilon_t \end{aligned} \tag{4.4}$$

Subtracting gdp_{t-1} from both sides (thus differencing the model), and adding and subtracting β_1 $energy_{t-1} + \beta_2$ $oil\ price_{t-1}$ from the right-hand side will then yield the following Error Correction Model (ECM):

$$\begin{aligned} \Delta gdp_t &= a_0 + a_1 \Delta energy_t + a_2 \Delta oil\ price_t \\ &\quad - a_3(gdp_{t-1} - \alpha_0 - \alpha_1\ energy_{t-1} - \alpha_2\ oil\ price_{t-1}) + \upsilon_t \end{aligned} \tag{4.5}$$

where

$$a_1 = \beta_1,\ a_2 = \beta_2,\ a_3 = (1 - \beta_3),\ a_0 = \beta_0 - a_3\alpha_0 = \beta_0 - (1 - \beta_3)\alpha_0,$$

$$\alpha_1 = (\beta_4 + \beta_1)/(1 - \beta_3) \quad and \quad \alpha_2 = (\beta_5 + \beta_2)/(1 - \beta_3)$$

Estimating equation (4.5) with OLS provides:

a_1 as the short-run elasticity of GDP with respect to energy consumption, a_2 as the short-run elasticity of GDP with respect to energy prices, and a_3 as the parameter indicating the speed of adjustment of the system to the long-term equilibrium path in response to short-term deviations of Δ*energy* and Δ*oil price* from their long-term mean values.

The case, in which *gdp* (*per capita* income) is the explanatory variable, this will yield *mutatis mutandis* the following Error Correction Model:

$$\begin{aligned} \Delta energy_t &= a_0 + a_1 \Delta gdp_t + a_2 \Delta oil\ price_t \\ &\quad - a_3(energy_{t-1} - \alpha_0 - \alpha_1 gdp_{t-1} - \alpha_2\ oil\ price_{t-1}) + \upsilon_t \end{aligned} \tag{4.6}$$

where

$$a_1 = \beta_1,\ a_2 = \beta_2,\ a_3 = (1 - \beta_3),\ a_0 = \beta_0 - a_3\alpha_0 = \beta_0 - (1 - \beta_3)\alpha_0,$$

$$\alpha_1 = (\beta_4 + \beta_1)/(1 - \beta_3) \quad \text{and}$$

$$\alpha_2 = (\beta_5 + \beta_2)/(1 - \beta_3)$$

Estimating equation (4.6) with OLS will provide:

a_1 as the short-run income elasticity of energy demand, a_2 as the short-run price elasticity of energy demand, and a_3 as the parameter indicating the speed of adjustment of the system to the long-term equilibrium path in response to short-term deviations of Δ*gdp* and Δ*oil price* from their long-term paths.

Presentation of regression results

In the following, we will present the various steps of the testing procedure with the results that have been obtained at each step. The objective is to allow readers to reproduce the results with the indicated data, techniques and testing procedures.

Testing for non-stationarity

Testing for non-stationarity of the time series of *per capita* income, total *per capita* energy consumption, *per capita* electricity consumption, *per capita* oil consumption and the oil price for the ten countries under consideration yields the following results:

Except for the oil price, the various time series have been tested for stationarity under the assumptions that they do possess an intercept and do not possess an autonomous trend (for a motivation see Elder and Kennedy, 2001, p. 140). The first assumption is justified by the fact that none of the countries started at zero levels of consumption or income. The second assumption is justified by the fact that none of the economies will be faced with ever increasing rates of either income or consumption. The case is different for the oil price, where we have less information on theoretical grounds before testing. We have therefore reported stationarity tests for the oil price in all three possible permutations. Given that all ten countries had at least one time series

Table 4.3 Testing for non-stationarity* (t-statistics for the Philipps-Perron test, Newey-West bandwith using Bartlett Kernel)

	GDP	Energy consumption	Oil consumption	Electricity consumption	Oil price
Argentina	−1,768***	−1,517***	−0,274***	−0,647***	no intercept,
Brazil	[−4,146]	−1,917***	[−2,694]	[−6,942]	no trend
Chile	0,407***	0,407***	−1,079***	2,766***	0,175***
China	1,530***	−0,996***	−1,061***	0,322***	
Egypt	−1,411***	−2,002***	−2,506***	−1,517***	intercept,
India	2,501***	0,507***	0,727***	0,899***	no trend
Indonesia	−1,948***	−0,019***	−2,162***	−1,294***	−2,704*
Kenya	[−3,871]	−1,109***	−1,886***	[−3,096]	
South Africa	−1,279***	−2,109***	−1,109***	[−6,008]	trend & intercept
Thailand	−0,706***	0,230***	−0,438***	−1,423***	−3,101**

Note: * Tested for the null hypothesis that the series (intercept but no trend except for the oil price, see discussion in text) have a unit root. The signs (*), (**) and (***) show the null hypothesis is confirmed at the 1 per cent, 5 per cent and 10 per cent level of significance respectively. The critical values for $M1$ (no intercept, no trend) are 1 per cent −2.642, 5 per cent −1.952, 10 per cent −1.610; for $M2$ (intercept, no trend) 1 per cent −3.662, 5 per cent −2.960, 10 per cent −2.619 and for $M3$ (intercept and trend) 1 per cent −4.285, 5 per cent −3.563, 10 per cent −3.215. Square brackets indicate the null hypothesis is rejected and the series is stationary.

Source: EViews.

that was non-stationary, we resorted to first differencing of the data. This gave the following results:

Table 4.4 Testing for non-stationarity – first differences* (t-statistics for the Philipps–Perron test, Newey–West bandwith using Bartlett Kernel)

	ΔGDP	ΔEnergy consumption	ΔOil consumption	ΔElectricity consumption	ΔOil price
Argentina	[−3, 912]	[−4, 226]	[−4, 010]	[−3, 830]	no intercept,
Brazil	[−3, 741]	[−3, 152]	[−2, 946]	[−2, 766]	no trend
Chile	[−3, 636]	[−4, 153]	[−4, 124]	[−4, 844]	[−5.108]
China	[−3, 789]	[−4, 335]	[−5, 815]	[−5, 421]	
Egypt	[−3, 267]	[−4, 898]	[−5, 138]	[−4, 446]	intercept,
India	[−6, 254]	[−5, 579]	[−11, 817]	[−4, 032]	no trend
Indonesia	[−3, 969]	[−5, 973]	[−7, 249]	[−2, 699]	[−5, 080]
Kenya	[−5, 252]	[−5, 641]	[−4, 717]	[−4, 944]	
South Africa	[−4.405]	[−5, 000]	[−8, 156]	[−2, 716]	trend & intercept
Thailand	[−3, 273]	[−3, 699]	[−3, 662]	[−3, 119]	[−5.259]

Note: * Tested for the null hypothesis that the series (intercept but no trend except for oil price, see discussion in text) have a unit root. The signs (*), (**) and (***) indicate the null hypothesis is confirmed at the 1 per cent, 5 per cent and 10 per cent level of significance respectively. The critical values for $M2$ (intercept, no trend) are 1 per cent −3, 679, 5 per cent −2, 968, 10 per cent −2, 623. Parentheses show the null hypothesis is rejected and the series is stationary.

Source: EViews.

Thus all time series were stationary at the level of first differences, which allows continuing with the next step of the testing strategy, the pair-wise testing for Granger causality.

Testing for Granger causality

The Granger causality test was performed by testing for bivariate causality, that is, by comparing (example given for a test between *per capita* energy consumption and *per capita* GDP) the significance of

$$gdp_t = \alpha_1 + \sum_{i=1}^{T} \alpha_{2i}\, gdp_{t-i} + \sum_{j=1}^{T} \alpha_{3j}\, energy_{t-j} + \varepsilon_t$$

with the significance of

$$gdp_t = \alpha_4 + \sum_{i=1}^{T} \alpha_{5i}\, gdp_{t-i} + \varepsilon_t,$$

and the significance of

$$energy_t = \alpha_6 + \sum_{i=1}^{T} \alpha_{7i}\, energy_{t-i} + \sum_{j=1}^{T} \alpha_{8j}\, gdp_{t-j} + \varepsilon_t,$$

with the significance of

$$energy_t = \alpha_9 + \sum_{i=1}^{T} \alpha_{10i}\, energy_{t-i} + \varepsilon_t$$

The Granger causality tests performed pair-wise for *per capita* income and total *per capita* energy consumption, *per capita* income and oil *per capita* consumption, as well as for *per capita* income and *per capita* electricity consumption did *not* show any significant link in eight of the countries tested (Argentina, Brazil, Chile, Egypt, Indonesia, Kenya, South Africa and Thailand) at the 5 per cent level of significance.

Notable exceptions were, however, the two largest countries in the sample, China and India. In China, both oil consumption and electricity consumption contribute to economic growth. In India, economic growth causes increases in both oil and electricity consumption. Extending the range of significance to the 10 per cent level, would allow concluding that *per capita* electricity consumption also Granger-causes *per capita* economic growth in Argentina and Kenya (as in China) and that *per capita* economic growth Granger-causes *per capita* total energy consumption in Brazil.

The detailed results are presented in Table 4.5. 'Yes' or 'no' indicate whether bivariate Granger causality is present. The figure in parentheses provides the F-statistic for the null-hypothesis that the variables in the first row do *not* Granger-cause the variables in the first column. For a sample size of 32 years and three degrees of freedom, the relevant tabulated value of the F-statistic, above which the null-hypothesis can be rejected with an error of less than 5 per cent, is 2.99.[8]

Estimating the long-term OLS equations

The Granger tests yield significant causal relations at the five per cent level only in the cases of China and India. Given that in the Chinese case both *per capita* electricity and oil consumption Granger-cause *per capita* GDP growth, it was natural to continue to research in this direction.

Table 4.5 Results of Granger causality tests (The table reports the existence of pair-wise Granger causality as well as the relevant *F*-statistics, the critical value at the 5 per cent level being 2,99; results significant at the 5 per cent level are in bold)

	GDP	Energy	Oil	Electricity
Argentina				
GDP	n.a.	no (0.518)	no (0.428)	no (2.782)
Energy	no (0.848)			
Oil	no (0.539)			
Electricity	no (0.580)			
Brazil				
GDP	n.a.	no (2.849)	no (1.439)	no (0.774)
Energy	no (2.854)			
Oil	no (0.577)			
Electricity	no (1.564)			
Chile				
GDP	n.a.	no (1.015)	no (1.269)	no (0.216)
Energy	no (0.341)			
Oil	no (0.805)			
Electricity	no (0.312)			
China				
GDP	n.a.	no (0.393)	**yes (4.818)**	**yes (3.270)**
Energy	no (0.829)			
Oil	no (1.788)			
Electricity	no (0.917)			
Egypt				
GDP	n.a.	no (1.168)	no (1.289)	no (1.782)
Energy	no (1.200)			
Oil	no (0.277)			
Electricity	no (1.317			
India				
GDP	n.a.	no (0.548)	no (1.505)	no (0.924)
Energy	no (1.096)			
Oil	**yes (3.658)**			
Electricity	**yes (3.283)**			
Indonesia				
GDP	n.a.	no (0.298)	no (0.584)	no (0.097)
Energy	no (0.476)			
Oil	no (0.829)			
Electricity	no (0.066)			

Continued

Table 4.5 Continued

	GDP	Energy	Oil	Electricity
Kenya				
GDP	n.a.	no (0.504)	no (0.707)	no (2.364)
Energy	no (0.440)			
Oil	no (0.006)			
Electricity	no (0.094)			
South Africa				
GDP	n.a.	no (0.688)	no (0.097)	no (0.357)
Energy	no (0.310)			
Oil	no (0.700)			
Electricity	no (0.725)			
Thailand				
GDP	n.a.	no (0.084)	no (0.566)	no (0.374)
Energy	no (0.656)			
Oil	no (1.135)			
Electricity	no (2.166)			

Source: EViews.

Box 4.1 The case of India

The case of India, in which *per capita* income growth causes both *per capita* oil and electricity consumption, offered a less clear direction to pursue. Looking separately at the links between GDP and electricity consumption as well as GDP and consumption did not offer any leads for the application of the Error Correction Model either. For GDP and oil, the variables are not cointegrated. (For GDP and electricity, they are cointegrated but, in the Error Correction Model, the GDP variable is not significant at the 5 per cent level.) The long-run relationship between *per capita* oil consumption and *per capita* income in India, including a lagged variable for *per capita* oil consumption accounting for the inertia in the adjustment of consumer behaviour can thus be estimated directly (parentheses below the coefficients indicate standard errors):

$$oil_t = -1.363 + 0.598\, gdp_t + 0.515\, oil_{t-1} + \varepsilon_t$$

$$(0.455) \quad (0.183) \quad (0.150)$$

All variables are significant at the 5 per cent level, R^2 is high at 0.974 and the Durbin–Watson statistic is satisfactory at 1.857. In the long run, a percentage increase in *per capita* income in India will increase *per capita* oil consumption by 0.6 per cent.

Source: EViews.

We thus tested for the long-run relationship between Chinese *per capita* electricity consumption (electricity), *per capita* oil consumption (oil) and *per capita* income growth (*gdp*) with the OLS method:

$$gdp_t = \alpha_0 + \alpha_1 \; electricity_t + \alpha_2 \; oil + \varepsilon \tag{4.7}$$

where α_1 and α_2 show the long-term elasticity of *per capita* income with respect to *per capita* electricity consumption and *per capita* oil consumption. This yields the following result (the standard errors are provided in brackets below the coefficients):

$$\underset{}{gdp_t} = \underset{(0.208)}{-\,0.674} + \underset{(0.058)}{1.239\; electricity_t} - \underset{(0.107)}{0.241\; oil_t} + \varepsilon_t \tag{4.7'}$$

While R^2 was high at 0.990, the Durbin–Watson statistic was excessively low at 0.330. Including a lagged variable for *per capita* income growth to account for the marked Chinese economic growth cycle, resulted in the following equation:[9]

$$gdp_t = \underset{(0.096)}{-0.175} + \underset{(0.069)}{0.347\; electricity_t} - \underset{(0.040)}{0.098 oil_t} + \underset{(0.057)}{0.751 gdp_{t-1}} + \varepsilon_t \tag{4.8}$$

All variables other than the intercept are significant at the 5 per cent-level, R^2 is high at 0.999 and the Durbin–Watson statistic improves to 1.349, greatly improved but not enough to warrant acceptance of the results. This demanded another strategy – the application of the Error Correction Model. We thus tested Chinese *per capita* income, *per capita* electricity consumption and *per capita* oil consumption for cointegration. The Johansen cointegration test identified two cointegrating relationships at the 5 per cent level of significance.

Table 4.6 Unrestricted cointegration rank test (Series: *per capita* income, *per capita* electricity consumption, *per capita* oil consumption)

No. of cointegrating equations	**Eigenvalue**	**Trace statistic**	**0.05 Critical value**	**Probability**
None*	0.472	33.904	24.276	0.002
At most 1*	0.321	14.766	12.321	0.019
At most 2	0.099	3.138	4.130	0.091

Trace test indicates two cointegrating equations at the 0.05 level.
* denotes rejection of the hypothesis at the 0.05 level.

Source: EViews.

Table 4.7 Estimating the error correction model

	ΔGDP_t as the dependent variable			
Variable	**Coefficient**	**Standard error**	**t-Statistic**	**Probability**
Constant	−0.017	0.0168	−1.032	0.312
$\Delta Electricity_{t-1}$	0.670	0.141	4.750	0.000
ΔOil_{t-1}	−0.119	0.090	−1.320	0.199
ΔGDP_{t-1}	0.705	0.172	4.100	0.000
Error correction term	−0.629	0.257	−2.450	0.021
R-squared	0.623	Mean dependent variable		0.070
Adjusted R-squared	0.563	S.D. dependent variable		0.035
Standard error regression	0.023	Akaike info criterion		−4.562
Sum squared of residuals	0.013	Schwarz criterion		−4.329
Log likelihood	73.434	F-statistic		10.339
Durbin–Watson statistic	1.615	Probability (F-statistic)		0.000

Estimating the Short-run dynamics with the error correction model

The existence of cointegration requires employing the Error Correction Model. The error correction terms are given by the lagged OLS equation (4.8):

$$ecm = e_t = gdp_{t-1} - \alpha_1 - \alpha_2 electricity_{t-1} - \alpha_3 oil_{t-1} - \alpha_4 gdp_{t-2} \quad (4.9)$$

Inserting the error correction term (4.9) and differentiating yields:

$$\begin{aligned}\Delta gdp_t = a_1 + a_2 \Delta electricity_t + a_3 \Delta oil_t + a_4 \Delta gdp_{t-1} - a_5 (gdp_{t-1} \\ - \alpha_1 - \alpha_2 electricity_{t-1} - \alpha_3 oil_{t-1} - \alpha_4 gdp_{t-2}) + \varepsilon_t\end{aligned} \quad (4.10)$$

Estimating equation (4.10) yields the following results:

$a_2 = 0.67$ is the short-run elasticity of *per capita* income with respect to *per capita* electricity consumption. $a_3 = -0.12$ is the (rather weak) short-run elasticity of *per capita* income with respect to *per capita* oil consumption; in addition the variable is significant only at a 0.2 level of significance. $a_4 = 0.70$ indicates the elasticity of current income to past income. Current income thus depends as much on current electricity consumption as on past income. $a_5 = -0.62$, finally indicates the speed of adjustment of the system. It implies that each year 62 per cent of any divergence from the long-term relationship will be removed. In other words, the impact of any shock will persist

Box 4.2 The Chinese economic growth cycle

In conclusion, we provide the results of an additional test performed outside the narrow scope of this chapter to present an application of the Error Correction Model. Regressing *per capita* income growth on *per capita* electricity consumption, *per capita* oil consumption and a sinus-shaped economic cycle of 13 years length, beginning in 1970, provides the following results with a near-perfect fit (the length of the cycle was estimated with the help of a Hodrick–Prescott Filter):

$$\begin{array}{llllll} gdp_t = & -0.812 & + 1.111\, electricity_t & - 0.067\, oil_t & + 0.0715\, cycle\, 13_t & + \varepsilon_t \\ & (0.058) & (0.007) & (0.010) & (0.007) & \end{array}$$

The variables are significant at any desired level, the R^2 is 0.999 and the Durbin–Watson statistic is 1.863. The results confirm the analysis based on the Error Correction Model: in China, electricity consumption is a key driver for economic growth.

Source: EViews.

roughly for only a year and a half before the system reverts to its long-term relationship. Testing for the properties of the residual, the Jarque-Bera test indicates the residuals follow a normal distribution with a probability of over 39 per cent.

Energy market implications of results and perspectives for future research

The results of the Granger causality tests, at the same time, contradict the current consensus in the literature ('there is an important relationship between energy consumption and economic growth') and confirm it ('even after twenty years of intensive study we do not know what the link looks like'). Eight out of ten countries considered did not show a link between various indicators of *per capita* energy consumption and *per capita* income at the five per cent level of significance. On the other hand, the results for China and India show solid relationships between the two. Extending the range of significance to ten per cent shows that electricity consumption also has an impact on growth in Argentina and Kenya.

Per capita electricity and oil consumption drive growth of *per capita* incomes in China to the extent that every percentage increase in electricity consumption increases economic growth by over one-half per cent. While China's economic development hardly needs any added stimulus, the results confirm the suspicion of researchers that the lack of enough power generation capacity is the major bottleneck for further economic development in China (Keppler and Méritet, 2004, p. 317).

We would like to point out there was no link between *per capita* income growth and total *per capita* consumption of energy (where coal, that provides more than two thirds of China's energy, figures prominently). The gradual decoupling of coal consumption from income growth in China, found in other studies, would be consistent with this finding (Masih and Masih, 1996b, p. 328). This could suggest that stricter policies on coal consumption (warranted both for national and global environmental reasons) might not harm economic growth as long as sufficient electricity production, for instance from nuclear energy, is guaranteed.

The weakly negative impact of *per capita* oil consumption on *per capita* income is econometrically less robust. Testing separately for the impacts before and after 1992 (the year that China turned from a net oil exporter to a net oil importer), however, consistently confirmed the negative sign. While this might be surprising at first, it is entirely logical. In China, domestic oil consumption, that is to say the difference between domestic production and the oil trade balance, *always* drains capital from more productive uses. When it exports, consumption raises the opportunity cost of not exporting precious oil. When it imports, consumption raises outward capital flows.

For India, the relationship runs from *per capita* income growth to *per capita* oil consumption. This is consistent with information about India's massive subsidization of oil consumption, notably in rural areas (see Keppler and Birol, 1999). According to this study, kerosene was sold in India in 1998, on the average, at roughly half its cost. Oil is thus a merit good, whose consumption depends on general welfare rather than its productivity in economic processes. For every one per cent increase in income, consumption levels of oil increase by 0.6 per cent.

The policy implications for India's decision-makers are far from clear-cut. Reducing subsidies and delinking energy consumption from growth could have undesirable social and political side-effects. Continuing current policies means continuing with inefficiencies that burden government budgets and growth. It is, perhaps, most useful to point out the general fact that support for socially weaker groups of society is best administered through direct income transfers rather than through price subsidies.

Questions about the link between energy consumption and income are here to stay. The divergence of national experiences with the energy consumption – income relationship also highlights that energy continues to be a policy area in which outcomes are not solely determined by decentralized market forces. Infrastructure provision, massive subsidization, trade policies, climate and cultural factors all play decisive roles shaping that relationship. Unfortunately, these are precisely the factors that are most difficult for econometricians to take into account. Carefully modelling them is nevertheless the most promising way forward. However, modelling them for several countries at a time to allow for general conclusions would be a hugely labour-intensive enterprise.

One specific issue for future research is including coal in the analysis. Another is the link between energy consumption (and, in particular, electricity consumption) and broader measures of welfare that are not captured in standard GDP accounting. Given the ample anecdotal evidence of the positive externalities of electricity consumption, it might be worthwhile to analyse the relationship between electricity consumption and the Human Development Index (HDI). The HDI is a synthetic index of quality of life developed by the United Nations Development Programme (UNDP, 2004) that also includes, other than GDP, life expectancy and adult literacy. Comparing the results for GDP and HDI regressions should allow casting added light on the relationship between energy demand and economic well-being. One thing is certain; the already rich literature on the energy–income link is destined to become richer still.

Notes

1 I would like to thank my colleagues Régis Bourbonnais, Carlo Pozzi and Marie Bessec for their expert comments during the preparation of this chapter, as well as Jacques Girod for his help in identifying the relevant literature on the subject. All have significantly contributed to the successful conclusion of this chapter. Any remaining errors of commission or omission are, of course, the sole responsibility of the author.

2 Throughout the study *per capita* levels of consumption and income are considered to normalize for demographic growth, the impact of which is not the object of this study. See the paper by Holtedahl and Joutz (2004) explicitly modelling the impact of urbanization on electricity demand for an alternative approach.

3 ELEC stands for *per capita* electricity consumption, OIL for *per capita* oil consumption, ENRGY for total *per capita* energy consumption and GDP for *per capita* income measured in 1995 dollars converted at exchange rates.

4 Upper case letters refer to real-valued economic variables, lower case letters to their natural logarithms. In practice, we will exclusively work with the natural logarithms of economic variables due to the fact that the parameter of an independent variable in a linear regression has convenient economic interpretability. Consider, for instance, the model $y_t = \alpha_0 + \alpha_1 x_t + u_t$, where y_t is energy consumption and x_t is income. In this case, α_1 can be considered the constant income elasticity of energy consumption.

5 The F-statistic is given by the equation $F_{K,N-K} = [(SSR_R - SSR_{NR})/(K_{NR} - K_R)]/[(SSR_{NR}/N - K_{NR})]$ where SSR indicates the sum of squared residuals, the subscripts R and NR indicate the restricted and the non restricted equation, K indicates the number of exogenous variables and N the number of observations. In the specific case of this chapter with 32 years of observation and seven exogenous variables in the non restricted case and four in the restricted case (given three lags and a constant), the above expression reduces to $F_{4,28} = [(SSR_R - SSR_{NR})/3)]/[(SSR_{NR}/25)]$.

6 In order to be cointegrated, the series need to have the same degree of non-stationarity; series of different degrees of non-stationarity will never be cointegrated. In the present paper, the issue does not arise since all data are $I(1)$.

7 Most previous studies do report links between energy consumption and economic growth. Apart from the issue of not using *per capita* figures, this might also be due to the known bias of reporting positive rather than negative results. One exception is Masih and Masih (1996a). While finding links in different directions for India, Indonesia and Pakistan, they report the absence of links between energy and growth for Malaysia, Singapore and the Philippines.

8 Testing for a three-year lag was found to provide the most significant results. Three years is also the period over which we would expect on the basis of heuristic analysis the link between energy consumption and income to be most significant.

9 Running a Hodrick–Prescott filter with the Chinese GDP data indicated a 13-year cycle from peak to peak.

References

Ambapour, S. and C. Massamba (2005) 'Croissance économique et consommation d'énergie au Congo: Une analyse en termes de causalité', *Document de Travail DT* 12/2005, Bureau d'application des méthodes statistiques et informatiques, Brazzaville.

Asafu-Adjaye, J. (2000) 'The Relationship between Energy Consumption, Energy prices and Economic Growth: Time Series Evidence from Asian Developing Countries', *Energy Economics*, vol. 22, pp. 615–25.

Bohi, D.R. and M.B. Zimmerman (1984) 'An Update on Econometric Studies of Energy Demand Behavior', *Annual Review of Energy*, vol. 9, pp. 105–54.

Bourbonnais, R. (2006) *Économétrie: Manuel et exercices corrigés* (Paris: Dunod).

Cheng, B.S. (1996) 'An Investigation of Cointegration and Causality between Energy Consumption and Economic Growth', *Journal of Energy and Development*, vol. 21, pp. 73–84.

Dahl, C.A. (1994) 'A Survey of Energy Demand Elasticities for the Developing World', *Journal of Energy and Development*, vol. 18, pp. 1–48.

Engle, R.F. and C.W.J. Granger (1987) 'Co-integration and Error-correction: Representation, Estimation, and Testing', *Econometrica*, vol. 55, pp. 251–76.

Engle, R.F. and C.W.J. Granger (eds.) (1991) *Long-run Economic Relationships: Readings in Cointegration*, (Oxford, Oxford University Press).

Elder, J. and P. Kennedy (2001) 'Testing for Unit Roots: What Should Students Be Taught?', *Journal of Economic Education*, vol. 31, pp. 137–45.

Granger, C. (1969) 'Testing for Causality and Feedback', *Econometrica*, vol. 37, pp. 424–38.

Hendry, D.F. and K. Juselius (2000) 'Explaining Cointegration Analysis: Part I', *The Energy Journal*, vol. 21, pp. 1–42.

Hendry, D.F. and K. Juselius (2001) 'Explaining Cointegration Analysis: Part II', *The Energy Journal*, vol. 22, pp. 75–120.

Holtedahl, P. and F.L. Joutz (2004) 'Residential Electricity Demand in Taiwan', *Energy Economics*, vol. 26, pp. 201–24.

IEA (2004a) *IEA Energy Prices and Taxes*, (Paris: OCDE/IEA).

IEA (2004b) *IEA Energy Statistics of Non-OECD Countries 1960–2002* (Paris: OECD/IEA).

IEA (2004c) *IEA Energy Statistics of OECD Countries 1960–2002* (Paris: OECD/IEA).

Johansen, S. (1988) 'Statistical Analysis of Cointegrating Vectors', *Journal of Economic Dynamics and Control*, vol. 12, pp. 231–54.

Keppler, J.H. and F. Birol (1999) *Looking at Energy Subsidies: Getting the Prices Right*, WEO Insights (Paris: OECD/IEA).

Keppler, J.H. and J. Lesourne (2002) *Electricity for All* (Paris: EDF).

Keppler, J.H. and S. Méritet (2004) 'Les perspectives énergétiques de la Chine', *Revue de l'énergie*, vol. 557, pp. 316–20.

Lee, C. (2005a) 'Energy Consumption and GDP in Developing Countries: A Cointegrated Panel Analysis', *Energy Economics*, vol. 27, pp. 415–27.

Lee, C. and C. Chang (2005b) 'Structural Breaks, Energy Consumption, and Economic Growth Revisited: Evidence from Taiwan', *Energy Economics*, vol. 27, pp. 857–72.

Masih, A.M.M. and R. Masih (1996a) 'Energy Consumption, Real Income and Temporal Causality: Results from a Multi-country Study Based on Cointegration and Error-correcting Modelling Techniques', *Energy Economics*, vol. 18, pp. 165–83.

Masih, A.M.M. and R. Masih (1996b) 'Stock–Watson Dynamic OLS (DOLS) and Error-Correction Modeling Approaches to Estimating Long- and Short-Run Elasticities in a Demand Function: New Evidence and Methodological Implications from an Application to the Demand for Coal in Mainland China', *Energy Economics*, vol. 18, pp. 315–34.

McKinnon, J.G. (1991) 'Critical Values for Cointegration Tests', in R.F. Engle and C.W.J. Granger (eds), *Long-run Economic Relationships: Readings in Cointegration*, (Oxford: Oxford University Press), pp. 267–76.

Narayan, P.K. and R. Smyth (2005) 'Electricity Consumption, Employment and Real Income in Australia: Evidence from Multivariate Granger Causality Tests', *Energy Policy*, vol. 33, pp. 1109–16.

UNDP (2004) *Human Development Report 2004: Cultural Liberty in Today's Diverse World* (New York: UNDP).

Yang, H. (2000) 'A Note on the Causal Relationship Between Energy and GDP in Taiwan', *Energy Economics*, vol. 22, pp. 309–17.

5

Economic Development and Energy Intensity: A Panel Data Analysis

Ghislaine Destais, Julien Fouquau and Christophe Hurlin

Observing and understanding the relationship between economic development and energy intensity

The energy–GDP ratio, or ratio of total national primary energy consumption to GDP, is a measure of the Energy Intensity of the economy (henceforward noted as EI). It represents the energy required to generate a unit of national output. Its evolution over time shows whether the economy becomes more or less energy intensive. Projections of national energy demand under different growth scenarios depend upon the explicit or implicit value of this ratio. It can also be used to define an objective of energy policy.

Another way of looking at the evolution of the energy–GDP ratio is to talk in terms of GDP-elasticity of energy consumption (noted 'e'). A constant energy–GDP ratio means energy consumption grows at the same rhythm as economic activity, in other words that the value of the elasticity is equal to one. A decreasing ratio corresponds to elasticity lower than one. But, as noted by Ang (2006), 'Unlike the energy–GDP ratio, the elasticity is often unstable. When the annual growth rate of GDP is close to zero and that of energy consumption is not, the coefficient is either a large positive or negative number, which is of little practical value'. In like manner, a constant decreasing rate of EI (2 per cent for example, which is the French objective beyond 2015) leads to a value of e inversely proportional to the rate of economic growth. The elasticity is equal to 0.5 if the economy grows at 4 per cent, 0 (stagnation of energy consumption) for a 2 per cent GDP growth, −1 for 1 per cent and is indeterminate in case of economic stagnation. Conversely, a constant elasticity leads to a linear relation between the evolution of EI and economic growth. There is then a double-log relation between EI and GDP allowing for various monotone functional forms according to the value of the income elasticity.

Since the middle of the twentieth century, energy economists have been trying to evaluate and compare the energy intensity of various economies to discover the trends in their evolution (see, for example, Putnam (1953),

Clark (1960), Percebois (1979), Martin (1988)). In general, these authors have shown that the energy intensity of a country first passes through a more or less strong and long growth phase, before reaching a turning point which is sometimes marked, sometimes in the form of a plateau, and then decreases (see Figure 5.1). This bell-shaped or Inverted-U curve that had also been observed by S. Kuznets (1955) for the relationship between income inequality and economic development, was popularized during the nineties under the name of 'Kuznets curve' by environment economists who found the same type of relation between environmental pollutants and economic activity (Müller-Fürstenberger *et al.* (2004)).

In addition, an apparent convergence phenomenon of the level of the EI is observed, the range passing from 1 to 15 at the beginning of the twentieth century to 1 to 3.5 at the beginning of the twenty-first century. However, it should be noted, along with Toman and Jemelkova (2003), that 'advanced industrialized societies [still] use more energy per unit of economic output (and far more energy per capita) than poorer societies'.

Although 'the interpretation of this ratio entails great care' (Ang, 2006), it is possible to identify at least three important explanations for these evolutions: the increase of energy efficiency, the different stages of economic development and inter-energy substitutions. Firstly, it has often been attributed to a

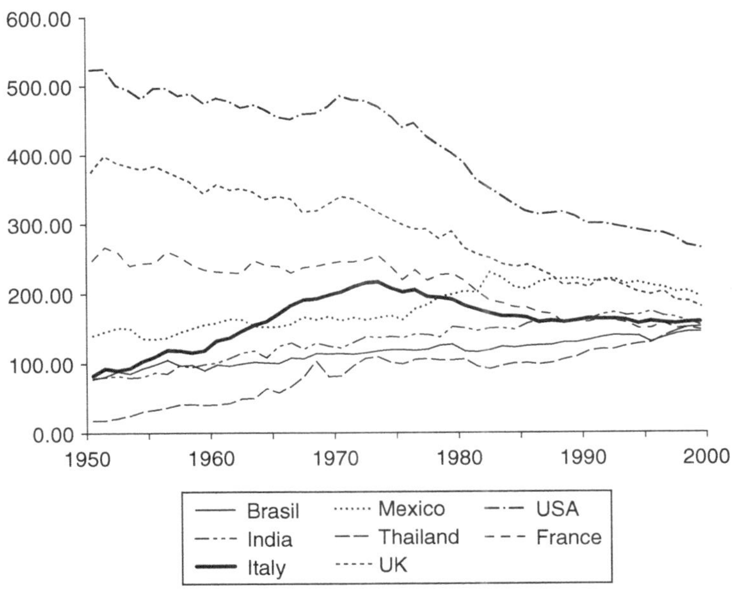

Figure 5.1 Commercial energy intensity in selected countries (kilo of oil equivalent per thousand 1990 Geary–Khamis $)

more efficient way of producing and using energy, due partly to autonomous technical progress but mainly to increasing energy prices. Secondly, many authors state that the energy intensity of a country first rises along with the economic development process during the industrialization phase, and then declines in the post-industrialization phase because of the increase of services and high technology industries, that is, with the dematerialization of the economy, despite the development of transportation. Quantification of these effects of structural changes on the evolution of energy intensity has been made by means of index decomposition analysis (see, for example, Schäfer, 2003). Thirdly, primary energy consumption is an aggregated value of the various energy sources used in an economy, each having its own efficiency. Substitution among them and the development of new energy sources will then influence the EI ratio independently of the delivered service, the main phenomenon until now being the development of the use of electricity and gas.

Other authors also point out the disparities between countries (Ang, 1987). For example, the United States and Canada have greater energy intensities than the other industrialized countries for a number of reasons already presented by Darmstadter *et al.* (1977): the very low price of fuel, geographical characteristics which lead to greater transportation needs, large houses and a high level of consumption in the electrical sector. Martin (1988) mentions the persistent influence of the past, like the availability of natural resources in the United States in the nineteenth century.

These observations make clear the problem of the homogeneity of worldwide energy models. Is it possible to assume the existence of a model for the evolution of long-term energy intensities which would pertain to all parts of the world, perhaps even over time or capable of being slowed down or accelerated? How can one take account of the individual specificities of the various countries of the world in the construction of a model for worldwide energy demand? These are some of the many questions which can only be approached using a cross-section or panel model. That is why in this chapter we begin by presenting a review of the various technical approaches used in cross-section or panel models to illustrate the question of homogeneity/heterogeneity of the energy models. Then we will propose an original panel model with a threshold and a smooth transition which makes it possible, in a global model, to test for and take account of any possible heterogeneity in the income elasticity of the energy demand.

Panel data analysis

Let us now consider a cross-section model of the relationship between income and energy demand. Like Zilberfarb and Adams (1981) or Shrestha (2000) let us consider a double-log specification of the energy demand equation. Defining c_i as the logarithm of the consumption of primary energy *per capita* of the ith country of a sample of N countries for the year studied, and y_i the logarithm of the corresponding *per capita* GDP, this approach leads to an estimation using the following model:

$$c_i = \alpha + \beta y_i + \varepsilon_i \quad i = 1, \ldots, N \tag{5.1}$$

where α and β are constants for one or several years and ε_i is *i.i.d.* $(0, \sigma_\varepsilon^2)$. In this simple model, the constant long-term elasticity is common for all the countries and is given by $e_i = \beta$, $\forall i$. The corresponding energy intensity is equal to:

$$\mathrm{EI}_i = \gamma^* Y_i^{(\beta-1)} \tag{5.2}$$

where Y is the level of GDP and γ is a constant. With 1989 data for 41 countries of various levels of development, Shrestha found an income elasticity of 1.6 for commercial energy consumption and 1.4 for both commercial and traditional energy.

A general drawback of the cross-section approach is that, as noted by Medlock and Soligo (2001), 'it suffers from implicitly assuming that the same regularities apply to all nations'. There are two ways to deal partially with this problem: the introduction of dummy variables and the pooling of countries by classes. Zilberfarb and Adams (1981) introduced dummy variables representing, among other things, the differences between countries at various levels of development, but they were unable to discover any 'development effect' in a data set of 47 developing countries in 1970–74–76. They found that the elasticity was 'in the neighbourhood of 1.35'.

Furthermore the log–log structural relationship has the great disadvantage of being intrinsically unable to reproduce the empirical evidence of the Inverted-U curve, which implies that the relationship between energy intensity and income is non-monotonic and, therefore, that income elasticity of energy demand may depend on income level. One way to deal with the problem is to use a quadratic logarithmic specification as Ang (1987) does and to consider the cross-section model:

$$c_i = \alpha + \beta y_i + \lambda y_i^2 + \varepsilon_i \quad i = 1, \ldots, N \tag{5.3}$$

where β is expected to be greater than 1 and λ negative. This quadratic form function can be viewed as an approximation to a more complex function and constitutes an alternative solution to non-parametric approaches (Judson *et al.*, 1999). It leads to an elasticity equal to $e_i = \beta + 2\lambda y_i$. In this case, then, energy intensity might depend on the level of economic development. Its maximum occurs when $e = 1$, that is when $\bar{y} = (1 - \beta)/2\lambda$. Ang concludes, with 1975 data for 100 countries pooled into four levels of *per capita* GDP, that 'commercial energy elasticities are consistently higher for developing than for developed countries'; for industrial countries, the best fit is to a double-log relation, yielding 1.73 for the value of the elasticity.

However, in this approach the temporal dimension is not explicitly dealt with, although Brookes (1973) had previously shown, with the use of year by year estimations of a log–log relationship for 22 countries from 1950 to 1965, that the elasticity would decrease over time. The development of *panel data econometrics* makes it possible to take into account the two-fold dimension, individual and temporal, of the related data. As stated by Hsiao (2003), panel data sets possess several major advantages over conventional cross-sectional or time-series data sets. Obviously, the fact of using data observed for N entities (countries, regions, cities, firms, and so on) over T periods gives the researcher a large number of observations, increasing the number of degrees of freedom and reducing the co-linearity among explanatory variables. Besides, it is well known that panel data models are better able to deal, in a more natural way, with the effects of missing or unobserved variables.

Two ways of using panel models can be found in the energy literature: the first is based on micro-panels (with a short time dimension and a very large number of entities) and is usually devoted to the study of the behaviour of energy producers or consumers (firms, households) (see for example, Baltagi and Griffin, 1997, and Garcia-Cerrutti, 2000). The second category, less developed, corresponds to macro-panels (with similar time and individual dimensions) which are devoted to global energy consumption. In this latter case, the panel models are generally estimated only on post-war data in order to allow using balanced samples with the same time dimension for all the countries.

If it is assumed that all the parameters of the quadratic demand function are identical for all the countries of the panel; the specification is the same as (5.3) with the introduction of time in the variables:

$$c_{it} = \alpha + \beta y_{it} + \lambda y_{it}^2 + \varepsilon_{it} \quad i = 1, \ldots, N \;\; t = 1, \ldots, T \tag{5.4}$$

where ε_{it} is *i.i.d.* $(0, \sigma_\varepsilon^2)$. As for the cross-section model, it is considered to be totally *homogeneous*; non-heterogeneity is considered in the energy demand model. It implies that, for a given level of *per capita* GDP, the average level of energy consumption *per capita E* (c_{it}), and that the energy-GDP ratio is the same for all the countries of the sample. If the panel includes Canada and Mexico, this assumption may be doubtful. It is, therefore, generally admitted that it is necessary to introduce a minimum of heterogeneity into the model in order to take account of the specificities of the various countries of the sample.

The simplest method for introducing parameter *heterogeneity* consists of assuming that the constants of the model (5.4) vary from country to country. This is precisely the specification of the well known *individual* or *fixed effect model (FEM)*:

$$c_{it} = \alpha_i + \beta y_{it} + \lambda y_{it}^2 + \varepsilon_{it} \tag{5.5}$$

The *individual effects* α_i (or individual constants) allow capturing all the time-less (or structural) dimensions of the energy demand model. More precisely, they capture the influence of all the unobserved time-less variables (climate, industrial organization, and so forth) that affect the level of the energy demand. These individual effects can be fixed or random. When individual effects are assumed to be fixed, the simple OLS estimator is the BLUE (Best Linear Unbiased Estimator) and is commonly called a *Within* estimator. When individual effects are specified as random variables, they are assumed to be *i.i.d.* and independently distributed over the explanatory variable, the level of *per capita* GDP. In this case, the BLUE is a GLS estimator (see Hsiao, 2003, for more details). The choice between these two specifications depends on the assumption of independence between α_i and y_{it}, and may be determined by a standard Hausman (1978) test.

However, this model only allows heterogeneity of the average level of *per capita* energy consumption; in other words it only affects the Y-axis intercepts of the Inverted-U curve. National intensities are displayed along homothetic parabolas; the gap between the national curves is determined by the level of individual effects α_i. In addition, the turning point of the quadratic function is identical for all the countries of the sample, since it depends only on β and λ. This model has been used in particular by Medlock and Soligo (2001) for a sectoral panel of 28 countries (1978–95). In this study, they provide various specification tests, including homogeneity tests. They show, for instance, that the industrial sectors are substantially more heterogeneous than the other sectors. This problem of heterogeneity/homogeneity is particularly important as shown by H. Vollebergh *et al.* (2005) who found that the Inverted-U curve of CO_2 emissions is very sensitive to the degree of heterogeneity assumed in the specifications and in the estimation techniques. These authors suggest leaving enough heterogeneity in order to avoid abusive correlations from estimations of reduced forms on panel data. Ignoring such parameter heterogeneity could lead to inconsistent or meaningless estimates of interesting parameters.

From an elasticity point of view, the slope parameters β and λ that determine the income elasticity (equal to $\beta + 2\lambda\, y_{it}$) are assumed to be cross-section homogeneous. Consequently, in this model, at a particular date, if the income elasticity for Canada is different from the income elasticity for Mexico, it is only due to the difference in their *per capita* GDP, that is the difference in y_{it}. Since the parameters that determine income elasticities are assumed to be homogeneous, when Mexico will have achieved the same *per capita* GDP as Canada, their income elasticities will be identical. This assumption may or may not be valid; that is not the question. The question is: does an econometrician have the right to impose *ex-ante* such an assumption?

An alternative consists of using a *heterogeneous panel model*. In such a model, the slope parameters of the energy demand model are assumed to be cross-sectionally heterogeneous:

$$c_{it} = \alpha_i + \beta_i\, y_{it} + \lambda_i\, y_{it}^2 + \varepsilon_{it} \tag{5.6}$$

where α_i denotes an individual effect (fixed or random) and ε_{it} is *i.i.d.* $(0, \sigma_\varepsilon^2)$. Many approaches can be used to estimate a heterogeneous panel model. The simplest consists of assuming that these *slope parameters* are *randomly distributed*. These models are generally called Random Coefficient Models (RCM). The most popular is the simple Swamy model (1970) in which we assume that the parameters β_i and λ_i are randomly distributed according to distributions with homogeneous means and homogeneous variances. The aim is then to estimate the mean and the variance (more precisely the variance-covariance matrix) of the distribution of the parameters of the model. Galli (1998) tried this approach on Asian emerging countries from 1973 to 1990 but could not obtain any significant income coefficient and went back to the FEM.

This kind of approach is statistically very attractive, but has some drawbacks. The simple assumption that an economic variable is generated by a parametric probability distribution function that is identical for all individuals at all times may not be a realistic one. Moreover it does not offer an economic interpretation of the heterogeneity of the slope parameters (and, therefore, of the income elasticities). It does not allow identifying a set of explanatory variables q_{it} that explain why income elasticities may be not equal for the same levels of GDP. Given these various observations, we propose another original solution to specify the heterogeneity of the energy demand models in a panel sample, based on threshold panel specifications.

Threshold panel specifications

One way to circumvent the previously mentioned issues is to introduce threshold effects in a linear panel model. In fact, the idea that income elasticity of energy demand depends on income level clearly corresponds to the definition of a threshold regression model: 'threshold regression models specify that individual observations can be divided into classes based on the value of an observed variable' (Hansen, 1999, p. 346). In this context, a natural solution consists of using a potentially linear relationship between energy demand and income that depends on the income level. In a simple Panel Threshold Regression (PTR) model (Hansen, 1999) the idea is very simple: at each date in the threshold model the countries are divided into a small number of classes with the same elasticity according to an observable variable, called the threshold variable. This threshold variable can, for example, correspond to *per capita* GDP. In a PTR, the transition mechanism between extreme regimes is very simple; at each date, if the threshold variable observed for a given country is smaller than a given value, called the threshold parameter, the income–demand relationship is defined by a particular model (or regime) which is different from the model used if the threshold variable is larger than the threshold parameter. The advantage of this model is that even if the extreme regime models are linear (and not quadratic as in the literature), the income elasticity depends on the level of the threshold variable. For example, let us consider a PTR model with two extreme regimes:

$$c_{it} = \alpha_i + \beta_0 y_{it} + \beta_1 y_{it} g(q_{it}, c) + \varepsilon_{it} \tag{5.7}$$

The variable q_{it} denotes a threshold variable, c is a threshold parameter and the transition function $g(q_{it}; c)$ corresponds to the indicator function:

$$g(q_{it}, c) = \begin{cases} 1 & \text{if } q_{it} > c \\ 0 & \text{otherwise} \end{cases} \tag{5.8}$$

In this two extreme regimes model, the income elasticity is equal to β_0 if the threshold variable (the income, for example) is smaller than c and is equal to $\beta_0 + \beta_1$ if the threshold variable is larger than c. Consequently, we have exactly the same situation as in the quadratic model; the income elasticity depends on the income level (or on other economic variables). The main difference is that we specify a functional form of this dependency in a threshold model. However, in a PTR model, the transition mechanism between the regimes is too simple to show interesting non-linear effects of the income level on the income elasticity. As is often shown in the threshold model literature, the solution is to use a model with a smooth transition function. This kind of model has been recently extended to panel data with the Panel Smooth Threshold Regression (PSTR) model proposed by Gonzalez, Teräsvirta and Van Dijk (2004).

Let us consider the simplest case with two extreme regimes and a single transition function. The corresponding PSTR energy demand model is defined as:

$$c_{it} = \alpha_i + \beta_0 y_{it} + \beta_1 y_{it}\, g(q_{it}; \gamma, c) + \varepsilon_{it} \tag{5.9}$$

In this case, the transition function $g(q_{it}; \gamma, c)$ is a continuous and bounded function of the threshold variable q_{it}. Gonzalez, Teräsvirta and Van Dijk (2004), following the work of Granger and Teräsvirta (1993) for the time series STAR models, consider the following transition function:

$$g(q_{it}; \gamma, c) = \left[1 + \exp\left(-\gamma \prod_{z=1}^{m} (q_{it} - c_z)\right)\right]^{-1}, \quad \gamma > 0, \quad c_1 \leq \ldots \leq c_m \tag{5.10}$$

The vector $c = (c_1, \ldots, c_m)'$ denotes an m-dimensional vector of location parameters and the parameter γ determines the slope of the transition function.

In our context, the PSTR energy demand model has three main advantages. The first is that it allows the parameters (and consequently the income elasticity) to vary between countries (heterogeneity issue) but also with time (stability issue). It provides a parametric approach to the cross-country heterogeneity and the time instability of the slope coefficients of the energy demand model. It allows the parameters to change smoothly as a function of the threshold variable q_{it}. More precisely, the income elasticity is defined by the weighted average of the parameters β_0 and β_1. For example, if the threshold variable q_{it} is different from the income level, the income elasticity for the *i*th country at time *t* is defined by:

$$e_{it} = \frac{\partial c_{it}}{\partial y_{it}} = \beta_0 + \beta_1 g(q_{it}; \gamma, c) \tag{5.11}$$

with, as defined by the transition function, $\beta_0 \leq e_{it} \leq \beta_0 + \beta_1$ if $\beta_1 > 0$ or $\beta_0 + \beta_1 \leq e_{it} \leq \beta_0$ if $\beta_1 < 0$.

The second advantage of the PSTR energy demand model is that the value of the income elasticity, for a given country, at a given date, can be different from the estimated parameters for the extreme regimes, that is parameters β_0 and β_1. As illustrated by the equation (5.11), these parameters do not directly correspond to income elasticity. The parameter β_0 corresponds to the income elasticity only if the transition function $g(q_{it}; \gamma, c)$ tends to 0. For example, if the threshold variable corresponds to the *per capita* GDP, the parameter β_0 denotes the income elasticity only when the *per capita* income (in logarithms) tends to $-\infty$. The sum of the parameters β_0 and β_1 corresponds to the income elasticity only if the transition function $g(q_{it}; \gamma, c)$ tends to 1. Between these two extremes, the income elasticity e_{it} is defined as a weighted average of the parameters β_0 and β_1. Therefore, it is important to note that it is often difficult to directly interpret the values of these parameters (as in a probit or logit model). It is generally preferable to interpret (i) as the sign of these parameters which indicates an increase or a decrease of the income elasticity with the value of the threshold variable and (ii) the time varying and individual elasticity given by the equation (5.11).

Finally, this model can be analysed as a generalization of the Panel Threshold Regression (PTR) model proposed by Hansen (1999) and the panel linear model with individual effects. Figure 5.2 shows the transition function for various values of the parameter γ in the case where $m = 1$. It can be seen that when the parameter γ tends to infinity, the transition function $g(q_{it}; \gamma, c)$ tends to the indicator function (5.8). Thus, when $m = 1$ and γ tends to infinity the PSTR model gives the PTR model. When $m > 1$ and γ tends to infinity, the number of identical regimes remains two, but the function switches between zero and one at c_1, c_2, and so on. When γ tends to zero the transition function $g(q_{it}; \gamma, c)$ is constant and the model is the standard linear model with individual effects (the so-called '*within*' model), that is with constant and homogeneous elasticities. The income elasticity is then simply defined by $e_{it} = \beta_0$, $\forall i = 1, \ldots, N$ and $\forall t = 1, \ldots, T$.

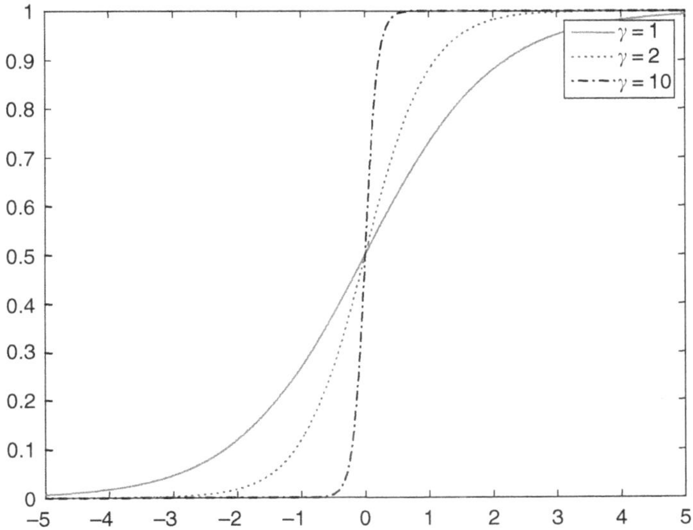

Figure 5.2 Transition function with $m = 1$ and $c = 0$: analysis of sensitivity to the slope parameter

This PSTR model can be generalized to $r + 1$ extreme regimes as follows:

$$c_{it} = \alpha_i + \beta_0 \, y_{it} + \sum_{j=1}^{r} \beta_j y_{it} \, g_j(q_{it}; \gamma_j, c_j) + \varepsilon_{it} \tag{5.12}$$

where the r transition functions $g_j(q_{it}; \gamma_j, c_j)$ depend on the slope parameters γ_j and on m location parameters c_j. In this generalization, if the threshold variable q_{it} is different from y_{it}, the income elasticity for the ith country at time t is defined by the weighted average of the $r+1$ parameters β_j associated to the $r + 1$ extreme regimes:

$$e_{it} = \frac{\partial c_{it}}{\partial y_{it}} = \beta_0 + \sum_{j=1}^{r} \beta_j \, g_j(q_{it}; \gamma_j, c_j) \tag{5.13}$$

The expression of the elasticity is slightly different if the threshold variable q_{it} is a function of income. For example, if we assume that the threshold variable corresponds to the income level, that is if $q_{it} = y_{it}$, the expression of the income elasticity is then defined as:

$$e_{it} = \frac{\partial c_{it}}{\partial y_{it}} = \beta_0 + \sum_{j=1}^{r} \beta_j \, g_j(y_{it}; \gamma_j, c_j) + \sum_{j=1}^{r} \beta_j \, y_{it} \frac{\partial g_j(y_{it}; \gamma_j, c_j)}{\partial y_{it}} \tag{5.14}$$

Such an expression authorizes a variety of configurations for the relationships between income and energy demand (or energy intensity) as will be discussed in the next section.

Estimation and specification tests

The estimation of the parameters of the PSTR model consists of eliminating the individual effects α_i by removing individual–specific means and then by applying non-linear least squares to the transformed model (see Gonzalez, Teräsvirta and Dijk, 2004, or Colletaz and Hurlin, 2006, for more details). Gonzalez, Teräsvirta and Van Dijk propose a testing procedure of order (i) to test the linearity against the PSTR model and (ii) to determine the number, r, of transition functions, that is the number of extreme regimes which is equal to $r+1$. Let us consider an energy demand model with only one location parameter ($m = 1$) and assume that the threshold variable q_{it} is known. Testing the linearity in a PSTR model (equation 5.5) can be done by testing $H_0 : \gamma = 0$ or $H_0 : \beta_0 = \beta_1$. But in both cases, the test will be non-standard since, under H_0 the PSTR model contains unidentified nuisance parameters. A solution consists of replacing the transition function $g_j(q_{it};\, \gamma_j,\, c_j)$ by its first-order Taylor expansion around $\gamma = 0$ and by testing an equivalent hypothesis in an auxiliary regression:

$$c_{it} = \alpha_i + \beta_0\, y_{it} \;+\; \theta_1\, y_{it}\, q_{it} \;+ \theta_2\, y_{it}\, q_{it}^2 + \cdots + \;\theta_m\, y_{it}\, q_{it}^m + \varepsilon_{it} \tag{5.15}$$

In this first-order Taylor expansion, the parameters θ_i are proportional to the slope parameter γ. Thus, testing the linearity against the PSTR model simply consists of testing $H_0 \; : \; \theta_1 \; = \; \ldots \; = \; \theta_m \; = \; 0$ in this linear panel model. If we denote SSR_0 the panel sum of squared residuals under H_0 (linear panel model with individual effects) and SSR_1 the panel sum of squared residuals under H_1 (PSTR model with two regimes), the corresponding F-statistic is then defined by:

$$LM_F = [(SSR_0 - SSR_1)/m] \,/\, [SSR_0/(TN - N - m)] \tag{5.16}$$

Under the null hypothesis, the F-statistic has an approximate $F(m, TN - N - m)$ distribution. The logic is similar when testing the number of transition functions in the model or, equivalently, the number of extreme regimes. The idea is as follows: we use a sequential approach by testing the null hypothesis of no remaining non-linearity in the transition function. For instance, let us assume that we have rejected the linearity hypothesis. The issue is then to test whether there is one transition function ($H_0 : r = 1$) or whether there are at least two transition functions ($H_0 : r = 2$). Let us assume that the model with $r = 2$ is defined as:

$$c_{it} = \alpha_i + \beta_0\, y_{it} \;+\; \beta_1 y_{it}\; g_1(q_{it};\, \gamma_1,\, c_1) + \;\beta_2 y_{it}\; g_2(q_{it};\, \gamma_2,\, c_2) + \varepsilon_{it} \tag{5.17}$$

The logic of the test consists of replacing the second transition function by its first-order Taylor expansion around $\gamma_2 = 0$ and then testing linear constraints on the parameters. If we use the first-order Taylor approximation of $g_2(q_{it}; \gamma_2, c_2)$, the model becomes:

$$c_{it} = \alpha_i + \beta_0 y_{it} + \beta_1 y_{it} g_1(q_{it}; \gamma_1, c_1) + \theta_1 y_{it} q_{it} + \cdots + \theta_m y_{it} q_{it}^m + \varepsilon_{it} \quad (5.18)$$

and the test of no remaining non-linearity is simply defined by $H_0 : \theta_1 = \ldots = \theta_m = 0$. Let us define SSR_0 as the panel sum of squared residuals under H_0, that is in a PSTR model with one transition function. Let us define SSR_1 as the sum of squared residuals of the transformed model (equation 5.18). As in the previous cases, the F-statistic LM_F can be computed according to the same definitions by adjusting the number of degrees of freedom. The testing procedure is then the following. Given a PSTR model with $r = r^*$, we will test the null $H_0 : r = r^*$ against $H_1 : r = r^* + 1$. If H_0 is not rejected, the procedure ends. Otherwise, the null hypothesis $H_0 : r = r^* + 1$ is tested against $H_1 : r = r^* + 2$. The testing procedure continues until the first acceptance of H_0. Given the sequential aspect of this testing procedure, at each step of the procedure the significance level must be reduced by a factor $\rho = 0.5$ in order to avoid excessively large models (Gonzalez, Teräsvirta and Van Dijk, 2004).

Data and results

In this study we considered a panel of 44 countries over the period 1950–99. The energy data base that we used was worked out in Grenoble by Jean-Marie Martin and is presently managed by the enterprise Enerdata. It evaluates worldwide primary energy consumption over the long run (nearly 200 years) on a geographic basis by distinguishing between 'commercial' consumption (including coal, petroleum products, gas and electricity) measured by country and 'biomass', evaluated at the level of world regions. Two special characteristics of these data should be mentioned. First of all, data available over a long period allow only an indirect evaluation of consumption starting from national production, increased by imports, decreased by exports and stored quantities and corrected by variations in stocks. Secondly, total consumption is the sum of consumption by source aggregated on the basis of its net calorific value and expressed in tonnes of oil equivalent by adopting the convention that 1 toe = 42 GJ. For primary electricity (of nuclear, hydraulic, geothermic, wind or solar origin) the consumption equivalence (1 kWh = 860 kcal) is retained, except for the nuclear case where 2600 kcal is used to take account of the efficiency of transformation of heat into electricity in these stations.

Population and GDP data have been gathered from the last publication of Maddison in OECD (2003). For international comparisons, the GDPs must be expressed in the same units. It is well known that the best converters are the purchasing power parities (ppp) which aim at neutralizing the effect of broad disparities of prices among countries, and Shrestha (2000) shows that choosing a wrong unit of measure of GDP (market exchange rates for example) may lead to misleading results in this area. The converters used by Maddison are the Geary–Khamis 1990$ ppp which allow multilateral comparisons by taking into account the ppp of currencies, and international average prices of commodities, and by weighting each country by its GDP.

As suggested by Hansen (1999), we consider a balanced panel since it is not known if the results of estimation and testing procedures presented below extend to unbalanced panels. This constraint led us to limit our study to the post-1950 data which detail the 'commercial consumption' of 44 countries. They have been set up using United Nations data, after some boundary changes and modifications of the equivalence coefficients to take into account the different qualities of fuels used over time and in various countries.

In our threshold specification, we consider two potential threshold variables. In the first model (called model *A*), we assume that the transition mechanism in the energy demand equation is determined by the income level, i.e. $q_{it} = y_{it}$. This specification corresponds to the standard idea that income elasticity of energy demand depends on income level. We also consider a second specification (called model *B*) in which the transition mechanism is based on the income growth rate, $q_{it} = y_{it} - y_{i,t-1}$. This model may be more suitable when the *per capita* GDP is not stationary.

The first step consists of testing the log-linear specification of energy demand against a specification with threshold effects. The results of these linearity tests and specification tests of no remaining non-linearity are reported on Table 5.1. For each definition of the threshold variable q_{it} (models *A* or *B*) we consider three specifications with one, two or three location parameters. For each specification, we compute the LM_F statistics for the linearity tests ($H_0 : r = 0$ versus $H_1 : r = 1$) and for the tests of no remaining non-linearity ($H_0 : r = a$ versus $H_1 : r = a+1$). The values of the statistics are reported until the first acceptance of H_0.

The linearity tests clearly lead to the rejection of the null hypothesis of linearity of the relationships between income and energy demand. The only exception is found in model *B* with $m = 1$. Whatever the choice made for the threshold variable, the number of location parameters, the LM_F statistics lead to strongly reject the null $H_0 : r = 0$. For the energy demand model *A*, the lowest value of the LM_F statistic is obtained with two location parameters, but even in this case the value of the test statistic is largely below the critical value at standard levels. This first result confirms the non-linearity of the energy demand, but more originally shows the presence of strong threshold effects determined either by income level or income growth rate. Given the values of the LM_F statistics, we can see that the threshold effects are stronger when income level is used to characterize the transition mechanism between demand regimes.

The specification tests of no remaining non-linearity (see Table 5.1) lead to identify an optimal number of transition functions (or extreme regimes) in all cases. The optimal number of transition functions is always inferior to the maximum number of transition functions authorized in the algorithm. In other words, in a PSTR model, a small number of extreme regimes is sufficient to capture the non-linearity of the energy demand, or equivalently the cross-country heterogeneity and the time variability of the income elasticity. Recall that a smooth transition model, even with two extreme regimes ($r = 1$), can be viewed as a model with an infinite number of intermediate regimes. The income elasticities are defined at each date point and for each country as weighted averages of the values obtained in the two extreme regimes. The weights depend on the value of the transition function. So, even if $r = 1$, this model allows a *continuum* of elasticities (or regimes), with each one associated with a different value of the transition function $g(.)$ between 0 and 1. Thus, the choice of r is just a question of specification of the model.

Finally, in the PSTR model, it is necessary to choose the number of location parameters used in the transition functions, that is the value of m. The choice of m is not very important as long as we determine the corresponding

Table 5.1 LM_f tests for remaining nonlinearity

Model	**Model *A***			**Model *B***		
Threshold variable	y_{it}			Δy_{it}		
Number of location parameters	$m = 1$	$m = 2$	$m = 3$	$m = 1$	$m = 2$	$m = 3$
$H_0 : r = 0$ vs $H_1 : r = 1$	551.5 (0.00)	291.8 (0.00)	206.6 (0.00)	1.66 (0.20)	9.19 (0.00)	6.17 (0.00)
$H_0 : r = 1$ vs $H_1 : r = 2$	2.36 (0.12)	0.001 (0.99)	8.65 (0.00)	–	0.96 (0.38)	3.54 (0.01)
$H_0 : r = 2$ vs $H_1 : r = 3$	–	–	13.2 (0.00)	–	–	0.12 (0.94)
$H_0 : r = 3$ vs $H_1 : r = 4$	–	–	2.10 (0.10)	–	–	–
$H_0 : r = 4$ vs $H_1 : r > 4$	–	–	–	–	–	–

Note: For each model, the testing procedure works as follows. First, test a linear model ($r = 0$) against a model with one threshold ($r = 1$). If the null hypothesis is rejected, test the single threshold model against a double threshold model ($r = 2$). The procedure is continued until the hypothesis of no additional threshold is not rejected. The LM_F statistic has an asymptotic $F[m, TN - N - (r + 1)m]$ distribution under H_0 where m is the number of location parameters. The corresponding p-values are in parentheses.

number of transition functions, denoted $r(m)$, which assures that there is no remaining non-linearity in the model. The model is so flexible that different models with different couples m, $r(m)$ give the same quantitative, as well as qualitative, results when we estimate the individual elasticities. In Table 5.2, for each assumed value of m we report the corresponding optimal number of transition functions deduced from the LM_F tests of remaining non-linearity. We estimate the PSTR models for each potential specification m, $r(m)$, and report the number of parameters and the residual sum of squares. We suggest here the use of two standard information criteria (the Akaike and the Schwarz

Table 5.2 Determination of the number of location parameters

Model	**Model *A***			**Model *B***		
Number of location parameters	$m = 1$	$m = 2$	$m = 3$	$m = 1$	$m = 2$	$m = 3$
Optimal number of thresholds	1	1	3	0	1	2
Residual sum of squares	108.9	109	98	149	137.5	137.5
AIC criterion	−2.979	−2.977	−3.067	−2.667	−2.744	−2.736
Schwarz criterion	−2.968	−2.964	−3.025	−2.664	−2.731	−2.707

Note: For each model, the optimal number of location parameters can be determined as follows. For each value of m, the corresponding optimal number of thresholds, denoted $r^*(m)$, is determined according to a sequential procedure based on the LM_F statistics of the hypothesis of non-remaining non-linearity. Thus, for each couple (m, r^*), the value RSS of the model is reported. The total number of parameters is $(r^* + 1) + r^*(m + 1)$.

Table 5.3 Parameter estimates for the final PSTR models

Specification threshold variable (m, r^*)	**Model *A* (1,1)**	**Model *B* (2,1)**
Income parameter β_0	1.569	1.1115
	(0.03)	(0.02)
Income parameter β_1	−0.800	0.1314
	(0.04)	(0.02)
Location parameters c_j		
First transition function	3.055	[0.0154 0.0154]
Second transition function	–	–
Slope parameters	1.296	494.2

Note: Model *A* corresponds to the threshold variable y_{it} and Model *B* to the threshold variable Δy_{it}. The standard errors in parentheses are corrected for heteroskedasticity. For each model and each value of m the number of transition functions r is determined by a sequential testing procedure (see Table 5.1). For the jth transition function, with $j = 1, \ldots, r$, the m estimated location parameters c_j and the corresponding estimated slope parameter g_j are reported.

Table 5.4 Individual estimated income elasticities

	Quadratic fixed		PSTR Model *A*		PSTR Model *B*	
Model	Average	Std	Average	Std	Average	Std
Argentina	1.036	7.01	1.110	9.80	1.202	2.18
Australia	0.802	12.0	0.719	21.0	1.183	0.61
Austria	0.871	18.4	0.824	29.6	1.189	1.55
Belgium	0.840	15.5	0.780	26.5	1.185	0.88
Brazil	1.295	15.5	1.367	10.5	1.194	1.74
Bulgaria	1.213	14.9	1.299	11.8	1.202	2.17
Canada	0.778	12.8	0.678	22.4	1.186	1.06
Chile	1.128	9.77	1.223	12.8	1.198	1.99
China	1.764	21.7	1.537	4.22	1.207	2.18
Colombia	1.295	11.6	1.378	8.51	1.183	0.95
EX Czechoslovakia	1.059	10.8	1.132	13.5	1.187	1.38
Denmark	0.781	13.7	0.683	23.7	1.185	1.17
Egypt	1.607	15.9	1.516	3.83	1.189	1.66
Finland	0.883	17.1	0.847	27.8	1.192	1.77
France	0.818	15.5	0.743	26.4	1.184	0.76
Germany	0.848	15.8	0.790	26.1	1.19	1.67
Hungary	1.157	11.4	1.252	11.1	1.192	1.80
India	1.801	11.3	1.553	1.36	1.191	1.48
Indonesia	1.608	17.4	1.513	5.05	1.200	2.09
Iran	1.314	16.1	1.380	10.4	1.212	2.32
Italy	0.888	18.4	0.849	29.1	1.190	1.41
Japan	0.924	27.9	0.870	38.8	1.201	2.36
South Korea	1.345	35.8	1.299	29.2	1.211	2.25
Malaysia	1.371	21.8	1.394	15.2	1.199	1.75
Mexico	1.191	12.9	1.283	12.0	1.190	1.68
Netherlands	0.812	13.8	0.734	23.8	1.186	1.09
New Zealand	0.826	7.62	0.762	13.6	1.190	1.79
Norway	0.819	17.4	0.749	29.3	1.185	0.72
Nigeria	1.756	7.66	1.550	0.89	1.203	2.39
Peru	1.303	6.34	1.395	4.23	1.195	2.06
Philippines	1.541	8.21	1.507	2.21	1.186	1.53
Poland	1.008	12.2	1.055	17.1	1.195	1.63
Romania	1.382	14.1	1.430	6.84	1.197	2.06
South Africa	1.276	6.12	1.375	4.33	1.185	1.24
Spain	1.042	22.0	1.063	28.1	1.195	1.97
Sweden	0.797	12.2	0.709	21.4	1.184	0.78
Switzerland	0.700	9.52	0.544	16.3	1.186	1.21
Taiwan	1.235	33.9	1.215	32.6	1.207	2.19
Thailand	1.483	25.8	1.441	13.8	1.201	2.08
Turkey	1.291	15.2	1.364	11.4	1.196	1.99
United Kingdom	0.825	11.5	0.759	20.1	1.183	0.66

Continued

Table 5.4 Continued

Model	Quadratic fixed		PSTR Model *A*		PSTR Model *B*	
	Average	Std	Average	Std	Average	Std
USA	0.694	11.9	0.543	19.3	1.186	0.91
EX URSS	1.161	10.8	1.258	11.2	1.196	2.15
Venezuela	0.913	3.74	0.917	6.50	1.197	2.07

Note: For each country, the average and standard deviation (in percentages) of the individual income elasticities are reported. The quadratic fixed effect model corresponds to a quadratic specification of the energy demand with individual fixed effects. For the PSTR models, Model *A* corresponds to the threshold variable y_{it} and Model *B* to Δy_{it}.

criteria) in order to choose a benchmark specification for each specification of the demand function. Consequently, we consider the specification with $m = 1$ and $r = 1$ as optimal for the model A ($q_{it} = y_{it}$) and the specification with $m = 2$ and $r = 1$ for the model B ($q_{it} = \Delta y_{it}$).

Table 5.3 contains the parameter estimates of the final PSTR models. Recall that the estimated parameters β_j cannot be directly interpreted as elasticities. As in logit or probit models, the value of the estimated parameters is not directly interpretable, but their signs can be interpreted. For instance, let us consider the model A with one transition function. A negative (or positive) parameter β_1 only signifies that when the threshold variable (income level) increases, the income elasticity decreases (or increases). This observation can be generalized in a model with more than one transition function ($r > 1$) even if things are slightly more complicated. In a model with two transition functions, if the parameter β_1 is positive and the parameter β_2 is negative, this implies that an increase of the threshold variable has two opposite effects on the income elasticity. The results of these two opposite effects will depend on the value of the (i) slope parameters γ_j and (ii) the location parameters c_j. No general result can be deduced here.

We can observe that the estimated transition function in model A is not sharp. Recall that when the slope parameter tends to infinity, the transition function tends to an indicator function as in the threshold model without smooth transition. We can see in Table 5.3 that the estimated slope parameter for the transition function in the model A is equal to 1.296. Consequently, this transition function is quite different from an indicator function. This point is particularly important, since it implies that the non-linearity of the energy demand cannot be reduced to a limited number of regimes with different income elasticities. Indeed, it is important to recall that, as opposed to a PTR model, a PSTR model with a smooth transition function can be interpreted as a model which allows a *continuum* of regimes. This *continuum* of regimes is clearly required when measuring the threshold effects of the energy demand (as assumed in the non-parametric approaches used, for instance, by Judson, Schmalensee and Stoker, 1999). This result also points out the fact that the solution which consists of grouping countries in a panel and estimating a relationship between income and energy demand, or energy intensity, may be unsatisfactory (even if the specification used is quadratic). It is well known that this approach neglects the heterogeneity of the relationships between the countries.

Individual income elasticities

In panel data models, published results usually refer solely to general values of the parameters whereas detailed results by country remain unpublished. Given the parameter estimates of our energy demand models, it is interesting and possible to compute, for each country of the sample and for each date, the time varying income elasticity, denoted $e_{it}, i = 1, \ldots, N$ and $t = 1, \ldots, T$ (see equation 5.14). The averages of these individual smoothed income elasticities, as well as their variances, are reported in Table 5.4 for the 44 countries of the sample. These averages and standard deviations correspond to:

$$\overline{e}_i = \frac{1}{T}\sum_{t=1}^{T} e_{it} \qquad s_{e,i} = \sqrt{\frac{1}{T}\sum_{t=1}^{T}(e_{it} - \overline{e}_i)^2} \qquad \forall i = 1, \ldots, N \tag{5.19}$$

In the case of model A (see Table 5.3 and equation 5.15), we have:

$$\begin{aligned} e_{it} = \frac{\partial c_{it}}{\partial y_{it}} &= 1.569 - \frac{0.800}{[1 + \exp(-1.296\,(y_{it} - 3.055))]} \\ &\quad - 0.800\,y_{it}\,\frac{1.296 \times \exp[-1.296(y_{it} - 3.055)]}{[1 + \exp(-1.296\,(y_{it} - 3.055))]^2} \end{aligned} \tag{5.20}$$

It is interesting to compare these elasticities to the estimated elasticities obtained in panel data models with quadratic specifications (Galli, 1998). For this comparison, we also report in Table 5.4 the average and the standard deviation of the elasticities based on a fixed effect model with a quadratic specification of the energy demand as proposed by Galli, 1998. Recall that in an FEM specification of a quadratic demand model (equation 5.5), the elasticity is country and year specific, and is equal to $e_{it}^q = \beta + 2\,\lambda\,y_{it}$. For each country, the corresponding average and standard deviations of income elasticities are given by:

$$\overline{e}_i^q = \frac{1}{T}\sum_{t=1}^{T} e_{it}^q = \beta + 2\lambda\,\overline{y}_i \qquad s_{e,i}^q = \sqrt{\frac{1}{T}\sum_{t=1}^{T}\left(e_{it}^q - \overline{e}_i^q\right)^2} \qquad \forall i = 1, \ldots, N \tag{5.21}$$

It is important to note that in the FEM approach the cross-country variance (and time variability) of the income elasticities is only due to the variance in the level of *per capita* GDP. Since the parameters β and λ are common to all countries, the international differences in income elasticities are only due to the international difference in the averages of *per capita* GDP. The richer the country, the more its income elasticity is important and the relationship between average income and income elasticity is strictly linear. On the other hand, in a PSTR model, the income elasticities are cross-country and specific for more subtle reasons. The smooth threshold effect allows a 'continuum' of income elasticity, given the threshold variable, the level of income. Consequently, the formal relationship between income and income elasticity is strongly non-linear as shown in our estimates (equation 5.17). It does not necessarily imply that the average elasticities (PSTR versus FEM) are strongly different. But, for some particular countries, the PSTR elasticities may be different from the FEM elasticities. For these countries, the energetic demand model is very different from that observed for the other countries; for the same *per capita* GDP, these countries would not have the same income elasticity of their energy demand.

In Table 5.4, the means and standard errors of the PSTR and FEM estimates of income elasticities are reported. Recall that, in both cases, the estimated income elasticities are time varying, so these values correspond to the averages (and standard deviations) of the national elasticities estimated over the period 1950–99. We can see that, when the level of *per capita* GDP is used, a threshold variable (columns 4 and 5, Table 5.4), the PSTR model gives approximately the same average estimates as those obtained with an FEM quadratic model at the average point (columns 2 and 3, Table 5.4). This result confirms the fact that, for most countries, the quadratic FEM can be viewed as a second order Taylor approximation of a PSTR model. This result is generally true when average elasticities are considered. However, it does not imply that the time varying elasticities have identical dynamics in both models. Indeed, the estimated income elasticities derived from the FEM quadratic model and the PSTR model A are reported in Figure 5.3 for a list of selected countries (the others are available on request).

For most of the 44 countries, the time profile of FEM and PSTR estimated elasticities are similar. This implies that for these countries, a quadratic homogeneous model is sufficient to approximate the elasticity dynamics derived from a heterogeneous model. On the other hand, for some countries of our panel, this result is not valid. This is, for example, the case at least for China, Egypt, India, Indonesia, Nigeria and Thailand. For instance, for Taiwan Galli (1998) found an estimated long-run elasticity equal to 1.18 in 1973 and equal to 0.63 in 1990. In our sample, the FEM gives an average elasticity over 1950–99 equal to 1.23. If the PSTR model is used we find a similar profile as that observed by Galli; the estimated elasticity for Taiwan is equal to 1.58 in 1973 and 1.22 in 1990. However, with a PSTR model, we show that

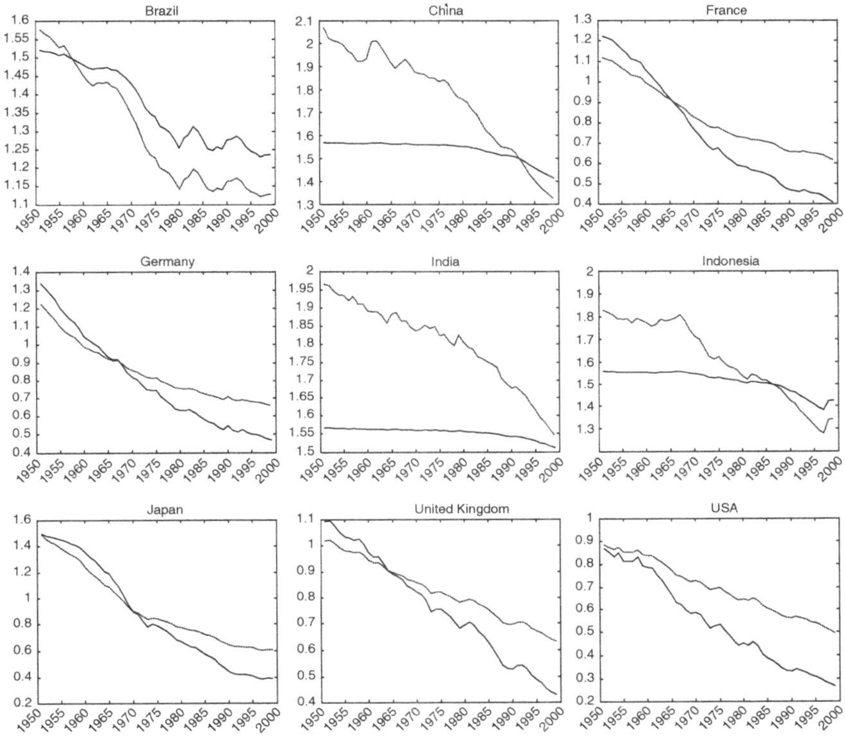

Figure 5.3 Individual PSTR and FEM income elasticities (1950–99)

Note: The blue continuous line corresponds to the estimated income elasticity obtained in the PSTR with $qit = yit$ (model *A*) and the dashed line corresponds to estimated elasticity obtained in the quadratic fixed effect model.

this decrease of the elasticity is considerably less important in our estimates than in the FEM estimates. Such heterogeneity would not have been taken into account with a homogeneous quadratic model. In our opinion, it is one of the main advantages of our threshold approach.

Another way to illustrate these advantages of the PSTR is to compare the estimated parameters of an FEM quadratic model for two sub-samples. In the first sample, denoted sample *A*, we consider 8 countries for which the PSTR and FEM models give different elasticity profiles. The second sample corresponds to the rest of the countries. As can be seen in Table 5.5, the homogeneous parameters estimated for both samples are substantially different, the parameter associated with the square of GDP in particular. In other words, this implies that, for the same *per capita* GDP level, these countries (samples *A* and *B*) do not have the same income elasticity of energy

Table 5.5 Quadratic energy demand function, fixed effects model

	Total sample	**Sample *A***	**Sample *B***
Income parameter β_0	1.78	1.72	1.94
	(63.6)	(26.7)	(55.9)
Squared income parameter $\beta 1$	−0.194	−0.179	−0.235
	(−23.4)	(−5.61)	(−24.8)
RSS	110.34	41.14	66.7

Note: Sample *A* corresponds to China, Egypt, India, Indonesia, Nigeria, the Philippines and Thailand. Sample *B* corresponds to all others countries.

demand. Only a PSTR model (or a random coefficient model) is able to take into account this heterogeneity.

Finally, when the GDP growth rate is used as a threshold variable (columns 6 and 7, Table 5.4), the PSTR model gives similar average estimated elasticities. This meaningless result can be interpreted as follows. Obviously, if the transition mechanism is not well specified, that is if the threshold variable is not well chosen, the use of the PSTR model implies associating countries according to fallacious criteria. Consequently, at each date the countries are split into a small number of randomly constituted groups and associated with different slope parameters, according to the value of the fallacious threshold variable. Therefore, the estimated slope parameters obtained in this context on random groups are not different from those estimated for the whole sample. Consequently, the fact that we obtain roughly the same individual estimated elasticities as those obtained in linear panel models may be interpreted as evidence that the threshold variable is not well identified. This conclusion is reinforced by the fact that the linearity tests lead to a stronger rejection of the linearity of model *A* than that observed for model *B* (Table 5.3). As suggested by Gonzalez *et al.* (2004), it is recommended to choose the threshold variable that leads to the largest value of the linearity test statistics.

Conclusion

In this chapter we propose an original method for specifying the heterogeneity and the time variability of the income elasticity of energy demand. This method is based on panel smooth transition regression models. Indeed, the issue of heterogeneity in panel approach is deeply linked to the non-linearity of the energy demand. Therefore, an alternative to parametric threshold models would consist of using a non-parametric method to estimate the relationship between income and energy demand. In this context, Judson, Schmalensee and Stoker (1999) propose the use of local regressions (knot-spline) in order to estimate this relationship for 123 countries over the period

1950–92. In particular, they show that when the *per capita* GDP is larger than $1500–1985, the income-elasticity is decreasing. These observations are not incompatible with our threshold representation.

References

Ang, B.W. (1987) 'A Cross-Sectional Analysis of Energy-Output Correlation', *Energy Economics*, October, pp. 274–85.

Ang, B.W. (2006) 'Monitoring Changes in Economy-wide Energy Efficiency: From Energy-GDP Ratio To Composite Efficiency Index', *Energy Policy*, vol. 34, no. 5, March, pp. 574–82.

Baltagi, B.H. and Griffin, J.M. (1997) 'Pooled Estimators vs. their Heterogeneous Counterparts in the Context of Dynamic Demand for Gasoline', *Journal of Econometrics*, vol. 77, pp. 303–27.

Brookes, L.G. (1973) 'More on the Output Elasticity of Energy Consumption', *Journal of Industrial Economics*, April, pp. 83–94.

Clark, C. (1960) *The Conditions of Economic Progress* (London: Macmillan).

Colletaz, G. and Hurlin, C. (2006) 'Threshold Effects in the Public Capital Productivity: An International Panel Smooth Transition Approach', Working Paper, University of Orleans.

Darmstadter, J., Teitelbaum, P.D. and Polach, J.G. (1971) *Energy in the World Economy: A Statistical Review of Trends in Output, Trade and Consumption since 1925* (Baltimore: Johns Hopkins University Press).

Darmstadter, J., Dunkerley, J. and Alterman, J. (1977) *How Industrial Societies Use Energy*, (Baltimore: Johns Hopkins University Press).

Galli, R. (1998) 'The Relationship between Energy Intensity and Income Levels: "Forecasting Long Term Energy Demand in Asian Emerging Countries"', *Energy Journal*, vol. 19, no. 4, pp. 85–105.

Garcia-Cerrutti, L.M. (2000) 'Estimating Elasticities of Residential Energy Demand from Panel County Using Dynamic Random Variables Models with Heteroskedastic and Correlated Terms', *Resource and Energy Economics*, vol. 22, pp. 355–66.

Gonzalez, A., Teräsvirta, T. and Van Dijk, D. (2004) 'Panel Smooth Transition Regression Model and an Application to Investment under Credit Constraint', Working Paper Stockholm School of Economics.

Granger, C.W. and Teräsvirta, T. (1993) *Modelling NonLinear Economic Relationships* (Oxford University Press).

Judson, R.A., Schmalensee, R. and Stoker, T.M. (1999) 'Economic Development and the Structure of the Demand for Commercial Energy', *Energy Journal*, vol. 20, no. 2, pp. 28–57.

Hansen, B.E. (1999) 'Threshold Effects in Non-Dynamic Panels: Estimation, Testing and Inference', *Journal of Econometrics*, vol. 93, pp. 345–68.

Hausman, J.A. (1978) 'Specification Tests in Econometrics', *Econometrica*, 46, pp. 1251–71.

Hsiao, C. (2003) *Analysis of Panel Data*, 2nd edn (Cambridge University Press).

Kuznets, S. (1955) 'Economic Growth and Income Inequality', *American Economic Review*, vol. 45, pp. 1–28.

Maddison, A. (2003) *L'économie mondiale, Statistiques historiques* (Paris: OCDE).

Martin, J.-M. (1988) 'L'intensité énergétique de l'activité économique dans les pays industrialisés : les évolutions de très longue période livrent-elles des enseignements utiles?', *Economie et Société*, no. 4, pp. 9–27.

Medlock, K.B. and Soligo, R. (2001) 'Economic Development and End-Use Energy Demand', *The Energy Journal*, vol. 22, no. 2, pp. 77–105.

Miketa, A. (2001) 'Analysis of Energy Intensity Developments in Manufacturing Sectors in Industrialized and Developing Countries', *Energy Policy*, vol. 29, pp. 769–75.

Müller-Fürstenberger, G., Wagner, M., Müller, B. (2004) *Exploring the Carbon Kuznets Hypothesis*, Oxford Institute for Energy Studies, EV 34.

Nachane, D., Nadkarni, R. and A. Karnik (1988) 'Cointegration and Causality Testing of the Energy-GDP Relationship: a Cross-Country Study' *Applied Economics*, vol. 20, pp. 1511–31.

Percebois, J. (1979) 'Le concept d'intensité énergétique est-il significatif?', *Revue d'économie politique*, no. 4, pp. 509–27.

Putnam, P.C. (1953) *Energy in the Future* (Princeton: D. Van Nostrand Co.).

Savvides, A. and Thanasis, S. (2000) 'Income Inequality and Economic Development: Evidence from the Threshold Regression Model', *Economics Letters*, vol. 69, pp. 207–12.

Schäfer, A. (2003) 'Structural Change in energy Use', *Energy Policy*, vol. 33, pp. 429–37.

Shrestha, R.M. (2000) 'Estimation of International Output–Energy Relation: Effects of Alternative Output Measures', *Energy Economics*, vol. 22, pp. 297–308.

Shurr, S.H. and Netschert, B.C. (1960) *Energy in the American Economy, 1850–1975* (Baltimore: Johns Hopkins University Press).

Swamy, P.A. (1970) 'Efficient Inference in a Random Coefficient Regression Model', *Econometrica*, vol. 38, pp. 311–23.

Toman, M.A. and Jemelkova, B. (2003) 'Energy and Economic Development: An Assessment of the State of Knowledge', *Energy Journal*, vol. 24, no. 4.

Vollebergh, H.R.J., Dijkgraaf, E. and Melenberg, B. (2005) *Environmental Kuznetz Curves for CO_2: Heterogeneity Versus Homogeneity*, Discussion Paper 25, Tilburg University.

Zilberfarb, B.Z. and Adams, F.G. (1981) 'The Energy–GDP Relationship in Developing Countries, Empirical Evidence and Stability Tests', *Energy Economics*, October, pp. 244–8.

6

The Causality Link between Energy Prices, Technology and Energy Intensity

Marie Bessec and Sophie Méritet

Introduction

This chapter deals with a field of renewed interest in energy economics: the relationship between energy prices and energy intensity, which is measured by the ratio of final energy consumption to total output (GDP).[1] For years, economic papers have been studying energy intensity through the decomposition of the energy demand (Wing and Eckaus, 2004, and Liu, 2005). The link between energy prices and energy intensity has not really been analysed and is nowhere nearly as well established as other relations. A third variable, technological progress, may interfere in this relation. In a first analysis, it appears that technological changes can be stimulated by energy price increases and more efficient equipment reduces the energy demand. At the same time, an increase of energy demand is possible through a change in habits of consumption (changes in energy services, or energy use, and so forth). The causality link is complicated by this variable technology and its effects on energy consumption.

Consequently, the purpose of this chapter is to assess the link between energy prices and energy intensity, taking into account the role of technological progress. This discussion has been stimulated by the recent energy price increase, especially in the oil market. Looking at past experience since the two oil price shocks should make it possible to assess the impact in the different countries of the current price increase on energy efficiency and energy consumption. This subject is currently of crucial concern, given the importance of the environmental costs concerning production and consumption of energy and proposals to reduce greenhouse gas emissions. Today climate change and security of energy supply are amongst the greatest challenges to the growth of the economy and the well-being of citizens. The present energy system is undergoing transformations on the supply side as well as on the demand side to satisfy sustainability criteria. A main underlying political question is how to reduce greenhouse gas emissions through reduction in energy consumption. Whether or not energy efficiency is effective in reducing energy consumption is the subject of an ongoing debate (see Howarth, 1997).

This chapter focuses on the oil market because of the importance of oil in the total energy consumption in countries of the Organization for Economic Cooperation and Development (OECD). Since the beginning of the last century, oil has been the major source of energy. It has replaced coal for the production of heat and for transport. Today, oil consumption accounts for 40 per cent of total primary energy production (EIA, 2004). Oil consumption is responsible for about 40 per cent of the carbon emissions and about 30 per cent of the greenhouse gas production (EIA, 2004). Furthermore, the recent increase in the oil price, which rose to near 70 US dollars a barrel during the summer of 2005, motivates the study of the interactions between oil prices, technical progress and oil consumption.

To this end, we use the multivariate Johansen's (1988) cointegration framework and Granger causality tests. More specifically, we use a vector error correction model (VECM) and test for the direction of the causality among the three variables. Such a framework has several advantages over traditional techniques, which consist of testing causality in vector autoregressive models (VAR) specified in first differences if the variables are integrated of order one. From a technical viewpoint, a VAR specified in first differences is incorrectly specified if the variables are cointegrated. Moreover, using a VECM rather than a VAR model allows us to distinguish between short-run and long-run causality among the variables.

We implement this approach in trivariate models. We could have performed the causality tests considering each pair of variables separately in bivariate models. This approach is widely used in the literature when examining causal relationships among variables, such as energy consumption and economic growth (Hondroyiannis *et al.*, 2002; Soytas and Sari, 2003; Jumbe, 2004). However, causality tests could lead to spurious conclusions if an important explicative variable is omitted (see, for example Glasure, 2002, for an illustration of this point in the energy field). Our results suggest that there is a clear dependence among the three variables. For this reason, a trivariate framework seems more relevant.

The analysis is applied to fifteen major industrialized OECD countries over the last 40 years. In this framework, we find a long-run relationship between oil intensity, oil price and technological progress in most countries. Moreover, the Granger causality tests reveal a causality running from prices to technical efficiency and from prices and technical efficiency to oil consumption in most OECD members. However, oil prices are found strongly exogenous except in major countries like the United States. These results show that the actual price increase induces energy conservation through an increase in energy efficiency. This result stimulates discussions on energy taxes by governments for the promotion of energy efficiency and energy conservation programmes.

The organization of this chapter is as follows. The following section presents an overview of the literature. The next section describes the data and the methodology used, while the following section presents the empirical results. In the last section, the conclusions of the analysis are summarized and the policy implications are discussed.

Overview of the literature

The question addressed in this chapter concerns the links between energy intensity, energy prices and technological progress. The energy intensity is usually considered to be the energy used to produce one unit of GDP. According to the literature, a change in energy intensity is due to either a structural effect (proportions of energy intensive industries), or a fuel substitution effect (shares of high quality energy inputs used) or a technical effect (it combines changes in energy/labour and energy/capital substitutions, and energy efficiency improvement).

Several remarks are appropriate:

- *Endogenous technological progress.* The three causes of changes in energy intensity can be summarized as follows (Azar and Dowlatabadi, 1999): price driven changes in demand, income driven changes in demand and autonomous energy efficiency improvements (AEEI). The difficulty arises in separating the various sources and especially the role of technological progress. In a deterministic trend, AEEI appears to be the 'left over' after the effects of other variables are removed. With cointegration, the analysis is different: it allows analysts to identify the factor responsible for AEEI.
- *Energy efficiency.* Energy efficiency is the inverse of intensity, but it measures the specific output and efficiency of a process. It depends on changes in industrial processes, consumption practices and technology. At a macroeconomic level, in many studies energy efficiency is unfortunately measured by energy intensity, thus disregarding that energy intensity is influenced by many factors including energy efficiency. The problem is to measure the energy intensity changes due only to the energy efficiency changes.
- *Rebound effect.* An increase of energy efficiency through technology progress will ultimately reduce demand for this energy resource. However, this decrease in demand and subsequent decrease in the cost of using the resource could cause a phenomenon called 'Rebound Effect'. Energy savings produced by efficiency improvement can be lost through higher consumption. The principle is the following: a person with a more efficient automobile may drive longer (direct effect), or he can choose to spend the money saved by buying other cars or other goods which use the same energy resource (indirect effect).

> The rebound effect arises from substitution and income effects linked to price variations of a resource and from consumption changes. It is important to remember that these losses in energy savings would generally be associated with improvements in consumer life quality: the recipient of a more efficient heater can choose to live in a warmer house or spend the energy cost savings on other consumer goods. This phenomenon has been studied extensively in the literature (see the surveys of Greening and Greene, 1998; and Schipper and Grubb, 2000).

Considering these elements, the main question can be formulated in two ways depending on the relationship studied: energy prices and technology, or technology and energy consumption.

What is the influence of energy price on technology?

Focusing on the first pair of variables, increases in energy prices promote technological progress and therefore reduce energy intensity. For example, energy saving innovations will allow a better use of energy in terms of consumption. Therefore, the influence of energy prices on technology should be to decrease energy intensity through a reduction of energy demand. However, this effect will be lessened by the rebound effect; the demand will not decrease as much as expected. For policy considerations, in particular for energy tax policy, the main question is what will be the effect of an increase of energy prices on energy consumption at a national level.

What is the influence of technology on energy consumption?

Focusing on the second relationship, AEEI is defined as a reduction in energy intensity that is not associated with energy prices. These non-price factors include technological changes usually considered as endogenous. Increasing energy efficiency, due to innovations, obviously reduces demand for energy since energy efficiency will reduce the quantity of energy used to produce one unit of GDP. However, the rebound effect could, again, reduce this decrease. Indeed, as the energy efficiency of a process improves, the process becomes cheaper and therefore provides an incentive to increase its use. It has long been realized that energy consumption changes less than proportionally to changes in physical energy efficiency. For policy concerns, the main question is, what will be the effect of energy efficiency on energy consumption? Are energy efficiency improvements policy driven or are they the result of an autonomous trend due to technological changes?

Various papers estimate the link between energy intensity, technology and energy prices. As far as the first question of price is concerned, the effect of higher energy prices initially reduces demand but in the longer term encourages greater efficiency (which can increase demand). In fact, the efficiency improvement is a response to the price increase, and therefore the reduction in demand is limited. According to Herring (1998), it will lead to 'a new balance between supply and demand at a higher level of supply and demand than if there had been no efficiency response'.

Various studies show contradictory results for the impact of oil prices increases in the 1970s (Berndt, 1990). On the one hand, Schurr (1985) found that energy efficiency increased more rapidly in periods of low energy prices. Technological progress is likely to flourish when the availability of an important resource like energy is high enough and at a low price so as to stimulate economic growth. On the other hand, the decline in energy intensity has been causally attributed by some analysts to energy saving innovation, induced by rising energy prices (Holdren, 2001). A significant amount of energy saving technological change responds to energy price increases (Newell *et al.*, 1999; Popp, 2001, 2002). Recent papers provide information on the degree to which energy price increases induce improvement in the energy efficiency of consumer products. For instance, Popp (2002) finds that increases of energy prices have a positive impact on the rate of patenting in the energy sector. Nevertheless, these studies do not establish a direct causal link between the changes in energy technology and energy use.

In terms of energy services, an innovation that reduces the amount of energy required to produce a unit of energy services lowers the effective price of these services. This may result in an increase in demand for energy services and therefore for energy (Binswanger, 2001). One important cause is that higher efficiency reduces energy costs which again increase demand (Khazzoom, 1980, 1989; Khazzoom *et al.*, 1990). The lower price of energy also results in an income effect (Lovins, 1988) that increases demand for all goods in the economy and, therefore, for energy. The rebound effect is less important than the initial innovation-induced reduction in energy use, so improvements in energy efficiency reduce total energy demand (Howarth, 1997). Khazzoom (1987) criticizes Lovins for ignoring the rebound effect (Lovins, 1988, and Khazzoom, 1989). Khazzoom *et al.* (1990) suggest that, in the household sector, micro-effects could be large enough to offset efficiency improvements but others disagree (Henly *et al.*, 1988).

As far as the second question is concerned, the link between efficiency improvements and the energy consumption of households has been a major issue among energy economists since the 1980s (Brookes, 2000; Greening *et al.*, 2000). The current debate on reducing greenhouse gas emissions is stimulating economic research. On the one hand, increased energy efficiency at an industry level leads to a reduction of energy use at this level. What is the effect on energy consumption at the national level? The conservationists, as they are called, use a 'bottom up' approach; they promote energy efficiency through prices as a means of reducing energy consumption.

Moreover, changes in energy intensity which are not linked to changes in the price of energy are called changes in the autonomous energy efficiency index (AEEI). The AEEI is expected to reduce energy intensity 0.5 to 1 per cent per year (Manne and Richels, 1992; Burniaux *et al.*, 1992). Manne and Richels (1995) assume that AEEI will equal 40 per cent of GDP growth rate in the twenty-first century. Manne and Richel (1992), analysing the economic costs arising from CO_2 emission limits, show that a higher value of the AEEI would reduce both energy use and greenhouse gas emission.

However, Brookes (1990) believes that widespread improvements in energy efficiency will not, by themselves, do anything to stop the emission of greenhouse gases. Reductions in the energy intensity of output are associated with increases rather than decreases in energy demand. Therefore, Brookes considers efficiency improvements to be inappropriate to reduce emissions of greenhouse gases (argument challenged by Grubb, 1990).

In a study of US data on the residential conservation programme, it was found that around 60–70 per cent of the initial savings were eroded by the rebound effect (Khazzoom, 1986). Khazzoom (1980, 1986) and Wirl (1997) came up with a precise definition of the rebound effect with respect to energy, whose existence was also supported by empirical research (Binswanger, 2001; Greening *et al.*, 2000).

Schipper and Grubb (2000) define a classification for the rebound effect:

- micro-rebound effect: direct feedback between energy efficiency improvements and the level of energy using activity.
- macro effects: efficiency improvements can stimulate economic growth which will stimulate more energy use.
- 're-spending effect': if households reduce energy use at constant energy prices with little outlay, they have money which may or may not be spent on energy consumption.

Under certain circumstances, the rebound effect could actually turn an increase in energy efficiency into an increase of demand.[2] (See Table 6.1.)

Table 6.1 Measured rebound effect on various devices

Device	Size of the rebound effect (%)	Number of studies
Space heating	10–30	26
Space cooling	0–50	9
Water heating	10–40	5
Residential lighting	5–12	4
Home appliances	0	2
Automobiles	10–30	23

Source: Gottron F. (2001).

In a survey using Norwegian data, in a programme of reducing oil consumption, Haugland (1996) shows that the rebound effect was about 40 per cent for households and 10 per cent for commerce. Applied to Norway, Grepperud (1999) underlines differences across sectors concerning both energy use and the consequences of the rebound effect. As Schipper and Grubb (2000) remark:

> Feedback effects are small in mature sectors of mature economies and only potentially large in a few cases; lowering energy intensities almost always leads to lower use than otherwise... We may find that over a sufficient period energy use has increased even if energy efficiency has improved. Our thesis ... is that the improvement in efficiency per se is only a small part of the reason why total energy use may have increased.

Recently economists have focused on the rebound effect (or 'take back') on energy and gasoline markets and on global climate change. A consumer who saves money on his heating bill may spend it on a more carbon-intense activity. Alternatively, the saving could be spent on a less carbon-intense activity. Energy efficiency improvements might increase rather than decrease consumption. Efforts supported by authorities to increase the use of energy saving technology may not produce the expected result because of the rebound effect. It could weaken arguments for increased efficiency requirements. The debate is open.

Data and method

Data and definition of the variables

The data consist of annual observations of the oil consumption, the constant GDP in 1995 prices and the oil prices in USD per barrel for OECD countries. Units used in energy consumption are thousands of tons of oil equivalent (ktoe). The oil consumption and GDP data are taken from the energy balances in OECD countries of the International Energy Agency (IEA). The oil prices are provided by the US department of Energy (DOE). They are annual averages of crude oil domestic first purchase prices and are inflation adjusted. Annual exchange rate data taken from the IMF's International Financial Statistics database are also used to convert oil prices into national currency units. Finally, fuel rate (miles per gallon) measured in the United States and provided by the US Department of Transportation is taken as a measure of technological progress.

The sample period spans from 1960 to 2002. We consider 15 OECD countries:[3] Australia (AU), Austria (AT), Canada (CA), Finland (FI), France (FR), Germany (DE), Greece (GR), Italy (IT), Japan (JP), the Netherlands (NL), New Zealand (NZ), Norway (NO), Sweden (SE), the United Kingdom (GB) and the

United States (US). Note that our sample only contains developed countries. Such a choice is of course not neutral.

The variables under study are:

- the oil intensity which is given by the ratio of total oil consumption to GDP and which measures the oil used per unit of economic output;
- the real oil prices converted from US Dollars into the national currency of each country;
- the fuel rate obtained by dividing fuel consumption by mileage of a motor vehicle and used as a proxy for technological progress. Such a measure seems relevant, given the high part of consumption due to road transport in the total consumption of oil products (see Table 6.2).

These three variables are expressed in logarithms. The model also includes a dummy variable to account for the two oil price shocks in 1973 and 1979–80.

The three variables exhibit a similar pattern in the 15 countries under study. All countries record an increase in their oil intensity until the beginning of the 1970s and then a sharp decrease during the rest of the period following the first oil shock. For example, 50.8 oil units are necessary today to produce one unit of GDP in the United States (46.7 in France) against 100 units in 1973. The exceptions are Greece, which shows only a slight slowdown in the energy use after 1973, and New Zealand, where the oil intensity increases after 1985.[4] The oil prices exhibit an upward trend from 1960 with spikes in 1973 and 1979–80. This pattern justifies the introduction of the oil price shocks

Table 6.2 Part of road transport in the total consumption of oil products in 2002

Country	Road consumption (ktoe)	Total consumption (ktoe)	RC/TC (%)
AT	6144	12270	50.07
AU	23015	36184	63.61
CA	39974	82467	48.47
DE	55688	120507	46.21
FI	28733	57700	49.80
FR	43776	88308	49.57
GB	39657	72758	54.51
GR	5747	14290	40.22
IT	38561	66558	57.94
JP	77558	223268	34.74
NL	3884	8922	43.53
NO	3175	8640	36.75
NZ	2564	6356	40.34
SE	6951	13350	52.07
US	508725	833254	61.05

Source: Energy Balances in OECD Countries, International Energy Agency.

dummy in the following treatment. Finally, we observe a large increase in automobile fuel efficiency measured in the United States since the middle of the 1970s. In 1960, average mileage was 14.3 miles per gallon versus 22 miles per gallon in 2002.

We will now conduct a causality analysis in a multivariate framework in order to assess how the three variables – oil intensity, technology and oil prices – interact to yield these patterns.

Method

We investigate the causal relationships among oil prices, oil intensity and technological progress relying on the Granger (1969) definition of causality. Basically, a variable Y does not Granger-cause a variable X if knowledge of past information on Y does not improve the prediction of X.

The study of causality between several variables depends on the order of integration of the series. If the variables are stationary, standard causality tests can be applied in a VAR model constructed with the variables taken in level (Granger, 1969). If the variables are integrated of order one, or I(1), the usual distributions of the test statistics are not valid. In particular, the significance of the causality statistics is overstated so that spurious results will be obtained (Granger and Newbold, 1974). Consequently, if the variables contain a unit root, the causality tests will not be conducted in a VAR model in level. Instead, if the series are cointegrated, the causality analysis must be conducted in a vector error-correction (VECM) model (Engle and Granger, 1987). In the absence of cointegration, a vector autoregressive (VAR) model in first differences is considered.

For this reason, a three-stage procedure is followed to examine the direction of causality among the three variables. First, unit root tests are applied to assess the order of integration of each variable. To this end, we use Augmented Dickey Fuller (ADF) and Perron tests (Dickey and Fuller, 1979, 1981, and Perron, 1989). As the oil intensity, the oil price and the fuel rate turn out to be I(1) for most countries, we test for cointegration among the three variables using the Johansen (1988) and Johansen–Juselius (1990) maximum likelihood procedure. Finally, we test for causality among oil intensity, oil price and technological progress using a trivariate VECM or VAR model specified in first differences according to the results of the cointegration tests.[5]

Results

Unit root tests

First, we implement a standard unit root test: the Augmented Dickey Fuller (ADF).[6] This test is conducted in two alternative models: a model including an intercept and a model with an intercept and a trend. We exclude the case of no intercept (and no trend), which is to say we rule out the unlikely case where the mean of the stationary variable is zero. It is noted by Davidson and McKinnon (1993, p. 702) that: 'Testing with a zero intercept is extremely restrictive, so much so that it is hard to imagine ever using it in economic time series'. The Akaike and Schwarz information criteria are applied to choose the optimal lag length.[7]

Given the presence of oil shocks, the usual unit root tests could lead to misleading conclusions. Consequently, we also conduct the unit root test developed by Perron (1989) in order to assess the non-stationarity in the presence of a structural break.[8] We test for a unit root when allowing first an exogenous change in the level of the series, then an exogenous change in the rate of growth of the series and, finally, allowing both effects to take place simultaneously. This structural break[9] is assumed to occur in 1973 (the first oil shock).[10] Again, the information criteria are applied to select the optimal lag length.

The results of the unit root tests for levels and first differences are reported in Tables 6.3 and 6.4. A unit root can generally not be rejected for the variables in level in all specifications, whereas it is rejected for the variables in first differences at the 5 per cent level. The unit root statistics for the levels of the oil intensity, the oil price and the fuel rate exceed the critical values. However, the test statistics are smaller than the critical values for the first differenced variables. Therefore, we consider, in the following, that the oil intensity, the oil price and the fuel rate processes are $I(1)$.

However, inconclusive results are obtained for the oil intensity in five countries: Austria, Germany, Finland, Italy and the Netherlands. In these

Table 6.3A ADF unit root tests – oil intensity

	With an intercept and a trend		**With an intercept**	
Country	**Statistics for C**	**Statistics for ΔC**	**Statistics for C**	**Statistics for ΔC**
AT	−4.05**	−4.71***	−1.38	−3.18**
AU	−2.76	−3.60**	0.78	−2.88*
CA	−2.25	−3.91**	0.17	−3.78***
DE	−6.00***	−3.90**	−1.07	−3.14**
FI	−4.47***	−3.72**	−1.30	−2.70*
FR	−3.23*	−3.53**	−1.08	−2.97**
GB	−2.82	−2.50	−0.80	−2.72*
GR	−1.68	−8.39***	−2.57	−7.51***
IT	−4.23***	−2.65	−1.43	−2.52
JP	−2.90	−2.31	−1.92	−2.78*
NL	−4.52***	−5.80***	−0.59	−5.65***
NO	−2.94	−5.47***	0.63	−4.97***
NZ	−2.43	−7.21***	−2.69*	−7.15***
SE	−2.47	−5.14***	1.10	−4.69***
US	−2.27	−3.94**	0.09	−3.91***

Table 6.3B ADF unit root tests – oil price

	With an intercept and a trend		With an intercept	
Country	Statistics for P	Statistics for ΔP	Statistics for P	Statistics for ΔP
AT	−2.08	−5.73***	−2.11	−5.80***
AU	−1.98	−6.18***	−1.85	−6.26***
CA	−1.85	−5.90***	−1.77	−5.97***
DE	−2.18	−5.97***	−2.11	−6.04***
FI	−2.03	−5.92***	−2.02	−6.00***
FR	−2.09	−6.13***	−2.08	−6.21***
GB	−2.09	−6.32***	−2.12	−6.40***
GR	−1.81	−5.69***	−1.83	−5.76***
IT	−1.94	−5.93***	−1.93	−6.01***
JP	−2.11	−5.75***	−1.93	−5.81***
NL	−2.19	−5.77***	−2.24	−5.84***
NO	−2.13	−5.84***	−2.16	−5.91***
NZ	−1.86	−5.27***	−1.86	−5.34***
SE	−1.95	−5.82***	−1.86	−5.88***
US	−1.55	−5.60**	−1.12	−5.65***

Table 6.3C ADF unit root tests – fuel rate

With an intercept and a trend		With an intercept	
Statistics for F	Statistics for ΔF	Statistics for F	Statistics for ΔF
−1.91	−4.77***	0.51	−4.67***

Note: The columns statistics for $x(\Delta x)$ contain the test statistics applied to the variable in level (first differences). The asterisks ***, ** and * denote the rejection of the unit root at 1 per cent, 5 per cent and 10 per cent levels respectively.

countries, the unit root is rejected in the specification with an intercept and a linear trend and is not rejected in the specification with an intercept only. As the trend coefficient is found significant, this variable may be rather stationary around a linear trend in these countries. Nevertheless, we consider in the following that the oil intensity is integrated of order one, but the results must be interpreted cautiously in these countries.

Cointegration test

Given that the three variables are generally found integrated of order one, the next step is to test for cointegration, that is to determine whether there exists a stationary long-run relationship among oil intensity, oil price and fuel rate. We apply the Johansen and Juselius Maximum Likelihood approach using the maximum eigenvalue and trace statistics. To determine the number r of

Table 6.4A Unit root tests with a structural break in 1973 – oil intensity

Country	With a dummy on the trend and the intercept		With a dummy on the trend		With a dummy on the intercept	
	Statistics for *C*	Statistics for Δ*C*	Statistics for *C*	Statistics for Δ*C*	Statistics for *C*	Statistics for Δ*C*
AT	−1.32	−7.14***	−0.35	−6.95***	−2.70	−6.04***
AU	−2.86	−9.17***	−2.93	−9.40***	−1.99	−9.11***
CA	−1.60	−4.88***	−0.74	−4.25**	−1.45	−4.90***
DE	−2.77	−5.59***	−1.54	−5.56***	−4.74***	−4.73***
FI	−1.53	−5.68***	−0.72	−5.73***	−3.29	−4.58***
FR	−1.59	−5.55***	0.18	−4.85**	−2.06	−5.10***
GB	−1.23	−5.79***	−0.13	−5.80***	−4.49**	−4.02**
GR	−3.32	−8.99***	−3.67*	−8.29***	−0.84	−8.92***
IT	−0.98	−6.88***	1.26	−5.81***	−5.64***	−3.70*
JP	−1.72	−7.30***	−0.05	−6.85***	−5.83***	−4.07**
NL	−3.10	−7.27***	−2.37	−6.30***	−3.85**	−6.65***
NO	−3.32	−6.49***	−1.87	−6.12***	−1.13	−6.47***
NZ	−2.01	−7.48***	−1.74	−7.62***	−2.35	−7.40***
SE	−1.38	−6.13***	−1.00	−5.99***	−1.68	−5.87***
US	−1.12	−4.21**	−1.22	−4.10	−0.83	−4.29**

Table 6.4B Unit root tests with a structural break in 1973 – oil price

Country	With a dummy on the trend and the intercept		With a dummy on the trend		With a dummy on the intercept	
	Statistics for *P*	**Statistics for Δ*P***	**Statistics for *P***	**Statistics for Δ*P***	**Statistics for *P***	**Statistics for Δ*P***
AT	−2.17	−5.60***	−2.16	−5.66***	−2.20	−5.67***
AU	−2.28	−6.05***	−2.06	−6.13***	−2.29	−6.13***
CA	−2.38	−5.98***	−2.06	−5.87***	−2.42	−6.07***
DE	−2.30	−5.81***	−2.22	−5.90***	−2.32	−5.88***
FI	−2.11	−5.82***	−2.19	−5.87***	−2.13	−5.90***
FR	−2.21	−6.11***	−2.23	−6.09***	−2.24	−6.20***
GB	−2.66	−6.42***	−2.47	−6.28***	−2.67	−6.51***
GR	−2.30	−5.58***	−2.08	−5.65***	−2.31	−5.66***
IT	−2.27	−6.00***	−2.16	−5.92***	−2.30	−6.08***
JP	−2.17	−5.63***	−2.16	−5.68***	−2.20	−5.71***
NL	−2.30	−5.69***	−2.21	−5.72***	−2.30	−5.77***
NO	−2.26	−5.79***	−2.17	−5.80***	−2.27	−5.87***
NZ	−2.23	−5.18***	−2.08	−5.22***	−2.26	−5.25***
SE	−2.05	−5.85***	−1.99	−5.78***	−2.05	−5.93***
US	−2.66	−6.15***	−2.29	−6.01***	−2.66	−6.22***

Table 6.4C Unit root tests with a structural break in 1973 – fuel rate

With a dummy on the trend and the intercept		**With a dummy on the trend**		**With a dummy on the intercept**	
Statistics for *F*	**Statistics for Δ*F***	**Statistics for *F***	**Statistics for Δ*F***	**Statistics for *F***	**Statistics for Δ*F***
−1.36	−5.66***	−1.40	−5.01***	−0.72	−5.76***

Note: The columns statistics for $x(\Delta x)$ contain the test statistics applied to the variable in level (first differences). The asterisks ***, ** and * denote the rejection of the unit root at 1 per cent, 5 per cent and 10 per cent levels respectively using the asymptotic critical values reported in Perron (1989) for a time of break relative to the total sample size equal to 0.3.

cointegrating relations, we proceed sequentially from $r = 0$ to $r = 2$, until we fail to reject. The critical values are taken from Osterwald–Lenum (1992).

We use the Johansen and Juselius procedure rather than the Engle and Granger (1987) approach to test for cointegration. This technique has several advantages. First, the Engle and Granger approach relies on a two-step estimation, so that an error in the first step is carried into the second step. Moreover, the Johansen and Juselius technique allows us to estimate and test for the presence of multiple cointegrating vectors, which is relevant in our trivariate framework. Furthermore, all variables are treated as endogenous, avoiding the arbitrary choice of the dependent variable. Finally, the Johansen and Juselius approach allows us to test restricted versions of the cointegrating vector and the speed of adjustment parameters, which is particularly useful for the causality analysis.

The Johansen–Juselius method relies on the error-correction representation of the VAR model. We choose the specification with a trend in the data and an intercept in the cointegrating space. The long-run equilibrium relationship among the three variables is unlikely to exhibit a linear trend. Moreover, the mean of the first differenced variables is unequal to zero, so that we have to introduce an intercept in the three equations of the VECM model. A dummy variable, accounting for oil shocks, is also included among the regressors of the VECM model.

The results of the sequential test procedure are reported in Table 6.5. The null value for the zero cointegrating vector is rejected in favour of one cointegrating vector, whereas the null of one cointegrating vector against two is not rejected at the conventional significance level, at least with one of the two statistics, except in three countries: Greece, Norway and New Zealand, where no cointegrating vector is found with the maximum eigenvalue and trace statistics. There exists a long-run relationship between oil prices, oil intensity and technological progress in the 12 other countries.

Table 6.5 Cointegration tests based on the Johansen ML procedure

Country	Cointegration rank	λ_{max} Statistics	λ_{trace} Statistics
AT	$r = 0$	20.66*	28.63*
	$r \leq 1$	7.84	7.97
	$r \leq 2$	0.13	0.13
AU	$r = 0$	22.78**	33.61**
	$r \leq 1$	10.19	10.83
	$r \leq 2$	0.64	0.64
CA	$r = 0$	23.72**	35.27**
	$r \leq 1$	11.46	11.55
	$r \leq 2$	0.09	0.09
DE	$r = 0$	27.02***	34.89**
	$r \leq 1$	7.56	7.86
	$r \leq 2$	0.30	0.30
FI	$r = 0$	21.55**	28.72*
	$r \leq 1$	7.16	7.18
	$r \leq 2$	0.01	0.01
FR	$r = 0$	19.26*	28.43*
	$r \leq 1$	8.88	9.17
	$r \leq 2$	0.28	0.28
GB	$r = 0$	18.11	27.94*
	$r \leq 1$	8.98	9.83
	$r \leq 2$	0.85	0.85
GR	$r = 0$	15.39	21.33
	$r \leq 1$	4.38	5.93
	$r \leq 2$	1.55	1.55
IT	$r = 0$	20.84*	29.79**
	$r \leq 1$	8.77	8.94
	$r \leq 2$	0.17	0.17
JP	$r = 0$	34.52***	43.77***
	$r \leq 1$	9.22	9.25
	$r \leq 2$	0.03	0.03
NL	$r = 0$	26.58***	34.52***
	$r \leq 1$	7.52	7.94
	$r \leq 2$	0.42	0.42
NO	$r = 0$	14.56	23.12
	$r \leq 1$	8.07	8.56
	$r \leq 2$	0.49	0.49
NZ	$r = 0$	14.50	19.60
	$r \leq 1$	5.04	5.10
	$r \leq 2$	0.06	0.06

Continued

Table 6.5 Continued

Country	Cointegration rank	λ_{max} Statistics	λ_{trace} Statistics
SE	$r = 0$	19.28*	32.99**
	$r \leq 1$	13.01*	13.71*
	$r \leq 2$	0.71	0.71
US	$r = 0$	26.05***	32.52**
	$r \leq 1$	6.33	6.47
	$r \leq 2$	0.14	0.14

Note: r denotes the number of cointegrating relationships. The asterisks *, ** and *** denote the rejection of the null hypothesis at the 10 per cent, 5 per cent and 1 per cent levels respectively using the critical values provided by Osterwald-Lenum (1992).

Causality tests

To examine the causal relationship between oil intensity, oil price and fuel rate, we next perform Granger causality tests in the VECM or in the VAR models.

In the absence of a cointegrating relationship among the three variables, the following VAR model specified in first differences is estimated:

$$\begin{pmatrix} \Delta C_t \\ \Delta P_t \\ \Delta F_t \end{pmatrix} = \begin{pmatrix} \mu_C \\ \mu_P \\ \mu_F \end{pmatrix} + \begin{pmatrix} \lambda_C d_t \\ \lambda_P d_t \\ \lambda_F d_t \end{pmatrix} + \begin{pmatrix} \Gamma_{CC,1} & \Gamma_{CP,1} & \Gamma_{CF,1} \\ \Gamma_{PC,1} & \Gamma_{PP,1} & \Gamma_{PF,1} \\ \Gamma_{FC,1} & \Gamma_{FP,1} & \Gamma_{FF,1} \end{pmatrix} \begin{pmatrix} \Delta C_{t-1} \\ \Delta P_{t-1} \\ \Delta F_{t-1} \end{pmatrix}$$
$$+ \cdots + \begin{pmatrix} \Gamma_{CC,p} & \Gamma_{CP,p} & \Gamma_{CF,p} \\ \Gamma_{PC,p} & \Gamma_{PP,p} & \Gamma_{PF,p} \\ \Gamma_{FC,p} & \Gamma_{FP,p} & \Gamma_{FF,p} \end{pmatrix} \begin{pmatrix} \Delta C_{t-p} \\ \Delta P_{t-p} \\ \Delta F_{t-p} \end{pmatrix} + \begin{pmatrix} \varepsilon_{C,t} \\ \varepsilon_{P,t} \\ \varepsilon_{F,t} \end{pmatrix} \quad (6.1)$$

where C, P and F represent the oil intensity, the oil price and the fuel rate respectively and d_t represents the dummy for the oil-price shocks.

Granger causality from the variable j to the variable i is evaluated by testing the null hypothesis $H_0 : \Gamma_{ij,l} = 0,\ l = 1, \ldots, p$ using standard Wald statistics.

In the countries where a cointegrating relationship is found, the following VECM model is applied:

$$\begin{pmatrix} \Delta C_t \\ \Delta P_t \\ \Delta F_t \end{pmatrix} = \begin{pmatrix} \mu_C \\ \mu_P \\ \mu_F \end{pmatrix} + \begin{pmatrix} \lambda_C d_t \\ \lambda_P d_t \\ \lambda_F d_t \end{pmatrix} + \begin{pmatrix} \Gamma_{CC,1} & \Gamma_{CP,1} & \Gamma_{CF,1} \\ \Gamma_{PC,1} & \Gamma_{PP,1} & \Gamma_{PF,1} \\ \Gamma_{FC,1} & \Gamma_{FP,1} & \Gamma_{FF,1} \end{pmatrix} \begin{pmatrix} \Delta C_{t-1} \\ \Delta P_{t-1} \\ \Delta F_{t-1} \end{pmatrix}$$
$$+ \cdots + \begin{pmatrix} \Gamma_{CC,p} & \Gamma_{CP,p} & \Gamma_{CF,p} \\ \Gamma_{PC,p} & \Gamma_{PP,p} & \Gamma_{PF,p} \\ \Gamma_{FC,p} & \Gamma_{FP,p} & \Gamma_{FF,p} \end{pmatrix} \begin{pmatrix} \Delta C_{t-p} \\ \Delta P_{t-p} \\ \Delta F_{t-p} \end{pmatrix}$$

$$+\begin{pmatrix} \alpha_C \\ \alpha_P \\ \alpha_F \end{pmatrix} (\beta_C \quad \beta_P \quad \beta_F \quad \rho_0) \begin{pmatrix} C_{t-1} \\ P_{t-1} \\ F_{t-1} \\ 1 \end{pmatrix} + \begin{pmatrix} \varepsilon_{C,t} \\ \varepsilon_{P,t} \\ \varepsilon_{F,t} \end{pmatrix} \tag{6.2}$$

In the VECM, it is possible to test for Granger non-causality among the three variables in both the short and the long-run. Globally, there is no causality running from the variable j to the variable i if $\Gamma_{ij,l} = 0, l = 1, \ldots, p$ and if $\alpha_i\beta_j = 0$. The restrictions $\Gamma_{ij,l} = 0, l = 1, \ldots, p$ can be interpreted in terms of short run non-causality since the rejection of this hypothesis indicates that the dependent variable responds to short-run shocks. The rejection of the second restriction $\alpha_i\beta_j = 0$ is referred to a long-run non-causality since it is related to the effect on the dependent variable of a variable contained in the long-run relationship.

Short-run causality from the variable j to the variable i is examined by testing $H_{01} : \Gamma_{ij,l} = 0, l = 1, \ldots, p$ with standard Wald statistics. The long-run causality will be assessed by testing the nullity of the long-run parameters. The variable j does not cause the variable i in the long-run if $\pi_{ij} = \alpha_i\beta_j = 0$. However, the usual distribution of the test statistics does not hold if $\alpha_i = \beta_j = 0$, that is to say if the parameters α_i and β_j are simultaneously equal to zero (Toda and Phillips, 1993). To overcome this problem, we apply the sequential test procedure as described in Toda and Phillips (1994). First, weak exogeneity of the dependent variable is assessed by testing for the significance of the speed of adjustment parameters $H_{02} : \alpha_i = 0$. For this purpose, LR statistics can be employed. Second, a test of exclusion of the variable j in the long-run relation $H_{03} : \beta_j = 0$ is conducted using LR statistics. If weak exogeneity and/or long-run exclusion are/is not rejected, there is no long-run causality from the variable j to the variable i. If H_{02} and H_{03} are rejected, we can reject the null of long-run non-causality $\pi_{ij} = \alpha_i\beta_j = 0$ without any additional testing in the case of one cointegrating vector.[11]

The results of estimations of the VAR and VECM models lead to the following remarks.[12] In the VAR specification, the price variation significantly and negatively affects the variation of the consumption in two countries – Greece and New Zealand. The price variation positively affects the fuel rate in three countries – Greece, New Zealand and Norway. In the VECM model, the coefficients of the long-run relationship generally have the expected signs exhibiting a negative relation between the oil intensity and the oil price and the technological progress variable. In the short run, the consumption growth is negatively correlated with the price variation and with the fuel rate change of the last period. The fuel rate change is positively correlated with the price change. The dummy variable is generally found significant and has the expected positive sign in the price equation and a negative sign in the consumption equation capturing the negative impact of the oil shocks on energy

Table 6.6 Results of the causality tests

Country	Model	Eq.	Source of causality: Short-run ΔC	Short-run ΔP	Short-run ΔF	Long-run α_C	Long-run α_P	Long-run α_F	Long-run β_C	Long-run β_P	Long-run β_F	Conclusion
AT	VECM	ΔC	–	0.03	0.06							$P \to C, F \to C$
		ΔP	0.97	–	0.78	0.00	0.98	0.04	0.00	0.35	0.00	–
		ΔF	0.04	0.04	–							$C \to F, P \to F$
AU	VECM	ΔC	–	0.01	0.01							$P \to C, F \to C$
		ΔP	0.18	–	0.33	0.01	0.03	0.31	0.25	0.00	0.15	–
		ΔF	0.83	0.01	–							$P \to F$
CA	VECM	ΔC	–	0.13	0.73							$P \to C$
		ΔP	0.11	–	0.46	0.07	0.00	0.04	0.20	0.01	0.18	–
		ΔF	0.36	0.06	–							$P \to F$
DE	VECM	ΔC	–	0.48	0.38							$P \to C, F \to C$
		ΔP	0.12	–	0.51	0.02	0.04	0.42	0.00	0.02	0.00	$C \to P, F \to P$
		ΔF	0.39	0.03	–							$P \to F$
FI	VECM	ΔC	–	0.04	0.61							$P \to C, F \to C$
		ΔP	0.94	–	0.72	0.01	0.48	0.26	0.00	0.00	0.00	–
		ΔF	0.03	0.00	–							$C \to F, P \to F$
FR	VECM	ΔC	–	0.02	0.26							$P \to C, F \to C$
		ΔP	0.84	–	0.66	0.01	0.43	0.07	0.00	0.06	0.00	
		ΔF	0.00	0.00	–							$C \to F, P \to F$
GB	VECM	ΔC	–	0.59	0.03							$P \to C, F \to C$
		ΔP	0.04	–	0.43	0.08	0.02	0.83	0.05	0.00	0.01	$C \to P, F \to P$
		ΔF	0.07	0.00	–							$C \to F, P \to F$

GR	VAR	ΔC	–	0.05	0.33							$P \to C$
		ΔP	0.39	–	0.51	–	–	–	–	–	–	–
		ΔF	0.35	0.18	–							–
IT	VECM	ΔC	–	0.00	0.90							$P \to C, F \to C$
		ΔP	0.98	–	0.74	0.00	0.70	0.10	0.00	0.07	0.00	–
		ΔF	0.02	0.00	–							$C \to F, P \to F$
JP	VECM	ΔC	–	0.00	0.06							$P \to C, F \to C$
		ΔP	0.71	–	0.70	0.01	0.83	0.00	0.00	0.03	0.00	–
		ΔF	0.00	0.00	–							$C \to F, P \to F$
NL	VECM	ΔC	–	0.17	0.41							$F \to C$
		ΔP	0.99	–	0.69	0.01	0.76	0.01	0.00	0.30	0.00	–
		ΔF	0.33	0.00	–							$C \to F, P \to F$
NO	VAR	ΔC	–	0.30	0.00							$F \to C$
		ΔP	0.72	–	0.43	–	–	–	–	–	–	–
		ΔF	0.69	0.08	–							$P \to F$
NZ	VAR	ΔC	–	0.00	0.51							$P \to C$
		ΔP	0.55	–	0.42	–	–	–	–	–	–	–
		ΔF	0.73	0.21	–							–
SE	VECM	ΔC	–	0.94	0.70							–
		ΔP	0.23	–	0.92	0.50	0.01	0.03	0.13	0.11	0.16	–
		ΔF	0.37	0.01	–							$P \to F$
US	VECM	ΔC	–	0.14	0.09							$P \to C, F \to C$
		ΔP	0.30	–	0.21	0.00	0.00	0.60	0.02	0.00	0.01	$C \to P, F \to P$
		ΔF	0.54	0.01	–							$P \to F$

Note: This table contains the p-values of the causality tests in the VAR or in the VECM model (including a dummy variable for oil-shocks). The columns ΔC, ΔP and ΔF contain the *p*-values of the Wald test for the joint nullity of the lagged variations of C (oil intensity), P (oil prices) and F (fuel rate) respectively. The columns α_C, α_P, and α_F report the *p*-values of the LR statistics of the speed of adjustment parameters. The columns β_C, β_P and β_F contain the *p*-values of the LR statistics for the exclusion of C, P and F from the long-run relationship. In the last column, '$\to$' denotes the direction of Granger-causality.

consumption. We also note a significant positive impact of the oil-price shock on the fuel rate. At last, the VAR and VECM models pass a series of diagnostic tests.

The results of the causality tests are reported in Table 6.6.

Oil consumption is affected by oil prices (Australia, Canada, Greece, New Zealand) and fuel rate (the Netherlands and Norway) or both (Austria, Finland, France, Italy and Japan). Fuel efficiency depends on the oil price, except in Greece and New Zealand and on oil intensity (Austria, Finland, France, the United Kingdom, Italy, Japan and the Netherlands). However, there is no causality from oil intensity or from fuel rate to oil prices, except in three major countries: Germany, the United Kingdom and the United States. The United States is the largest oil consumer and importer in the world. Consequently, it is not surprising to find that oil prices are not exogenous in this country. Note also the peculiar results for Greece and New Zealand where the only causality link we find runs from oil price to oil consumption. Recall however that the oil intensity series are atypical in these two countries, showing no decrease after the two oil price shocks.

These results can be summarized as follows. We find:

- a unidirectional causality running from prices to oil intensity in 12 countries and a causality from the fuel rate to the oil intensity in 11 countries with a feedback effect from oil intensity to fuel rate in 7 countries.
- in 13 countries a relationship running from price to fuel rate and in 7 countries a causality running from oil intensity to fuel rate.
- strongly exogenous oil prices, except in three countries (Germany, the United Kingdom and the United States); this means that this variable is generally unaffected by the changes in fuel rate and in oil intensity except in major countries like the United States.

Our main question was how two variables, energy prices and energy intensity, interact, taking into account a third variable: technological progress. We consider two relations: energy prices and technology, and technology and energy consumption.

Concerning the first link between energy prices and technology, the empirical results provide evidence consistent with a clear relationship between energy prices and technological progress measured by the fuel rate variable. In particular, they highlight the strong impact of the price increase on technology. In fact, we find a causality running from the oil price to the oil efficiency in most countries. The higher prices faced by consumers since the 1970s have resulted in lower rates of consumption: automobiles with better mileage, homes and commercial buildings better insulated and improvements in industrial energy efficiency.

The results also show the impact of the overall increase in oil prices on oil consumption since the first oil shock. Demand is sensitive to high price. The

Asian crisis in 1997–98 is an illustration of this sensitivity, with a collapse of the demand. The developed countries have tried to reduce their oil dependence since 1973 by reducing the quantity of oil used per unit of economic output. This can be explained by structural transformations of the gross value added, the aforementioned technological innovations and by a substitution of petroleum products for another energy sources where possible. We can quote as an example the French policy of energy diversification, where nuclear plant construction following the first oil shock has led to an increase in nuclear power from a value of 25 per cent to 50 per cent of the total energy consumed in the country.

Conclusion

This chapter uses a cointegration analysis and Granger causality tests to examine in 15 major OECD countries the causal relationships between oil prices, oil consumption and technological progress measured by the fuel rate in road transport. In most countries, the three series appear to be non-stationary in level, but stationary in first-differences. Then, we find evidence of cointegration among the three variables in 12 countries out of the 15 considered. Finally, Granger causality tests suggest a causality running from prices to fuel rate and a causality from prices and fuel rate to oil consumption in most OECD countries.

These results have important policy implications. In particular, the positive impact of high energy prices on energy efficiency can be taken into consideration. Discussions of the effects of energy taxes by governments on the promotion of energy efficiency and energy conservation are stimulated. The debate in France on the '*TIPP flottante*' is a good illustration. The decrease of taxation to reduce the impact of the actual oil price increase considered in some countries, can have negative effects in terms of energy efficiency; price increases promote technological innovations leading to increased energy efficiency and energy saving. This idea supports the decision of the 25 members of the European Union not to take such measures during the informal meeting in Manchester (September 2005). Nevertheless, the potential for energy efficiency improvements is still very high. The question is crucial at this time, given the importance of the environmental costs related to the production and consumption of energy and proposals to reduce greenhouse gas emissions.

There are a number of extensions possible to this chapter. First, we could examine the causality among the three variables when taking into account different relationships according to the price level using a threshold VEC model. The relationships among the three variables may, in fact, be nonlinear, so that causality may depend on the energy price level. Second, it could be interesting to apply the same analysis to a sample of developing countries; countries like China, India or South Korea show a very fast growth in oil consumption over the last 20 years. We could assess whether energy price increases can also encourage less developed countries to improve energy efficiency, to move towards cleaner technologies and to develop alternative sources of energy without hampering their economic development.

Notes

1 We do not analyze the link with economic growth presented in Chapter 5.
2 On the importance of the rebound effect, see Lovins (1988).
3 The OECD countries account for almost 2/3 of worldwide daily oil consumption.
4 See Hondroyiannis *et al.* (2002) for a discussion of the energy consumption in Greece.
5 Recall that we could have performed the causality tests considering each pair of variables separately in bivariate models. This approach is widely used in the literature when examining causal relationships among variables. However, causality tests could lead to spurious conclusions if an important explicative variable is omitted. From the results of estimations shown in the following section, we see a clear dependence among the three variables. For this reason, we conduct the causality tests in a trivariate model.
6 The ADF regression tests for a unit root $\rho = 1$ in the following specification $y_t = D_t + \rho y_{t-1} + \varepsilon_t$ where $D_t = 0$, μ or $\mu + \beta t$. See Chapter 3 for a detailed presentation of the Dickey Fuller tests.
7 Given the frequency of data and the limited number of observations, the maximum lag length that we consider is 2.
8 Perron (1989) modifies the usual Dickey Fuller specification $y_t = D_t + \rho y_{t-1} + \varepsilon_t$ where $D_t = 0$, μ or $\mu + \beta t$, by introducing three alternative definitions of the deterministic trend function D_t which contains one break at time T_B. The crash model allows for a one-time change in the intercept of the trend function: $D_t = \mu + dD(T_B)$ with $D(T_B) = 1$ if $t = T_B + 1$, 0 otherwise. The changing growth model allows for a change in the slope of the trend function $D_t = \mu_1 + (\mu_2 - \mu_1)DU_t$ where $DU_t = 1$ if $t > T_B$, 0 otherwise. Both effects are allowed in the third model $D_t = \mu_1 + dD(T_B) + (\mu_2 - \mu_1)DU_t$.
9 This test has also been performed with a break point in 1980. As the results are similar, they are not reported here, but they are available from the authors on request.
10 If uncertainty exists about the timing of the structural change, other statistics can be applied (see for example Zivot and Andrews, 1992; Vogelsang and Perron, 1998). There are also tests for the case of more than one structural break in the series (see among others Vogelsang, 1997).
11 For $r > 1$, the null hypothesis $H_{04} : \sum_{c=1}^{r} \alpha_i^c \beta_j^c = 0$ must additionally be tested. Since the nullity of $\alpha_i^c, c = 1, \ldots, r$ and $\beta_j^c, c = 1, \ldots, r$ has been previously rejected, standard *t*-statistics can be applied in this case (see Toda and Phillips, 1994).
12 Again, for sake of parsimony, the results of estimation and the diagnostic tests are not reported here but are available from the authors on request.

References

Azar, C. and Dowlatabadi, E. (1999) 'A Review of Technical Change in Assessment of Climate Policy', *Annual Review of Energy Environment*, vol. 24, pp. 513–44.

Berndt, E. (1990) 'Energy Use, Technical Progress and Productivity Growth: A Survey of Economic Issues', *Journal of Productivity Analysis*, vol. 2, pp. 67–83.

Binswanger, M. (2001) 'Technological Progress and Sustainable Development: What About the Rebound Effect?', *Ecological Economics*, vol. 36, pp. 119–32.

Brookes, L. (1990) 'The Greenhouse Effect: The Fallacies in the Energy Efficiency Solution', *Energy Policy*, March, pp. 199–201.

Brookes, L. (2000) 'Energy Efficiency Fallacies Revisited', *Energy Policy*, vol. 2, pp. 355–66.

Burniaux, J-M., Martin, J.P., Nicoletti, G. and Oliveira-Martins, J. (1992) 'Green – A Multi-Sector, Multi-Region Dynamic General Equilibrium Model for Quantifying the Costs of Curbing CO2 Emissions: A Technical Manual', *OECD Economics and Statistics Department Working Papers*, no. 104 (June).

Davidson, R. and McKinnon, J.G. (1993) *Estimation and Inference in Econometrics* (Oxford: Oxford University Press).

Dickey, D.A. and Fuller, W.A. (1979) 'Distribution of the Estimators for Autoregressive Time Series with a Unit Root', *Journal of the American Statistical Association*, vol. 74, pp. 427–31.

Dickey, D.A. and Fuller, W.A. (1981) 'Likelihood Ratio Statistics for Autoregressive Time Series with a Unit Root', *Econometrica*, vol. 49, pp. 1057–72.

EIA (2004) 'Annual Energy Outlook 2004', *Energy Information Administration* (Washington, DC: US Department of Energy DOE).

Engle, R. and Granger, C.W.J. (1987) 'Cointegration and Error-Correction: Representation, Estimation, and Testing', *Econometrica*, vol. 55, pp. 251–76.

Glasure, Y. (2002) 'Energy and National Income in Korea: Further Evidence on the Role of Omitted Variables', *Energy Economics*, vol. 24, pp. 355–65.

Gottron, F. (2001) 'Energy Efficiency and The Rebound Effect: Does Increasing Efficiency Decrease Demand?', *CRS Report for Congress RS 20981*, Resource, Science and Industry Division, July, 30.

Granger, C.W.J. (1969) 'Investigating Causal Relations by Econometric Models and Cross-Spectral Methods', *Econometrica*, vol. 37, pp. 424–38.

Granger, C.W.J. and Newbold, P. (1974) 'Spurious Regressions in Econometrics', *Journal of Econometrics*, vol. 2, pp. 111–20.

Greening, L. and Greene, D. (1998) 'Energy Use, Technical Efficiency and the Rebound Effect: A Review of the Literature', Hagler Bailly Services, Colorado, *USA. Final Report*, January.

Greening, L., Greene D. and Difiglio, C. (2000) 'Energy Efficiency and Consumption – The Rebound Effect – A Survey', *Energy Policy*, vol. 28, pp. 389–401.

Grepperud, S. (1999) 'A General Equilibrium Assessment of Rebound Effects', *Prosus Report* 2/99, available at Http://Www.Prosus.UIO.No/Publikasjoner/Rapporter/Index.Htm.

Grubb, M. (1990) 'Energy Efficiency and Economic Fallacies – A Reply', *Energy Policy*, vol. 18, no. 8, pp. 783–85.

Haugland, T. (1996) 'Social Benefits of Financial Investment Support in Energy Conservation Policy', *Energy Journal*, vol. 17, no. 2, pp. 79–102.

Henly, L., Ruderman, H. and Levine, M. (1988) 'Energy Savings Resulting from the Adoption of More Efficient Appliances: A Follow-Up', *Energy Journal*, vol. 2, pp. 163–70.

Herring, H. (1998) 'Does Energy Efficiency Save Energy? *The Economists Debate*', EERU Report No. 074 – July 1998.

Holdren, J. (2001) 'Searching for a National Energy Policy', *Issues in Science and Technology*, vol. 17, no. 3, pp. 43–51.

Hondroyiannis, G., Lolos, S. and Papapetrou, E. (2002) 'Energy Consumption and Economic Growth: Assessing the Evidence From Greece', *Energy Economics*, vol. 24, pp. 319–36.

Howarth, R. (1997) 'Energy Efficiency and Economic Growth', *Contemporary Economic Policy*, vol. 25, pp. 1–9.

Jevons, S. (1865) 'The Coal Question – Can Britain Survive?', *Extracts in Environment and Change*, 1974, Macmillan.

Johansen, S. (1988) 'Statistical Analysis of Cointegration Vectors', *Journal of Economic Dynamics and Control*, vol. 12, pp. 231–54.

Johansen, S. and Juselius, K. (1990) 'Maximum Likelihood Estimation and Inferences on Cointegration with Application to the Demand for Money', *Oxford Bulletin of Economics and Statistics*, vol. 52, pp. 169–210.

Jumbe, C. (2004) 'Cointegration and Causality Between Electricity Consumption and GDP: Empirical Evidence from Malawi', *Energy Economics*, vol. 26, pp. 61–8.

Khazzoom, J. (1980) 'Economic Implications of Mandated Efficiency Standards for Household Appliances', *Energy Journal*, vol. 1, no. 2, pp. 21–40.

Khazzoom, J. (1986) *An Econometric Model Integrating Conservation Measures in the Estimation of the Residential Demand for Electricity* (Greenwich, CN: JAI Press).

Khazzoom, J. (1987) 'Energy Saving Resulting from More Efficient Appliances', *Energy Journal*, vol. 8, no. 4, pp. 85–9.

Khazzoom, J. (1989) 'Energy Savings from More Efficient Appliances: A Rejoinder', *Energy Journal*, vol. 10, no. 1, pp. 157–66.

Khazzoom, J. Shelby, M. and Wolcott, R. (1990) 'The Conflict Between Energy Conservation and Environmental Policy in The U.S. Transportation Sector', *Energy Policy*, vol. 18, no. 5, pp. 456–8.

Liu, C. (2005) 'An Overview for Decomposition of Industry Energy Consumption', *American Journal of Applied Science*, vol. 2, no. 7, pp. 1166–8.

Lovins, A. (1988) 'Energy Saving Resulting from the Adoption of More Efficient Appliances: Another View', *Energy Journal*, vol. 9, no. 2, pp. 155–62.

Manne, A. and Richels, R. (1992) *Buying Greenhouse Insurance* (Cambridge, MA: MIT Press).

Manne, A. and Richels, R. (1995) 'The Greenhouse Debate: Economic Efficiency, Burden Sharing and Hedging Strategies', *Energy Journal*, vol. 16, no. 4, pp. 1–37.

Newell, R., Jaffe, A. and Stavins, R. (1999) 'The Induced Innovation Hypothesis and Energy-Saving Technological Change', *Quarterly Journal of Economics*, vol. 114, pp. 941–75.

Osterwald-Lenum, M. (1992) 'A Note with Quantiles of the Asymptotic Distribution of the Maximum Likelihood Cointegration Rank Test Statistic', *Oxford Bulletin of Economics and Statistics*, vol. 54, pp. 461–72.

Perron, P. (1989) 'The Great Crash, the Oil Price Shock and the Unit Root Hypothesis', *Econometrica*, vol. 57, pp. 1361–401.

Popp, D. (2001) 'The Effect of New Technology on Energy Consumption', *Resource and Energy Economics*, vol. 23, pp. 215–39.

Popp, D. (2002) 'Induced Innovation and Energy Prices', *American Economic Review*, vol. 92, pp. 160–80.

Schipper, L. and Grubb, M. (2000) 'On The Rebound? Feedbacks Between Energy Intensities and Energy Uses in IEA Countries', *Energy Policy*, vol. 20, pp. 367–88.

Schurr, S. (1985) 'Energy Conservation and Productivity Growth – Can We Have Both?', *Energy Policy*, vol. 13, no. 2, pp. 126–32.

Soytas, U. and Sari, R. (2003) 'Energy Consumption and GDP: Causality Relationship In G-7 Countries and Emerging Markets', *Energy Economics*, vol. 25, pp. 33–7.

Toda, H.Y. and Phillips, P.C.B. (1993) 'Vector Autoregression and Causality', *Econometrica*, vol. 61, pp. 1367–93.

Toda, H.Y. and Phillips, P.C.B. (1994) 'Vector Autoregression and Causality: A Theoretical Overview and Simulation Study', *Econometric Reviews*, vol. 13, pp. 259–85.

Vogelsang, T.J. (1997) 'Wald-Type Tests for Detecting Breaks in the Trend Function of a Dynamic Time Series', *Econometric Theory*, vol. 13, pp. 818–49.

Vogelsang, T.J. and Perron, P. (1998) 'Additional Tests for a Unit-Root Allowing for a Break in the Trend Function at an Unknown Time', *International Economic Review*, vol. 39, pp. 1073–100.

Wing, I. and Eckaus, R. (2004) 'The Decline in U.S. Energy Intensity: Its Origins and Implications for Long-Run CO_2 Emission Projections', *Journal of Policy Modeling*, vol. 19, no. 4, pp. 417–40.

Wirl, F. (1997) *The Economics of Conservation Programs* (Dordrecht: Kluwer).

Zivot, E. and Andrews, D.W.K. (1992) 'Further Evidence on the Great Crash, the Oil-Price Shock and the Unit-Root Hypothesis', *Journal of Business and Economic Statistics*, vol. 10, pp. 251–70.

7
Energy Substitution Modelling

Patricia Renou-Maissant

Introduction

The analysis of substitution among energy sources remains one of the main issues in energy economy and policy. The extent of substitution in energy demand can bring about important changes in energy balance sheets and cause profound changes in energy supply. An obvious example is the substitution of oil for natural gas, which has occurred in many countries over the last 30 years, in power generation, industry and households.

Interfuel substitution may be caused by shifts in relative fuel prices which lead to changes in the degree of utilization of individual fuels but can also be caused by events such as energy policy, political and institutional constraints, emergence of new technologies and processes, changes in economic activity and specific characteristics within individual countries. Reliable information on interfuel substitution possibilities is particularly useful in evaluating the effects of public policies on the pricing of fuels. Decision makers want to know the potential impact of alternative policies that may be adopted. Many of the policies put forward by energy policy makers will, through their effects on fuel prices, affect fuel utilization indirectly. Industrial energy demand is often thought to have the greatest potential for interfuel substitution.

During the 1970s, the dramatic rise in the price of oil, combined with an unprecedented series of new energy policies, was expected to result in interfuel transition away from oil to other domestically abundant sources of energy. More recently, an investigation of interfuel substitution among different types of energy sources has shown increasing relevance, from an environmental regulation point of view, because the consumption of different types of energy is associated with different levels of CO_2, SO_2 and other emissions. If the various sources of energy are close substitutes, it is relatively easy to obtain reductions in CO_2 and SO_2 emissions from industry by altering the *pattern* of energy sources. New carbon dioxide emission taxes in Europe and a BTU tax in the US are intended primarily to encourage end users to switch away from coal and oil products in favour of cleaner burning fuels such as natural gas or electricity generated by hydro or nuclear power.

In this chapter, an analysis of interfuel substitution in the industrial sector of two European countries, France and the United Kingdom, over the 1978–2002 period is performed using translog (Christensen, Jorgenson and Lau, 1973) and linear logit (Considine and Mount, 1984) models. A comparison between these results and those obtained over the period 1960–88 is also carried out.

The chapter is organized as follows: the first section focuses on econometric methodology for analysing interfuel substitution. The second section presents a review of current literature. The third section presents data for French and British industrial sectors. The fourth section describes the interfuel substitution models, while the next section provides empirical results. The sixth section outlines the energy market implications and the final section presents conclusions.

Econometric methodology

A complete set of theoretically consistent own and cross-price elasticities is needed to forecast the extent of fuel substitution that would result from tax-induced relative fuel prices changes. The demand for energy is a derived demand related to the stock of appliances. The adjustment of demand factors to price changes is constrained by technological factors and the adjustment of the capital stock and other fixed factors of production. Most capital equipment was designed to consume a certain kind and amount of energy, so that capital and energy must be used together, which is to say that they are complementary inputs to production in the short run. But in the long run, when energy prices increase, producers have the flexibility to shift to more capital-intensive and less energy-intensive processes of production. Furthermore, producers often make input decisions on the basis of expected prices, so their response to relative price changes takes time. For these reasons, interfuel substitution response is expected to be limited in the short run but potentially significant in the long run when adjustments have been made. It is of importance to analyse substitution both in the short run and in the long run; the demand function should incorporate a stock effect as well as some assumptions about the adjustment of these stocks over time. It would also be desirable to have a direct estimate of the length of time required before the long-run response would be completed.

Energy substitution modelling within a dynamic framework involves trade-offs between empirical tractability and theoretical sophistication. On the one hand, there are models which consider the interrelated disequilibrium of the adjustment process (Nadiri and Rosen, 1969) by generalizing the Koyck adjustment mechanism for a single equation to the case of n inputs. These models provide relatively simple formulations because stock variables are not needed for estimation, but the role of economic theory is limited in that economic factors affecting the time path of adjustment from short to long run are not formally introduced. On the other hand, there are models which are based explicitly on dynamic economic optimization, incorporating costs of adjustment for the quasi-fixed factors. Speeds of adjustment of quasi-fixed factors to their long-run equilibrium levels are endogenous and time varying. These models are particularly well adapted to the analysis of substitution among aggregated factor inputs. In other respects, in situations where the empirical researcher is constrained by lack of information on capital stocks and other fixed inputs, the former alternative provides the advantage of greater empirical applicability.

In attempting to measure the substitutability among fuels, a useful starting point is the theory of production function. This approach is based on neoclassical theory assuming that, in the industrial sector, factor inputs are chosen to minimize the total cost of production. Industrial energy demand must be treated using a two-stage approach.

The technical structure of industrial production can be summarized by the production function:

$$y = f\,(K,\ L,\ EN\,(O,\ E,\ G,\ C), M) \tag{7.1}$$

where y is the industrial level of output associated with any combination of inputs K, L, EN and M (capital, labour, energy and raw materials, respectively). EN is an aggregate weakly homothetically separable from the other inputs. The variables O, E, G and C represent, respectively, the quantities of oil, electricity, natural gas and coal consumed. Interfuel substitution models require separability assumptions in order to reduce the number of parameters that must be estimated.

If the factor prices and output level are exogenously determined, the production structure described by (7.1) can alternatively be described by a cost function, which is also separable:

$$C = g\,(P_K,\ P_L,\ P_{EN}(P_O,\ P_E,\ P_G,\ P_C), P_M,\ y) \tag{7.2}$$

where P_i is the price of the individual fuel i and P_{EN} is the aggregate price of energy. The useful feature of (7.2) is that the properties of the production function, in particular its input substitution elasticities, can be determined from the dual cost function alone. Most interfuel substitution studies assume that energy is weakly separable from labour, capital, and raw materials, which implies that the energy cost function can be estimated separately:

$$P_{EN} = h(P_O,\ P_E,\ P_G,\ P_c) \tag{7.3}$$

Weak separability means that the cost minimizing mix of fuels is independent of the optimal mix and level of labour, capital and raw materials, even though the level of total energy use is not. This cost structure implies that producers follow a sequential optimization process, first selecting individual fuels to minimize energy costs and then choosing the level of all inputs, including aggregate energy expenditures.

The usual approach in empirical applications is to specify an empirical cost function and to derive the system of demand equations by applying Shepard's lemma:

$$X_i = \frac{\partial C}{\partial P_i} \quad i = O, E, G, C \tag{7.4}$$

$$S_i = \frac{P_i X_i}{C} = \frac{P_i \left(\frac{\partial C}{\partial P_i}\right)}{\sum_{j=1}^{n} P_j X_j} = \frac{P_i \left(\frac{\partial C}{\partial P_i}\right)}{\sum_{j=1}^{n} P_j \left(\frac{\partial C}{\partial P_j}\right)} \quad i = O, E, G, C \tag{7.5}$$

where C is total cost, X_i is the quantity of input i and S_i is the input cost share for input i.

The Allen partial elasticity of substitution for inputs i and j is defined as follows:

$$\sigma_{ij} = C \frac{\frac{\partial^2 C}{\partial P_i \partial P_j}}{\left(\frac{\partial C}{\partial P_i}\right)\left(\frac{\partial C}{\partial P_j}\right)} \tag{7.6}$$

The cross-price elasticity can be written:

$$\eta_{ij} = S_j \sigma_{ij} \quad i \neq j \tag{7.7}$$

η_{ij} is the elasticity of the demand of fuel i with respect to the price of fuel j. When η_{ij} is positive i and j are substitutes; when η_{ij} is negative i and j are complements.

It is necessary to specify the input demand functions more completely. Economic theory does not suggest any particular functional form, but rather one that satisfies the regularity conditions. A neoclassical cost function must have the usual properties; that is it is non-decreasing, continuous, homogeneous of degree one and concave in input prices. For cost minimizing producers, the conditional demand equations must be non-negative and homogeneous of degree zero in prices. The Hessian matrix derived from the cost function must be symmetric and negative semi-definite.

Literature review

The choice of functional form can be viewed as a choice between regularity and flexibility. It is preferable for the functional form to be as little constrained as possible. Analysis of multi-input systems requires more flexible functional forms than the traditional Cobb–Douglas and CES production functions. These functions satisfy the regularity conditions but are very restrictive. The elasticities of substitution between any pairs of inputs are equal to one for the Cobb–Douglas function and equal for all pairs of inputs for the CES function. That is why more general functions, which place no restrictions on the Allen partial elasticities of substitution, have been developed.

The flexible functional forms, which are defined as an approximation of the underlying cost function, have been proposed. Most often, these functions can be viewed as a second order approximation to any arbitrary twice-differentiable cost function and are locally flexible. The generalized Box–Cox (Berndt and Khaled, 1979) belongs to this class. It includes the generalized Leontieff (Diewert, 1971) and generalized square-root quadratic forms as special cases. The translog form (Christensen, Jorgenson and Lau, 1973) appears as a limiting case. A potential problem with these local approximations is that they are 'well-behaved' for only a limited range of relative prices, in the neighbourhood of a point. Outside this specific range, regularity conditions such as positive cost shares and negative own-price elasticities are not satisfied. Many studies of the theoretical properties of various functional forms reveal the limitations of local approximation methods; there is nothing to guarantee that these second-order forms will approximate the underlying cost function or its derivatives over a region of the price space. This may cause some trouble if the model is built for simulation purposes. Imposing concavity on these functions considerably reduces their flexibility. For example imposing concavity constraints on the translog function causes it to collapse to a Cobb–Douglas function. New functional forms, such as the generalized Barnett and McFadden cost functions, in which concavity conditions can be imposed globally, provide an alternative (Diewert and Wales, 1987). These models require many additional parameters. In empirical studies using aggregate time-series data, degrees of freedom are considerably limited, so these functions cannot be used easily.

The Fourier function was introduced by Gallant (1981, 1982, 1984); it is based on a Fourier series expansion form that provides greater flexibility. Furthermore, Gallant (1981) and Gallant and Golub (1984) show that the parametric constraints, which allow testing or imposing certain usual conditions characterizing the producer behaviour (separability and concavity), do not disturb the flexibility of the Fourier form. However, increased flexibility is achieved through a significant increase in the number of parameters and, therefore, it is not clear that the Fourier form provides a practical approximation method in the small samples encountered in most analyses. Furthermore, the Fourier form results in considerable oscillation in estimated elasticities. The cycling of signs and magnitudes of elasticities seem to be unacceptable (Renou-Maissant, 2002). All applied research involves theoretical and empirical trade-offs. The translog function is the most popular because of its ease of use and the quality of results obtained for elasticities in most studies (Griffin, 1977; Pindyck, 1979; Hall, 1986; Taheri, 1994; Renou-Maissant, 1999, 2002).

The use of dynamic adjustment mechanisms with flexible functional forms leads to theoretical and empirical difficulties. The adjustment process must be specified in terms of input shares rather than in input levels, as theory and intuition would suggest. Dynamic optimization is not explicitly taken into account and thus consistency with theory is not assured. In such models, the short-run own-price elasticities may be larger in absolute value than the corresponding long-run own-price elasticities.

Another approach is to specify demand functions that verify, or at least have a potential to verify, the neoclassical assumptions. Considine and Mount (1984) propose, in this context, the linear logit model. Although linear logit models are often associated with discrete choice problems, such as the choice of mode of transport (McFadden, 1974), this model can be used for a variety of empirical problems. In a discrete choice problem, a multinomial logit model is used to represent probabilities in order to ensure that they are non-negative and sum to one. These properties must also hold for shares, and the use of a logit form to represent shares is, therefore, a natural one. Previous models were specified in terms of market shares (Baughman and Joskow, 1976) but these models assume the independence of irrelevant alternatives and lead to substantial restrictions on the elasticities. That seems to be an implausible assumption to employ in the specification of a demand system. The logit model presented by Considine and Mount is not subject to these restrictions because it is specified in terms of cost shares. The logit model has several advantages: cost fuel shares non-negative, concavity and symmetry conditions more easily assured than with the flexible functional forms. In other respects, the logistic function is particularly well suited for incorporating dynamic adjustment mechanisms by including lagged quantities. Recent applications of the logit model can be found in Considine (1989a, 1989b, 1990), Jones (1995, 1996), Moody (1996), Bjorner and Jensen (2002), Urga and Walters (2003) and Brännlund and Lundgren (2004).

Data for French and British industrial sectors

An application of the translog and logit models will be considered in this chapter for analysing interfuel substitution in the industrial sector of two European countries, France and the United Kingdom, between 1978 and

2002. The data used in this study are annual data on total industrial fuel consumption in the non-energy producing industrial sector, excluding the iron and steel industry by reason of its specificity. This choice is motivated by the desire to consider a sector to be as homogeneous as possible. Fuels used by the industrial sector for non-energy purposes, such as coking coal, petrochemical feed-stocks, or lubricants, have few available substitutes. Jones (1995) shows that taking account of non-energy uses in the aggregate consumptions leads one to underestimate elasticity prices.

The fuels under consideration are the four major fuels: steam coal, oil (all petroleum products for energy use), electricity and natural gas. Annual fuel quantity data are collected from the Energy Balance Sheet compiled by the OECD. All quantities are measured in ktoe. The fuel prices, on a heat equivalent basis, are inclusive of taxes and are taken from Energy Prices and Taxes (OECD/IEA). They are measured in national currencies: in euros for France and in pounds sterling for United Kingdom. Only energy consumption and energy prices are necessary to estimate translog and logit models.

Table 7.1 presents market shares of fuels in the industrial energy demand. France and the United Kingdom have very similar energy consumption patterns. Important interfuel substitution occurred on the period 1978–2002. This period is characterized by a drop in oil consumption and an increase in electricity and gas demands. The demand for coal remains low in both countries.

Considering Figure 7.1, which shows the evolution of expenditure shares of fuel in the two countries over the period 1978–2002, strong similarities become apparent. Because of the weak valorization of coal, the expenditure shares of coal are very low; they are, on the average, only 4 per cent for both countries. On the other hand, the strong valorization of electricity leads to high expenditure shares for electricity; on average, electricity held a 54 per cent share in France and 59 per cent in the United Kingdom. With regard to natural gas, the evolution is more contrasted: natural gas benefited from

Table 7.1 Market shares of fuels in France and the United Kingdom

	France			United Kingdom		
(%)	Mean	1978	2002	Mean	1978	2002
Oil	30.6	57.2	20.8	25.5	40.1	22.0
Electricity	30.4	20.5	32.8	25.6	17.7	31.8
Gas	31.0	17.0	41.4	38.3	32.4	42.7
Coal	8.0	5.3	5.0	10.6	9.8	3.5

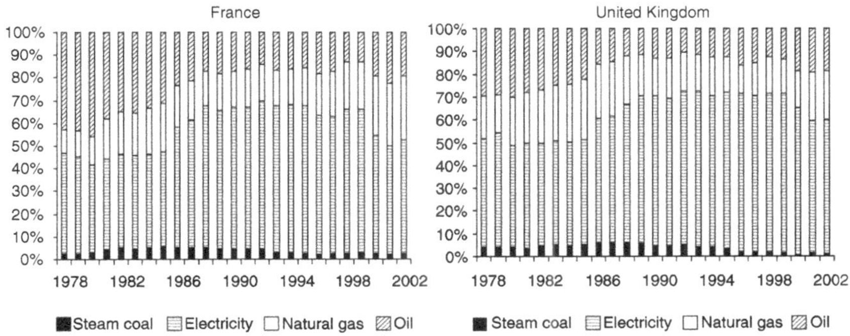

Figure 7.1 Energy cost shares in French and British industrial sectors in per cent

development support in French industry over the entire period whereas it remained stable in the United Kingdom.

The interfuel substitution models

In this section, the translog and linear logit models are presented. Static and dynamic specifications and useful forms for estimation and price elasticities of demand are developed for each model. The aim of this section is to present only the essentials from an empirical point of view; details relating to calculations and demonstrations can be found in pioneer articles.

The translog model

The homothetic translog cost model can be written:

$$LnC = \alpha_0 + \sum_{i=1}^{n} \alpha_i \, LnP_i + \frac{1}{2}\sum_{i=1}^{n}\sum_{j=1}^{n} \beta_{ij} \, LnP_i \, LnP_j \quad i,j = 1,\ldots,n \tag{7.8}$$

where αs and βs are the unknown parameters.

We assume that the cost function is homogeneous of degree one in prices; that implies:

$$\sum_{i=1}^{n} \alpha_i = 1 \tag{7.9a}$$

$$\sum_{j=1}^{n} \beta_{ij} = 0 \tag{7.9b}$$

Assuming cost minimizing behaviour, we may determine the expenditure shares equations by partially differentiating (7.8) with respect to the logarithm of the price of the *i*th fuel under the hypothesis of symmetry ($\beta_{ij} = \beta_{ji}, \forall i \neq j$) and homogeneity of degree one in prices:

$$S_i = \alpha_i + \sum_{j=1}^{n} \beta_{ij}\, LnP_j \quad i = 1, \ldots, n \tag{7.10}$$

The Allen partial elasticities of substitution and the price elasticities of demand can be computed from equations (7.6) and (7.7).

Price elasticities of demand are given by:

$$\eta_{ij} = \frac{\beta_{ij}}{S_i} + S_j \quad \text{when } i \neq j, \quad \eta_{ii} = \frac{\beta_{ii}}{S_i} + S_i - 1 \tag{7.11}$$

This formulation assures that

$$\sum_{j=1}^{n} \eta_{ij} = 0 \quad i = 1, \ldots, n \tag{7.12}$$

As with all flexible forms, the translog form does not impose any restrictions on the Allen partial elasticities of substitution, which vary over time according to S_i. It is also common practice to verify the concavity conditions of the cost function expost by imposing them from the outset, since that prevents exclusion of complementarity between inputs.

An ad hoc dynamic process, which is based on lagged shares is considered:

$$S_{it} = \alpha_i + \sum_{j=1}^{n} \beta_{ij}\, LnP_{it} + \lambda S_{it-1} \quad i = 1, \ldots, n \tag{7.13}$$

where λ is the dynamic rate of adjustment; this parameter is common to all share equations and can be interpreted as the rate of adjustment in total fuel use.

In the long run the model becomes:

$$S_{it} = \frac{1}{1-\lambda}\left[\alpha_i + \sum_{j=1}^{n} \beta_{ij}\, LnP_{jt}\right] \tag{7.14}$$

Long-run price elasticities may also be computed by formula (7.11).

The logit model

The linear logit model of cost shares does not require the specification of a cost function. Under constant returns to scale, there is no theoretical reason requiring the formulation of a cost function because the cost shares yield all the necessary information on the cost structure (Considine, 1989a).

A linear model of input demand can be derived by representing a set of n cost shares by a logistic function. Consider a set of n non-homothetic cost share equations with non-neutral technical changes approximated by a logistic model:

$$S_i = \frac{\exp(f_i)}{\sum_{j=1}^{n} \exp(f_j)} \quad i = 1, \ldots, n \tag{7.15}$$

with the function f specified as:

$$f_i = \eta_i + \sum_{j=1}^{n} c_{ij} \, LnP_j + \varepsilon_i \quad i = 1, \ldots, n \tag{7.16}$$

where η_i and c_{ij} are the unknown parameters and ε_i are random error terms. The predicted shares are guaranteed to be positive and sum to 1, given the exponential form of the logistic function. The necessary conditions of neoclassical demand theory can be imposed by restrictions on the parameters in (7.16) (Considine and Mount, 1984).

Homogeneity of degree zero in prices can be imposed if:

$$\sum_{j=1}^{n} c_{ij} = d \quad \text{for all } i \tag{7.17}$$

where d is an arbitrary constant than can be set to zero. Symmetry conditions can be imposed with the following constraint:

$$c^*_{ij} = c^*_{ji} \quad \text{for all } i \neq j \tag{7.18}$$

$$\text{in which } c^*_{ij} = c_{ij}/S^*_j \quad \text{for all } i \neq j \tag{7.19}$$

where S^*_j are specific cost shares that ensure that the property of symmetry is fulfilled.

In Considine and Mount (1984), local symmetry is imposed by replacing the set of specific cost shares with the time invariant sample averages. But global symmetry may be imposed if the predicted shares are used in the estimation (Considine, 1990). When imposing global symmetry, parameter estimates are obtained through a two-step iterative estimation method, described below.

Using the redefined parameters (7.18) to restate the homogeneity constraint (7.17) and imposing (7.19), the share equation model can be specified as follows:

$$Ln\,(S_i/S_n) = (\eta_i - \eta_n) + \sum_{k=1}^{i-1} (c^*_{ki} - c^*_{kn})\, S^*_k\, Ln(P_k/P_n)$$

$$- \left(\sum_{k=1}^{i-1} S^*_k c^*_{ik} + \sum_{k=i+1}^{n} S^*_k c^*_{ik} + S^*_i c^*_{in} \right) Ln(P_i/P_n)$$

$$+ \sum_{k=i+1}^{n-1} (c^*_{ik} - c^*_{kn})\, S^*_k\, Ln(P_k/P_n) + (\varepsilon_i - \varepsilon_n) \tag{7.20}$$

$$\text{where } S^*_i = \frac{\exp(f_i - f_n)^p}{\sum_{j=1}^{n-1} (\exp(f_i - f_n)^p + 1)} \tag{7.21}$$

and according to (7.15), $(f_i - f_n)^p$ are the predicted logarithmic share ratios from equation (7.20).

The $(\varepsilon_i - \varepsilon_n)$ are assumed to be normally distributed random disturbances. In the two factors case, the linear logit model reduces to a CES input demand function.

The price elasticities are:

$$\eta_{ij} = \left(c^*_{ij} + 1\right) S^*_j \quad \text{when } i \neq j \tag{7.22}$$

$$\eta_{ii} = (c^*_{ii} + 1)\, S^*_i - 1 = - \left(\sum_{k=1}^{i-1} S^*_k c^*_{ki} + \sum_{k=i+1}^{n} S^*_k c^*_{ik} \right) + S^*_i - 1 \tag{7.23}$$

The linear logit model can also be extended to explicitly capture dynamic effects by including lagged quantities, rather than lagged shares (Considine and Mount, 1984). Equation (7.16) becomes:

$$f_{it} = \eta_i + \sum_{j=1}^{n} c_{ij}\, LnP_{jt} + \lambda\, LnQ_{it-1} + \varepsilon_{it} \tag{7.24}$$

This adjustment process insures that long-run elasticities will never be smaller than short-run elasticities and provides a direct estimate of the rate of demand adjustment to price changes. The dynamic version of the linear logit model is:

$$
\begin{aligned}
Ln\,(S_{it}/S_{nt}) = {} & (\eta_i - \eta_n) + \sum_{k=1}^{i-1} \left(c_{ki}^* - c_{kn}^*\right) S_{kt}^* \, Ln(P_{kt}/P_{nt}) \\
& - \left(\sum_{k=1}^{i-1} S_{kt}^* c_{ik}^* + \sum_{k=i+1}^{n} S_{kt}^* c_{ik}^* + S_{it}^* c_{in}^* \right) Ln(P_{it}/P_{nt}) \\
& + \sum_{k=i+1}^{n-1} \left(c_{ik}^* - c_{kn}^*\right) S_{kt}^* \, Ln(P_{kt}/P_{nt}) \\
& + \lambda \, Ln(Q_i/Q_n)_{t-1} + (\varepsilon_{it} - \varepsilon_{nt})
\end{aligned}
\tag{7.25}
$$

which is similar to the static version (7.20), except for the presence of the lagged-quantity ratio terms, whose common coefficient λ measures the rate of dynamic adjustment.

The long-run price elasticities are calculated as:

$$
\eta_{ij}^{LR} = \eta_{ij}/(1 - \lambda) \quad \text{for all } i, j \tag{7.26}
$$

The necessary conditions of symmetry and homogeneity are imposed on all models before estimation. Concavity, a sufficient condition for cost minimization, is not imposed but is tested at the sample mean as well as at each point of the sample. The concavity conditions require that the matrix of second partial derivatives of cost with respect to price be negative and semi-definite. Considine (1990) shows that the eigen values of the matrix are all less than or equal to zero or, equivalently, that the principal minors alternate in sign starting with a negative sign.[1]

Empirical results

In a complete system of demand equations, the expenditure shares sum to one, the disturbance covariance matrix is singular; consequently, for the translog model, one demand equation must be dropped from the system before estimation. Both models have three regression equations and it is likely that their disturbances are correlated. It is, therefore, necessary to use multivariate regression, particularly because joint estimation is the only way of imposing cross equation restrictions on parameters.[2]

An iterative Zellner estimator (1963) for seemingly unrelated regressions is used to obtain the parameter estimates. Berndt and Savin (1975) show that, when the same exogenous variables appear in all equations, the estimation of parameters is invariant with respect to the suppressed equation, provided that the estimation of the variance–covariance matrix of residuals is based on an estimation by OLS, applied successively to each equation. Moreover, an estimator converging to the Maximum Likelihood Estimator is obtained by iterating on the variance–covariance matrix of residuals. For the logit model, parameter estimates are not dependent on the selection of the base input, when using the iterative Zellner estimator. As a first step, we use the actual shares for the endogenous variables S^* that appear on the right-hand side of equation (7.28). This stage yields initial estimates for the coefficients in the cost share equations. The second stage consists of taking the initial predicted cost shares from (7.24), substituting into (7.28) and re-estimating using Zellner's method. The predicted cost shares from this iteration are used on the right hand side of the next estimation of (7.28). This process is repeated until convergence. In this way the linear logit model is guaranteed to be symmetric for all predicted cost shares in the sample. However, symmetry cannot be guaranteed for out of sample forecasts.

The coal demand equation has been dropped in the translog models and coal is the base input for the logit models. Only results concerning the dynamic models are presented here, their superiority compared to the static specifications being clearly established. The standard errors for the dynamic models are substantially lower than those of the static models. Furthermore, for static models, the residuals from each equation indicate the presence of serial correlation.

In the case of France, 71 per cent of the estimated coefficients are not statistically significant in a two-tailed test at the 5 per cent level for the translog model. For the United Kingdom, one notes a stronger level of significance of the estimated coefficients. All except one of the slope coefficients are statistically significant for the logit model. On the other hand, the two specifications reveal a problem of serial correlation in the residuals. The rate of adjustment parameter is always strongly significant for both countries. Long-run price elasticities and concavity conditions are evaluated at the sample mean cost shares and are presented in Table 7.2. Only long-run elasticities are reported because estimated long-run elasticities are very low and it is well known that substitution possibilities among fuels are limited in the short run. The eigen values of the matrix of second partial derivatives of cost are not all less than or equal to zero. Both models violate the concavity conditions at the sample mean and over most of the sample. Moreover, own-price elasticities do not have the right sign: coal own-price elasticity is positive for the two countries and whatever the specification. Electricity own-price elasticity, estimated with the logit model, is also positive. Note that negative own-price elasticities do not necessarily imply concavity, although concavity does imply the former.

The poor performance of these models leads us to exclude coal because coal consumption is very low over the entire period and the market share of coal in the industrial sector remains low despite the fact that its price is competitive. The drop in coal consumption must be explained by the decline in high coal-intensive industries and the emergence of new equipment using gas

Table 7.2 Long-run mean price elasticities for a four-fuels model for the period 1978–2002

	France			
	Steam coal	Electricity	Natural gas	Oil
Translog				
Steam coal	2.48	−1.86	−0.08	−0.54
Electricity	−0.13	0.06	−0.04	0.11
Natural gas	−0.02	−0.13	−0.25	0.39
Oil	−0.08	0.25	0.29	−0.45
Eigenvalues	0.00	0.05	0.15	0.38
Logit				
Steam coal	10.37	−5.92	−5.30	0.85
Electricity	−0.42	0.33	0.12	−0.03
Natural gas	−1.09	0.35	−0.22	0.95
Oil	0.14	−0.07	0.76	−0.82
Eigen values	−0.04	0.00	0.00	0.07
	United Kingdom			
	Steam coal	**Electricity**	**Natural gas**	**Oil**
Translog				
Steam coal	0.09	0.05	0.35	−0.49
Electricity	0.00	−0.10	0.03	0.07
Natural gas	0.07	0.08	−0.38	0.23
Oil	−0.10	0.21	0.24	−0.35
Eigen values	−0.00	0.04	0.07	0.28
Logit				
Steam coal	1.56	−1.64	2.32	−2.24
Electricity	−0.11	0.12	−0.08	0.07
Natural gas	0.46	−0.25	−0.50	0.29
Oil	−0.47	0.21	0.31	−0.05
Eigen values	−0.03	−0.00	0.00	0.03

and electricity in the 1970s and 1980s. Furthermore, coal requires additional handling and room on manufacturing sites, which leads to added production costs. During the 1970s and 1980s, environmental regulations were implemented in response to rising levels of particulates and acid rain precursors. This contributed to the decreases in coal consumption.

The gas demand equation has been dropped in the translog model and gas is the base input for the logit model. For France, many estimated coefficients remain statistically of no significance. For the United Kingdom, all the slope coefficients are statistically significant for all models but the residuals from oil and electricity equations indicate the presence of serial correlation. Results concerning the three-fuels models are presented in Table 7.3. The constraints of concavity are neither checked for France nor for the United Kingdom. For the translog model, all own-price elasticities have the right sign but for the logit model, electricity price elasticity is positive.

Table 7.3 Long run mean price elasticities for a three-fuels model for the period 1978–2002

	France		
	Electricity	**Natural gas**	**Oil**
Translog			
Electricity	−0.05	−0.03	0.08
Natural gas	−0.08	−0.15	0.23
Oil	0.17	0.18	−0.35
Eigen values	−0.00	−0.00	0.14
Logit			
Electricity	0.12	−0.05	−0.07
Natural gas	−0.14	−0.21	0.35
Oil	−0.16	0.26	−0.11
Eigen values	−0.01	−0.00	0.01
	United Kingdom		
	Electricity	**Natural gas**	**Oil**
Translog			
Electricity	−0.07	0.03	0.04
Natural gas	0.08	−0.30	0.22
Oil	0.14	0.23	−0.37
Eigen values	−0.00	0.05	0.28
Logit			
Electricity	0.07	−0.03	−0.04
Natural gas	−0.10	−0.57	0.67
Oil	−0.12	0.71	−0.59
Eigen values	−0.04	0.00	0.01

These results are very disappointing. The usual models do not perform well to explain the substitution which occurred in the French and British industrial sectors. In addition, these results are very different from those published in the literature, since they do not make it possible to highlight the superiority of the logit model over the translog model with regard to theoretical aspects. In fact, the constraints of concavity are not checked. Moreover own-price elasticities do not have the right sign for the logit model. However, the choice of countries, period and type of data used can explain the differences obtained. Most of the studies use older data for the period 1960–90 (Considine and Mount, 1984; Considine, 1989; Jones, 1995, 1996; and Urga and Walters, 2003). The most recent studies use panel data (Bjorner and Jensen, 2002 and Brännlund and Lundgren, 2004); furthermore, few studies

Table 7.4 Long-run mean price elasticities for a four-fuels model for the period 1960–88

	France			
	Steam coal	**Electricity**	**Natural gas**	**Oil**
Translog				
Steam coal	−1.30	0.33	1.47	−0.51
Electricity	0.06	−0.05	−0.15	0.14
Natural gas	0.91	−0.50	−1.00	0.59
Oil	−0.12	0.18	0.23	−0.29
Eigen values	−0.02	0.00	0.00	0.09
Logit				
Steam coal	−2.26	0.53	0.93	0.81
Electricity	0.10	−0.16	−0.23	0.29
Natural gas	0.57	−0.77	−0.03	0.23
Oil	0.19	0.38	0.09	−0.67
Eigen values	−0.04	−0.03	0.00	0.01
	United Kingdom			
	Steam coal	**Electricity**	**Natural gas**	**Oil**
Translog				
Steam coal	−0.63	−0.23	0.95	−0.09
Electricity	−0.05	−0.08	0.04	0.09
Natural gas	0.56	0.11	−0.98	0.31
Oil	−0.03	0.16	0.19	−0.32
Eigen values	−0.01	0.00	0.06	0.16
Logit				
Steam coal	−1.04	0.28	1.00	−0.24
Electricity	0.05	−0.28	−0.04	0.27
Natural gas	0.59	−0.13	−0.65	0.19
Oil	−0.08	0.46	0.11	−0.49
Eigen values	−0.05	−0.03	−0.00	0.00

concern France and the United Kingdom, except in the case of panel data (Jones, 1996). In attempting to make a comparison with previous studies, the models were estimated over the period 1960–88. The data are not completely homogeneous with those based on the period 1978–2002. The prices over the period 1960–78 come from the Baade report (1981). The coefficients are much more significant. The residuals from the translog model and those of the logit model estimated for the United Kingdom are not serially correlated. Results for four-fuels models over this period are presented in Table 7.4. Own-price elasticities have the right sign; the constraints of concavity were checked for the logit model estimated for the United Kingdom whereas concavity has not been verified for the translog model. Moreover, the logit model satisfies the concavity conditions at every data point. These results are similar to those presented in the literature.

Energy market implications

The results obtained show the difficulty in modelling energy substitution and demonstrate that it is particularly difficult to maintain global regularity conditions when estimating the demand for energy. As Waverman (1992) has pointed out, after several decades of empirical investigation, it is still hard to find a complete set of theoretically consistent fuel price elasticity estimates for the industrial sector. All applied research involves theoretical and empirical trade-offs. A compromise must be made concerning the theoretical validity of the model, the statistical quality of the estimates and the economic relevance of estimated elasticities. One of the major criteria for a sensible model of interfuel substitution is having the correct sign for own-price elasticities. For this reason, translog three-fuels model is seen to be the preferred model over the 1978–2002 period. Models perform better for the United Kingdom than for France: most of the estimated coefficients are statistically significant for the United Kingdom, while for France several are not.

The estimates of the adjustment parameter indicate that the adjustment is faster in the United Kingdom than in France. With regard to the translog model for France, less than 20 per cent of the long-run adjustment occurs in the same year as a price change, with 50 per cent of the adjustment being attained about halfway through the period (3.7 years following the year of the price change). For the United Kingdom, 41 per cent of the long-run adjustment occurs in the same year as a price change; the median lag is 1.3 years. This response lag seems quite reasonable for France but is very short for the United Kingdom. The logit model provides slower adjustments, which seem more plausible; in particular the median lag is 4.8 years for France and 4.4 years for the United Kingdom. These results are consistent with the range of 3 to 15 years predicted by Pindyck.

Estimated elasticities are very similar for France and the United Kingdom; they are slightly higher in the United Kingdom. The demand for oil seems to be more sensitive to own-price changes compared to the demand for natural gas and electricity. With regard to the translog three-fuels model, the long-run own-price elasticity for oil ranges from −0.35 to −0.37. The long-run own-price elasticity for natural gas is slightly smaller, ranging from −0.15 to −0.30, while the demand for electricity is the least elastic, with long-run own-price elasticity close to −0.08. Statistically significant substitutability exists but it is generally small in magnitude. Oil and gas and oil and electricity are substitutes. The oil demand is the more elastic; elasticity of oil demand with respect to electricity price varies from 0.14 to 0.17 and elasticity of oil demand with respect to natural gas price varies from 0.18 to 0.23. Gas and electricity are weak substitutes in the United Kingdom while they are weak complements in France. Cross-prices elasticities of electricity demand are very low.

The inelasticity of electricity demand is linked to the specificity of electricity. The period is characterized by the diffusion of new processes using electricity which require important investment to change energy. Multi-fuel equipment allows easy shifts between oil and gas but for electricity it implies additional expensive investments. Finally, the electricity price is an average expost price and does not exactly represent the price paid by firms. High electricity consumers profit from lower prices and have opportunities to negotiate price. Therefore, an average price does not explain a firm's response to electricity price variations.

Whatever the model, all the price elasticities are less than 0.6 in absolute value; they are lower than those estimated by Taheri (1994) and Jones (1995) but closer to those estimated by Urga and Walters (2003) with similar models. Long-run demand is very inelastic. The weakness of elasticities and the fact that many coefficients are not significant would seem to indicate that prices were not the determining factor in the choice of fuels. The poor performance of estimations for France is probably linked to the weakness of price variations for the period 1978–2002. The variability of energy prices measured by the standard deviation has been divided by six for coal, three for electricity and five for natural gas and oil between the two periods 1960–88 and 1978–2002. The energy prices are, thus, not enough to explain the energy substitution that occurred in the industrial sector over the period 1978–2002.

The period 1970–86 is a period of unprecedented price instability in the energy markets, coupled with overwhelming policy-induced pressure to achieve a greater interfuel substitution transition away from oil in French and British industries. The relative stability of oil prices during the 1990s cannot explain the extensive substitution of oil for natural gas and electricity. Moreover, energy generally represents only a small proportion of total costs; it is less than 5 per cent of the total cost in most industrial branches. Prices are not, therefore, essential to the choice of production processes, especially during a period of relative price stability. Finally, until recently, gas and electricity industries were accustomed to operate in an environment protected from competition, which did not *a priori* favour inter-energy competition. The liberalization of energy markets during the nineties had probably led to increased intra-energy competition but had not promoted high inter-energy competition.

Other elements must be taken into account in order to understand the increase in electricity and natural gas consumption. With the oil shocks, France and the United Kingdom initiated deliberate energy policies to improve the efficiency of their economies and diversified both the sources of imported energy and suppliers. These programmes included the emergence of new technologies and processes, modifications of consumer behaviour, and the development of transport and distribution networks for natural gas. Furthermore, during a period of 25 years, the countries experienced dramatic changes in the composition of their industries, with the decline of heavy manufacturing and low-technology industries and the expansion of high-technology industries. These changes in economic activity led to shifts towards less carbon-intensive fuels.

To explain the weakness of price elasticities over the period 1978–2002, one can also refer to the studies carried out during the 1990s, which highlight the asymmetry of the demand for energy with respect to variations of the energy price. They show that the response of energy demand to the fall in energy price of the mid-1980s was much weaker than the response to the increase in the 1970s. The rise in price considerably reduced demand; consumers saved energy and changed energy types. The subsequent collapse of prices did not reverse the process completely. These studies were intended to analyse the responses of demand (energy or oil) to variations of own-prices and did not study energy substitution. The developed models thus do not include potential substitutes' prices and relate to only one equation of demand (total energy or oil), which can bias estimated elasticities. Wirl (1991) and Kaufmann (1994) outline the importance of a memory effect and high price anticipations in the near future to explain the weakness of the growth of energy demand following the fall in oil price. The work of Hassett and Metcalf (1993) also emphasizes the role of future uncertainty on energy prices and the strong price volatility in investment decisions. The irreversibility of technical progress and improvements in energy efficiency as well as the considerable cost of adjustment are extensively considered by Wirl (1991), Walker and Wirl (1993), Gately (1993) and Dargay and Gately (1994, 1995). According to Dargay and Gately, another aspect of the imperfect price reversibility of oil demand is the possibility that adjustments to price increases are not as significant as in the past. The least difficult and least expensive economies and substitutions were already carried out and oil was already replaced by other energies for many uses.

Conclusions

The purpose of this chapter was to estimate how the choice of fuel mix in the industrial sector changes as the relative prices of various fuels changes.

Estimations were carried out using both dynamic translog and linear logit functional forms. This study emphasizes the restricted role of prices for explaining interfuel substitution in the French and British industrial sectors over the period 1978–2002. Statistically significant substitutability exists but it is generally very small in magnitude. Oil and gas and oil and electricity are weak substitutes.

An interesting conclusion from a policy point of view is a strong uncertainty as to what authorities can expect, in the industrial sector alone, from a signal on carbon use in the form of a tax. The weakness of elasticities suggests that it is difficult to obtain reductions in CO_2, and SO_2 emissions from industry by altering the energy source pattern with environmental taxes.

Finally, it is necessary to point out the limits of such modelling. First, the assumption of homothetic separability of the aggregate production function was made in order to be able to estimate an independent energy sub-model. Nevertheless, it seems reasonable to think that variations of oil prices lead to energy substitution but also contribute to reducing the consumption of total energy by substitution among aggregate factors of production. The assumption of separability selected can also explain the weakness of elasticities relating to electricity and the problems of modelling coal. Then aggregation bias must be considered, especially in view of the significant differences among industrial branches. Moreover, a study on an aggregated level (sector) requiring the use of average prices for gas and electricity can mask strong disparities between industrial branches. In this respect, a study of panel data (on the level of branches or companies) could make it possible to better represent energy substitution behaviours. Unfortunately, the lack of micro-data makes such a study difficult.

Notes

1 Details concerning calculations of eigen values can be found in Considine (1990).
2 It is necessary to impose cross equation restrictions on parameters because the same parameters appear in each share equation.

References

Baade, P. (1981) *International Energy Prices 1955–1980*, International Energy Evaluation Systems, United States Department of Energy, December.

Baughman, M. L. and P. L. Joskow (1976), 'Energy Consumption and Fuel Choice by Residential and Commercial Consumers in the United States', *Energy Systems and Policy*, vol. 1, no.4, pp. 305–23.

Berndt, E. R. and M. S. Khaled (1979) 'Parametric Productivity Measurement and Choice among Flexible Functional Forms', *Journal of Political Economy*, vol. 87, no. 6, pp. 220–45.

Berndt, E. R. and N. E. Savin (1975) 'Conflict among Criteria for Testing Hypotheses in the Multivariate Linear Regression Model', *Econometricia*, vol. 45, no. 5, pp. 1263–77.

Bjorner, T. B. and H. H. Jensen (2002) 'Interfuel Substitution within Industrial Companies: An Analysis Based on Panel Data at Company Level', *Energy Journal,* vol. 23, no. 2, pp. 27–50.

Brännlund, R. and T. Lundgren (2004) 'A Dynamic Analysis of Interfuel Substitution for Swedish Heating Plants', *Energy Economics,* vol. 26, pp. 961–76.

Christensen, L. R., D. Jorgenson and L. Lau (1973) 'Transcendental Logarithmic Production Frontiers', *Review of Economics and Statistics,* no. 55 (February), pp. 28–45.

Considine, T. J. and T. D. Mount (1984) 'The Use of Linear Logit Models for Dynamic Input Demand Systems', *Review of Economics and Statistics,* no. 66, pp. 434–43.

Considine, T. J. (1989a) 'Separability, Functional Form and Regulatory Policy in Models of Interfuel Substitution', *Energy Economics,* vol. 11, pp. 89–94.

Considine, T. J. (1989b) 'Estimating the Demand for Energy and Natural Resource Inputs: Trade-Offs in Global Properties', *Applied Economics,* vol. 21, pp. 931–45.

Considine, T. J. (1990) 'Symmetry Constraints and Variable Return to Scale in Logit Models', *Journal of Business and Economic Statistics,* vol. 8, pp. 347–53.

Dargay, J. and D. Gately (1994) 'Oil Demand in the Industrialized Countries', *Energy Journal,* vol. 15, pp. 39–67.

Dargay, J. and D. Gately (1995) 'The Imperfect Price Reversibility of Non-Transport Oil Demand in The Oecd', *Energy Economics,* vol. 17, no.1, pp. 59–71.

Diewert, W. E. (1971) 'An Application of the Shephard Duality Theorem: A Generalized Leontief Production Function', *Journal of Political Economy,* vol. 79 (May), pp. 481–507.

Diewert, W. E. and T. J. Wales (1987) 'Flexible Functional Forms and Global Curvature Conditions', *Econometrica,* vol. 55, no. 1, pp. 43–68.

Gallant, A. R. (1981) 'On the Bias in Flexible Functional Forms and an Essentially Unbiased Form', *Journal of Econometrics,* vol. 15, pp. 211–45.

Gallant, A. R. (1982) 'Unbiased Determination of Production Technologies', *Journal of Econometrics,* vol. 20, pp. 285–323.

Gallant, A. R. (1984) 'The Fourier Flexible Form', *American Agricultural Economics Association,* (May), pp. 204–08.

Gallant, A. R. and G. H. Golub (1984) 'Imposing Curvature Restrictions on Flexible Functional Forms', *Journal of Econometrics,* vol. 26, pp. 295–321.

Gately, D. (1993) 'The Imperfect Price-Reversibility of World Oil Demand', *Energy Journal,* vol. 14, no. 4, pp. 163–82.

Griffin, J. M. (1977) 'Interfuel Substitution Possibilities: A Translog Application to Intercountry Data', *International Economic Review,* vol. 18, no. 3 (October), pp. 755–70.

Hall, V. B. (1986) 'Major OECD Country Industrial Sector Interfuel Substitution Estimates 1960–79', *Energy Economics,* (April), pp. 74–89.

Hassett, K. A. and G. E. Metcalf (1993) 'Energy Conservation Investment. Do Consumers Discount The Future Correctly?' *Energy Policy* (June), pp. 710–16.

Jones, C. T. (1995) 'A Dynamic Analysis of Interfuel Substitution in U.S. Industrial Energy Demand', *Journal of Business and Economic Statistics,* vol. 13, pp. 459–65.

Jones, C. T. (1996) 'A Pooled Dynamic Analysis of Interfuel Substitution in Industrial Energy Demand By The G-7 Countries', *Applied Economics* (July), vol. 28, no. 7, pp. 815–21.

Kaufmann, R. K. (1994) 'The Effect of Expected Energy Prices on Energy Demand: Implications for Energy Conservation and Carbon Taxes', *Resource and Energy Economics,* vol. 16, pp. 167–88.

McFadden, D. A. (1974) 'Conditional Logit Analysis of Qualitative Choice Behavior', in P. Zaremka (ed.), *Frontiers of Econometrics* (New York: Academic Press), pp. 105–43.
Moody, C. E. (1996) 'A Regional Linear Logit Fuel Demand Model for Electric Utilities', *Energy Economics*, vol. 18, pp. 295–314.
Nadiri, M. I. and S. R. Rosen (1969) 'Interrelated Factor Demand Functions', *American Economic Review*, vol. 59, no. 3, pp. 457–71.
Pindyck, R. S. (1979) 'Interfuel Substitution and Industrial Demand for Energy: An International Comparison', *Review of Economics and Statistics*, vol. 61, pp. 169–79.
Renou-Maissant, P. (1999) 'Interfuel Competition in the Industrial Sector of Seven OECD Countries', *Energy Policy*, vol. 27, pp. 99–110.
Renou-Maissant, P. (2002) 'Analyse des Comportements de Substitutions Energétiques dans le Secteur Industriel des Sept Grands Pays de l'OCDE', *Revue Economique*, vol. 53(5), pp. 983–1011.
Taheri, A. A. (1994) 'Oil Shocks and the Dynamics of Substitution Adjustments of Industrial Fuels in the US', *Applied Economics*, vol. 26, pp. 751–6.
Urga, G. and C. Walters (2003) 'Dynamic Translog and Linear Logit Models: A Factor Demand Analysis of Interfuel Substitution in US Industrial Energy Demand', *Energy Economics*, vol. 25, pp. 1–21.
Wales, T. J. (1977) 'On the Flexibility of Functional Forms', *Journal of Econometrics*, vol. 5, pp. 183–93.
Walker, I. O. and F. Wirl (1993) 'Irreversible Price-Induced Efficiency Improvements', *Energy Journal*, vol. 14, pp. 183–205.
Waverman, L. (1992) 'Econometric Modeling of Energy Demand: When are Substitutes Good Substitutes?', in D. Hawdon (ed.), *Energy Demand: Evidence and Expectations* (Academic Press, London).
Wirl, F. (1991) 'Energy Demand and Consumer Price Expectations: An Empirical Investigation of the Consequence of Recent Oil Collapse', *Resource and Energy*, vol. 13, pp. 241–62.
Zellner, A. (1963) 'Estimators for Seemingly Unrelated Regression Equations: Some Exact Finite Sample Results', *Journal of the American Statistical Association*, vol. 58, pp. 977–92.

8

Delineation of Energy Markets with Cointegration Techniques

Régis Bourbonnais and Patrice Geoffron

Presentation of the energy issue: what are the frontiers and internal dynamics of energy markets in a context of liberalization and globalization?

The question of market 'frontiers' is a constant issue in energy economics. The first and second oils shocks, during the 1970s, impacted national economies – to various degrees – in all OECD countries, resulting in a growing globalization of the oil markets or, at least, close links between regional markets. The move towards liberalization of energy markets, starting during the 1980s in the US and progressively reaching Europe, extended this process to all categories of energy and geographical markets. At the same time, improved availability of price information decreased transactions costs and also contributed to integrating energy markets even more than previously. These combined movements explain that research on the delineation of market boundaries and tests of the law of 'one price' are nowadays 'classics' in the field of energy economics.[1]

These works are generally based on cointegration methods that allow the consideration of persistent phenomena: in a stationary world, any shock will finally disappear, while it may leave permanent effects in a non-stationary environment. The presence of price series cointegration between different geographical (or product) markets is evidence of market integration, with a common stochastic trend for prices.

In energy economics, cointegration econometrics has various functionalities:

- For regulators and antitrust authorities, cointegration enables the definition of the relevant market and the appraisal of firms' market power.
- Cointegration tools may improve the definition and the 'fine tuning' of government policies of supply security.
- For industrial firms or financiers, cointegration is appropriate for the analysis of investments between markets (interconnections, capacities of

transport or storage, and so on) or within markets (forecasting of returns on investments).

The organization of the chapter is as follows. The first section presents a review of cointegration methods and an overview of its applications to the field of energy economics. The second section describes the Vector Error Correction Model (VECM)[2] we will use to analyse the integration of national gas markets within the European Union and the next section presents our empirical results. In the final section, these results are discussed and we present our conclusions on the efficiency of cointegration techniques for energy economics.

The econometric methods used for analysing the integration of energy markets

We propose here to discuss the general principles of cointegration analysis and ECM modelling and to review the literature based on such methods in the field of energy economics.

Review of the general principles[3]

In 2003, Robert F. Engle and Clive W. J. Granger were awarded the Nobel Prize for their work on cointegration of time series, especially for a paper they jointly published in 1987.Cointegration is a method designed to distinguish between a long-run and a short-run relationship among variables. As an engineer might separate 'signal' from 'noise', an economist tries to distinguish between a random fluctuation and feedback to equilibrium, an objective that assumes the ability to regress non-stationary variables. But regressing such series may lead to meaningless economic conclusions, qualified as 'spurious'. Spurious regressions accept a false relation ('Type I error') or reject a true relation ('Type II error').

This problem can be solved by using cointegration. Usually, the combination of two non-stationary time series is also non-stationary, but it sometimes leads to stationarity. In such a circumstance, the data are said to be cointegrated. This means that, even if these cointegrated series are individually non-stationary, they will not drift apart without limit.

More precisely, two series x_t and y_t are cointegrated if:

- They share a common stochastic trend of the same order of integration.
- A linear combination of these series leads to a series of lower integration order and with a stationary long-term residual. If this linear transformation exists, the time series are cointegrated, since regression indicates that the difference between the time series varies randomly around a fixed level.

In such a case, it is possible to distinguish between a long-run and a short-run relationship between x_t and y_t. The long-run relationship captures the cointegration, while the short-run relationship describes deviations of x_t and y_t from their trends. The mechanism designed for this differentiation is the error correction model (ECM) (Engle and Granger, 1987). ECM models reveal an error-correction term that describes the speed of adjustment of each series back to long-run equilibrium.

One virtue of ECM is, among others, to eliminate simultaneity bias, observed when there is feedback from the dependent variable to the explanatory variable. If the variables considered are prices for homogeneous goods, the long-run economic relationship reveals that the series are 'included' in a common market. As energy markets commonly organise transactions on rather homogeneous goods, cointegration methods are particularly appropriate in this context. In a complex context, with no evidence of a relationship between variables, a Vector Error Correction Model – the vectorial version of the ECM – is employed. And that is what we intend to do in this chapter.

Literature review: from 'oil' to 'non-oil' market cointegration analyses

The use of cointegration methods in the context of energy debates is originally linked to a controversy over oil market delineation. Many studies have been performed regarding the degree of integration of oil markets (and the interdependence between crude and refined oil markets) and, progressively, cointegration techniques have been extended for the same purpose to electricity, coal and gas markets.

Adelman (1984) originally stated that: 'the world oil market, like the world ocean, is one great pool'. He introduced this 'great pool' concept, because of the degree of integration of the world oil market, that is, the existence of one single market for crude oil as opposed to several regional markets. The aim was to determine to what extent prices might be distorted in one part of the world without influencing prices in other areas. Weiner (1991) challenged this 'great pool' scheme with correlation and regression techniques applied to price adjustment on crude oil monthly data. His starting point is that long-term contracts would not be necessary within the limits of an integrated market. He concludes that the world oil market is far from completely unified and points out that these findings could be due to the ability of sellers to engage in price discrimination. His results are consistent with efforts of many importing countries to seek arrangements for 'secure supply' from exporters, contracts that are without strategic utility in a global market.

Many researchers have tried to determine whether Adelman's or Wiener's interpretation was the more consistent. Sauer (1994), by means of a VECM and innovative accounting (impulse response analysis and variance decomposition), finds that Weiner's approach implies an adjustment over a far too short period (one month) for determining the integration of markets, but that adjustments may continue for as much as five months. More correctly,

Sauer underlines shortcomings in using correlation analysis for such applications: in markets combining more than two regions, bivariate correlation analysis may be influenced by effects coming from other parts, so that they become inappropriate for recognizing feedback effects.

Ripple and Wilamoski (1998) argue that Weiner failed to account for greater price transparency following the introduction of crude oil futures contracts. They examine the implications of these contracts using tests of cointegration and VECM models to estimate the speed of adjustment coefficients and variance decompositions. They confirm that crude-oil market integration increased with the development of futures and spot markets and they highlight the growing importance of the US market in influencing prices in other areas.

Gülen (1997) also clearly indicates that, despite the existence of long-term contracts, the oil market is, nevertheless, unified and prices do not deviate for the same quality of crude oil from different regions (over the 1980–95 period). Gülen (1999) proposes a comparison of two sub-periods for complementary results. Even if Weiner's intuition of regionalization is still rejected, it is interesting that local prices tend to deviate more during periods of rising prices. The explanation is that during a period of surging global demand, there is a greater economic rationale to substitute crude of different qualities.

In addition, research has been designed to test the long-run relationship between crude oil and refined product prices in the US or in Europe, from Serletis (1994) to Asche *et al.* (2003). More recently Lanza *et al.* (2005) consider ten price series of crude oil and fourteen price series of petroleum products for Europe and the Americas. They check to see if an ECM is appropriate for anticipating the evolution of crude oil prices, rather than a model in first differences, which does not include any cointegration relationship, but find mixed results depending on the area considered.

As of the late 1990s, cointegration analyses have been extended to every category of energy. For electricity, De Vany and Walls (1999) use a VECM to provide evidence of cointegration among eleven regional markets in the US. Note that Haldrup and Nielsen (2006) preferred a Markov switching fractional integration model to analyse the Nordic power exchange (Nord Pool), because the dynamics of the market can differ in a context of congestion. Without congestion, prices are fractionally cointegrated in the sense that their differences are equal to zero, but in a congestion state, bivariate prices can be fractionally cointegrated in a more conventional way or the prices can appear not to cointegrate. This choice is due to the fact that the standard Vector Error Correction Model (VECM) usually assumes a constant co-integration space.[4]

For the coal industry, Wårell (2006) tests the existence of a unique market by analysing whether Japanese and European prices are cointegrated between 1980 and 2000 and, separately, during the 1980s and the 1990s with ECM models. The results – both for coking coal and steam coal – indicate the existence of a world market for the global period, but show that the steam coal market cannot be considered cointegrated in the 1990s, probably as a consequence of the market power of merged companies.

With respect to gas, the literature has long been limited to the regional level. Most of the studies (De Vany and Walls, 1995; Serletis, 1997; and Serletis and Herbert, 1999) have been centred on the North American market, showing increasing price integration as liberalisation proceeded in the 1980s. The literature on Europe remains sparse (which is why we will later propose an application in this area). The most interesting work is probably Asche *et al.* (2002) that focuses on German imports, with an examination of beach prices from Russia, Norway and the Netherlands in the period 1990–98. Their cointegration tests show that prices move proportionally over time, so that the Law of One Price holds.

In a more global perspective, Siliverstovs *et al.* (2005) try to determine if the regional areas evolved into a global market, as an emulation of the world oil markets. Traditionally, three main regional gas markets are delineated, resulting in a lack of pipeline infrastructure and insufficient availability of liquefied natural gas (LNG) transport capacity: Europe, North America and Japan/South Korea. The main findings of Siliverstovs *et al.* suggest that integration of trans-Atlantic gas markets has not taken place, whereas regional markets in Continental Europe and North America are highly integrated and the European and Japanese markets are integrated.

A method to determine the integration of national gas markets in Europe

Error correction models have thus gained increased support for estimations of market integration in energy industries. We now propose to enter into technical detail with the development of a VECM dedicated to examination of market integration in the European gas market. In this section we will, first of all, explain the interest in determining the degree of integration of national gas markets within the EU and then discuss in detail a VECM.

Issues regarding the homogeneity of European national gas markets

Astonishingly, little attention has been paid to the integration of national gas markets within the European Union. Even Asche *et al.* (2002), whose paper is entitled 'European market integration for gas?' do not consider this issue, as their research is, in fact, centred on imports into the German market from various origins. Despite this, it would be interesting to now consider the building of the 'European gas economic area'. This interest is, at least, threefold.

Firstly, the internal dynamics of gas markets are particularly complex because of the imbrications of long-term contracts. The logic of long-term take-or-pay gas sales contracts is based on the sellers' need to secure suppliers before engaging sunk costs into extraction or transportation facilities, and the buyers' need to secure their supply. Even if the spot markets leave some space to more 'pure' market mechanisms, the economic logic of long-term contracts determines the price equilibria. This situation is evolving with liberalization: in the most advanced countries, like the UK and the US, the share of long-term contracts remains above 50 per cent. But, mainly, Europe is today a 'kaleidoscope' of indexation price rules.

Secondly, the question of the homogeneity of the European market is of high policy relevance. Given the low carbon dioxide emissions, natural gas is likely to take a larger part in the energy mix in Europe. According to the IEA, the share of natural gas in the primary energy demand is expected to increase from 23 per cent to 32 per cent in 2020. With indigenous gas reserves declining in the Netherlands, most gas imports will come from Russia, Norway and Algeria, even if Europe is in a favourable situation with close to 80 per cent of the world reserves within economic transportation reach (see Figure 8.1).

Thirdly (and most important) Europe is progressively experiencing structural changes by introducing a new regulatory framework. The Directive 2003/55/EC concerning common rules for the internal market in natural

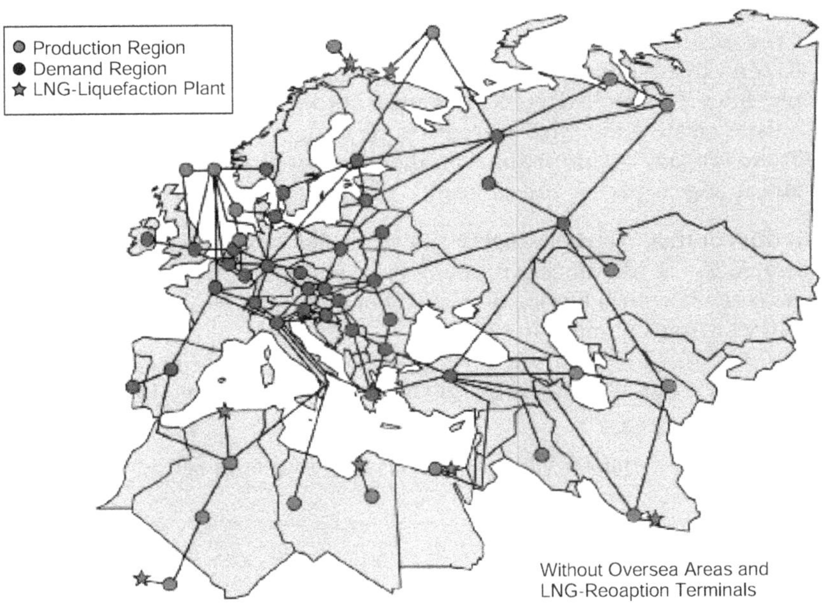

Figure 8.1 Gas network and interconnection map of Europe

Source: Seeliger and Perner (2004).

gas is a major step. These rules concern non-discriminatory network access, operation of the transmission and distribution systems (operated through legally separate entities where vertically integrated undertakings exist) and specification of the functions of the regulatory authorities. These redefinitions of the rules are accompanied by a movement towards privatization of public incumbents.

But this process of integration is still in its infancy, with an absence of price convergence across the EU and a rather low level of cross-border trade. For example, price differences for industrial users are close to 100 per cent between the most and the least expensive countries. However, wholesale price levels have started to converge in some neighbouring countries and the development of regional markets, as an intermediate step, is plausible.

Nevertheless, the preliminary report on the inquiry conducted by the European Commission on the electric and gas market foresees a very severe outlook for the EU with area dysfunctions:[5]

- At the wholesale stage, a high level of concentration is maintained, the incumbent firms remaining dominant in their traditional markets.
- In spite of the EU rules on third party access and on unbundling, new entrants lack effective access to networks. Contracts between producers and incumbents restrain the capacity of incoming firms to access gas in the upstream markets.
- Cross-border sales do not exert competitive pressure, as available capacity on cross-border import pipelines is limited. The capacity of transit pipelines is controlled by incumbents and congestion management mechanisms create difficulties in securing even small volumes on short-term.
- There is a lack of information on the markets: access to networks, transit and storage capacity, and so forth.

In this context, our econometric analysis in the next section will be mainly dedicated to the identification of any progress in the growth of integration of gas markets within Europe on a global or a regional basis (that is, between countries with a common frontier).

Presentation and specifications of the vector error correction model

Dynamics and VECM

Assume a representation VAR(p) in k variables in matrix form:

$$Y_t = A_0 + A_1\ Y_{t-1} + A_2\ Y_{t-2} + \cdots + A_p\ Y_{t-p} + \varepsilon \text{ with:}$$

Y_t : vector in $(k \times 1)$ dimensions made up of the k variables $(y_{1t}, y_{2t}, \ldots, y_{kt})$,

A_0 : vector of dimension $(k \times 1)$,

A_i : matrix of dimension $(k \times k)$

This model can be written in primary differences in two ways:

$$\Delta Y_t = A_0 + (A_1 - I)\Delta Y_{t-1} + (A_2 + A_1 - I)\Delta Y_{t-2} \\ + \cdots + (A_{p-1} + \cdots + A_2 + A_1 - I)\Delta Y_{t-p+1} + \pi Y_{t-p} + \varepsilon$$

or else as a function of Y_{t-1}:

$$\Delta Y_t = A_0 + B_1 \Delta Y_{t-1} + B_2 \Delta Y_{t-2} + \cdots + B_{p-1} \Delta Y_{t-p+1} + \pi Y_{t-1} + \varepsilon$$

the matrices B_i being functions of the matrices A_i and $\pi = (\sum_{i=1}^{p} A_i - I)$.

This representation corresponds to a VECM 'Vector Error Correction Model'.

The matrix π can be written in the form $\pi = \alpha\ \beta'$ where the vector α is the return force towards equilibrium and β is the vector whose elements are the coefficients of the long-term relations among the variables. Each linear combination represents, therefore, a cointegration relation.

If all the elements of π are zero (the rank of the matrix π is equal to 0 and, therefore, $A_{p-1} + \cdots + A_2 + A_1 = I$), then we cannot retain an error correction specification. If the rank of π is equal to k, it is then implied that all the variables are $I(0)$ and the problem of cointegration does not occur (the estimation of the level VAR model is identical with the estimation of the difference VAR model).

If the rank of the matrix π (noted r) lies between 1 and $k-1$ $(1 \leq r \leq k-1)$, then there are r relations of cointegration and the ECM representation is valid so that:

$$\Delta Y_t = A_0 + B_1 \Delta Y_{t-1} + B_2 \Delta Y_{t-2} + \cdots + B_{p-1} \Delta Y_{t-p+1} + \alpha\ e_{t-1} + \varepsilon$$

$$\text{with } e_t = \beta' Y_t$$

The rank of the π matrix determines the number of cointegration relations. Johansen (1988) proposes a test based on the proper vectors corresponding to the highest proper values of the π matrix.

Progress of the estimation test

We can synthesize the major steps associated with the estimation of a VECM model:

- *Step 1*: Determination of the number of lags p in the model according to the AIC or SC criterion on the level VAR.
- *Step 2*: Estimation of the π matrix and the Johansen test making it possible to know the number of cointegration relations.
- *Step 3*: Identification of the cointegration relations, that is to say, the long-term relations between the variables.

- *Step 4*: Estimation by the maximum likelihood method of the vectorial error correction model (test of the significance of the validation coefficients of the representation).

Results of the VECM for the industrial gas market in Europe

We start by presentating our data on industrial gas prices to end-users over the 1991–2005 period and then in the next section proceed to the determination of the integration order of the variables. We then make various cointegration bivariate tests for the whole period and for two sub-periods and, finally, propose a VECM centred on the relationship between the German and the French markets. The results obtained will be discussed in detail in the next section.

Presentation of the data

We have chosen data provided by Eurostat, biannually from 1991 to 2005 (see Figure 8.2). Variables are prices before taxes in euros per MWh. To anticipate market movements it is preferable to consider the industrial rather than household use of gas, as price determinations leave more space for market mechanisms in the industrial case. A 'hypothetical firm' is built with a consumption profile of 11.63 GWh per year. Six main national markets have been selected, each one being interconnected to at least one of the five other

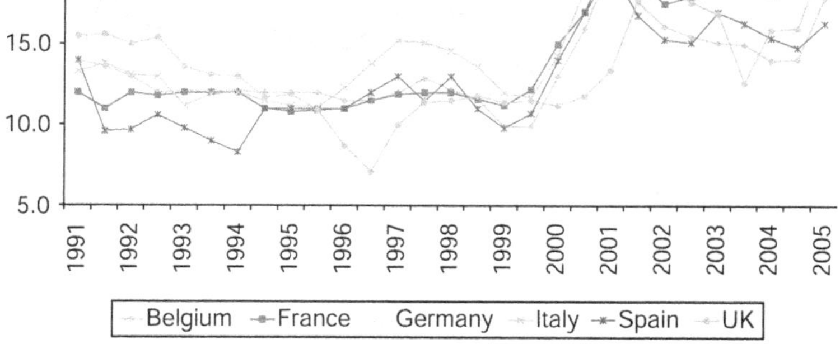

Figure 8.2 Biannual evolution of the price of gas for industrial use (in €/MWh before taxes)

Source: EUROSTAT.

countries (see Figure 8.1). To fix orders beyond these six markets, note that the mean in the EU 15 was, for the first semester of 2005, 21.1 €/MWh, the maximum being 29.1 € in Sweden and the minimum 16.2 € in the Netherlands.

Obviously, direct observation of the data is sufficient to conclude, roughly, that there is an absence of global convergence inside a narrow band of prices. Of course, as gas import contracts use variable indexation rules, wholesale price variations as well as end-user prices are not simply the result of changes on the supply or the demand side. However, cointegration techniques are precisely designed to capture more intimate links between variables. That is what we intend to illustrate.

Integration order of the variables

This first step is to determine the stochastic properties of the variables: stationary process, DS or TS type non-stationary process (see Chapter 3). In fact, the cointegration problem only exists in the DS type non-stationary processes.

The Dickey–Fuller, Augmented Dickey–Fuller and Phillips–Perron tests are carried out on previously transformed series by passage to logarithms.[6]

We have put into practice the sequential test strategy in order to determine the type of underlying process. Table 8.1 sums up the results relative to the model with constant term (the other models without constant terms or with deterministic trends not being significant).

Table 8.1 Dickey–Fuller and Phillips–Perron unit root tests (model with constant)

	Dickey–Fuller test *t* statistic Critical probability	Phillips–Perron test *t* statistic Critical probability
Belgium	−2.08 25%	−1.36 58%
France	0.15 96%	0.09 95%
Germany	−1.49 52%	−1.43 55%
Italy	−1.09 69%	−1.22 64%
UK	−1.16 67%	−1.29 61%
Spain	−1.46 53%	−1.52 50%

The first column shows the results of the simple or Augmented Dickey–Fuller tests when the lags are significant, according to the Schwarz information criterion: Italy = 2 lags, Germany and Belgium = 1 lag.

The Phillips–Perron test results are shown in the second column (truncation = 2).

Beneath each of the t statistics the H_0 hypothesis critical probabilities are shown for the existence of a unit root. Examining the results, we conclude that the series are non-stationary (H_0 hypothesis rejected). It is a DS type process without constant; the order of integration of gas prices is, therefore, $I(1)$.

Note that the study of the correlograms of the series in first differences shows that all of the difference series are white noise processes, with the exception of Italy.

The annual evolution of the price of gas for these five European countries follows, therefore, a random walk model, which means that it is impossible to make predictions.

Cointegration bivariate tests for 1991–2005

The price series being type $I(1)$ integrated, the existence of a cointegration vector is possible. We therefore resort to the Johansen–Juselius test and, in view of the preceding data and the results obtained using the second specification, tests with other specifications and different numbers of lags confirm the robustness of the results.

The critical value for a threshold of 5 per cent is equal to 19.96 for the H_0 hypothesis : $r = 0$ against $H_1 : r > 0$. There are, therefore, only two cointegration relations between the gas prices in two countries (see Table 8.2).

- Belgium – France (weakly).
- Germany – France.

Since the annual evolutions of gas prices in Spain, Italy and the UK are not cointegrated among themselves, we can, therefore, conclude that the gas markets themselves are also independent for these countries. On the other hand, we observe

Table 8.2 Synthesis of Johansen–Juselius cointegration test results

	Belgium	**France**	**Germany**	**Italy**	**Spain**	**UK**
Belgium						
France	21.96					
Germany	12.78	28.91				
Italy	12.50	13.81	8.60			
Spain	12.03	11.00	10.96	19.20		
UK	15.41	11.49	12.87	7.92	10.42	

Source: EViews.

strong integration, over the period considered, between the gas markets of Germany and France and, to a lesser extent, between Belgium and France.

On the basis of these first results, we now propose to divide the analysis into two periods, one between 1991–98 and the other between 1999–2005 and then to estimate a VECM to analyse in more detail the relation between France and Germany.

Bivariate cointegration tests for 1991–98 and 1999–2005

A similar test conducted for the period 1991–98 leads to the following results (see Table 8.3)

The critical value for a threshold of 5 per cent is equal to 19.96 for the H_0 hypothesis : $r = 0$ against $H_1 : r > 0$. There are, therefore, only two weakly significant cointegration relations between the gas prices of two countries, shown in italics in the table:

- Belgium – UK.
- Germany – UK.

Table 8.3 Synthesis of the Johansen–Juselius cointegration tests (period 1991–98)

	Belgium	France	Germany	Italy	Spain	UK
Belgium						
France	19.52					
Germany	19.78	17.23				
Italy	18.42	13.76	11.03			
Spain	10.48	14.66	6.17	10.50		
UK	22.50	9.14	21.10	15.86	7.84	

Source: EViews.

Since the annual evolution of gas prices in Spain, Italy and France are not cointegrated, we can, therefore, conclude that the gas markets, for the period 1991–98, are also independent for these countries.

A second study deals with the period 1999–2005 for which Table 8.4 shows a synthesis of results.

The critical value for a threshold of 5 per cent is equal to 19.96 for the H_0 hypothesis : $r = 0$ against $H_1 : r > 0$. There are, therefore, only two cointegration relations between the gas prices in two countries (see Table 8.4).

- France – Italy
- France – Germany
- France – Spain
- Germany – Spain
- UK – Spain

Table 8.4 Synthesis of Johansen–Juselius cointegration tests (period 1999–2005)

	Belgium	France	Germany	Italy	Spain	UK
Belgium						
France	18.69					
Germany	9.26	23.51				
Italy	17.84	25.15	22.55			
Spain	15.09	20.80	17.61	15.55		
UK	17.11	13.34	19.29	19.49	25.24	

Source: EViews.

Note that, since 1999, the integration of the European markets in terms of price is much stronger.

Estimation of a VECM for Germany and France

Knowing that there is a cointegration relation between gas prices between Germany and France over the entire period 1991–2005 and that this relation is unique (by its intensity) in Europe, we can, therefore, estimate a Vectorial Error Correction Model (VECM).

Estimation of the number of lags in the VAR

We calculate the Akaike (AIC) and Schwarz (SC) information criteria on the level VAR for three lags; the criteria are minimal for 2 lags. The VECM is, therefore, estimated with a single lag (see Table 8.5)

Table 8.5 Number of VAR lags

Lag	3	2	1
AIC	−4.740639	−5.088105	−4.194355
SC	−4.063202	−4.608166	−3.908883

Source: EViews.

Following are the estimation results (see Table 8.6)

The residual derived from the long-term relation is white noise.

We can see that the quality statistic of the long-term relation is very significant (Student's $t = 17.47$).

The coefficients of the dynamic model are almost all significant and the coefficient (−0.94) of the return term really has the expected negative sign and is significantly different from 0. The correlogram of the residuals shows them to be Gaussian white noise. The error correction representation is validated.

Table 8.6 Estimation of the France–Germany VECM (1992–2005)

Cointegrating Eq:	**CointEq1**	
LGERMANY(-1)	1.000000	
LFRANCE(-1)	−0.833354 (0.04768) [−17.4790]	
C	−0.728293	
Error Correction:	**D(LGERMANY)**	**D(LFRANCE)**
CointEq1	−0.949317 (0.19143) [−4.95907]	−0.866118 (0.20084) [−4.31249]
D(LGERMANY(-1))	0.319239 (0.13155) [2.42677]	0.376047 (0.13801) [2.72469]
D(LFRANCE(-1))	0.291462 (0.23557) [1.23725]	−0.510111 (0.24715) [−2.06397]
C	−0.000177 (0.01134) [−0.01561]	0.028229 (0.01190) [2.37210]

Note: Standard errors in ( ) & *t*–statistics in []

Source: EViews.

Comments on the results: an integration process yet to be achieved

Our results confirm that cointegration analysis is efficient for highlighting more subtle relationships between variables than those bounded by correlation procedures and that it is appropriate for overcoming the problem of 'spurious' regression.

Considering the European gas region, the main results that deserve comment are, from our point of view, the following:

i) The principal national gas markets do not form any kind of 'pool' over the entire 1991–2005 period. Such an observation is not surprising, since we know that the DG Energy (2006) inquiry – at the end of the period under review – leads to the conclusion that there is little space for market mechanisms in the European gas area, for technical reasons (capacity of transport and storage) as well as economic reasons (market power of incumbents). Over the long run, the relationship between the German and the French markets is the only one that presents a significant profile of cointegration (and, to a lesser degree, the Belgian and German markets). This intimate link between France and Germany is confirmed by the results of the VECM.

ii) To present an analysis with more contrast, we have separately treated the periods 1991–98 and 1999–2005. Our object was to determine whether differences in terms of cointegration are observable before and after 1998. Indeed, this year was the (prudent) starting point for liberalization with the Directive 98/30/EC of the European Parliament and of the Council concerning 'common rules for the internal market in natural gas', that was a precursor to the Directive 2003/55/EC. 1998 also marks the opening of the UK–Belgium inter-connector gas pipeline, establishing a relationship between gas markets that were previously independent of one another. Our conclusions are somewhat reserved, because the amount of data for each period is rather limited (about fifteen observations for each sub-period). Without pushing our conclusions too far, however, we see that the period 1999–2005 shows more cointegrated relationships than previously (2 against 6). We will not try to infer a more precise conclusion on the 'peer-to-peer' relationship, that is, on the specific links between two national markets in the latter period. However, these results may indicate more common trends after 1998 than before.

iii) The explanations of the heterogeneity that continues, roughly, to prevail in Europe, are to be found in three domains. Firstly, import strategies present diversity. For example, in 2004 the UK imported 80 per cent from Norway and Spain, 57 per cent from Algeria. Secondly, indexation rules are also diverse and, thirdly, local market powers have a strong influence on price levels. Wholesale trading is characterized by *de facto* monopolies (for example, Gaz de France in France, ENI in Italy, ENAGAS in Spain) or by a very narrow oligopoly (for example, E.ON-Ruhrgas, RWE and Wintershall in Germany) which allows room for strategic behaviour.

iv) The persistent differences in terms of gas prices for industrial use are a real trade issue in the internal market. As mentioned before, the current state of the gas markets in the EU leads to differences of 100 per cent between the most expensive and the least expensive countries. This situation impacts the production costs of European firms. Similar differences also may be observed for electricity, but they sometimes reflect local choices in terms production techniques (in particular, the nuclear part). As for gas, European countries are importers; the hypothesis that the market power of national incumbents plays a greater role in the persistent heterogeneity of national markets should be considered carefully and tested.

v) According to the IEA, global gas consumption will increase by more than 95 per cent by the year 2030 and Europe will not be a part of this general process. That means that the current situation of acute independence of markets will be profoundly modified in the next decade, for regulatory reasons with the increasing influence of the 2003 gas Directive and because the growth of demand will impact import strategies and technologies. From that point of view, Liquefied Natural Gas seems to be the most reasonable and effective option to increase supply diversification and to reduce bottlenecks in the pipeline network and storage capacity.

Conclusion

Recourse to cointegration tests is a classical econometric procedure whenever it is a question of testing for the presence of long-term equilibrium relations. The idea that a long-term equilibrium relation can be defined between variables that are, nevertheless, individually non-stationary is the basis of the theory of cointegration. The existence of such an equilibrium relation is tested with the aid of statistical procedures, of which the most useful are those of Engle and Granger (1987) and of Johansen (1988). We have shown in this chapter that the approach, in terms of cointegration and recourse to the ECM, are commonly used in the area of energy economy to determine the interrelationships between markets, starting 'historically' with oil, but then extending to the ensemble of primary energy prices. We have decomposed the method by applying it to the integration of European gas markets with results that illustrate the weak degree of cointegration of national markets and the relative evolution of this phenomenon with the deregulation to which the European authorities are committed.

Notes

1 Observed when relative prices are constant.
2 See also Chapter 6.
3 A more extensive development of cointegration is presented in Chapter 4.
4 Thus Haldrup and Nielsen show that even in a context of highly liberalized markets there is scope for authorities to closely monitor market behaviour, as the relevant market boundaries evolve with congestion. Consequently, a single player (or a group of players) can have huge market power and extract rents due to congestion.
5 DG Energy (2006) 'Sector Inquiry under Art 17 Regulation 1/2003 on the Gas and Electricity Markets', Preliminary Report, European Commission.
6 See Chapter 3 for a detailed presentation of the Dickey–Fuller tests.

References

Adelman, M.A. (1984) 'International Oil Agreements', *Energy Journal*, vol. 5, pp. 1–9.

Andreadis, I. and Serletis, A. (2004) 'Random Fractal Structures in North American Energy Markets', *Energy Economics*, vol. 26, pp. 389–99.

Asche, F., Gjølberg, O. and Volker, T. (2003) 'Price Relationships in The Petroleum Market: An Analysis of Crude Oil and Refined Product Prices', *Energy Economics*, vol. 25, pp. 289–301.

Asche, F., Osmundsen, P. and Tveter, R. (2002) 'European Market Integration for Gas? Volume Flexibility and Political Risk', *Energy Economics*, vol. 24, 249–65.

Chen, L.H., Finney, M. and Lai, K.S. (2005) 'A Threshold Cointegration Analysis of Asymmetric Price Transmission from Crude Oil to Gasoline Prices', *Economic Letters*, vol. 89, pp. 233–39.

De Vany, A.S. and Walls, W.D. (1995) *The Emerging New Order in Natural Gas – Market Versus Regulation* (Westport, CN: Quorum Books).

De Vany, A.S. and Walls, W.D. (1999) 'Cointegration Analysis of Spot Electricity Prices: Insights on Transmission Efficiency in the Western US', *Energy Economics*, vol. 21, pp. 435–48.

DG Energy (2006) 'Sector Inquiry under Art. 17 Regulation 1/2003 in the Gas and Electricity Market', European Commission, 16 February 2006.

Engle, R.F. and Granger, C.W.J. (1987) 'Co-integration and Error Correction Representation, Estimation, and Testing', *Econometrica*, vol. 55, pp. 251–76.

Gülen, S.G. (1997) 'Regionalization in the World Crude Oil Market', *Energy Journal*, vol. 18, pp. 106–79.

Gülen, S.G. (1998) 'Efficiency in the Crude Oil Futures Market', *Journal of Energy Finance and Development*, vol. 3, pp. 13–21.

Gülen, S.G. (1999) 'Regionalization in the World Crude Oil Market: Further Results', *Energy Journal*, vol. 20, no. 1, pp. 125–39.

Haldrup, N. and Nielsen, M.Ø. (2006) 'A Regime Switching Long Memory Model for Electricity Prices', *Journal of Econometrics*, vol. 135, pp. 349–76.

Hendry, D.F. and Juselius, K. (2000) 'Explaining Cointegration Analysis: Part I', *Energy Journal*, vol. 21, pp. 1–42.

Hendry, D.F. and Juselius, K. (2001) 'Explaining Cointegration Analysis: Part II', *Energy Journal*, vol. 22, pp. 75–120.

Hua, P. (1998) 'On Primary Commodity Prices: The Impact of Macroeconomic/Monetary Shocks', *Journal of Policy Modeling*, vol. 20, pp. 767–90.

Indjehagopian, J.P., Lantz, F. and Simon, V. (2000) 'Dynamics of Heating Oil Market Prices in Europe', *Energy Economics*, vol. 22, pp. 225–52.

Johansen, S. (1988) 'Statistical Analysis of Cointegrating Vectors', *Journal of Economic Dynamics and Control*, vol. 12, pp. 231–54.

Johensen, S. and Juselius, K. (1990) 'Maximum Likehood Estimation and Inference on Cointegration with Application to the Demand for Money', *Oxford Bulletin of Economics and Statistics*, vol. 52, pp. 169–209.

Juncal, C. and Perez De Gracia, F. (2003) 'Do Oil Price Shocks Matter? Evidence for Some European Countries', *Energy Economics*, vol. 25, pp. 137–54.

Lanza, A., Manera, M. and Giovannini, M. (2005) 'Modeling and Forecasting Cointegrated Relationships among Heavy Oil and Product Prices', *Energy Economics*, vol. 27, no. 6, pp. 831–48.

Lien, D. and Root, T.H. (1995) 'Convergence to the Long-Run Equilibrium: The Case of Natural Gas Markets', *Energy Economics*, vol. 21, pp. 95–110.

Modjtahedi, B. and Movassagh, N. (2005) 'Natural-Gas Futures: Bias, Predictive Performance, and he Theory of Storage', *Energy Economics*, vol. 27, pp. 617–37.

Narayan, P.K. and Smyth, R. (2005) 'The Residential Demand for Electricity in Australia: An Application of the Bounds Testing Approach to Cointegration', *Energy Policy*, vol. 33, pp. 467–74.

Panagiotidis, T. and Rutledge, E. (2004) 'Oil and Gas Market in the UK: Evidence from a Cointegration Approach', mimeo.
Ramanathan, R. (1999) 'Short- and Long-Run Elasticities of Gasoline Demand in India: an Empirical Analysis Using Cointegration Techniques', *Energy Economics*, vol. 21, pp. 321–30.
Rautava, J. (2004) 'The Role of Oil Prices and the Real Exchange Rate in Russia's Economy – A Cointegration Approach', *Journal of Comparative Economics*, vol. 32, pp. 315–27.
Ripple, R.D. and Wilamoski, P. (1998) 'Is the World Oil Market "One Great Pool"?: Revisited, Again', *Portland School of Finance and Business Economics Working Paper Series*, vol. 98, p. 19.
Root, T.H. and Lien, D. (2003) 'Can Modelling The Natural Gas Futures Market as a Threshold Cointegrated System Improve Hedging and Forecasting Performance?', *International Review of Financial Analysis*, vol. 12, pp. 117–33.
Sauer, D.G. (1994). 'Measuring Economic Markets for Imported Crude Oil', *Energy Journal*, vol. 2, pp. 107–23.
Seeliger, A. and Perner, J. (2004) 'Prospects of Gas Supplier to the European Market until 2030 – Results from the Simulation Model EUGAS', *Utilities Policy*, vol. 12, no. 4, pp. 291–302.
Serletis, A. (1994) 'A Cointegration Analysis of Petroleum Future Prices', *Energy Economics*, vol. 16, no. 2, pp. 93–7.
Serletis, A. (1997) 'Is there an East–West Split in North American Natural Gas Markets?', *Energy Journal*, vol. 1, pp. 47–62.
Serletis, A. and Herbert, J. (1999) 'The Message in North American Energy Prices', *Energy Economics*, vol. 21, pp. 471–83.
Serletis, A. and Rangel-Ruiz, R. (2004) 'Testing for Common Features in North American Energy Markets', *Energy Economics*, vol. 26, pp. 401–14.
Shawkat, H. and Choi, K. (2006) 'Behavior of GCC Stock Markets and Impacts of US Oil and Financial Markets', *Research in International Business and Finance*, vol. 20, no. 1, pp. 22–44.
Shawkat, H., Dibooglu, S. and Aleisa, E. (2004) 'Relationships among US Oil Prices and Oil Industry Equity Indices', *International Review of Economics and Finance*, vol. 13, pp. 427–53.
Siliverstovs, B., L'Hégaret, G., Neumann, A. and Von Hirschhausen, C. (2005) 'International Market Integration for Natural Gas?', *Energy Economics*, vol. 27, pp. 603–15.
Wårell, L. (2006) 'Market Integration in the International Coal Industry: A Cointegration Approach', *Energy Journal*, vol. 27, no. 1, pp. 99–118.
Weiner, R. (1991) 'Is the World Oil Market One Great Pool', *Energy Journal*, vol. 12, pp. 95–107.

9
The Relationship between Spot and Forward Prices in Electricity Markets

Carlo Pozzi

Introduction

The functional relationship linking spot and forward power prices has been long debated. In this chapter, we rely on a modified interpretation of the storage theory and draw on an approximation of residual generation capacity in the German power system to model the difference between future and spot prices (price *basis*) registered at the European Energy Exchange (EEX). We accommodate various econometric specifications to three years of daily data time series. Statistical significance is achieved in all cases. Best results are obtained with an exponential GARCH estimation. Restated residual capacity is able to accurately drive the observed basis. This provides some evidence of the increasing rationality of power markets and their dependence on production and distribution constraints.

The liberalization of the electricity sector has brought about new marketplaces where power can be traded in standardized form, in a manner similar to the way in which other traditional commodities like oil, ores or crops are traded. To cite a few, Nordpool, PJM, EEX or Powernext, are today familiar names for commodity traders in Europe and North America. They identify financial exchanges, matched to one or more power grids, where producers of electricity (or traders having access to production) can offer, for a fixed price, the supply of a predetermined amount of energy (usually measured in megawatts, MW) during one or more hours of the next day, while buyers (such as industrial consumers or local distribution companies) can bid for the purchase of an equal amount of energy, during the same time-slot.

According to the settlement model followed in each marketplace, bids and offers can be matched in diverse ways. In marketplaces where trades are organized on a continuous basis, bids and offers are paired on the spot. A bid can thus be placed for a time slot in the immediate future (like the next hour) and is settled – and a sale contract established – as soon as a seller makes available an offer (1) for an equal or lower price and (2) a corresponding amount of energy to be delivered during the same period. If, instead, trades are settled by auction, buyers and sellers must communicate their undisclosed bids and offers to the market authority generally one day ahead of their delivery time. Bids and offers are subsequently stacked according to their proposed prices, and different demand and supply schedules are built for every future time slot in which they are to be delivered. The intersection between each pair of schedules then yields the settlement price at which power will be exchanged in every next-day time period of reference. Accordingly, this price is taken as the performance basis for agents who are assigned contracts in the auction process.

This brief illustration provides some insight into *spot* power trading, specifically on the settlement mechanism of bids and offers placed for quasi-immediate delivery. But in power markets generators may commit to provide power to their customers well ahead of when it is needed. Likewise, buyers can forecast their seasonal necessities and place bids accordingly. In several existing power exchanges, contracts for *forward* delivery have thus thrived, giving rise to *futures* markets where agents can trade electricity for short-to-medium maturities.

The coexistence of spot and forward power markets makes available different prices for a single megawatt-hour (MWh) to be delivered in a power system over different maturities. In this regard, power markets have thus developed similarly to other commodity markets, whose prices for immediate or future delivery have long been available to traders. Yet power prices seem to escape the application of the traditional asset-pricing relationships which are commonly employed to link spot and term prices in other commodity markets. It is indeed still largely unexplained why spot electricity prices may trade for some time below future prices, then suddenly soar well above the latter and reach levels several times in excess of their previous values. This limitation in many ways thwarts the liquid functioning of electricity exchanges which, for mainstream financial practitioners, remain somewhat awkward marketplaces. On the other hand, the same is not true for researchers who look at power exchanges and their partially unknown pricing processes as an interesting area of investigation.

The non- or limited storability of electricity is often invoked to justify the lack of a well-defined relationship between spot and forward power prices. Electricity cannot be directly amassed in large reserves and is thus stored as potential energy through its means of production (water, coal, oil, natural gas and uranium). The *storage theory* (Kaldor, 1939; Working, 1948) illustrates why this may have a significant effect on power prices. According to the theory, firms trading storable commodities (hence not power) hold inventories in order to respond to unanticipated demand oscillations. This surely exposes them to storage and opportunity costs, but makes possible the selling of retained stocks when goods are most desired – a valuable advantage commonly called *convenience yield*. Therefore, when demand is high and commodity reserves scarce, traders dislike the postponed delivery associated with forward contracts and prefer to gain immediate possession of contracted goods. As a result, storage and opportunity costs become secondary, the convenience yield acquires a crucial importance, spot prices rise above forward prices, and the market is said to *backward*. Conversely, when low demand and abundant inventories increase the importance of storage and opportunity costs, the convenience of having reserves is quasi-irrelevant, and spot prices quote below forward prices (*contango*).[1] With electricity, this is not easily observed. Power inventories have a blurred nature and very indistinct magnitude, so no reliable metric is available to functionally link the significant oscillations of the difference between future and spot power prices to power reserves.

However, if power reserves could be measured in an alternative fashion, it is, in principle, admissible that the storage theory could also have some explanatory role on power prices. In this chapter, using real data from the German power market (EEX), we test the hypothesis that an implicit measure of power reserves may explain the oscillations followed by the *basis* – the algebraic difference between forward and *adjusted* spot power prices. In order to do this, (1) we rely on power load measures (in MWh) as released by the Transmission System Administrators (TSOs) that manage the entire German grid and (2) we extract from them a measure of available power reserves by proxy (hereinafter, *implicit reserves*) to which we econometrically link the simultaneous basis observed on the most liquid futures contract traded at the EEX. The remainder of the chapter is organized as follows. The next section illustrates the existing state of the research on the subject. The following section explains the explicit hypotheses which are subjected to econometric testing, while the third section discusses the employed econometric methods. The fourth section describes the dataset under investigation. The next one presents the estimation results and the final section provides a discussion of the conclusions which can be drawn from this study.

Background: the storage theory and the forward price of commodities

For the storage theory, the relationships linking forward and spot prices of a commodity can be derived from the *cash-and-carry* rationale. Agents agreeing to sell an asset at a future date may cover their commitment by immediately buying and carrying until maturity what they will then need to deliver. In this way, they incur the opportunity cost of readily purchasing the asset, but profit from the utility of possessing and being able to trade it until maturity.[2] Therefore, for these agents the return of buying a commodity today (that is, at time t) and delivering it at maturity (T) should at least be equal to:[3]

$$F(t,T) - S(t) = S(t)R(t,T) + W(t,T) - Y(t,T) \tag{9.1}$$

Here $F(t, T)$ represents the commodity forward price, $S(t)$ is the spot price, $S(t)R(t, T)$ is the opportunity cost of investing cash in a unit of commodity, $W(t, T)$ is the marginal cost of storing the commodity through the delivery period, and $Y(t, T)$ tracks the convenience yield of holding the asset. By moving the second term on the left-hand side of (9.1) to the right-hand side, a statement for the forward price of a commodity is obtained. This statement, in complete markets, yields the theoretical value at which commodity futures written on storable commodities for maturities equal to T should trade at t.

As explained in the introduction, when commodity inventories become scarce, prices tend to back up. Therefore, with low inventories, the left-hand side of (9.1) becomes significantly negative and matches the growth of $Y(t, T)$ on the right-hand side; while the reverse is true with abundant inventories. The literature on the empirical estimation of this prediction is relatively extensive. Notwithstanding the difficulty of modelling storage costs and the convenience yield, for various types of storable commodities (either seasonal, like agricultural products or semi-processed foods, or non-seasonal, like metal ores or hydrocarbons) researchers have been able to significantly show that, as expected, convenience yields and the timely differences between forward and spot prices $[F(t, T)-S(t)]$ decrease when the inventory level of a commodity declines relative to its trading volumes. Indeed, surveys not only confirm the basic insight of the storage theory, but also show that inventory levels drive the difference between forward and spot prices in a strongly non-linear fashion. To cite a few relatively recent studies, readers may refer to Fama and French, 1987 and 1988; Brennan, 1991; Deaton and Laroque, 1992; Ng and Pirrong, 1994; and Pyndick, 1994.

Electricity, on the other hand, is patently non-storable. Hence many deem that trying to use the storage theory to estimate power prices is nonsense. But this is perhaps an excessively exaggerated standpoint. In fact, since power can be stored in potential form, power inventories may possibly be tracked in some analogous form. For instance, where electricity is mainly produced with hydroelectric reserves (as in the Nordic countries) researchers have partially validated the relationship between water levels in hydraulic reservoirs and the forward-spot difference (see Gjoilberg and Johnsen, 2001; and Botterud *et al.*, 2003). Hence, estimating no-arbitrage statements akin to (9.2) on power prices may not be altogether futile. The challenge, though, is to measure indirect power reserves in a way that validly approximates inventories as they are tracked in other commodity markets; particularly when water reserves are not available or just unimportant. The following section illustrates how we propose to tackle this task using German data.

Hypothesis: power implicit reserves

In order to accumulate power reserves and be ready to respond to additional demand, power generators need to indirectly store electricity through its means of production: water, coal, oil, natural gas and uranium. In addition, they need to have production plants capable of processing more raw materials and generate more MWh when they are needed. In developed economies, this ability to cope with greater demand must also be firm. Consumers in Europe and North America, in fact, assume the continuous supply of electricity to their premises to be a basic right. As a result, this entails two consequences. First, the maximum overall supply capacity in a western power system (as mandated by supervisory authorities) is greater than what is normally needed, and this additional capacity is defined as *reserve capacity*. Second, power producers can use reserve capacity to process primary energy reserves to supply more power when needed. In this case, they respond with varying delays to additional demand, depending on several explanatory factors such as the production fuel, the generation technology, the location of the plant, and so forth. It follows that in periods of great demand, reserve capacity gets eaten up and the use of additional capacity translates into additional supply with some delay. When present, the mechanism of balancing markets takes care of the very short-term re-equilibration of the system towards greater supply and this has a signalling effect. Bidders start to increase prices ahead of time in order to secure readily available output. Settlement prices jump above their normal levels and, the greater the reserve capacity to be used, the higher the pressure on prices to avoid blackouts, hence the higher the spikes in spot price processes.

In this manner, reserve capacity makes up for direct inventories and measures the ability of a power system to resort to primary sources of energy, in a timely manner, in order to cope with demand swings. Assuming that raw materials are available for production, the greater the level of reserve capacity with respect to the normal level of output, the lower the convenience it provides. Conversely, the lower the capacity to be set aside for use in normal circumstances, the higher the utility of possessing an extra MW to satisfy demand.

We refer to *power implicit reserves* as the floating level of reserve capacity in a power system with respect to its normal level of supply. Since the maximum production capacity in a power system is a relatively stable measure (it basically represents the summation of the capacity of all existing and operating plants) and is probably never reached in actual terms, this datum can be approximated as the highest supply level attained over a sufficiently long period of time. The timely level of residual production capacity in a power system can thus be defined as the difference between its maximum and timely levels over the time window $(t-n, t-n+1, \ldots, t-1, t)$:

$$RL(t) = \max_{t}\,[L(t)] - L(t) \tag{9.2}$$

where $L(t)$ represents the total load of electricity supplied in a power system at time t expressed in MW and $RL(t)$ stands for residual load.

It follows that *power implicit reserves*, $IR(t)$, can be defined as:

$$IR(t) = f\left(RL(t) - \frac{\sum_{t=1}^{t-n}[RL(t)]}{n}, RL(t) - \frac{\sum_{t=1}^{t-p}[RL(t)]}{p} \right) \tag{9.3}$$

If time is measured in days, equation (9.3) hypothesizes that implicit reserves are a function of (1) the conditional expectation of the residual load level (over the entire set of n days considered) and (2) some short-run mean specification (over a subset of p observations, with $p < n$). The idea is that market agents track inventory levels by looking at two pieces of information: the current residual capacity with respect to its normal level and the latest trend in its evolution (possibly on a weekly basis, ($p \leq 5$)). This provides insight both on long-run consumption intensity and on the immediate possibility to cope with demand oscillations and, hence, on the overall utility of possessing available residual capacity.

Now, ignoring marginal storage costs,[4] equation (9.1) can be rewritten as:

$$F(t,T) - [S(t) + S(t)R(t,T)] = -Y(t,T) \tag{9.4}$$

In the expression above, the square bracket on the left side represents the future value of the spot price on maturity. Using continuously compounded rates, equation (9.4) thus becomes:

$$F(t,T) - S(t)e^{r(T-t)} = -Y(t,T) \tag{9.5}$$

where r is an approximation of the risk-free continuous rate. We define the left-hand side of (9.5) as *adjusted basis* (adjusted by the opportunity cost of capital) and we posit that this term represents the profit of having reserve capacity of power production. This profit is, therefore, a sort of convenience yield in electricity markets and may be significantly driven by implicit power reserves as tracked by equation (9.3).

Econometric methodology

In order to test this hypothesis, an explanatory relation linking $[S(t) - S(t)e^{r(T-t)}]$ to $IR(t)$ should be estimated based on trading data. With electricity prices, this poses some methodological complications. First, the hypothesis that residual production capacity drives forward-spot price differentials may not be thoroughly accommodated by the way $IR(t)$ are modelled by (9.3). Equation (9.3) indeed tries to provide an intuitive specification of implicit reserves. But price time series may have complex lag structures in their functional dependence on exogenous drivers. Buyers and sellers of electricity in a competitive market may, in fact, use information they learn at different points in time to orient their exchange activities. This implies that, most likely, significant serial correlation will affect estimation residuals after simple regression models are initially fit to price and load data.[5] Second, the rigidity of power demand, paired with the impossibility of directly storing it, causes power prices to oscillate greatly when consumption surges unexpectedly. Spot power price time series are, in fact, characterized by the periodic observation of high positive jumps followed by immediate negative jumps (that is, *spikes*), which tend to cluster in times of market crisis. Hence, on the one hand, numerous price spikes confer significant non-normality to power price data.[6] On the other hand, they also cause large estimation errors (which also concentrate in time), when estimation models are fit to actual datasets. This fact generates, in turn, significant heteroskedasticity in cross-sectional disturbances.[7]

Now, normality in regression estimation errors is the fundamental assumption to derive the properties and the statistical significance of ordinary least square (OLS) estimators. The same holds true for the assumption of their non-autocorrelation and homoskedasticity.[8] With power prices, the validity of OLS estimations may, therefore, be seriously limited. This requires us to tackle the problem of estimating a functional relationship between $[S(t) - S(t)e^{r(T-t)}]$ and $IR(t)$ by using different techniques. Let us review the viable alternatives.

The presence of serial correlation in disturbances after fitting a simple OLS regression on data between $-Y(t)$ and $IR(t)$, may require us to find alternative ways to model the independent variable, so as to mimic the possible trading behaviour of market agents, given their information on power load data. This can be done, (1) by relaxing the way equation (9.3) models residual power loads $RL(t)$ and (2) with the express insertion of auto-regressive (AR) and/or moving average (MA) terms in the model specification, in order to more accurately capture the relationship between past observations of $RL(t)$ in the generating process of $IR(t)$ and current observations of $-Y(t)$. Therefore, an *auto regressive moving average* (ARMA) model, whose specification will be guided by the measurement of partial serial correlation statistics between error terms (discussed later) provides a first methodological improvement.[9]

The simultaneous (and interrelated) presence of heteroskedasticity and non-normality in estimation errors may then suggest *robust estimation* methods in the fitting of the ARMA model to a dataset. In this way, regression coefficients linking reserve load observations to the adjusted basis can be corrected to consider the varying scale of estimation errors. However, if after this, disturbances still remain highly non-normal, the most credible hypothesis is that the econometric estimation is not thoroughly able to cope with the occurrence of high power price spikes. Estimation errors may, in fact, be large when spot prices jump well above or below forward prices, sending

$|-Y(t)|$ to very extreme levels. If this is the case, given the chosen ARMA specification, it means that some correlation between the chosen regressors (the explanatory variables) and the estimated disturbances (after the ARMA structure has been considered) still exists. In this instance, it may be possible to try to further improve estimation with the support of *instrumental variables*. Instrumental variables are a set of alternative regressors that enter the estimation model instead of the original ones. A correct identification of instrumental variables requires them to be significantly correlated with the original regressors, but not with estimation disturbances (in other words, they should therefore respect the *orthogonality* condition with respect to the disturbance vector). Therefore, if a set of instrumental variables is available, it can be profitably employed in estimation techniques like the *two stage least squares* (TSLS) and the *generalized method of moments* (GMM) that may afford some better results.

An alternative and, possibly, more powerful approach is to simultaneously take care of heteroskedasticity and non-normality in estimation errors (due to price spikes), by using a *generalized auto-regressive conditional heteroskedastic* (GARCH) model. This type of approach relies, in fact, on the separate estimation of two regression equations – a *mean* and a *variance* equation – which take into account both the conditional mean and conditional variance of estimation errors. Specifically, the *mean equation* regresses the adjusted basis, $-Y(t)$, on present and past reserve load data, using an ARMA as specification seen above. Whereas the *variance equation* just models the estimation error in the first equation by treating its variance as a dependent variable of two separate terms: (1) the square of one or more estimation errors at different lags from time t (between $t-1$ and $t-p$), and (2) the variance of the same lagged errors, up to a different delay order (between $t-1$ and $t-q$). In this manner, GARCH models are able to anticipate times of large price swings – that is, times of large estimation errors in the mean equation – by exploiting the tendency of power price spikes to cluster over time, hence to confer increasing past local variance to estimation errors. The implication is that GARCH models should normalize, to the highest possible extent, the distribution of estimation errors after all measurable causes of price spikes have been accounted for.[10]

Dataset: power prices and power load in the German power system

In this study we focus on the German power exchange (EEX). In this competitive arena, almost three years of daily price observations and intra-daily power load and consumption data are available. This, combined with its acceptable (though still limited) liquidity and the availability of a consistent array of financial forward contracts, provide good grounds for empirical testing.

Located in Leipzig, the EEX market – European Energy Exchange is the result of the merger in 2002 of the Leipzig Power Exchange and the European Energy Exchange, located in Frankfurt. For the moment, this market can be viably matched to the overall power system administered by the four German TSOs: EnBW, EON, RWE and Vattenfal. Spot trading is available at the EEX both on a continuous and auction basis, with the latter market making up the bulk of trading volume.[11] Every day, two single weighted average price indexes – the *Phelix Base* and *Phelix Peak* – representing that day's spot prices during two different time windows, are determined on the basis of 24-hourly prices. Time windows (base-load and peak-load windows, from hour 1 through 24 and hour 9 through 20, respectively) are defined according to normal patterns of consumption, and their price indexes are taken as a settlement reference for their respective futures contracts.

Futures contracts are then available for numerous increasing monthly, quarterly and yearly maturities (for instance, traded base-load monthly futures for which an open interest existed in MWh on 2 May 2005, were available for deliveries through the following six months; quarterly futures for the following seven quarters; and yearly futures up to 2011). All of these mentioned contracts are to be settled in cash against Phelix indexes reported through their respective delivery periods. In fact, for most power futures, delivery is over an entire period of time, not at a single date. Hence, the performance of futures begins upon maturity, which is the beginning of the delivery period, and ends with the end of the delivery period (so, according to EEX trading rules, a monthly future for delivery in June 2003, traded on 9 May 2003, has 20 days of residual trading and will be performed, and thus cash settled, through that entire month of June).

Various futures have diverse liquidity. Base-load contracts are more liquid than peak-load futures. Among the former, monthly contracts are more traded than quarterly contracts, which in turn are more numerous than yearly ones. Among monthly contracts, the most traded is the one which is to be delivered during the month that follows the month to which a current trading day belongs. Given its higher liquidity, it may be conjectured that this contract presents better pricing data; hence it provides a more adequate testing dataset. Accordingly, we test the hypothesis spelled out earlier on its price time series.

In order to perform econometric investigations, future prices must be juxtaposed on spot prices. By using the Greek letter τ to designate the beginning of the maturity period for the one-month base-load futures mentioned above, we indicate with $F_t(\tau, T)$ the future price traded at t for the one-month ahead delivery period $(\tau, \tau + 1, \ldots, T)$.[12] This price can be compared to the Phelix base-load daily mean in t, $S(t)$. Likewise, $F_{t-1}(\tau, T)$ can be compared to $S(t-1)$; $F_{t-2}(\tau, T)$ to $S(t-2)$, and so forth, so that two time series of prices are built backwards to $t-n$. Note that, going from t to $t-n$ over a time set in excess of one month, entails periodically rolling back the beginning and the end of the maturity periods (τ, T) for the tracked futures and choosing forward prices accordingly.[13] (τ, T) are thus also variable dates which are a scaled function of t. To avoid clumsiness, we do not represent this in the (τ, T) notation. However, we employ an algorithm to select, among all available future prices, the one for the contract which is for delivery in the month subsequent to which each trading day in the $(t - n, t - n + 1, \ldots, t - 1, t)$ set belongs. Since future prices are available at EEX on each working day from Monday through Friday (not for weekends), this procedures yields a dataset (selected after the merger of the power exchange in Leipzig with the one in Frankfurt) of 560 pairs of forward-spot prices, between 3 January 2003 and 25 April 2005.

Equation (9.5) requires then that the basis be determined after spot prices are adjusted for their opportunity cost of capital until delivery. This entails determining $S(t)e^{r(T-t)}$ as follows. Each observed $S(t)$ is multiplied by an exponential function of r for the $(T - t)$ period that includes a variable number of days to be split in two time slots: $(T - \tau)$, which is always one month and is approximated with the median value of a fortnight; $(\tau - t)$, that, given EEX trading rules, can go from a minimum of three days to a maximum of a month, and is directly determined on t. Continuous-time risk-free rates, r, are approximated with the most appropriate (given $(T - t)$) discrete-time Euribor rate in the weekly-to-sixty-day maturity term-structure, subsequently converted into its continuously-compounded equivalent.

Given $F_t(\tau, T)$ and $S(t)e^{r(T-t)}$, a time series of adjusted bases $-Y_{t-i}(t, T)$, with $i \in (n, \ldots, 0)$, is obtained. This time series is the dependent variable which, in our tests, must be regressed on a measure of power implicit reserves as defined earlier. To model implicit reserves, we track the evolution of power loads in the German grid so as to determine maximum and retained production capacities. All of the four German TSOs administering the national power grid release historical data on the total amount of power in MW they injected in the system every quarter hour, since June 2003.[14] This information is available online from their websites. The summation of each TSO's load provides the German national load. The arithmetic mean of national load across the 96 slots of 15 minutes that make up a base-load day (as set to determine the Phelix price basis), averaged across the four TSOs, provides the daily mean load in the whole German grid (previously indicated as $L(t)$). The maximum load over the time series of daily loads between 1 June 2003 and 25 April 2005 provides – according to (9.2) – the foundation to determine the corresponding time series of daily residual loads, $RL(t)$. This series is thus obtained under the assumption that the maximum observed load over the sampled period represents a quasi-complete utilization of production capacity. As a result, power loads treated in this manner define a (normally weekly) pattern of capacity utilization. This time series, finally yields the explanatory variable that hypothetically guides the adjusted basis of power prices over the entire sampled period.[15]

Estimation and results

Basic OLS estimation

The research objective of this paper is to verify that forward prices tend to move away from spot prices according to some function of the residual capacity that, in a power system, is available to satisfy demand. Figure 9.1 below presents, therefore, a preliminary graphic comparison between the independent variable $RL(t)$ (residual capacity measured in GW of residual load) and the dependent variable $-Y(t)$ (measured in € per MW).

This basic association does not really suggest a functional dependence linking the two variables, although some slight similarities between their trajectories may be at times observed. However, a simple OLS regression of the adjusted basis on a log-restatement of equation (9.3) already yields some interesting results, provided that the whole dataset is divided into single working days, and five estimations per each working day (from Monday through Friday) are separately conducted. Here, implicit reserves are simply modelled as:

$$IR(t) = \left\{ rl(t) - \frac{\sum_{t=1}^{t-n} [rl(t)]}{n} \right\} + \left\{ rl(t) - \frac{\sum_{t=1}^{t-p} [rl(t)]}{p} \right\} \tag{9.6}$$

(where $rl(t) = \lambda \ln[RL(t)]$). The estimated model at this preliminary stage of investigation is possibly the most streamlined:

$$-Y(t) = \alpha + \beta IR(t) + \varepsilon(t) \tag{9.7}$$

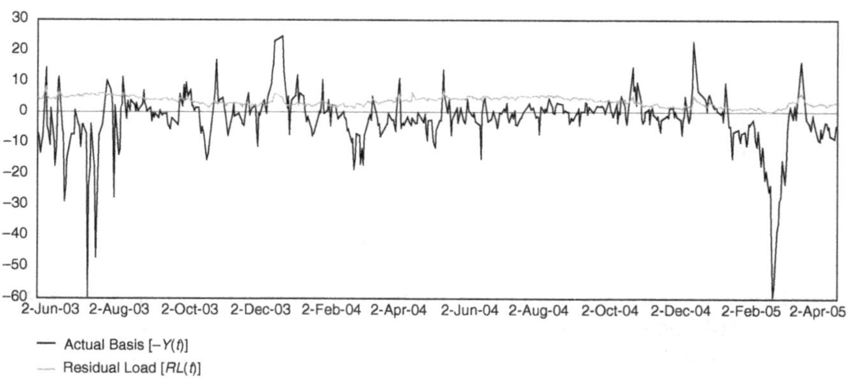

Figure 9.1 Adjusted basis vs. residual load

In it, $IR(t)$ are fed to equation (9.7) and determined as in (9.6) with $p = 7$ and $\lambda = 10$ for estimation optimization. Estimation statistics are apparently relatively good for all days, with all regression coefficients significantly different from zero at least at the 95 per cent level. Table 9.1 provides some highlights (there are 92 observations per day).

Table 9.1 OLS statistics for single business day estimations

Statistic	Monday	Tuesday	Wednesday	Thursday	Friday
α	−2.147108	−3.565482	−3.484542	−3.425387	−1.396168
$t(\alpha)$	−3.298438	−3.082761	−4.383150	−4.091367	−2.107090
Prob. $t(\alpha)$	0.0014	0.0027	0.0000	0.0001	0.0379
β	0.672074	0.117438	0.416443	0.975429	0.821897
$t(\beta)$	7.678897	2.081058	4.959429	8.538555	9.532839
Prob. $t(\beta)$	0.0000	0.0403	0.0000	0.0000	0.0000
Adjusted R^2	0.389120	0.035310	0.205906	0.441399	0.496890
Durbin–Watson	1.349961	1.281113	1.190776	1.034494	1.559369

However, the Durbin–Watson statistic presented in Table 9.1 is quite bad in all cases, since, with perfectly uncorrelated residuals, this should have a value of two. The Ljung-Box Q-statistics and the Breusch–Godfrey LM test further confirm this fact. In both tests, and for all trading days, the probabilities associated with the Q-statistics and the χ^2 distribution of the Breusch–Godfrey's $N \times R^2$ statistic (not reported here) reveal a significant autocorrelation in the residuals, at multiple lags. Serial correlation in estimated residuals strongly biases OLS regression coefficients (α, β in equation (9.7) above) and suggests to employ more involved methodologies that account for its presence in the estimation. Moreover, OLS residuals from these regressions are then plagued by the presence of significant heteroskedasticity.[16] This problem is also discussed and tackled in the following subsections.

ARMA specification

We tackle serial correlation by directly inserting lagged error terms as regressors in the econometric specification to be tested. For this reason, using Ljung-Box Q-statistics to target significant lagged disturbance terms, we fit an ARMA model directly to residual load values, $RL(t)$, as determined in (9.2). The estimation of the ARMA specification below is now conducted on a single sample comprising all business days:

$$-Y(t) = \alpha + \beta^1 RL(t) + \beta^2 u(t-1) + \beta^3 u(t-4) + \beta^4 \eta(t-5) + \varepsilon(t) \quad (9.8)$$

In equation (9.8), $u(t)$ are AR terms, while $\eta(t)$ is an MA term.[17]

This ARMA specification captures market pricing patterns within one week of trading and has the highest overall significance among all specifications satisfying the hypothesis spelled out in earlier (the second absolute highest among all tested specifications).[18]

The estimation output is summarized in Table 9.2. As can be seen, the first auto-regressive term has the highest significance in the model, while all other terms are significant at least above the 95 per cent level (all AR and MA inverted roots are also comfortably within the unit root circle). Figure 9.2 elucidates the graphic comparison between actual basis values, $-Y(t)$, and fitted values obtained by using the right-hand side of (9.8) (except the error term). The fit is graphically good, although the model appears to cope with

Table 9.2 ARMA estimation statistics

Statistic	α	β^1	β^2	β^3	β^4
Value	−20.23092824	5.036562971	0.6760196261	0.1627462608	0.1220492011
T	−7.658950	10.00908	18.56121	4.247654	2.434448
Prob. T	0.0000	0.0000	0.0000	0.0000	0.0153
F			179.0564		
Prob. F			0.000000		
Adjusted R^2			0.610710		
Durbin–Watson			2.161843		

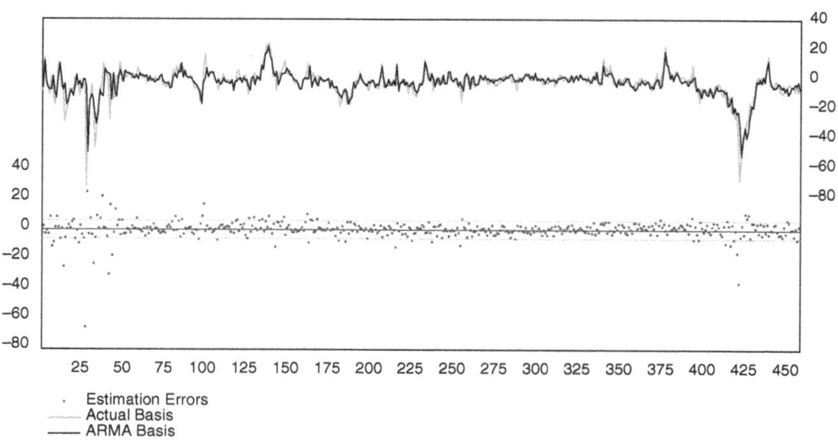

Figure 9.2 Adjusted basis vs. ARMA modelled residual load

innovations with delay. The bottom part shows the plot of ARMA residuals. Note that they tend to increase when innovations are large (that is, on or around price spikes).[19] Note that the Durbin–Watson statistic provided in Table 9.2 now has a value much closer to two. This suggests that, (1) serial correlation of residuals is relatively small after fitting the ARMA specification in (9.8), and (2) no major terms have been forgotten in the estimation. The other two serial correlation tests mentioned in the previous subsection also confirm this fact.

On the other hand, the White test does not reject the presence of heteroskedasticity among ARMA residuals.[20] EViews allows for improving ARMA estimations in the presence of such a drawback by supporting *robust estimation* through the White estimator – which is a heteroskedastic consistent estimator – for the same model specification. Unfortunately, this additional technique does not really improve estimation results and this suggests tackling the problem of heteroskedasticity in a more direct way. This is done with GARCH estimation at the end of this section.

Generalized estimation

As discussed earlier, after fitting the ARMA model on data, numerous estimation errors still have large values (which plot outside the jagged confidence lines in Figure 9.2). This gives significant kurtosis (39.86) to their distribution. Accordingly, the Jarque–Bera test – a test which controls the normality of the distribution of estimated residuals – applied to the whole set of n ARMA errors, rejects normality with high power.[21] The ARMA model is thus partially unable to capture large positive price spikes when or before they occur. This inability generates large errors when power prices jump and may cause the regressors to co-vary with estimation residuals, thus violating the underlying assumption of exogenously chosen explanatory variables which accompanies all regression estimations.

Controlling whether there exists some covariance between each of the regressors in (9.8) and the ARMA disturbance error vector, actually confirms some lack of independence between them. Hence, using an estimation method that generalizes the disturbance generating process in the variance–covariance matrix of the residuals (thus excluding normality) can possibly provide some improvement. But in order to do this, it is first necessary to identify a set of instrumental variables correlated to regressors in the original specification, but uncorrelated to the ARMA error vector (that is, variables which are orthogonal to errors).

Lagged values of the original vectors of regressors can be preliminarily used to create a set of instrumental variables and avoid the under-identification of a generalized estimation.[22] Therefore, it is sufficient to find one or more vectors of instrumental variables for the exogenous regressor in (9.8) so as to make the estimation possible. To do this, we use an algorithm to simulate

Table 9.3 GMM estimation statistics

Statistic	α	β^1	β^2	β^3	β^4	β^5
Value	−32.57230	9.037821	0.551878	0.126734	0.155170	0.125565
T	−4.885180	4.682371	8.725179	2.411225	2.468386	2.583626
Prob. T	0.0000	0.0000	0.0000	0.0163	0.0140	0.0101
J-statistic			0.006479			
Adjusted R^2			0.574862			
Durbin–Watson			1.949849			

vectors of values with zero covariance with ARMA errors and pre-defined covariance with regressors.[23] Once this is done, we introduce the appropriate instrumental variables into the estimation.

Eview supports a TSLS estimation for the same ARMA specification presented above. Unfortunately, this does not provide any significant improvement to the results presented in Table 9.2. However, with a slight modification of the ARMA specification in (9.8) into the following AR model:

$$-Y(t) = \alpha + \beta^1 RL(t) + \beta^2 u(t-1) + \beta^3 u(t-2) + \beta^4 u(t-4) + \beta^5 u(t-5) + \varepsilon(t) \tag{9.9}$$

it is possible to estimate an over-identified GMM model.[24]

Table 9.3 presents the estimation results for this estimation.[25] While the significance of regressors and the goodness of fit is not perceptibly lost (and serial correlation not introduced), some improvements in the normality of residuals are possible, after the AR specification in (9.9) is accommodated to the dataset. Their kurtosis diminishes to 34.01 and the Jarque–Bera test, while still rejecting normality, has a better statistic.[26] This is, however, a small amelioration that does not significantly change the ability of the model to replicate actual basis trajectories.

GARCH estimation

Note that so far heteroskedasticity in residuals (detected earlier) has not been directly tackled. GARCH models provide the possibility to model the variance of residuals in the estimation. So, by leveraging on the linkage between the latter and lagged error information, it may be possible to better capture the local error variability generated by the concentrated occurrence of price spikes.[27] To do this, we begin by estimating an exponential GARCH(1,1) model (which we call EGARCH) with the same ARMA specification used in (9.8).[28]

The choice of an EGARCH(1,1) responds to the possibility of modelling both in an asymmetric and exponential way the effect of volatility on the conditional variance $\sigma^2(t)$. In plain GARCH(1,1) models, the conditional variance is a function of, (1) a constant, (2) the estimation of the conditional variance until the last observation before t, $\sigma^2(t-1)$, and (3) information about innovations in the previous period $\varepsilon(t-1)$. Given the presence of large spikes in electricity prices, it, therefore, makes sense to imagine that in this type of market, positive price innovations have different effects from negative innovations. An EGARCH(1,1) specification models the conditional variance in a logarithmic way, as described below:

$$\ln[\sigma^2(t)] = \omega + \gamma^1 \ln[\sigma^2(t-1)] + \gamma^2 \left| \frac{\varepsilon(t-1)}{\sigma(t-1)} \right| + \gamma^3 \frac{\varepsilon(t-1)}{\sigma(t-1)} \tag{9.10}$$

Here, if γ^3 is different from zero, the effect of an innovation is, therefore, asymmetric and exponential.

With this EGARCH estimation, improvements with respect to residual normality are excellent, without material loss in either the significance of regressors or in the goodness of fit. Unfortunately, using the same ARMA specification as in (9.8) introduces some serial correlation in residuals. Therefore, we need to circumvent this problem by re-specifying the lag structure of our ARMA model (within the maximum time window of one week of trading) as:

$$\begin{aligned} -Y(t) = \alpha + \beta^1 RL(t) + \sum_{i=1}^{4} \beta^{1+i} u(t-i) + \beta^6 \eta(t-1) \\ + \beta^7 \eta(t-3) + \varepsilon(t) \end{aligned} \tag{9.11}$$

Table 9.4 presents EGARCH estimation statistics and Figure 9.3 provides a comparison between the actual and the modelled basis.[29] Notice that in Figure 9.3 some visual improvement is detectable with respect to Figure 9.2, particularly in the ability of this approach to capture large basis swings. Moreover, with a modified lag structure residuals no longer present significant serial correlation. Table 9.5 specifically illustrates a comparison between the normality of the distribution of GMM and EGARCH residuals, which clearly supports the better performance of the latter.

Table 9.4 EGARCH estimation statistics

Mean equation (ARMA specification in (9.11))			
Statistic	**Value**	**Z**	**Prob. Z**
α	−17.78400	−5.678035	0.0000
β^1	4.921593	18.84899	0.0000
β^2	0.093774	1.864278	0.0623
β^3	0.371047	23.01242	0.0000
β^4	0.846726	56.00497	0.0000
β^5	−0.348952	−7.082831	0.0000
β^6	0.464834	238.6482	0.0000
β^7	−0.787020	−311.7142	0.0000

Mean equation (cont'd)	
F	69.09332
Prob. F	0.000000
Adjusted R^2	0.622618
Durbin–Watson	1.900707

Variance equation (as of (9.10))				
Statistic	ω	γ^1	γ^2	γ^3
Value	−0.102128	0.315226	−0.126205	0.951777
Z	−1.739489	5.563972	−3.615108	59.43451
Prob. Z	0.0819	0.0000	0.0000	0.0000

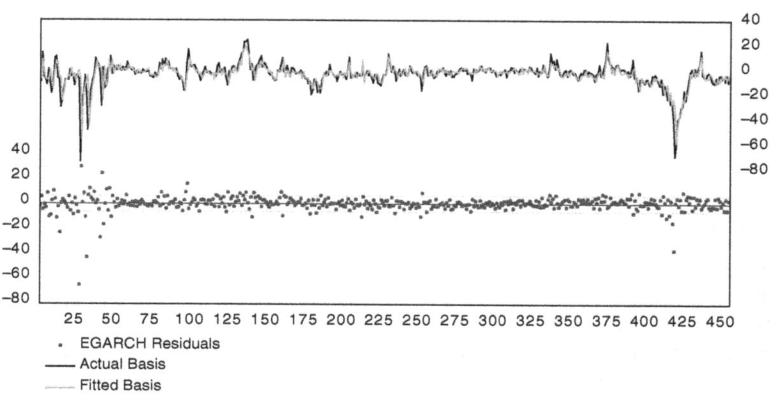

Figure 9.3 Adjusted basis vs. EGARCH modelled residual load

Table 9.5 Residual distribution statistics

Statistic	GMM	EGARCH
Mean	0.002801	−0.015712
Maximum	27.54331	3.204043
Minimum	−65.14843	−7.191287
Median	0.404030	0.019234
Std. Dev.	6.246448	1.042347
Skewness	−3.199416	−1.061752
Kurtosis	34.01387	8.670481
Jarque–Bera	18593.68	695.0812
Probability	0.000000	0.000000

Discussion of results and conclusions

In this chapter, we tested the hypothesis that differences between forward and spot prices in an electricity marketplace – the German one – may be explained by leveraging on an interpretation of the storage theory through which the impossibility of directly observing power inventories is bypassed by the construction of a measure of retained power production capacity. Using daily residual load observations in the German power grid, it has been shown that, in our dataset, available residual capacity maintained to cope with unanticipated demand swings has a significant role in driving the power spot-forward price basis.

This result may possibly provide some grounds for two separate considerations. On the one hand, it may suggest that electricity is not altogether different from other tradable commodities. Certainly, non-storability in a direct fashion and the necessity to declare before time bids and offers for its exchange, give particular features to the trading of this secondary source of energy. However, the fact that a specific economic factor, residual production capacity, seems to replace the role of inventories in guiding the convenience of inter-temporal exchanges, may mean that power trading does not respond to a pricing rationale different from that of other industrial commodities.

This leads to a second observation. As the exchange of power in dedicated financial markets is still greatly undeveloped when compared to the trading of mature commodities, the existence of a non-heterodox explanation that possibly bears a functional relationship between term and spot power prices, might anticipate the ability of power markets to evolve towards greater completeness. Experience shows that, even in the presence of challenging financial innovations, traded asset prices tend to respond to an identifiable rationale, if minimum liquidity is present and information is available (McKinlay and Ramaswamy, 1988). Financial actors follow a learning process in their trading activities. Their ability to develop rational bidding behaviour and eliminate arbitrage opportunities that plague young markets, improves over time. Therefore, provided some basic transparency and liquidity are at work, power exchanges may not, in the end, be relegated to the realm of financial exoticism and might, perhaps, assume a greater role in giving enhanced public utility to the liberalization of electricity markets.

Notes

1 For an alternative explanation that relates the difference between spot and forward commodity prices to inventories via the implicit performance guarantee that reserves provide to firms that short their products in future markets, see Bresnahan and Spiller, 1986. See also Fama and French (1987) for an empirical comparison between different theoretical interpretations.
2 In finance this is a *no-arbitrage* relationship. Traded assets and their likes built by replication need having convergent prices in complete markets.
3 Here, forward prices are modelled through the formulation proposed by Fama and French, 1987.
4 Power requires generators to build large facilities in order to store water or fuels. Within certain ranges, additional storage may actually have marginal costs close to zero, until the long-term investment of building a new facility needs to be undertaken.
5 For a discussion on serial correlation and the drawbacks it entails on OLS estimations, we refer readers to previous chapters in this book.
6 Price spikes can be seen as observations significantly off the conditional price mean over the entire sample of n power prices. When a distribution accommodates numerous extreme values, its bell-shaped curve has relatively fat tails. It is then said to be leptokurtic.
7 Heteroskedasticity occurs when observations on the central diagonal of the variance–covariance matrix of estimated errors ($\Sigma \equiv E[\boldsymbol{\varepsilon\varepsilon}'|\mathbf{X}]$) are different from σ^2, so the scale of estimation errors is not constant.
8 Disturbances are spherical when their matrix of variance-covariance is $\Sigma \equiv E[\boldsymbol{\varepsilon\varepsilon}'|\mathbf{X}] = \sigma^2\mathbf{I}$. Therefore, disturbances are non-spherical when their matrix of variance–covariance is $\Sigma \equiv E[\boldsymbol{\varepsilon\varepsilon}'|\mathbf{X}] = \sigma^2\boldsymbol{\Omega}$, where $\boldsymbol{\Omega}$ is another matrix of some known or unknown form which differs from $\mathbf{I}$.
9 We refer the reader for an explanation on ARMA models and their fitting on time series to previous chapters in this book.
10 For a general treatise on GARCH models, we refer the reader to Greene, 2003.
11 According to EEX data, throughout the first five months of 2005, continuous trading has reported actual trading volumes only in 37 out 138 business days. Mean volume exchanged has been for continuous and auction trading of 1250.3 MWh and 219,032.9 MWh, respectively.
12 So, for instance, if t is 9 May 2005, τ is 1 June 2005 and T is 30 June 2005.
13 In other words, starting from 9 May 2005 and going backwards, requires tracking the future price of the [τ = 1 June 2005/ T = 30 June 2005] futures contract when t belongs to May 2005, the price of the [τ = 1 May 2005/ T = 31 May 2005] futures when t belongs to April 2005, and so on.
14 In these time series of data, a few observations are missing for reasons unspecified

by TSOs. Missing data have been simulated by the author given the weekly and hourly pattern of German power consumption.

15 Residual load values are determined with the exclusion of Saturdays and Sundays for which forward prices, hence basis values, are not available.

16 White heteroskedasticity tests conducted on all regressions considered in Table 9.1 reject the hypothesis of no heteroskedasticity with high significance in all cases.

17 For a discussion on ARMA estimations, we refer the reader to previous chapters.

18 Using the partial correlation statistics it is indeed possible to identify at least another (slightly) more significant ARMA specification, using higher order MA terms. In this case however, the estimated structure does not fully comply with the weekly pattern of trading followed in the EEX power market.

19 The skewness of ARMA residuals is negative. Errors therefore tend to be more negative than positive. This indicates that errors are larger and/or more numerous when the basis plummets, that is, when spot prices mark positive spikes.

20 The statistics for this test are 5.089417 and 10.02073 for the F-statistic and the $N \times R^2$ value, which confirms heteroskedasticity beyond the 99 per cent level.

21 The Jarcque–Bera statistic, which is distributed as a χ^2, has, in this case, a value of 26,779.12 and rejects normality above the 99 per cent confidence level.

22 An under-identified generalized model is one in which the number of instrumental variable vectors is less than the number of parameters to be estimated (that is 5 parameters in equation (9.8)). Over-identification occurs instead when instrumental variable vectors are greater than the parameters to be estimated.

23 Using the same estimation results presented in Table 9.2, the covariance of $RL(t)$ in (9.8) with the fitted basis is $\text{Cov}[RL(t), -Y(t)] = 63.55$. We set an algorithm that, through randomization of log-values of $RL(t)$, finds j instrumental variable vectors, $\mathbf{IV}(t) = (IV_1(t), IV_2(t), \ldots, IV_j(t))$, for which $\text{Cov}[\mathbf{IV}(t), \varepsilon(t)] = 0$ is verified, and the covariance with $RL(t)$ is equal to $\text{Cov}[\mathbf{IV}(t), RL(t)] = \theta \times 63.55$, where θ assumes values between zero and two. Best weighted results between normality in residuals and goodness of fit in the estimation (R^2) are achieved with one vector of instrumental variables and θ set around unit values.

24 EViews does not support the estimation of MA terms in GMM estimations.

25 Estimation is here performed with the automatic bandwidth selection of the weighting matrix for the disturbance generating process of the variance–covariance matrix. Moments are determined following Andrews' autoregressive methodology.

26 The χ^2 value of the Jarque–Bera test here goes down to 18,593.84 as compared to the value of 26,779.12 that was obtained using the ARMA specification in (9.8).

27 See the discussion in the earlier section.

28 The numbers in parentheses indicate the lag order of the GARCH specification. Other specifications with respect both to (1) the ARMA structure of regressors in (9.8) and (2) the lagged structure of the variance equation, provide slightly better results. The choice of referring to the same specification adopted in (9.8) is nonetheless preferred to maintain the highest consistency across the different estimation approaches.

29 In the estimation of (9.10), different distributions for errors can be assumed. EViews in fact estimates GARCH models by maximizing the likelihood function of error variance, given their distribution. Here we choose a generalized error distribution (GED) with a parameter of 1.5. In this way, we inform the estimation on the fat-tailed nature of our disturbances (that is, of the presence of price spikes).

References

Bessembinder, H. and M. L. Lemmon (2002) 'Equilibrium Pricing and Optimal Hedging in Electricity Forward Markets', *Journal of Finance,* vol. 57, no. 2.

Borestein, S. (2001) 'The Trouble with Electricity Markets (and Some Solutions)', *Program on Workable Energy Regulation Working Paper.*

Botterud, A., A. Bhattacharyya and I. Marija (2003) 'Futures and Spot Prices – An Analysis of the Scandinavian Electricity Market', *Norwegian Research Council Working Paper.*

Brennan, M. (1991) 'The Price of Convenience and the Pricing of Commodity Contingent Claims', in D. Lund and B. Oksendal (eds), *Stochastic Models and Option Values* (New York: Elsevier).

Bresnahan, T. and P. Spiller (1986) 'Futures Market Backwardation under Risk Neutrality', *Economic Inquiry,* vol. 24 (July).

Copeland, T. and F. Weston (1992) *Financial Theory and Corporate Policy* (Reading, MA: Addison-Wesley).

Deaton, A. and G. Laroque (1992) 'Commodity Prices', *Review of Economic Studies,* vol. 59, no. 1.

Escribano, A., J. Pena and P. Villaplana (2002) 'Modeling Electricity Prices: International Evidence', *Universidad Carlos III de Madrid Working Paper.*

Fama, E. and K. R. French (1987) 'Commodity Futures Prices: Some Evidence on Forecast Power, Premiums, and the Theory of Storage', *Journal of Business,* vol. 60, no. 1.

Fama, E. and K. R. French (1988) 'Business Cycles and the Behavior of Metal Prices', *Journal of Finance,* vol. 43, no. 5.

Gjolberg, O. and T. Johnsen (2001) 'Electricity Futures: Inventories and Price Relationships at Nord Pool', *Discussion Paper.*

Greene, W. (2003) *Econometric Analysis* (Englewood Cliffs, NJ: Prentice-Hall).

Hull, J. (1993) *Options, Futures, and Other Derivative Securities* (Englewood Cliffs, NJ: Prentice-Hall).

Kaldor, D. (1939) 'Speculation and Economic Stability', *Review of Economic Studies,* 7.

McKinlay, C. and K. Ramaswamy (1988) 'Index-Futures Arbitrages and the Behavior of Stock Index Futures Prices', *Review of Financial Studies,* vol. 1, no. 2.

Mork, E. (2004) 'The Dynamics of Risk Premiums in Nord Pool's Futures Market', *24th USAEE/IAEE North American Conference Proceedings.*

Ng, V. and C. Pirrong (1994) 'Fundamentals and Volatility: Storage, Spreads, and the Dynamics of Metal Prices', *Journal of Business,* vol. 67, no. 2.

Pindyck, R. S. (1994) 'Inventories and the Short-Run Dynamics of Commodity Prices', *Rand Journal of Economics,* vol. 25, no. 1.

Pirrong, C. (2001) 'The Price of Power: The Valuation of Power and Weather Derivatives', *Oklahoma State University Working Paper.*

Routledge, B., D. Seppi and C. Spatt (2000) 'Equilibrium Forward Curves for Commodities', *Journal of Finance,* vol. 55, no. 3.

Woo, C., I. Horowitz and K. Hoang (2001) 'Cross Hedging and Forward-Contract Pricing of Electricity', *Energy Economics,* vol. 23.

Working, H. (1948) 'Theory of the Inverse Carrying Charge in Futures Markets', *Journal of Farm Economics,* vol. 30.

Working, H. (1949) 'The Theory of the Price of Storage', *American Economic Review,* vol. 39.

10

The Price of Oil over the Very Long Term

Sophie Chardon

Presentation of the energy issue

Identifying the stochastic processes governing energy prices is relevant for both energy policymakers and private energy actors. On the one hand, producers have to run energy price forecasts in order to motivate investment decisions related to resource exploration or reserve development. On the other hand, policymakers need to assess the future trends that energy prices may follow in order to adjust the timing of their energy policies. Indeed, the consequences of the oil price shock in terms of economic growth have highlighted the impact of energy price fluctuations.

The point is that energy investments are typically irreversible and need to be made in a long-run perspective, that is to say, over time horizons as long as twenty or thirty years. Irreversible investment decisions involve real options that are used to assess corporations' optimal capital investment decisions. In this case, second moment matters a great deal, so that an investment decision based on a mean reverting process could turn out to be quite different from one based on a random walk.

The most important among the various energy prices is, probably, the price of oil studied in this chapter. Ideally, we would like to be able to explain oil prices in fundamental terms, that is, in terms of movements in supply and demand. However, the determinants of those movements (inventory levels, production capacity and demand growth) are not so easy to anticipate. The use of such models in long-run forecasting would certainly lead to rather fragile results. As a consequence, industry forecasts are often extrapolations in which prices are assumed to grow in real terms at some fixed rate.

Alternatively, without any attempt at structural modelling, forecasts can be realized using stochastic processes that might be consistent with oil price long-run behaviour. We will, in fact, consider that oil prices are mean-reverting, but the rate of mean reversion is slow, so that the trends to which prices revert also fluctuate over time. Such stochastic fluctuations, both in the level and slope of the trend, are also consistent with a basic model of exhaustible resource production, (Hotelling, 1931).

However, the use of such models reflects some statistical properties of the series, notably in terms of mean reversion features. We will see in the next session the specific econometric techniques that are to be implemented in this long-run context.

Analysis of the movements in real energy prices and comments on required econometric techniques

We examine the real price of crude oil over the 143-year period 1861–2004. These annual data come from *BP Statistical Review of World Energy* (June 2004). From 1861 through 1944 the data were obtained from US average prices, and for 1945 to 1983 the Arabian Light price, posted at Ras Tanura, was used as a benchmark of crude oil price. Finally, from 1985 onwards, Brent prices were available. This nominal series has been deflated to 2005 dollars and we took the natural logarithm of the deflated series.

This econometric study of oil price, notably of its long-run movements, presents several specific challenges. Econometric techniques implemented in this chapter will be related to time series analysis and particularly mean reversion investigation.

The first intuitive reaction when facing a time series consists of extracting a trend that could show the path the process follows. Different techniques can be implemented, and we will present the results of the quadratic trend and Hodrick–Prescott Filter techniques. We will show the results of such tools and then we will present more sophisticated econometric techniques that can be used to forecast oil price future paths.

Descriptive analysis of oil prices

Considering the whole range of data available, it is clear that we can fit the series to a quadratic U-shaped time trend. We observe that oil prices fell until 1900–10, a period during which the production of this resource had been developed on a large scale. There were, in fact, more and more producers and many new fields were discovered and explored at decreasing cost, as a result of the technological changes put into effect at this time. Then, through the oil shock, oil prices continued to fluctuate but stayed generally close to an average value of about $15 per barrel (in 2005 dollars). This might suggest that the oil price exhibits mean-reverting characteristics. From 1973 to 1981, the price increased dramatically, but then it returned – still in 2005 dollars – to levels not much higher than those of thirty to eighty years earlier. Finally, a price increase occurred in 2004 due to the growing demand for oil products linked to economic development and the expectation of a future lack of petroleum products.

Table 10.1 Quadratic trend estimated on the sample (1865; 2004)

Variable	Coefficient	Std. error	*t*-Statistic	Prob.
Constant	3.907950	0.119442	32.71830	0.0000
t	−0.034035	0.003683	−9.241709	0.0000
t^2	0.000227	2.40*E* − 05	9.442796	0.0000
R-squared	0.394455	Mean dependent var		3.001672
Adjusted R-squared	0.385615	S.D. dependent var		0.529636
S.E. of regression	0.415143	Akaike info criterion		1.100807
Sum squared resid	23.61105	Schwarz criterion		1.163842
Log likelihood	−74.05646	*F*-statistic		44.62127
Durbin-Watson stat	0.365878	Prob(*F*-statistic)		0.000000

Source: EViews.

Quadratic trend

A different kind of trend can be extracted to describe the long-run movements of time series. In our case, the U-shaped series requires a non linear treatment. It is usual to draw a quadratic trend which can be estimated by running an OLS regression of the log price using a constant, time, and time squared:

$$p_t = \alpha + \beta t + \gamma t^2 + \varepsilon_t$$

where t is a vector of time [1865, 1866, ..., 2004]. The results of the regression on the sample [1865; 2004] are presented in Table 10.1.

This first tool remains a very rough estimation, as shown by the determination coefficient of the regression through the whole sample: 39 per cent of the variance of the log price of oil is explained by this trend specification. Moreover, this technique is very sensitive to the starting date chosen by the modeller, as shown in Figure 10.1. Note that we are able to use the OLS regression results to extend the path the oil price would follow under the assumption that it is well estimated by the equation presented above (we just need to extend the vector t until 2025 and then apply the OLS estimates of the parameters α, β and γ). Even if the R^2 statistic suggests the opposite, we performed this exercise to underline once again the sensitivity of this technique to the estimation starting date.

Hodrick–Prescott filter

We now implement a more sophisticated econometric technique, namely the Hodrick–Prescott filter (HP filter). This is a smoothing method that is widely used among macroeconomists to obtain a decomposition of a series into a long-run component, that is the trend, and a short-term component,

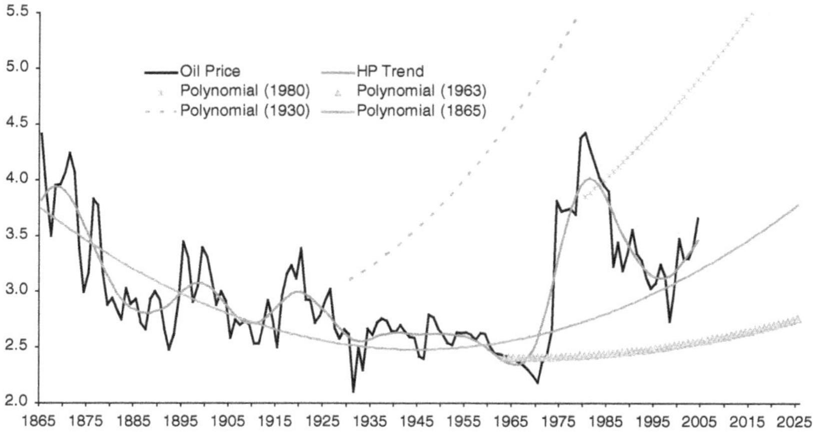

Figure 10.1 Log price of crude oil in 2005 dollars (1865–2004)

Note: HPtrend: Trend obtained with the Hodrick–Prescott filter. Polynomial (x): Quadratic trend obtained by regressing on the sample [1865; x] the log price of crude oil over time variables as described below.

corresponding to fluctuations around this trend. The method was first used in a working paper (circulated in the early 1980s and published in 1997) by Hodrick and Prescott to analyze post-war US business cycles.

Technically, it is a two-sided linear filter that computes the smoothed series s of a y series by minimizing the variance of y around s, subject to a penalty that constrains the second difference of s. The minimization programme can be written as:

$$\underset{s}{\mathrm{Min}} \sum_{t=1}^{T} (y_t - s_t)^2 + \lambda \sum_{t=2}^{T-1} ((s_{t+1} - s_t) - (s_t - s_{t-1}))^2$$

where λ is the smoothness parameter which penalizes the variability in the growth component, s. As λ goes to infinity, this corresponds to a linear trend. That is to say, the smaller this penalty parameter, the smoother the trend. For annual data, Hodrick and Prescott recommend using $\lambda = 100$. This technique makes it possible to reduce the long-run movement fluctuations of the process due to short term components. In our case (Fig. 10.1, line *HP Trend*), we can observe a first decreasing trend broken by the 1979 oil shock, followed by another increase.

This analysis suggests that the oil real price is mean reverting in the sense that it reverses to a trend. One of this chapter's challenges will be to examine whether oil prices are, in fact, mean reverting. Prices are usually considered as unit root processes, but we will show that classical unit root tests are likely to be inconclusive in the case of oil prices, for time series spanning several decades. Indeed, examining the long-run time series of real oil prices spanning a century, suggests non-linearity because of the existence of several breaking points. For example, OPEC behaviour in 1973–74 may be a candidate for a structural break. When working with classical regression models, this assumption can be checked using different testing procedures (Wald test, Hansen test, Cusums test, Lagrange multiplier statistic, and so forth) depending on whether the timing of the break is known or not. Once the structural breaks are identified, restricted regression and what is known as a spline function can be used to achieve the desired effect. In the context of time series, Perron (1989) has proved that the presence of structural breaks in the data may introduce a bias in the conclusions of unit root tests. Thus, taking structural change into account in a model is important in order to obtain a relevant statistical test.

In our case, a first step will be to show, thanks to a Wald test (usually called Chow test when applied on time series) that the regression, on which classical unit root tests are based, provides different estimates depending on the sample used (before or after the 1973 oil shock). Consequently, we implement specific unit root tests (Perron 1989, 1990) that take into account the possibility of a break in the data. Thus we will consider the 1973 oil shock as a structural break point after having checked this assumption with the Chow test for a structural break. This methodology leads us to a conclusion about the mean reversion feature of oil prices over the long term.

Finally, we will consider this oil price series as a stochastic process that reverses to trend lines with slopes and levels that may shift continuously and unpredictably over time. This thesis was first developed by Pindyck (1999). It interprets this trend line economically as a proxy for long-run marginal costs, according to the Hotelling model for depletable resources. Pindyck (1999) uses the Kalman filter to estimate this trend and to produce a forecast of the path oil prices could follow during the next two decades. In fact, long-run marginal cost is an unobservable variable: no data series can reflect this concept. So this trend will be considered as the state variable of the Kalman filter model. Its main advantage in our context is that this technique is forward looking and thus can be applied for forecasting purposes.

Literature review

An important issue in the literature has been the mean reversion features of oil prices. The presence of structural breaks in the series such as the oil price shock in 1973 suggests implementing specific unit root tests. Perron (1989, 1990) derives test statistics which make it possible to distinguish between a unit root process and stationary fluctuations around a mean or a trend function which contains a one-time break. He shows that standard unit root tests tend to reject the unit root hypothesis when a change in the constant or linear trend of the Data Generating Process (DGP) exists, and he proposed tests for the unit root hypothesis using a model with a structural break in a deterministic term. While the purpose of his paper is to test the unit root hypothesis in the whole sample period, it demonstrates the importance of considering structural breaks in a model. He applies this test to the Nelson–Plosser data set and to the post-war quarterly real GNP series. For 11 of the 14 series analysed by Nelson and Plosser, and judged by the latter as random walks, he finds that the unit root hypothesis can be rejected at a high confidence level. Fluctuations are indeed stationary around a deterministic trend function which contains a one-time break. Perron considers the 1929 crash and the 1973 oil price shock as *a priori* known. This point is quite interesting because it leads to an important debate in econometric theory. Perron (1989) was criticized by Banerjee, Lumsdaine and Stock (1992), Christiano (1992) and Zivot and Andrews (1992) because he assumed that the break point is known, while these studies insist that the break point must be unknown and decided upon according to the data. However, as explained by Perron (1994), there are situations where the break is known and, therefore, it seems appropriate to consider the testing problem for both cases of a known and unknown break point, depending on the situation.

The mean reversion of commodity prices to a marginal cost of production has been demonstrated a number of times in the literature (see, for instance, Geman and Nguyen (2002) for the case of agricultural commodities). The present study will be mainly based on Pindyck (1999). He applies a multivariate version of the Ornstein–Uhlenbeck process to the energy price long-run evolution which could take into account that the marginal cost may fluctuate in slope and level over time. We will see that this idea is supported by the famous Hotelling (1931) model for depletable resource production.

Unit root testing when the presence of a break is allowed

In this section we present the mean reversion features of oil prices. The presence of structural breaks in the series, such as the oil price shock in 1973, suggests implementing specific unit root tests. Perron is one of the leading econometricians working on the topic of structural breaks. He first demonstrated the failure of classical and widely-used unit root tests to account for such breaks, and, as a result, the spuriously high estimates of degrees of persistence.

We will, therefore, first briefly describe the usual unit root test results and point out their drawbacks in the context of our study. Then we will prove the existence of a break in 1973 in the DGP underlying the oil price process using the Chow test for structural breaks. Finally, we will apply Perron's methodology in order to test for unit roots in a DGP in which a break is allowed.

Table 10.2 Results of unit root tests

	Test-statistics *(Constant and trend in the equation test)*		
	1930–2004	1930–73	1974–2004
Augmented Dickey–Fuller unit root test	−2.299	−3.572**	−4.626**
Elliott-Rothenberg-Stock DF-GLS unit root test	−2.231	−3.683**	−2.705
Kwiatkowski–Phillips–Schmidt–Shin stationarity test	0.089	0.151+	0.112

Note: * and ** indicate that a unit root can be rejected at the 10 per cent and 5 per cent levels, respectively, + indicates that stationarity can be rejected at the 5 per cent level.

Source: EViews.

Note that all the tests do not always lead to the same conclusion. On the whole, we can conclude that the unit root can be rejected for oil price data of conventional test size when working on sub-samples but not over the whole period. Alternatively, these results may be explained by shifts in the slope of the trend line or in the mean of the process. In any case, a failure to reject a unit root does not imply an acceptance of a unit root; it simply leaves the question open.

Testing for a structural break

In specifying a regression model, we presume that its usual assumptions, notably the mean reversion, apply for all the observations in our sample. As demonstrated by Perron (1989, 1990), the degree of persistence of a given time series will be exaggerated if the investigator fails to recognize the presence of a break in the mean or in the trend of the process. Thus, before drawing any firm conclusions about oil price persistence, it is important to obtain formal econometric evidence about the presence or absence of structural breaks in this series.

In this section, we will show that structural parameters estimated in the ADF test implemented above are not constant over the time of the analysis, thanks to a simple but very useful test. In fact, structural change testing is one of the more common applications of the Wald test. In this context, the Wald test is also called a breakpoint test of Chow (1960). The testing procedure is quite simple. We run the same regression over the full sample, and then divide it into two sub-samples around the break date, which must be known *a priori*. The ADF specification can be written as:

$$y_t = \mu + \alpha y_{t-1} + \sum_{i=1}^{k} c_i \Delta y_{t-i} + e_t$$

As has already been shown, the ADF procedure tests the null hypothesis that the process exhibits a unit root ($\alpha = 1$). More precisely, Perron (1989, 1990) demonstrated that an exogenous shock in the deterministic part of the equation may lead one to accept the unit root hypothesis.

The Chow test procedure aims at comparing the parameter estimates obtained by OLS in order to check if they are statistically identical over different periods of time. The statistics are calculated as follows:

$$F = \frac{\dfrac{(SSR_r - (SSR_1 + SSR_2))}{K}}{\dfrac{(SSR_1 + SSR_2)}{(T - 2K)}}$$

where SSR_r represents the sum of squared residuals of the regression over the full sample, SSR_1 and SSR_2 are the sums of squared residuals on the subsamples, K is the number of parameters estimated, and T is the number of observations in the whole sample. The statistics thus follow a $F(2K, T - 2K)$ distribution, under the null hypothesis of equality of the parameters over the whole period of estimation.

In our case, the Chow test implies the rejection of the null hypothesis at the 1 per cent level:

Chow breakpoint test: 1973

F-statistic	3.783421	Probability	**0.001222**

This test permits us to conclude that using ADF regression to test for unit roots of oil prices from 1930 to 2004 is a misspecification. In fact, it does not take into account the change in the level of the parameters – in particular the intercept – due to the structural break implied by the 1973 first oil price shock.

Perron's test for unit roots

Perron (1989, 1990) derives test statistics which make it possible to distinguish between a unit root process and stationary fluctuations around a mean/trend which contains a one-time break. So, we can wonder if the 1973 oil shock is not the point that leads classical unit root tests to reject unit roots for oil price data. This example shows how important it is to take into account structural changes in a model for statistical tests. Perron (1989, 1990) shows that standard unit-root tests tend not to reject the unit root hypothesis when a change in a constant and/or a linear trend exists, and he proposed tests for a unit-root using a model with a structural break in a deterministic trend.

Perron's methodology considers the classical Dickey–Fuller (1979) type of regression of the form:

$$y_t = \mu + \alpha y_{t-1} + \sum_{i=1}^{k} c_i \Delta y_{t-i} + e_t$$

and allows for a change in the mean; that is to say that μ is impacted by a structural break. The usual characterization is generalized, however, to allow a one-time change in the structure of the series occurring at a time $T_B (1 < T_B < T)$. Formally, this equation can be rewritten as follows:

$$y_t = \mu + \gamma DU_t + dD(T_B)_t + \alpha y_{t-1} + \sum_{i=1}^{k} c_i \Delta y_{t-i} + e_t$$

with $DU_t = 0$ if $t \leq T_B$ and 1 otherwise, and $D(T_B) = 1$ if $t = T_B$. Perron (1990) proposes tables that permit hypothesis testing. The critical values are obtained via simulation methods and depend also on the parameter $\lambda = T_B/T$.

We implement this model and estimate the regression using OLS on the sample 1930–2004. The time of break is set to the first oil shock, that is to say $T_B = 1973$. The number of lags k of the autoregressive part of the equation is determined by minimizing Akaike information and the Schwarz criteria, and checking the good features of the residuals.

Table 10.3 Perron test's equation

Variable	Coefficient	Std. error	*t*-Statistic	Prob.
C	0.910557	0.225015	4.046643	0.0001
DU	0.320203	0.091616	3.495042	0.0009
DT_B	0.885044	0.199213	4.442698	0.0000
LBRENT(−1)	0.643941	0.087556	7.354636	0.0000
DLBRENT(−1)	−0.018725	0.096161	−0.194726	0.8462
DLBRENT(−2)	0.083094	0.093977	0.884199	0.3798
DLBRENT(−3)	0.084657	0.091752	0.922675	0.3596
DLBRENT(−4)	0.127428	0.091357	1.394836	0.1678
DLBRENT(−5)	0.312374	0.093469	3.342000	0.0014
DLBRENT(−6)	0.222660	0.097834	2.275885	0.0262
R-squared	0.918687	Mean dependent var		2.946182
Adjusted R-squared	0.907428	S.D. dependent var		0.580746
S.E. of regression	0.176696	Akaike info criterion		−0.505207
Sum squared resid	2.029395	Schwarz criterion		−0.196208
Log likelihood	28.94524	*F*-statistic		81.59731
Durbin–Watson stat	2.027888	Prob(*F*-statistic)		0.000000

Note: LBRENT (−1) is the first lag of the log of oil price, DLBRENT(−*i*) = LBRENT(*i*) − LBRENT (*i* − 1).

Source: EViews.

As in the case of classical unit root tests, we calculate the t-statistic associated with the OLS estimate of α to test the hypothesis $\alpha = 1$:

$$t_{\hat{\alpha}} = (0.644 - 1)/0.087 = -4.07$$

In our case, $\lambda = T_B/T = 0.58$ and the percentage points of distribution of $t_{\hat{\alpha}}$ simulated by Perron (1990) are presented in Table 10.4.

Table 10.4 Critical values of the asymptotic distribution of t_α when $\lambda = 0.4 - 0.6$ according to Perron's simulations

p.value/Sample size	1.0%	2.5%	5.0%	10%	90%	95%	97.5%	99%
$T = 50$	−4.11	−3.71	−3.43	−3.08	−0.74	−0.37	−0.11	0.26
$T = 100$	−4.03	−3.68	−3.38	−3.05	−0.74	−0.42	−0.10	0.23

Source: EViews.

The unit root hypothesis is easily rejected with a p-value lower than 0.025 ($T = 74$, our sample is [1930; 2004]). Moreover, the coefficients are highly significant, which confirms the existence of a break in the data. In particular, $\alpha = 0.64$ shows substantial mean reversion effects.

In summary, we have shown, thanks to Perron's methodology, that the shift observed in the trend line can bias the conclusions of traditional unit root tests. Since we could not introduce the quadratic trend shown in Figure 10.1 into the equation test, we have worked with a constant mean on a smaller sample. This statistical test allows us to use oil price as a mean reverting process on sub-periods. This conclusion is consistent with the fact that stochastic models that have been investigated for stock and interest rates over the last 30 years are now adjusted to commodity markets.

Presentation and specification of mean reversion models of commodity price processes

Even if sharp rises are observed during short periods for specific events such as weather or political conditions in producing countries, commodity prices tend generally to revert to 'normal level' over a long period. This may be viewed as unsurprising: if demand is constant or slightly increasing over time as in the case of coffee, for example, and if supply adjusts to this pattern, prices should stay roughly the same on average. In the case of the oil market, we can observe, over time, an increase of demand to which supply has to adjust. The resulting properties of oil price are a consequence of the general behaviour of mean-reversion combined with spikes in prices caused by shocks in the supply/demand balance. For instance, suppose we observe that oil prices jump from \$53/bl to \$59/bl due to an unexpected event (for example, cold wave, plant disruption, and so on). Most market practitioners would agree that it is highly probable that prices will eventually return to their average level once the cause of the jump goes away.

A theoretical justification for the movements in trend level and slope: Hotelling model

This analysis is in line with models of exhaustible resource production that incorporate exploration and proven reserves accumulation over time, as well as technological change. Let us consider the basic Hotelling model of a depletable resource production. Hotelling (1931) assumes that the resource is produced in a competitive market. According to energy economics literature, this hypothesis holds for oil production, over the long term, although OPEC has succeeded in pushing oil prices above competitive levels for periods of time. Indeed, a large part of recent extraction exhaustible resource models, which are used to assess the impact of substitution behaviours between different kinds of resources or taxes on energy consumption, is based on the Hotelling model, and thus on this assumption of competitive production.

In this model, the price trajectory is $dP/dt = r(P - c)$, with c the constant marginal cost and r the interest rate. We set $P_t = P_0 \cdot e^{rt} + c$. If the demand function is isoelastic with unitary elasticity, that is to say a demand function of the form $Q_t = AP_t^{-1}$, the rate of production is given by $Q_t = A(c + P_0e^{rt})^{-1}$. The cumulative production over the life of the resource must equal the initial reserve level, $R_0 : R_0 = \int_0^{\infty} A(c + P_0e^{rt})^{-1}\,dt$. Performing the integration: $R_0 = \frac{A}{rc}\log(\frac{c+P_0}{P_0})$, so that the price level is given by:

$$p_t = c + \left(\frac{ce^{rt}}{(e^{rcR_0/A} - 1)}\right)$$

This implies that the slope of the price trajectory derived from the model is:

$$\frac{dP_t}{dt} = \frac{rce^{rt}}{(e^{rcR_0/A} - 1)}$$

Thus, change in demand, extraction costs, and reserves all affect this slope. For example, an increase in A causes this slope to increase, while increases in c or R_0 cause the slope to decrease. In addition, increases in A or c lead to an increase in the price level, whereas an increase in R_0 causes a decrease in this level. If, as Pindyck (1999) argues, these factors fluctuate in a continuous and unpredictable manner over time, then long-run energy prices should revert to a trend that itself fluctuates in the same way.

Stochastic modelling of oil price processes

Pindyck (1999) argues that a model of long-run energy price evolution should incorporate both a reversion to the trend of long-run total marginal cost, and continuous random fluctuations in the level and the slope of that trend. These two characteristics correspond to a general version of the multivariate Ornstein–Uhlenbeck (OU) process. This kind of stochastic process was first introduced by Vasicek in 1977. He used it in order to describe the short term rate dynamic.

First, if we assume that the oil price follows a simple trending OU process, where the trend is quadratic, it means that the detrended price follows an arithmetic process. That process can be written:

$$d\bar{p} = -\gamma\bar{p}dt + \sigma dz$$

where, in our case, $\bar{p} = p - \alpha_0 - \alpha_1 t - \alpha_2 t^2$ is the detrended price. Hence, the parameter $-\gamma$ represents the mean reversion toward the quadratic trend.

A bivariate (price and trend) OU process is written in continuous time as:

$$d\bar{p} = (-\gamma\bar{p} + \lambda x)dt + \sigma dz_p \tag{10.1}$$

Box 10.1 An introduction to stochastic modelling

The oil spot price over time, starting now, constitutes a stochastic process $p(t)$. Our concern is to find the most appropriate mathematical structure for p. The choice of this stochastic process should lead to a probability distribution for the random variable $p(T)(T > t)$ that agrees with the empirical features in terms of empirical moments and dynamics already observed above. We will present the most general motion used to describe the mathematical structure of a process, i.e. the *Arithmetic Brownian process* (for more details, see Geman, 2005). A process p is called 'an arithmetic Brownian motion' if it satisfies the stochastic differential equation:

$$dp_t = \alpha dt + \sigma dz_t$$

where α and σ are real numbers, σ being strictly positive; dp_t represents the change in p over an infinitesimal time interval dt; dz_t represent the differential of Brownian motion (z_t) and follows a normal distribution with mean 0 and standard deviation $\sqrt{n}$.

Hence, dispersion of the change in p around its expected mean αdt increases with σ, the fundamental volatility parameter.

where x represents the long-run total marginal cost. It is itself an OU process:

$$dx = -\delta x dt + \sigma_x dz_x \tag{10.2}$$

dz_p and dz_x can be correlated. This pair of equations simply says that $\bar{p}$ reverts to $(\lambda/\gamma)x$ rather than 0, and x is mean-reverting around 0 if $\delta > 0$ and a random walk if $\delta = 0$.

So far, we have described a price process that reverts to a trend which is subject to continuous random fluctuations in level. We will finally implement a more general model that allows for fluctuations in both the level and slope of the trend. It can be written:

$$d\bar{p} = (-\gamma\bar{p} + \lambda_1 x + \lambda_2 yt)\, dt + \sigma dz_p \tag{10.3}$$

$$dx = -\delta_1 x dt + \sigma_x dz_x \tag{10.4}$$

$$dy = -\delta_2 y dt + \sigma_y dz_y \tag{10.5}$$

Recall that eqn. (10.3) is written in terms of the detrended price. If we replace $\bar{p}$ by p, we obtain:

$$dp = [-\gamma(p - \alpha_0 - \alpha_1 t - \alpha_2 t^2) + \alpha_1 + 2\alpha_2 t + \lambda_1 x + \lambda_2 yt]\, dt + \sigma\, dz_p$$

$$\Leftrightarrow dp = (-\gamma p - \alpha_0 - \alpha_1 t - \alpha_2 t^2 + \lambda_1 x + \lambda_2 yt) dt + \sigma\, dz_p \tag{10.6}$$

Equation (10.6) describes a process in which the log price of oil, p, reverts to the long-run total marginal cost with a level (eqn. (10.4)) and slope (eqn. (10.5)) that fluctuate stochastically, and which may be unobservable. These equations lead to the following discrete-time model:

$$p_t = \rho p_{t-1} + b_1 + b_2 t + b_3 t^2 + \phi_{1t} + \phi_{2t} t + \varepsilon_t \tag{10.7}$$

$$\phi_{1t} = c_1 \phi_{1,t-1} + \upsilon_{1t} \tag{10.8}$$

$$\phi_{2t} = c_2 \phi_{2,t-1} + \upsilon_{2t} \tag{10.9}$$

This set of three equations will be econometrically estimated. ϕ_{1t} and ϕ_{2t} describe the long-run marginal cost of oil at time t and thus will be treated as unobservable. This state variable model is naturally estimated using Kalman filter methods, since we make the further assumption that the distribution of the error terms ε_t, υ_{1t} and υ_{2t} is multivariate normal and that ε_t is uncorrelated with υ_{1t} and υ_{2t}. Moreover, in order to simplify the estimation procedure, we assume that υ_{1t} and υ_{2t} are uncorrelated.

Given that the series for the optimal linear estimate (minimum mean-square error) of the unobservable variables ϕ_{1t} and ϕ_{2t} is conditional on past information, and given the variance of the estimation errors in t, the Kalman filter procedure calculates the log-likelihood function, which depends on the parameters of the model. This is a recursive algorithm for sequentially updating the one-step ahead estimate of the state mean and variance, given new information. Thus, this method is well suited for forecasting.

Box 10.2 Linear state space models and the Kalman filter

The following system of equations represents a linear state space model for a n^*1 vector y_t.

$$y_t = c_t + Z_t \alpha_t + \varepsilon_t$$

$$\alpha_{t+1} = d_t + T_t \alpha_t + \upsilon_t$$

where α_t is a m^*1 vector of possibly unobserved variables (known as state variables), and c_t, Z_t, α_t, d_t and T_t are conformable vectors and matrices, and where ε_t and υ_t are error vectors following Gaussian distributions with zero mean. In this model, we assume that the unobserved state vector moves over time as a first-order vector regression. Hence, we usually refer to the first set of equations as the 'signal' equations and the second as the 'state' equations.

We specify that the disturbance vectors ε_t and υ_t are serially independent, such that: $\Omega_t = \text{var}\begin{bmatrix} \varepsilon_t \\ \upsilon_t \end{bmatrix} = \begin{bmatrix} H_t G_t \\ G_t Q_t \end{bmatrix}$ where H_t is an n^*n symmetric variance matrix, Q_t is an m^*m symmetric variance matrix, and G_t is an n^*m matrix of covariances.

We can define the mean and the variance matrix of the conditional distribution:

$$\alpha_{t|s} \equiv E_s(\alpha_t)$$

$$P_{t|s} \equiv E_s[(\alpha_t - \alpha_{t|s})(\alpha_t - \alpha_{t|s})']$$

where s indicates that expectations are taken using the conditional distribution for that period.

If we assume that $s = t - 1$ and that errors are Gaussian, $\alpha_{t|t-1}$ is the minimum mean square error estimator of α_t and $P_{t|t-1}$ is the mean square error (MSE) of $\alpha_{t|t-1}$.

Given the one-step ahead state conditional mean, we obtain the linear minimum MSE one-step ahead estimate of y_t:

$$\tilde{y}_t = y_{t|t-1} \equiv E_{t-1}(y_t) = E(y_t | \alpha_{t|t-1}) = c_t + Z_t \alpha_{t|t-1}$$

The one-step ahead prediction error is given by:

$$\tilde{\varepsilon}_t = \varepsilon_{t|t-1} \equiv y_t - \tilde{y}_{t|t-1}$$

and the prediction error variance is defined as:

$$\tilde{F}_t = F_{t|t-1} \equiv \text{var}(\varepsilon_{t|t-1}) = Z_t P_{t|t-1} Z_t' + H_t$$

The Kalman filter is a recursive algorithm for sequentially updating the one-step ahead estimate of the state mean and variance, given new information. Given initial values of the state mean and covariance, the Kalman filter may be used to compute one-step ahead estimates of the state and the associated mean square error matrix, the contemporaneous or filtered state and mean variance, and the one-step ahead prediction, prediction error, and prediction error variance.

To implement the Kalman filter, we need to replace any unknown elements of system matrices by their estimates. Under the assumption that the ε_t and υ_t are normally distributed, the sample log likelihood can be written:

$$\log L(\theta) = -\frac{nT}{2}\log 2\pi - \frac{1}{2}\sum_t \log[\tilde{F}_t(\theta)] - \frac{1}{2}\sum_t \tilde{\varepsilon}_t'(\theta)\tilde{F}_t(\theta)^{-1}\tilde{\varepsilon}_t(\theta)$$

Then, numerical optimization methods are required to maximize this log-likelihood function with respect to the unknown parameters θ (for more details, see Hamilton, 1994).

Estimation methodology and forecasting results

One issue that arises when using the Kalman filter is that initial estimates for the parameters and state variables are needed to begin the recursion. Typically, we use OLS estimates obtained by assuming that the state variables are constant parameters. Thus, we run the following regression over the first several data points (1865–90).

According to this estimation, we can set priors concerning the mean of our state variables, $MPRIOR = \begin{bmatrix} 4.253 \\ -0.19 \end{bmatrix}$, and their standard deviation, $VPRIOR = \begin{bmatrix} 2.32 & 0 \\ 0 & 0.008 \end{bmatrix}$. In addition, note that we drop the term t^2 in the signal equation in order to obtain convergence of our estimates. The system can finally be written:

$$\text{signal equation}: lbrent_t = \beta_1 * lbrent_{t-1} + \beta_2 * t + sv1_t + sv2_t * t + \varepsilon_t$$

$$\text{state equation 1}: sv1_t = \gamma_1 sv1_{t-1} + v_{1t}$$

$$\text{state equation 2}: sv2_t = \gamma_2 sv2_{t-1} + v_{2t}$$

Table 10.5 OLS initialization of the Kalman filter

Variable	Coefficient	Std. error	*t*-Statistic	Prob.
Constant	4.253136	1.522750	2.793063	0.0125
LBRENT(-1)	0.345191	0.219684	1.571308	0.1345
@TREND	−0.194557	0.089526	−2.173184	0.0442
(@TREND)2	0.003928	0.002023	1.941647	0.0689
R-squared	0.755707	Mean dependent var		3.198443
Adjusted R-squared	0.712597	S.D. dependent var		0.491436
S.E. of regression	0.263459	Akaike info criterion		0.339805
Sum squared resid	1.179980	Schwarz criterion		0.538761
Log likelihood	0.432052	*F*-statistic		17.52955
Durbin–Watson stat	1.433627	Prob(*F*-statistic)		0.000019

Source: EViews.

Estimations for the full sample are shown in the following table. The table shows the estimates of the parameters, along with the final year (2004) estimates of the state variables, $sv1_T$ and $sv2_T$.

Table 10.6 Kalman filter estimation

Variable	Coefficient	Std. error	Z-Statistic	Prob.
β_1	0.803004	0.065791	12.20531	0
β_2	0.005189	0.001655	3.135239	0.0017
γ_1	0.950575	0.011696	81.27525	0
γ_2	0.893105	0.015833	56.40795	0
	Final state	**Root MSE**	**Z-Statistic**	**Prob.**
$sv1_T$	0.003468	0.000467	7.429206	0
$sv2_T$	−5.64E-08	1.02E-08	−5.545514	0
Log likelihood	0.631206	Akaike info criterion		0.049908
Parameters	4	Schwarz criterion		0.13599
Diffuse priors	0	Hannan–Quinn criter		0.084889

Source: EViews.

We estimate the preceding system using data for the sub-samples 1865–1973, 1865–1980, 1865–1990, 1865–1996, 1865–2000, and 1865–2004. In each case, we used the estimates of the parameters, along with the final year estimates of the state variables, $sv1_T$ and $sv2_T$ to forecast the log price out to the years 2025.

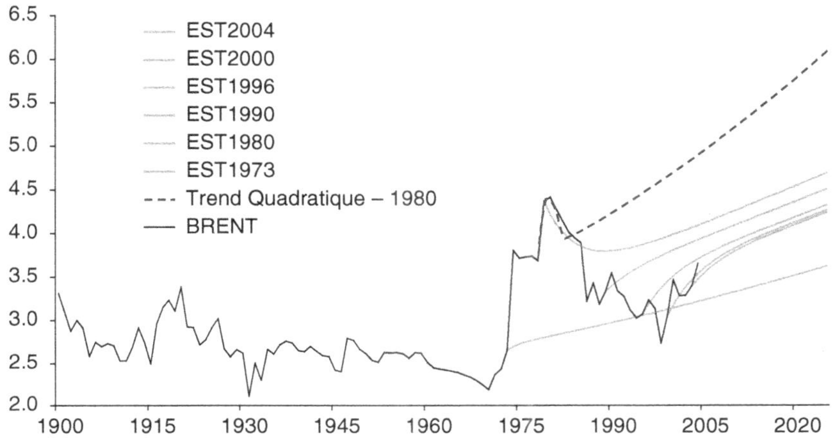

Figure 10.2 Log oil price forecasts

Note: EST(x) = Result of Kalman Filter forecast on the sample [x + 1; … ; 2025] when the model is estimated using the sample [1865; …; x].

First, observe that the forecasts which begin at several dates, spanning a range of 31 years (1973–2004) converge quite well to a narrow band for the years 2005 to 2025. Of course the forecast beginning in 1970 is a bit lower than the others because of the impact of oil shocks, but the other forecasts reach, on the average, 80 dollars (constant 2005 dollars). Assuming a yearly inflation of 3 per cent, this corresponds to 151$/bl in current dollars in 2025. This is much more relevant than the results of trend forecasts, which are much more dependant on the starting date (see Figure 10.1).

Energy market implications

These non-structural models perform well in forecasting oil prices, but Pindyck (1999) showed that they perform less well for coal and natural gas. Indeed, Kalman Filter use requires initialization that is very sensitive to the first few observations. Nonetheless, these models are quite promising because they utilize a non-structural framework which does not require formulating structural hypotheses on demand, market structure or other variables. The Hotelling model for depletable resources supports this view of a mean reversion to a stochastically fluctuating trend. It enables us to forecast the price of a barrel of oil at 80 dollars (constant 2005 dollars), or 151 current dollars in 2025. This kind of estimation makes feasible new investments that could have appeared too expensive before.

References

Banerjee A., Lumsdaine, R.L. and Stock, J.H. (1992) 'Recursive and sequential tests of the unit-root and trend-break hypothesis: theory and international evidence', *Journal of Business and Economic Statistics*, vol. 10, pp. 271–87.

BP Statistical Review of World Energy (June 2004).

Chow, G. (1960) 'Tests of equality between sets of coefficients in two linear regressions', *Econometrica*, vol. 28, pp. 591–605.

Christiano, L.J. (1992) 'Searching for a break in GNP', *Journal of Business and Economics Statistics*, vol. 10, pp. 237–50.

Geman, H. (2005) *Commodities and Commodity derivatives. Modeling and Pricing for Agricultural, Metals and Energy.* Wiley Lasa.

Greene, W.H. (2003) *Econometrics Analysis*, 5th edn (Englewood Cliffs, NJ: Prentice-Hall).

Hamilton, J.D. (1994) *Times Series Analysis*, Princeton, NJ: (Princeton University Press).

Hodrick, R.J. and Prescott, E.C. (1997) 'Postwar US Business Cycles: An Empirical Investigation', *Journal of Money, Credit, and Banking*, vol. 29, pp. 1–16.

Hotelling, H. (1931) 'The economics of exhaustible resources', *Journal of Political Economy*, vol. 39.

Nelson, C.R. and Plosser, C.I. (1982) 'Trends and random walks in macroeconomics time series', *Journal of Monetary Economics*, vol. 10, pp. 139–62.

Perron, P. (1989) 'The great crash, the oil price shock, and the unit root hypothesis', *Econometrica*, vol. 57, pp. 1361-401.

Perron, P. (1990) 'Testing for a unit root in a time series with a changing mean', *Journal of Business and Economics Statistics*, vol. 8, pp. 153–62.

Geman, H. and Nguyen, V.N. (2005) 'Soybean Inventory and Forward Curves Dynamics' *Management Science*, vol. 51, issue 7.

Perron, P. (1994) 'Trend, unit root and structural change in macroeconomic time series', in Rao, B.B. (ed.) *Cointegration for the Applied Economist* (Basingstoke: Macmillan), pp. 113–46.

Pindyck, R.S. (1999) 'The long-run evolution of energy prices', *Energy Journal*, vol. 20, pp. 1–27.

Vasicek, O. (1977) 'An equilibrium characterization of the term structure', *Journal of Financial Economics*, vol. 5(3), pp. 177–88.

Zivot, E. and Andrews, W.K. (1992) 'Further evidence on the great crash, the oil-price shock, and the unit root hypothesis', *Journal of Business and Economics Statistics*, vol. 10, pp. 251–70.

11
The Impact of Vertical Integration and Horizontal Diversification on the Value of Energy Firms

Carlo Pozzi and Philippe Vassilopoulos

Introduction

We analyse the long-run return performance of 27 value-weighted equity portfolios based on a classification of the US energy sector that follows traditional industrial organization categories. When adjusted to market and fuel risks, portfolio returns show that both vertical integration and horizontal diversification failed to produce shareholder value during the 1990–2003 period. This confirms the theoretical predictions of both financial economics and industrial organization and shows that the wave of corporate restructuring that has interested US energy industries over the last decade may have occurred at a net cost to firm shareholders.

Economic theory posits both positive and negative impacts of horizontal diversification on firm value. It also maintains that vertical integration produces value when firms internalize functions which may not be adequately performed in the market. Nonetheless, there is much empirical evidence indicating that horizontal diversification across multiple activities is generally harmful to stock value, while vertical integration has at best mixed effects. For instance, various authors show the presence of a discount in the value of diversified firms with respect to single business companies in various industries. Likewise, in an era of growing commoditization, the rationale of vertical integration is increasingly challenged by the possibility of outsourcing various stages of firm value chains. And both facts seem to be significant throughout time and across countries.

Is this the case also in the energy sector? To answer this question, two separate aspects should be taken into account. The first has to do with the relative scarcity of industry-based literature on the value of fuel diversification and vertical integration in the energy sector. Mainstream research seems to have little interest in the financial value of these strategies; hence some novel empirical analyses may be useful. The second aspect regards some evident idiosyncrasies of the industry. There are proven complementarities in the production of various fuels (for example, between oil and natural gas in their extraction) or in the transformation of a primary source of energy into a secondary source, as Hunt (2002) illustrates, in the cogeneration of power and steam. Therefore, it could be hypothesized that the energy sector enjoys some special conditions, for which both horizontal diversification and vertical integration possibly have inherent value.

In this chapter we measure the financial value of these conducts by focusing on the equity return of a large sample of energy listings in the United States. Using daily portfolio returns, adjusted by systematic and fuel risks, we find little evidence to support the value-creating character of both phenomena. While our analysis shows some limited value linked to vertical integration, there seems to be a significant diversification discount across various US energy industries. This confirms previous empirical findings in other industries and seems to refute the specificities of the energy business. The claimed synergies stemming from vertical and horizontal expansions do not easily materialize and this may attest both to the inferior ability of firms, with respect to equity markets, to allocate capital among their various businesses and to the negative effect of agency costs on equity value when firm executives engage in vertical expansion.

The remainder of the chapter is organized as follows. First we briefly summarize the existing empirical literature on the topic, then we illustrate the econometric methodology through which we determine the risk-adjusted performance of energy equities. The next section describes the dataset of equity returns under investigation. We then present our results. In the final sections we draw some inferences from the econometric findings.

Literature background

Vertical integration

In his classic contribution, Coase (1937) sets the foundation of the theory of the firm. Corporations and markets are alternative choices with respect to production organization, and transaction costs are the cornerstone. Corporations vertically expand until the marginal cost of internalizing production equals the marginal cost of outsourcing it in the market. This occurs, for instance, when firms integrate production upwards in order to avoid potential losses linked to the opportunistic behaviour of strong external suppliers. Or, similarly, when they internalize distribution downwards if confronted by high concentration among their customers.

Within this general rationale, various authors have further discussed different justifications of firm expansion. Bain (1956, 1959) points out that vertical integration is not only a way to defend against market power, but also to create it. Tirole (1988) sees it as a profitable response to the cost of contiguous monopolies. Others think it may facilitate price discrimination (Perry, 1978), or it can be used to raise rivals' costs by increasing their costs of entry in the industry (Aghion and Bolton, 1987; Ordover, Salop and Saloner, 1990; Hart and Tirole, 1990). Finally, Stigler (1951) advances a life-cycle theory arguing that, in an infant industry, vertical integration is more likely because the demand for specialized inputs is too small to support their independent production. To summarize, it appears that contractual incompleteness, combined with asset specificity, complexity and uncertainty, play a central theoretical role in justifying transaction costs and the increase of the probability that opportunistic behaviour may plague market relations (Carlton, 1979).

With this abundance of hypotheses, empirical studies have obviously thrived in industrial organization and have attempted to assess the factual importance of different factors as transaction cost drivers. Most of these surveys are product-based and focus on single industries (automobile components, coal, aerospace systems, aluminum, chemicals, timber). For an extensive review of this literature, we refer the reader to Joskow (2003) who provides a complete survey of studies which, as a whole, confirm the role of asset specificity and market concentration as crucial in the provision of a strong incentive to internalizing production stages in single industries.

Horizontal diversification

Horizontal diversification consists, instead, of corporate expansion across industries not necessarily related to each other. Vis-à-vis vertical integration, the theoretical grounding behind horizontal diversification is less defined and, in particular, is characterized by two partially competing explanations.

On the one hand, industrial organization suggests that because of commonalities in technology or economies of scale firms may profit from synergies through the allocation of internally generated cash flows across different businesses (Williamson, 1975). So firms diversify internally and can expand without the risk of having to pay transaction costs linked to the exploitation of synergies in a contractual fashion. As a result, diversification usually occurs throughout related industries, although conglomerates at times claim substantial synergies from non industry-specific economies of scale and scope.

On the other hand, financial economics points out that firms should not do internally what their shareholders can more efficiently accomplish in the capital market. If shareholders wish to diversify their holdings, they can do that by mixing their equity portfolios with stocks issued by firms engaged in different businesses. In this way, they can replicate horizontal diversification at virtually no cost, and avoid any externality.

Indeed, as Jensen and Meckling (1976) point out, the decision to internally expand a firm has an explicit cost for shareholders, since it is often conditioned by a divergence of interest between firm managers and shareholders. Shareholders normally do not enjoy the possibility of perfectly monitoring managers, so after appointing executives, they give them discretional power in the performance of their duties. Managers may therefore promote corporate expansion in order to appropriate value for themselves, rather than to reap real synergies. This potential appropriation is an *agency cost*; a type of transaction cost which may ultimately end up destroying shareholder value.

Given this theoretical debate, empirical work has had a thorny problem to deal with and as a result its findings have been more controversial. However, the current availability of an extensive dataset on stock prices and their fine statistical basis has increasingly given the lead to financial research. We refer the reader to three representative studies which provide a broad overview of the general effect of horizontal diversification and do not leave much doubt about its financial consequences. Morck, Schleifer, and Vishny (1990), Lang and Stulz (1994) and Berger and Ofek (1995), through different approaches, find that in most cases diversified firms experience negative stock value adjustments as a result of their strategy. So, because of different agency problems,[1] it appears that horizontal diversification is often unable to produce the value that it could theoretically create, particularly when unrelated activities are considered.

The following sections extend the empirical testing of the value of vertical integration and horizontal diversification in energy businesses. As said in the introduction, because of technological and business commonality, energy activities could theoretically liberate valuable synergies when integrated more than other sectors. We factually verify this from the shareholders' standpoint.

Methodology

Tracking the value creation of vertical integration and horizontal diversification among energy firms requires forming different equity portfolios that separate a representative sample of energy firm stocks in two dimensions:

1) the fuel/energy that firms produce and/or trade – namely, oil, natural gas, power, coal and their combinations;
2) the vertical stage of business in which firms are involved – customarily defined in the energy business as *upstream*, *midstream* or *downstream* activities, and their integrations.

In this manner, it is possible to separately observe the value performance of:

a) portfolios of pure players – that is, firms engaged in a single productive stage of one type of energy;
b) portfolios of horizontally diversified firms – that is, companies involved in the production/trade of two or more types of energy, whether involving one or more stages of production;

c) portfolios of vertically integrated firms – that is, companies involved in the integrated production of a single type of energy across two or more stages of their value chain, by measuring their risk-adjusted returns over a sufficiently long time window.

The analysis of portfolio returns is preferable to the investigation of individual firm returns, since portfolios, by pooling more equities in a single asset, yield returns less affected by firm specificities and statistical disturbances. Here we exploit this property extensively (although in two cases, because of lack of data, two portfolios include only one firm) while maintaining the ability of portfolios to single out firm strategies by drawing the aggregation rationale directly from the industrial organization literature. As a result, we can avoid the traditional Standard Industrial Classification (SIC) through which census authorities separate firms according to their activities – a form of classification often used in financial studies of this type – and thus eliminate the risk of forming portfolios according to a taxonomy which is somewhat irrelevant for the purpose of this study.

A preliminary aggregation is presented in Table 11.1. Pure-player *basic* portfolios, which pool single-fuel and single-segment firms, are first identified.[2]

Notice that these preliminary nine basic portfolios do not manage to represent all firm activities in the sector. For instance, firms engaged in the extraction and distribution of oil – oil integrated firms – need to be tracked by a portfolio which results from the unification of OU and OD portfolios. As a result, starting from portfolios in Table 11.1 we identify 13 other *integrated* portfolios that complete the initial taxonomy and provide a list of 22 basic and integrated portfolios presented in Table 11.2 below. These 22 portfolios include 681 energy equities listed in the US according to the breakdown shown above and cover the entire set of activities observed in the sector.

In order to further imitate the diversification strategies discussed in the industrial literature, we consolidate most of the 22 portfolios (according to their business nature) and obtain five *aggregated* portfolios: pure oil firms (PO), pure natural gas firms (PG), pure power firms (PP), aggregated oil and natural gas firms (OG) and aggregated natural gas and power firms (GP). The

Table 11.1 Basic portfolios

	Tranformation stage	Oil O	Natural gas G	Power P	Coal C
Generation/Upstream	UP–U	OU	GU	PU	CO
Transmission/Transport	MID–M		GM	PM	
Distribution/Retail	DOWN–D	OD	GD	PD	

Table 11.2 Basic and integrated portfolios

No.	Portfolios	Portfolio codes	Firms
1	Oil upstream	OU	11
2	Oil up-downstream	OU + OD	3
3	Gas integrated and oil up-downstream	OU + OD + GU + GM + GD	17
4	Oil and gas upstream	OU + GU	330
5	Oil upstream and gas up-midstream	OU + GU + GM	8
6	Gas integrated and oil upstream	OU + GU + GM + GD	3
7	Oil downstream	OD	35
8	Gas mid-downstream and oil downstream	OD + GM + GD	7
9	Gas upstream	GU	6
10	Gas integrated	GU + GM + GD	5
11	Gas integrated and power up-downstream	GU + GM + GD + PU + PD	1
12	Gas up-midstream and power upstream	GU + GM + PU	1
13	Gas midstream	GM	11
14	Gas mid-downstream	GM + GD	39
15	Gas downstream	GD	39
16	Power upstream	PU	6
17	Power integrated	PU + PM + PD	77
18	Power and gas integrated	PU + PM + PD + GU + GM + GD	4
19	Power integrated and gas mid-downstream	PU + PM + PD + GM + GD	59
20	Power integrated and gas downstream	PU + PM + PD + GD	6
21	Power downstream	PD	3
22	Coal	CO	10

rationale of this consolidation in connection with the horizontal possibilities of fuel diversification in the energy sector is self-evident.

Daily returns on each of the 27 portfolios identified so far are then determined by adding daily individual firm returns weighted by firm daily market capitalization. *Value-weighted* portfolio returns therefore give an economically focused and normalized measure of performance. Portfolio weighted returns are, in fact, just an absolute measure of value creation. They track the change in the value of a portfolio of energy firms for an unspecified shareholder, but do not correct this change by considering the various types of risk that may be of interest for an investor who buys and holds energy stocks in the long term or by considering his ability to diversify his holdings through portfolio management.[3] *Risk-adjusted* portfolio returns, instead, can better track a correct measure of performance, since they correct absolute performance by risk. But in order to determine them it is necessary to identify various types of risk factors (typologies of risk exposures) that are of relevance for an unspecified investor in energy equities. Specifically, two broad categories of exposure appear to be significant:

1) On the one hand, as financial theory suggests, measuring the relative covariance of energy portfolio returns with market-wide weighted portfolio returns (determined across all main US equity bourses) provides a measure of the *systematic* risk borne by energy equities. Systematic risk is the risk of herding with market trends; namely, the possibility that energy equities fail to protect their holders from value losses when the whole market is plummeting.
2) On the other hand, measuring the relative covariance of energy portfolio returns with daily fuel price returns (determined using fuel prices registered in US commodity markets) provides a measure of the *fuel* risks that affect energy equities. Energy firms, in fact, produce and trade fuels, so they maintain a large part of their working capital invested in them. Their stocks may thus simply follow commodity market trends and fail to insulate their holders from value losses when fuel prices diminish.

Starting from portfolio absolute returns, with (1) market portfolio and (2) fuel price data we determine risk-adjusted returns using two complementary approaches which are elucidated in the following two sub-sections.[4]

Fama–French approach

First, we employ the well-known Fama and French (1993, 1996) approach in order to econometrically link our firm portfolio returns to three explanatory market factors (modelled as US market-wide portfolios). These three factors (as calculated by CRSP, see next section) are, respectively:

1) the daily weighted return of the US market-wide portfolio (Factor 1);
2) the daily time series of two special types of average portfolio returns, constructed from six benchmark portfolios, which divide US firms according to their value size and their market-to-book ratios (Factors 2 and 3).

The first of the latter two series (Factor 2) is the average daily return difference between the yield of small value firms and large value firms (*small-minus-large* – SML, a measure of size risk). The second of the latter two series (Factor 3) is the daily return difference between the returns of high growth firms and low growth firms (*high-minus-low* – HML, a measure of growth risk).

Using this method, we estimate an econometric specification of the type:

$$R_{it} = \beta_i^1 M_t + \beta_i^2 SMB_t + \beta_i^3 HML_t + \varepsilon_t \tag{11.1}$$

All daily returns fed to each of the four terms on both sides of equation (11.1) are determined as *excess-returns*, which are rates in excess of the daily yield on US treasury bonds (an approximation of the risk-free investment rate, R_{ft}, the yield profited by an investor for holding a risk-less asset that pays an interest with certainty. In other words, the time value of money). Therefore, portfolio returns R_{it} in (11.1) are excess-returns determined as $R_{it} = R^*_{it} - R_{ft}$, where R^*_{it} are total portfolio weighted-returns determined on day t for each of the 27 portfolios presented above (thus, with $i = (1, 2, \ldots, 27)$). As such, R_{it} solely measures the compensation that an investor receives for bearing a risky asset in the form of an energy equity portfolio.[5] Likewise, M_t, SMB_t and HML_t are the part of the daily return, on each of the portfolios chosen as a risk factors, that exceeds the risk-free rate. Betas, $\beta_i^1, \beta_i^2, \beta_i^3$, are then regression coefficients (that is, factor sensitivities). Finally, ε_t is an error term.

In (11.1), the first regression coefficient – the market beta, β_i^1 – represents the most relevant piece of information, since it tracks the systematic risk borne by an energy portfolio. Because of the partial correlation between all explanatory factors, its estimation is here adjusted by the presence of the other two return factors (SMB_t and HML_t) and gives a specific measure of the sensitivity of an energy portfolio to market risk.[6] Therefore, measuring how much an energy portfolio yields in a given time window, and subsequently weighting such return performance by its market beta, provides the risk-adjusted measurement of return that we need.

But equation (11.1) lends itself to further utilization. Note that it is rather simplistic to imagine that the portfolio sensitivity to risk factors $(\beta_i^1, \beta_i^2, \beta_i^3)$ remains stable over long periods of time. It is indeed conceivable that, as time passes, energy firms modify their technology as well as their management regime and, thus, experience changes in their ability to protect investors from market (and other) risks. This implies that a single estimation of (11.1) on a given dataset, along the entire time window of the time series that it comprises, may not be the best methodological choice, since it constrains the estimation of β_i^1, β_i^2 and β_i^3 to single values.

A better approach is to employ *rolling regressions*. Suppose there is a large dataset of past observations between today (t) and a remote earlier date ($t - m$). Given the large number of available observations, it is possible to preliminarily estimate our model over an early part of the entire dataset (that is, between $t - m$ and $t - n$, with $t - n$ being a later date than $t - m$), beginning from the oldest observation. This first estimation (the *in-sample* estimation) assesses the preliminary explanatory role of our three factors for energy firm returns. Once this has been done, our estimated model can then be used to determine what the (*out-of-sample*) return on an energy portfolio should have been on the first day after the estimation interval ($t - n + 1$). This is done by plugging into the three factor terms their return for that day ($t - n + 1$), and by using previously estimated beta values (in the in-sample estimation). This *fitted* (that is, predicted) return can then be compared with the actual return observed during that day. The difference between the $(t - n + 1)$'s actual and fitted returns yields a second type of *excess-return* estimation (not only in excess of the risk free rate, but also in excess of what an investor's compensation should have been, given the risk factor value that very date), a datum that measures whether the energy portfolio has abnormally yielded more or less than expected.

Repeating this in-sample-out-of-sample procedure every subsequent day (that is, by *rolling* the estimation of a daily regression between $t - n + 2$ and t) permits building a time series of abnormal returns for each energy portfolio. The evolution of these excess-returns over time provides in turn some relevant information on the dynamic behaviour (by the factors considered) of the risk-adjusted performance of energy portfolios. One complication with this method is establishing how many observations should enter in the in-sample estimation window of each daily regression (that is, finding the value of $m - n$). Predetermined rules are not available, but a consistent approach is to choose the estimation length that minimizes the average absolute value of excess returns, since this implies minimizing the out-of-sample error of the model.

Multi-factor approach

As mentioned above, energy portfolio returns may significantly covariate with fuel prices. However, in a de-segmented market like the US, informed shareholders have the ability to diversify their portfolios by directly investing in fuels, which are tradable commodities. Therefore, we assume that energy equities should compensate investors and produce positive risk-adjusted returns, not only to the extent that they offer protection against market risks, but also if they shield unbiased investors from fuel price risks and provide a good alternative to direct investments in fuels. Consequently, we integrate equation (11.1) with additional return factors which specifically track fuel risks. To do this, we first convert daily fuel prices into daily fuel excess returns by using the statement:

$$R_{jt} = \frac{(P_{jt} - P_{jt-1})}{P_{jt-1}} - R_{ft} \tag{11.2}$$

where R_{jt} is a daily excess return on the j-th fuel on day t, P_{jt} is the j-th fuel price on the same day. Different time series of returns on J fuels can now be used as return factors and equation (11.1) can be integrated as follows:

$$R_{it} = \beta_i^1 M_t + \beta_i^2 SMB_t + \beta_i^3 HML_t + \sum_{j=1}^{J} \gamma^j R_{jt} + \varepsilon_t \tag{11.3}$$

whereby gammas represent portfolio return sensitivities to daily fuel returns. This model can then be employed in the same manner as described in the previous subsection for the classic Fama–French three factor model. Hence risk-adjusted (by market and fuel risk) performance and excess-returns on various energy portfolios can be measured.

Estimation

Coming to the estimation issue, we should first observe that the simpliest method to find betas and gammas in (11.1) and (11.3) is to use ordinary least squares (OLS) over the entire available time window. This would yield a single value for all regression coefficients (β_i and γ_i) in the equations. But given the long period of time involved in the estimation, these OLS parameters would probably suffer from two limitations: (1) they would be sensitive to several outlying observations that plague longitudinal datasets as a result of market crises and unanticipated events; (2) they would not be able to track changes in the sensitivity of equity portfolios to risk factors (that is, changes in β_i and γ_i) and would just average them out in a conditional mean.[7]

With respect to these problems, several estimation methods may provide some improvements vis-à-vis OLS. For instance, *robust* estimation, *generalized autoregressive conditional heteroskedastic* (GARCH) models and *Bayesian* methods may in various ways take care of outliers, but only partially address the problem of temporal changes in the assessment of factor regression coefficients.[8]

In this study we hold temporal modifications of return sensitivity to risk factors in great importance and, as described above, we take care of their impact in a direct fashion. Therefore, instead of relying on a single estimation that uses all observations in the time series to improve the determination of regression coefficients, we prefer to observe their evolution over time through rolling regressions. Note that since this entails estimating a multiple set of regressions, each of them could make use of one of the methodologies just described and could theoretically address both the problem of bias and volatility of regression coefficients. However, since we allow the number of observations that enter the estimation window of each rolling regression to vary and optimize the number according to the daily out-of-sample predictive ability of in-sample estimations, we deem that – given the large number of regressions involved in this study – using an approach different than OLS represents a very minor improvement at the cost of some significant information on coefficient volatility.

Data

Stock data used in this study are collected in the form of daily returns from the Center for Research in Security Price (CRPS). Our dataset comprises 14 years of daily observations (from 1990 through 2003) for 681 energy firms listed in the US equity markets. Sampled firms encompass four energy industries: oil, gas, power and coal.

To assess the business nature of firms considered here, we bypass the SIC used by CRSP, since recent studies have shown that this specification may suffer from relevant limitations.[9] Instead we individually match all firms to one of the 22 structural portfolios presented above by analysing their core business. Our analysis is based on: (1) business information directly released by the firm; (2) business news information as archived by Lexis–Nexis and Factiva; and (3) CRSP industrial segments, when no other source of information is available.

Except for aggregated portfolios, the attribution of a firm to the 22 basic and integrated portfolios in Table 11.2 is univocal; a firm that is inserted in one portfolio is not included in any other. Our portfolio taxonomy is kept stable throughout the time window considered in the study. This implies that, over time, new firm listings and firm de-listings modify two measures, namely: (1) the number of firms tracked by each portfolio, and (2) the total market value of each portfolio. Since we customarily determine portfolio returns as the weighted average of the singular daily returns on each listing, using market capitalization as a weight,[10] we do not keep track of delisting returns unless they are specifically tracked by CRSP. As a result, this may introduce some bias in our measure of portfolio performance.[11] However, given the large pool of tracked data and the relative concentration of energy industries, firm de-listings, which generally apply to small businesses, have limited overall effects on our estimations.

As far as fuels are concerned, we use data as provided by the Energy Information Agency (EIA) of the US government. We employ three different series: (1) oil prices as given by the West Tewas Intermediate (WTI) FOB daily index; (2) natural gas prices as given by Henry Hub wellhead daily observations; (3) power prices are instead tracked in the form of monthly observations (since daily observations are unavailable) of the US state-mean industrial cost (¢/KWh) deflated by the aggregate US consumer cost index.

Results

As a premise to the analysis of the historical performance of all equity portfolios presented in Section 11.2 – both along the vertical and horizontal dimensions – a few general aspects which concern the entire energy sector shall be highlighted.

First, it should be observed that the largest investments in energy equities in the US concern oil firms. In Figure 11.1, portfolios are plotted as pies in a Cartesian space where market betas, β_i^1, are measured along the x-axis, while the y-axis measures mean yearly observed portfolio returns. In this and the following figures, unless otherwise specified, β_i^1 are determined by estimating equation (11.1) through OLS over the entire dataset. Their statistical significance is, therefore, reduced. However, their values – hence the horizontal positioning of portfolios – approximate mean values determined

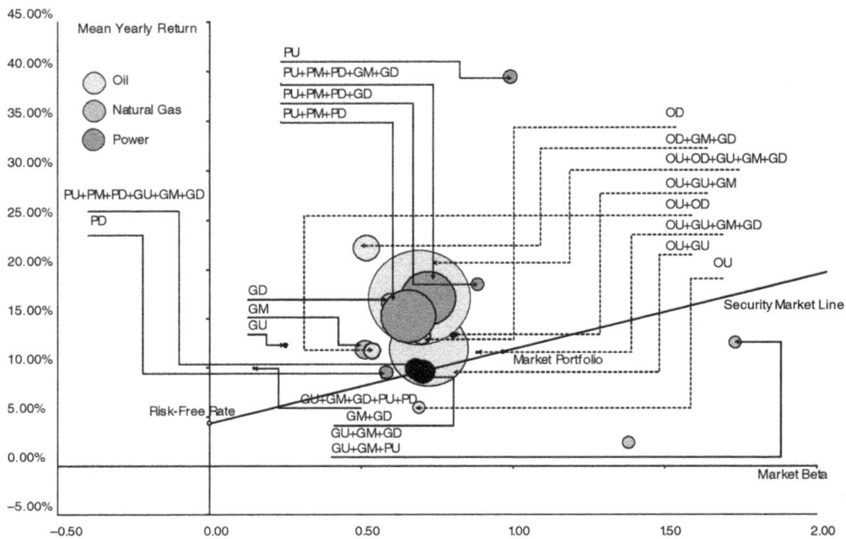

Figure 11.1 Portfolio positioning and value in the mean-return/market beta space

from estimations conducted with rolling regressions (Table 11.3 at the end of this chapter summarizes OLS estimation values and statistics). Pies are then scaled according to the total market capitalization of each portfolio on 31 December 2003 and, as shown, different graphical patterns are attributed to different fuels.

The two largest portfolios are those which include vertically and horizontally integrated oil and natural gas firms (Portfolio 3) and integrated upstream oil and natural gas firms (Portfolio 2). Specifically, Portfolio 3 includes all of the largest global oil and gas companies (such as Exxon–Mobil, for instance). From the graph it is evident how oil pies outsize and sometimes completely cover all the others. Utility portfolios are hardly comparable to oil portfolios, while natural gas portfolios are striking for their overall irrelevance by value in the US economy.

Note that the Cartesian space is crossed by an upward sloped thick line called Security Market Line (SML). This line connects two points: the observed risk-free yearly rate over the 1990–2003 period (equal to 4.38 per cent) and associated to the beta = 0 position on the x-axis, with the mean yearly return yielded by the overall US equity market portfolio (equal to 11.46 per cent), as determined by CRSP, including all dividends paid by all US listed firms over the same time period, and associated to the beta = 1 position. According to financial theory, the SML can be seen as the plot of all possible combinations of market risk (betas on the x-axis) and associated compensation for

Table 11.3 Equation (11.1): OLS statistics, full dataset – basic and integrated portfolios

No.	Portfolios	β_i^1	β_i^2	β_i^3	R^2	F
1	OU	0.684	0.099	0.659	0.153	212.944
2	OU + OD	0.536	−0.204	0.477	0.109	144.550
3	OU + OD + GU + GM + GD	0.688	−0.392	0.497	0.284	466.902
4	OU + GU	0.727	0.232	0.661	0.218	327.402
5	OU + GU + GM	0.804	0.005	0.676	0.190	276.079
6	OU + GU + GM + GD	0.882	0.681	0.870	0.101	132.696
7	OD	0.698	−0.052	0.602	0.225	342.254
8	OD + GM + GD	0.497	0.214	0.454	0.097	126.561
9	GU	0.252	0.267	0.231	0.007	8.189
10	GU + GM + GD	1.288	0.202	1.325	0.142	195.065
11	GU + GM + GD + PU + PD	0.147	−0.002	0.113	0.022	26.947
12	GU + GM + PU	1.731	0.386	1.363	0.129	174.430
13	GM	0.512	0.163	0.456	0.141	193.879
14	GM + GD	0.704	0.150	0.613	0.364	672.696
15	GD	0.594	0.164	0.495	0.365	676.022
16	PU	0.998	0.355	0.665	0.129	174.810
17	PU + PM + PD	0.656	−0.257	0.782	0.382	727.710
18	PU + PM + PD + GU + GM + GD	0.678	−0.213	0.916	0.281	460.216
19	PU + PM + PD + GM + GD	0.721	−0.153	0.773	0.346	621.653
20	PU + PM + PD + GD	0.886	−0.174	1.049	0.228	346.607
21	PD	0.583	−0.477	0.707	0.244	378.642
22	CO	0.953	0.085	0.690	0.173	246.093

holding an asset (returns on the y-axis) that an unbiased equity investor can obtain by diversifying his portfolio across all available securities in the US market (by mixing risky assets with governmental securities).[12] Therefore, the space north-west of the SML represents an area of positive excess-risk-adjusted-returns, since it contains return-risk combinations that yield more to investors than what they would normally obtain through portfolio diversification (that is, by diversifying their equity portfolios across available securities in the market). By the same token, the space south-east of the SML represents an area of negative excess-risk-adjusted-returns.

Here two general aspects are of interest. On the one hand, the large majority of energy portfolios have market beta β_i^1 less than one. Therefore, they shield investors from systematic risk better than holding the entire market portfolio would do. On the other hand, owning equity in an energy business is substantially better than just investing in the market portfolio, government bonds or in any combination of the two. In fact, most portfolios fall above the SML. Only drilling oil in isolation (Portfolio 1) and integrating the various production stages in the natural gas industry (Portfolios 10 and 12) yield less than what portfolio diversification would return to investors. It is difficult to determine which of the industries, oil or power, is the better of the two, although it seems that pure power generation creates tremendous value for stockholders (Portfolio 16).

In the following two subsections, we first present results obtained by single OLS estimation of (11.1) on the entire dataset. According to Section 11.3, we further detail these results in the subsequent subsections by including fuel prices as risk factors and by moving onto rolling regression estimations.

Value performance along the vertical dimension

Oil industry

Vertical integration in the oil industry produces acceptable value performance. Observe that reproducing vertical integration as a corporate strategy through portfolio diversification implies replicating Portfolio 2 (OU + OD) by simply mixing single-segment firms included in Portfolio 1 (OU) and 7 (OD). Figure 11.2 shows that, provided an investor mixes equities with comparable values, this is tantamount to obtaining a mimicking portfolio that would position between the plotting of each single-segment portfolio (since portfolio returns and market betas are linear quantities with respect to the return and risk of the equities they include). Here, we observe that vertically integrated activities (Portfolio 2) actually do better than simply averaging the performance of single segment portfolios, as they position above and to the right of the virtual equally-weighted mimicking portfolio. Nonetheless, vertical integration does not manage to create risk adjusted returns more than downstream businesses do in isolation (Portfolio 2 indeed plots at a distance above the SML which is slightly less than the one of Portfolio 7).

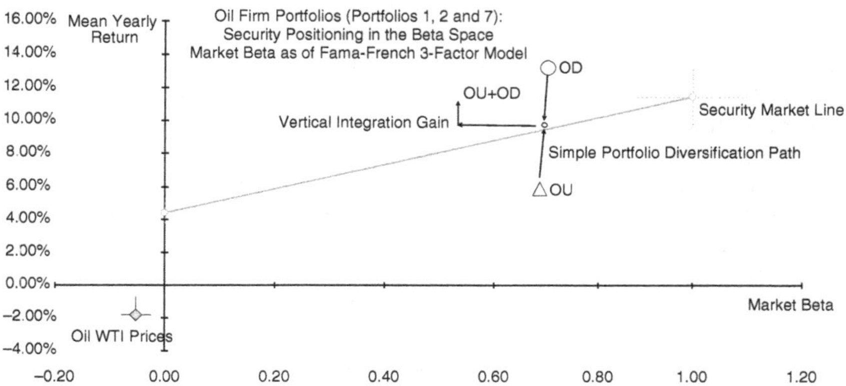

Figure 11.2 Vertically integrated vs. non-integrated oil portfolios: risk-adjusted returns

Natural gas industry

Vertical integration in natural gas businesses, compared to the oil industry, does not produce comparable value performance. Integrated natural gas concerns systematically compensate shareholders with less risk-adjusted returns than pure players. In Figure 11.3, integrated gas companies are either on or below the SML, while single-stage businesses are always well above the market-wide portfolio diversification boundary. Portfolio 10 is then particularly inefficient and manages to create less value than investing in natural gas prices in isolation.

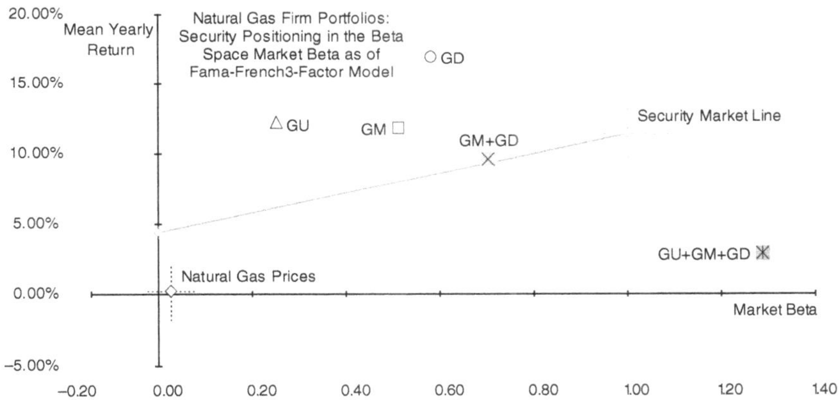

Figure 11.3 Vertically integrated vs. non-integrated natural gas portfolios: risk-adjusted returns

Power industry

Vertical integration in the power industry, similarly, has little power. However, some specificities complicate the analysis here. Consider absolute returns first. Figure 11.4 shows the performance of $100 of original investment in different power activities. Upstream activities not only seem to produce much more value than downstream businesses, but also more than investments in integrated activities. For shareholders, synergies from controlling the entire value chain in the industry seem, therefore, to be almost irrelevant and they would be better off concentrating their holdings in specialized generation firms (Portfolio 16). This is true, however, only throughout the 1997–2001 period, since, after the beginning of 2001, the value performance of upstream businesses has significantly diminished.

But such a negative result appears to be greatly mitigated when risk-adjusted returns are considered. In Figure 11.5, all power portfolios fall above the SML and vertical integration compares acceptably to pure portfolio diversification. Integrated companies yield, in fact, more than pure downstream firms. They dominate the SML and are closer to their theoretical mean positioning between the highest performers (Portfolio 16) and the lowest performers (Portfolio 21) than in any other case concerning integrated businesses. In substance, downstream businesses expose stockholders to very little risk, but yield irrelevant excess-returns, whereas upstream firms are the most rewarding (their distance north-west of the SML is the largest among all energy portfolios), but require stockholders to bear very significant systematic risk (their beta positioning is the rightmost). This admittedly seems to match the regulatory structure of the US power industry, where downstream activities have been traditionally regulated, while upstream activities have been partially opened to competition since 1998.

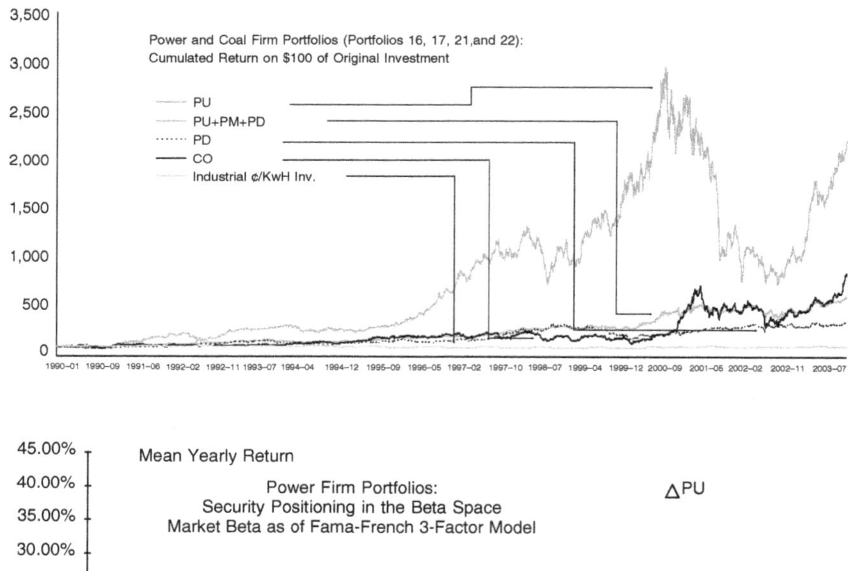

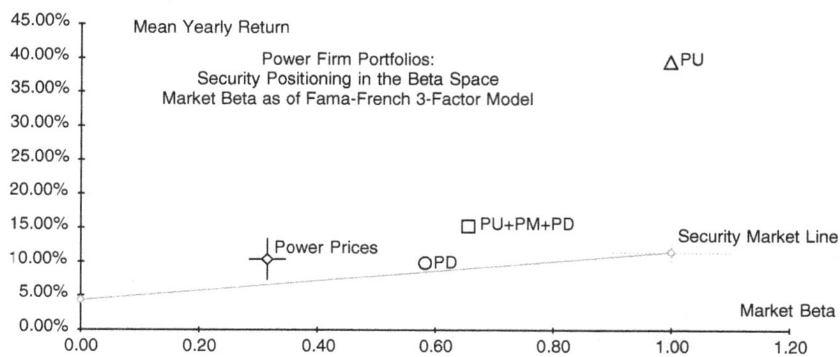

Figures 11.4 and 11.5 Vertically integrated vs. non-integrated power portfolios: portfolio values and risk-adjusted returns I and II

Figure 11.4 also presents the value performance of the integrated coal portfolio. In the US power industry, coal represents half of the total generation capacity (according to the EIA). Since we do not have daily power prices and coal prices, the coal portfolio may in this industry provide a proxy for a introductory fuel price risk analysis. Analysis the graph, it is evident how power firm portfolios (particularly generators) significantly correlate with the coal portfolio from 2000 onwards. This may imply a partial inability of power firms to insulate their shareholders from underlying price dynamics. However, here we offer this fact as preliminary information because of its visual evidence. The issue of fuel-risk diversification is addressed later in this section, where results of the estimation of (11.2) are further discussed.

Value performance along the horizontal dimension

Oil with natural gas

Figure 11.6 shows the cumulated return for $100 of original investment in pure player portfolios vs. diversified firm portfolios. The absolute value creation of most diversified businesses is lower than that of fuel concentrated activities. Only in one case (Portfolio 8) did diversified ongoing concerns outperform pure players and this occurs when firms specialize in downstream activities.

The same facts are confirmed when risk is considered. In Figure 11.7, (statistics for the OLS estimation of equation (11.1) on aggregated portfolios are provided in Table 11.4). It is evident how horizontal diversification between oil and gas does not significantly create value, even in terms of risk-adjusted returns. First, all diversified portfolios fall to the right of pure players' portfolios and it seems that firms load risk when they diversify between fuels. Second, while all portfolios dominate the SML, in no case diversified firms do better than pure natural gas players. Only Portfolio 3, which includes large oil and natural gas majors, manages to outperform pure oil players. This may suggest that business diversification pays off only to the extent that firms have sufficient size and business expertise to fully profit from it.

Natural gas with power

What was observed for diversification between oil and natural gas is further confirmed when power utilities diversify into natural gas. Figures 11.8 and 11.9 show these facts.

The first graph shows how in all cases diversified businesses produce less portfolio value than pure players. Diversification in upstream activities (Portfolio 12) outperforms other portfolios for a while, but fails to maintain a constant result in the long run (notice, however, that this portfolio, like Portfolio 11, includes only one firm, Williams Cos.; thus it has low statistical significance). The poor performance of horizontal diversification in risk-adjusted terms is even more compelling. Diversifying across energies is bad news for shareholders. The vertical distance between pure player portfolios and the SML dominates all other cases, with power production being the best type of investment. Only Portfolio 11 apparently reduces systematic risk in a significant way.[13]

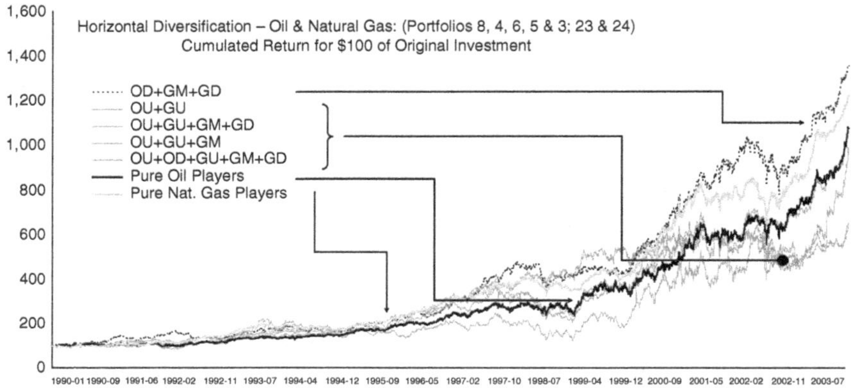

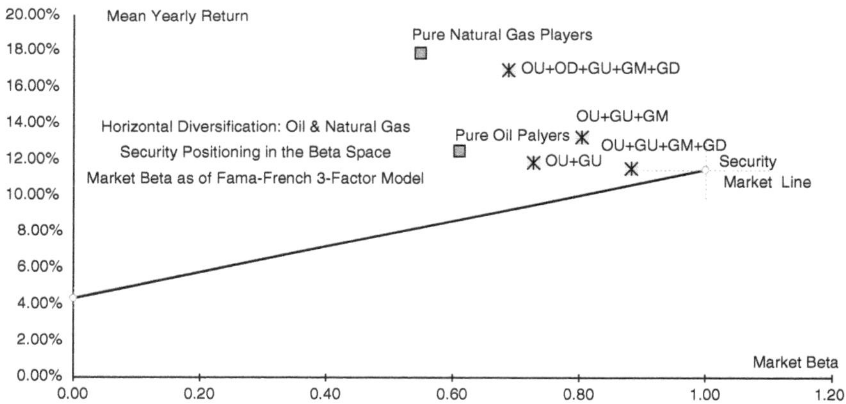

Figures 11.6 and 11.7 Horizontal diversfication between oil and natural gas: absolute and risk-adjusted returns I and II

In Figure 11.10, all the empirical evidence on horizontal diversification is summarized in a single graph. To avoid low significance, only aggregated portfolios (from 23 through 27) are considered here. Results do not significantly change. The arrows highlight the return-risk effect of diversification. While the summation of oil and natural gas increases the performance of the former, it does not really create value through synergies in terms of better positioning above the SML (diversified oil and natural gas firms yield slightly more than natural gas firms, but for significantly more risk); diversification between power and natural gas appears to be value-destroying. Diversified

Table 11.4 Equation (11.1): OLS statistics, entire dataset – aggregated portfolios

No.	Portfolios	β_i^1	β_i^2	β_i^3	R^2	F
23	Pure oil players	0.610635493	−0.07738109	0.549148708	0.206926475	306.9255272
24	Pure gas players	0.544807523	0.15276079	0.492217746	0.276660068	449.9191127
25	Pure power players	0.856008198	0.067612305	0.670805375	0.223461798	338.5095044
26	Oil & natural gas	0.686801506	0.109486071	0.603567433	0.286834067	473.1191696
27	Natural gas & power	0.776890559	−0.01845229	0.696130998	0.309650626	527.6347988

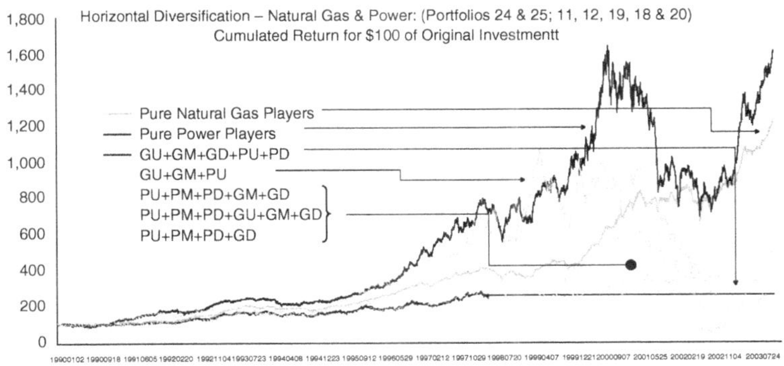

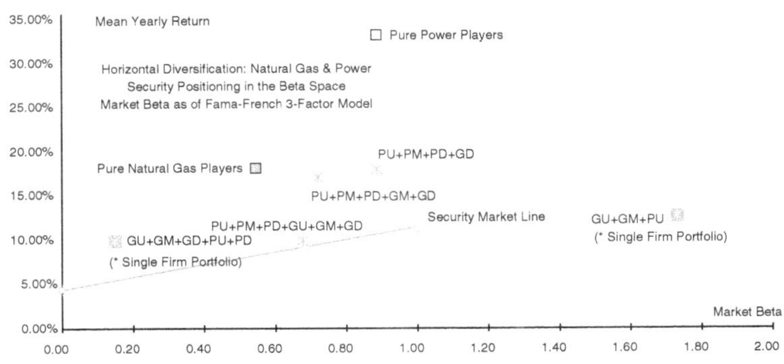

Figures 11.8 and 11.9 Horizontal diversification between natural gas and power: portfolio values and risk-adjusted returns I and II

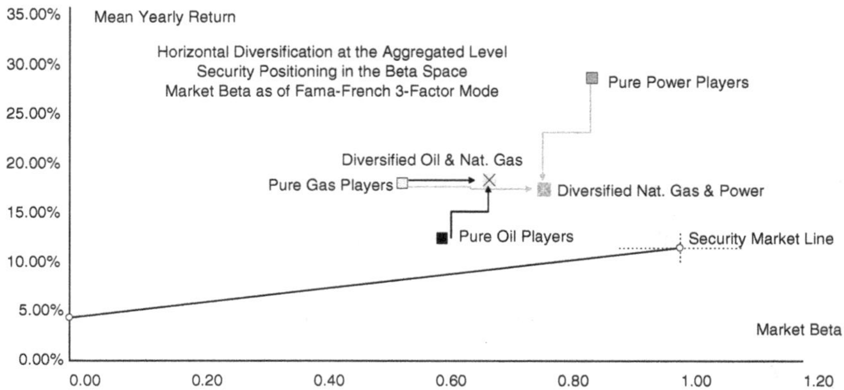

Figure 11.10 Horizontal diversification: all fuels, aggregated portfolios

utilities plot below both pure power players and natural gas firms. Their horizontal integration does not significantly protect investors from market risk; on the contrary, it pushes equities towards the SML.

Value performance jointly considering market and fuel risks

As explained in Section 11.3, a more thorough assessment of the risk-adjusted performance of energy portfolios requires considering fuel in addition to market risks. Moreover, in order to better track changes in the strategies of firms, we should also consider the information that rolling regressions may provide. Therefore, we present in this subsection the results obtained by rolling daily regressions between 1992 and 2003 for equation (11.2). For simplicity and better statistical significance, all results presented in this subsection are relative to aggregated portfolios only. Since fuel diversification is the aspect at stake, we only focus here on the horizontal dimension.

As explained before, equation (11.2) considers all market regressors of the Fama–French specification (11.1) plus multiple fuel price time series as additional regressors. Table 11.5 provides estimation statistics of equation (11.2) for all observations. Daily power price time series obtained from monthly EIA time series are never significant and, accordingly, are discarded as a regressor. Oil and natural gas prices are only insignificant in the case of the Pure Power Players Portfolio. The analysis conducted with Fama–French regressors presented in the previous subsection can thus be considered to be more representative for this latter type of firm.[14]

Rolling regressions require us, then, to specify the in-sample estimation windows. Using the Pure Oil Players Portfolio (Portfolio 23) as a reference, we employ mean excess–returns obtained by rolling regressions of (11.2) over the entire dataset (1990–2003) with various estimation window lengths (from ten

Table 11.5 Equation (11.2): OLS statistics, entire dataset – aggregated portfolios

Variable	Coefficient	St. error	t-statistic	prob.
Pure oil players				
M_t	0.64888	0.022375	29.00021	0
SMB_t	−0.058661	0.030675	−1.912321	0.0559
HML_t	0.599412	0.037827	15.84598	0
Oil prices	0.111269	0.006083	18.2929	0
Natural gas prices	0.009888	0.002601	3.801241	0.0001
R^2		0.283417		
Adjusted R^2		0.282604		
Pure natural gas players				
M_t	0.567829	0.015403	36.86406	0
SMB_t	0.172334	0.021117	8.160857	0
HML_t	0.530634	0.026041	20.37691	0
Oil prices	0.030491	0.004187	7.281642	0
Natural gas prices	0.009147	0.001791	5.107992	0
R^2		0.302599		
Adjusted R^2		0.301808		
Pure power players				
M_t	0.890003	0.030144	29.52469	0
SMB_t	0.121083	0.041326	2.929915	0.0034
HML_t	0.730614	0.050962	14.33636	0
Oil prices	0.006163	0.008195	0.752128	0.452
Natural gas prices	−0.00243	0.003504	−0.69342	0.4881
R^2		0.228136		
Adjusted R^2		0.22726		
Diversified oil & natural gas				
M_t	0.7202	0.019017	37.87057	0
SMB_t	0.132095	0.026072	5.066574	0
HML_t	0.65001	0.032151	20.21743	0
Oil prices	0.078211	0.00517	15.12834	0
Natural gas prices	0.011721	0.002211	5.301777	0
R^2		0.343786		
Adjusted R^2		0.343041		
Diversified natural gas & power				
M_t	0.7202	0.019017	37.87057	0
SMB_t	0.132095	0.026072	5.066574	0
HML_t	0.65001	0.032151	20.21743	0
Oil prices	0.078211	0.00517	15.12834	0
Natural gas prices	0.011721	0.002211	5.301777	0
R^2		0.343786		
Adjusted R^2		0.343041		

to 1,000 observations) as a selection criterion. Mean excess–returns are first negative and then positive and equate to zero when the estimation window length is between 470 and 480 observations (slightly less than two years of trading data). Therefore, we present here results obtained with an estimation window of 478 observations, a length that implies the possibility of using rolling regressions to draw inferences only between 1992 and 2003. Table 11.6 summarizes the estimation statistics for 3025 daily regressions run over this time interval.

Table 11.6 Rolling regressions: estimation statistics, equation (11.2)

Variable	Mean R^2	Mean F	Mean coefficient	Mean t-statistic
Pure oil players				
M_t			0.674499	10.02243
SMB_t			−0.0249	−0.23938
HML_t	0.326756	47.78727	0.512348	4.670318
Oil prices			0.119628	6.690151
Natural gas prices			0.062815	1.832097
Pure natural gas players				
M_t			0.553433	13.73188
SMB_t			0.233349	4.497297
HML_t	0.375016	61.82351	0.450891	6.859716
Oil prices			0.02198	2.003611
Natural gas prices			0.103771	3.416432
Pure power players				
M_t			0.935163	10.40324
SMB_t			0.148713	1.260548
HML_t	0.239628	30.94384	0.637687	4.309876
Oil prices			−0.00468	−0.1785
Natural gas prices			0.007417	−0.13609
Diversified oil & natural gas				
M_t			0.733627	12.88214
SMB_t			0.212098	2.849652
HML_t	0.366653	60.73669	0.540424	5.780866
Oil prices			0.07715	5.074656
Natural gas prices			0.058541	2.813889
Diversified natural gas & power				
M_t			0.779397	12.80209
SMB_t			−0.01209	−0.43301
HML_t	0.355421	55.53761	0.649565	6.357107
Oil prices			0.015822	0.692453
Natural gas prices			0.022738	1.193331

Figure 11.11 shows the effect of diversifying between fuels. The similarity with Figure 11.10 is patent and no new fact is evident. Considering fuel prices as regressors does not significantly change the value of market betas. The only appreciable difference is that, using equation (11.2), the integration between natural gas and power results is to be performed with a relatively more significant increase in market risk than with a simple Fama–French estimation (Portfolio 27 falls further to the right). It appears, therefore, to be further confirmed that, with both market and fuel risks energy firms fail to offer value to shareholders by diversifying.

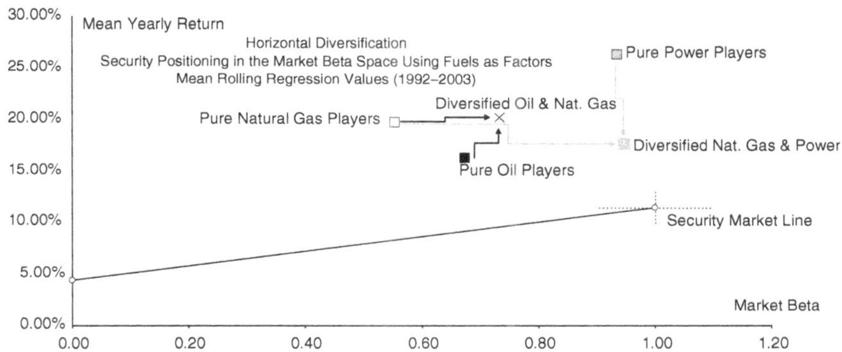

Figure 11.11 Horizontal diversification: mean rolling regressions results

Rolling regressions allow us, then, to track modifications in market risk as a result of firms' longitudinal efforts to adapt business strategies to their evolving environment. Figure 11.12 shows how mean yearly returns, coupled with market betas, have moved portfolio positioning during the 1992–2003 period. Three times windows of four years are analysed: 1992–95, 1996–99 and 2000–03. Two separate aspects clearly emerge:

1) All firms have become increasingly vulnerable to systematic risk during the passage from the first to the second set of four years. Both solid black and grey arrows in the figure show that portfolios have progressively shifted to the right, while maintaining similar vertical height. Only pure oil firms (PO) appear to have improved performance as they were increasing risk and thus represent the only equity portfolio which has increased its risk-adjusted performance (its vertical distance from the SML) during the first eight years.
2) Equity portfolios made up of pure power players (PP) and diversified natural gas and power utilities (GP) – grey arrows – have consistently diminished their return performance throughout the entire 12 years, while all other types of firm – black arrows – after a first negative period, seem to have positively corrected their performance.

Here the overall story seems to be one of fuel prices. Power-related portfolios appear to be conditioned by the effect of liberalization. Since, in deflated terms, mean power prices have diminished in the US, the opening of the industry to competition has increasingly exposed them to market trends and their risk, while integration into natural gas has failed to produce the synergies that were expected, particularly in terms of risk diversification (the GP portfolio is the one showing the largest shift to the right during the second of the two time periods). On the other hand, after an initial negative period, oil and natural gas firms have probably benefited from a moderate increase in industrial commodity prices (the oil price boom of the last two years is excluded from this study) and the full effect of their restructuring that took place during the second part of the nineties.

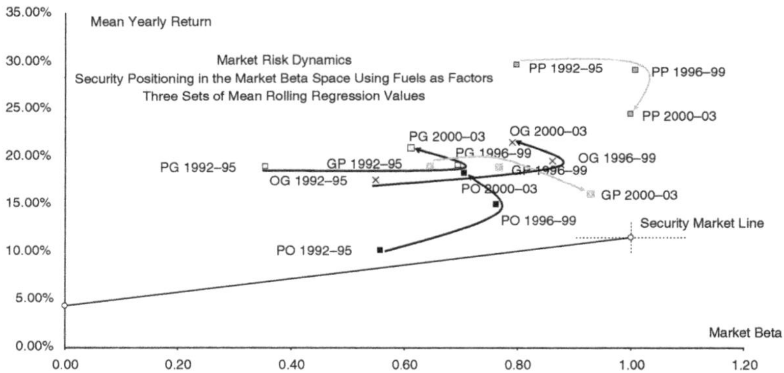

Figure 11.12 Market risk dynamics

Finally, by using rolling regressions, it is possible to determine out-of-sample excess-returns. These returns can be modelled as the yield that an investor would enjoy if he were to be compensated daily for buying and holding equities, given the exposures that equation (11.2) tracks. Such a yield represents, therefore, a positive or negative additional compensation that investors receive.

As usual, we gauge the value evolution of $100 invested in each aggregated portfolio at this excess yield. Figure 11.13 shows results and a daily break down of the market and fuel risk-adjusted performance of aggregated energy equity portfolios shown in Figure 11.12. With the partial exception of diversified natural gas and power activities and (less so) pure oil businesses, investing in energy seems to be a good choice on a daily basis. At least four cycles seem to be identifiable: 1992–94, 1996–98, 1999–2001 and

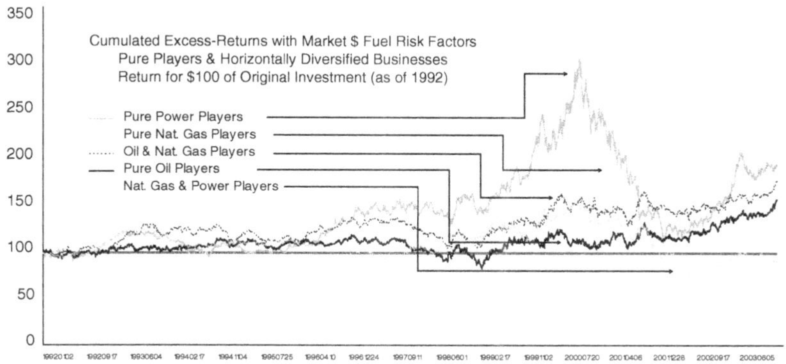

Figure 11.13 Cumulated excess returns

2002–03. During these periods, portfolio values have bulged, following first increasing then contracting underlying general stock and energy trends. With respect to the analysis in Figure 11.12, integration between oil and natural gas seems to yield some better synergic results, particularly in the 1996–98 triennium. On the other hand, integration between natural gas and power appears even more to be driven by the tremendous performance of pure power firms and always yields less than simple portfolio diversification by shareholders would yield. Finally, it even fails to rebound when pure power equities peak again during the 2002–03 period and ends up below the positive cumulated excess-return region.

Conclusions

In this study we investigate the ability of vertical integration and horizontal diversification to create value for US energy firm shareholders. Our results are mixed and appear to partially confirm the postulations of industrial organization, as far as the first type of corporate strategy is concerned, and of financial economics, with respect to fuel diversification.

On the one hand, vertical integration within energy portfolios seems to produce little risk-adjusted return performance for all types of energy firms. For industrial organization theory this may, perhaps, indicate that asset specificity and the possibility of opportunistic behaviour across various stages of production are not a sufficient cause to release material synergies as a result of upstream or downstream integration. Across the various types of energy, this is all the more true for the natural gas industry, a type of activity which, as a result of vertical integration, has experienced the worst results in the time window considered. Only power utilities seem to partially escape this reality, possibly because of their ability to create value by being integrated upstream into generation – a relatively small industry (see Figure 11.2) that, in isolation, has experienced the best equity performance among all energy portfolios. US antitrust authorities, in both their praxis and their periodical reports, treat energy industries as relatively non-concentrated. Accordingly, they have largely permitted the significant wave of corporate restructuring through mergers and acquisitions that reshaped the US energy sector during the last decade. Given the linkage between concentration and opportunistic behaviour (see Section 11.2), industrial structure may, therefore, be the cause of the contained performance of vertical integration in the sector. *A fortiori* this may also suggest that firm management might promote vertical integration beyond its strict transactional cost rationale, admittedly showing that corporate expansion decisions could be grounded in motivations unrelated to firm value maximization.

This last remark becomes still more evident when results of horizontal diversification are considered. Whether including or excluding fuel risk as a return factor, in no case does diversifying across energies through corporate expansion outperform simple shareholders' portfolio diversification. Figures 11.10 and 11.11 show, with little doubt, that firm horizontal strategies fail to produce value for shareholders, while Figure 11.12 illustrates that, even if some partial mitigation of this fact were to be observed during the 2000–04 period, it would most likely be due to a general amelioration of the overall performance of oil and natural gas industries that interested both diversified and pure players (pure power players and diversified portfolios including power, on the other hand, continued and even deepened their decline in the period considered) rather than to better synergies. Such evidence, perhaps disappointing with respect to the theoretical value of economies of scope, plainly confirms contemporary corporate financial theory, while not refuting the explanatory power of transaction cost economics. The residual loss in equity value associated with corporate expansion (a transaction cost) probably outweighs the possible synergic value of unrelated mergers and acquisitions. Clearly, we do not empirically test here if this is effectively explained by failures in the agency relationship between firm managers and their shareholders, although this seems to be suggested by our results.

Notes

1 See, for example, the contributions of Comment and Jarrell (1993), Lamont (1997), Scharfstein and Stein (1997), Scharfstein (1998), Dennis and Sarin (1997), and Zingales, Servaes, and Rajan (2000).

2 Note that certain pure-player portfolios that could theoretically be identified, but would not have actual meaning in business practice, have been discarded.

3 In other words, simple portfolio returns do not take into account both (1) the risks that shareholders bear by holding a certain type of equity and (2) their ability to hedge against these risks through portfolio diversification by mixing their holdings. For an introductory treatise, see Copeland and Weston (1992).

4 Relying on daily returns in medium-to-long-run performance analyses may actually expose risk-adjusted return measurements to the danger of accounting for

irrelevant daily shocks. Nonetheless, at the cost of some accuracy, we employ daily observations since we precisely intend to track portfolio risk-adjusted returns with respect to the ability of energy firm shareholders to diversify fuel price risk, which may be daily relevant.

5 Note that, in (11.1) there is no term for an intercept. Using excess-returns indeed requires eliminating the intercept, which would represent the portfolio return observed when all betas equal zero. But as betas track risk sensitivities, this return would be the one associated to the absence of risk. Thus, as R_f has been subtracted here from all vectors in (11.1) betas' estimation can be constrained to the absence of an intercept.

6 In multiple regression models estimated with ordinary least squares, betas are not only a function of the covariance between dependent and independent variables, but also a function of the covariance between the latter. Therefore, unless independent variables are perfectly orthogonal to each other, the estimation of a single beta in a multivariate setting yields a finer assessment of the elasticity of R_{it} with respect to each independent variable than in a simple univariate regression.

7 For a complete treatise of market beta estimations, see Marafin *et al.* (2006).

8 More specifically, *robust* estimation methods may perform better as far as the first problem is concerned since they weight observations in the dataset differently and reduce the importance of outlying observations. *Generalized autoregressive conditional heteroskedastic* (GARCH) models, by expressly factoring in the variance of errors in the estimation, can alternatively address the same problem in a more direct fashion (for a discussion on GARCH methods, see previous chapters in this book). Finally, *Bayesian* estimations, by assuming that estimated regression coefficients can be drawn from a certain statistical population (the so-called *posterior* distribution) can improve their estimation with respect to some bias that OLS coefficients may have by functionally relating this distribution to a separate distribution (the *prior* distribution) that represents the population of true regression coefficients. However, if such distributional information is not available, prior distribution parameters are drawn from the return dataset. This implies that estimated Bayesian regression coefficients tend to more closely converge to the OLS coefficients, the greater the volatilities of β_i and γ_i.

9 CRSP segments follow SIC codes as specified by the US Bureau of Census.

10 Formally, given a set of K firms included in the i-th portfolio, each daily portfolio return R_{it} results from, $R_{it} = \sum_{k=1}^{K} R_{kt} w_{kt}$ with $w_{kt} = v_{kt} / \sum_{k=1}^{K} v_{kt}$. In this equation, v_{kt} and R_{kt} are, respectively, the daily market value and the daily return of each firm included in the portfolio.

11 Not keeping track of de-listing returns is tantamount to assuming that an investor holding a portfolio is able to anticipate a de-listing on its previous day and simultaneously sell off the interested security. Hence new listings have an impact on portfolio returns that are first verified on the second day of their listings, while de-listings (which may generate a 100 per cent daily return) do not impact portfolio returns since they do not have market capitalization on the day of their de-listing. CRSP provides correcting information to account for this. However, this information may be partially incomplete. See Shumway (1997) for an extensive discussion.

12 Here, unusually, we draw on Cochrane (1999) and identify the SML in a mean return/market beta Cartesian space instead of doing it in a mean return/standard deviation of return setting.

13 Portfolio 11 is the other diversified portfolio that suffers from low significance, as it includes only one firm, Keyspan Energy Corporation, which was de-listed in 1998

as the result of a merger. Its beta estimation, therefore, is not conducted over the same time-window as the other portfolios.

14 Note that this model specification is robust with respect to serial correlation, which is not significantly detected on estimation errors. Residuals are also relatively well behaved in terms of their normality. Their skewness and kurtosis are contained between zero and one and five and six, respectively, in all cases, except for the case of Pure Power Players, for which, it has been already signalled that equation (11.2) is not the best specification. However, the Jarque–Bera statistics reject normality in all estimations. This is most likely the result of outlying observations which confer heteroskedasticity to the dataset. White heteroskedasticity tests indeed find that OLS estimation errors are driven by some or all of the squared regressors in (11.2) for all portfolios. In the presence of heteroskedasticity, OLS estimated coefficients may be flawed. Given the purpose of this study, we test if regression coefficients are significant and, in the case of market betas, if they have different values, by running a GARCH(1,1) specification on different sub-windows of the entire dataset. In all cases, except for the case of Pure Power Players, regression coefficients are significant. GARCH estimated market beta values converge to the OLS values at the second decimal. Therefore, we do not reject the significance of OLS results.

References

Aghion, P. and P. Botton (1987) 'Contacts as a Banner to Entry' *American Economic Review*, reprinted in *Industrial Economics*, Ed. Oliver Williamson (London: Edward Elgar).

Bain, J. (1956) *Barriers to New Competition* (Cambridge, MA: Harvard University Press).

Bain, J. (1959) *Industrial Organization* (New York: John Wiley).

Berger, P.G. and E. Ofek (1995) 'Diversification's Effect on Firm Value', *Journal of Financial Economics*, vol. 37.

Bollerslev, T. (1986) 'Generalized Autoregressive Conditional Heteroskedasticity', *Journal of Econometrics*, vol. 31.

Carlton, D. (1979) 'Vertical Integration in Competitive Markets Under Uncertainty', *Journal of Industrial Economics*, vol. 27.

Coase, R.H. (1937) 'The Nature of the Firm', *Economica*, vol. 4.

Cochrane, J.H. (1999) 'New Facts in Finance', *Economic Perspectives*, Federal Reserve Bank of Chicago, vol. 23.

Comment, R. and G.A. Jarrell (1993) 'Corporate Focus and Sock Returns', *Bradley Policy Research Center Paper*, University of Rochester (1993).

Copeland, T. and F. Weston (1992) *Financial Theory and Corporate Policy* (Reading, MA: Addison-Wesley).

Denis, D.J., D.K. Denis and S. Atulya (1997) 'Agency Problems, Equity Ownership and Corporate Diversification', *Journal of Finance*, vol. 52.

Denis, D. and A. Sarin (1997) 'Agency Problems, Equity Ownership and Corporate Diversification', *Journal of Finance*, vol. 52, pp. 135–160.

Elberfeld, W. (2002) 'Market Size and Vertical Integration: Stigler's Hypothesis Reconsidered', *Journal of Industrial Economics*, vol. 50.

Engle, R.F. (1982) 'Autoregressive Conditional Heteroscedasticity with Estimates of the Variance of United Kingdom Inflation', *Econometrica*, vol. 50, no. 4.

Fama, E.F. and K.R. French (1993) 'Common Risk Factors in the Returns on Stocks and Bonds', *Journal of Financial Economics*, vol. 33.

Fama, E.F. and K.R. French (1996) 'Multifactor Explanations of Asset Pricing Anomalies', *Journal of Finance*, vol. 51.

Hart, O. and J. Tirole (1990) 'Vertical Integration and Market Foreclosure', *Brookings Papers on Economic Activity* (Boston, MA: Massachusetts Institute of Technology (MIT)).

Hunt, S. (2002) *Making Competition Work in Electricity* (New York: John Wiley).

Jensen, M. and W. Meckling (1976) 'Theory of the Firm: Managerial Behavior, Agency Costs and Ownership Structure', *Journal of Financial Economics*, vol. 3.

Joskow, P.L. (2003) 'Vertical Integration', in C. Ménard and M.M. Shirley (eds) *Handbook of New Institutional Economics* (Berlin: Springer-Verlag).

Lamont, O.A and C. Polk (2000) 'Does Diversification Destroy Value? Evidence from Industry Shocks', *NBER Working Paper*.

Lamont, O.A and C. Polk (1999) 'The Diversification Discount, Cash-Flows vs Returns', *NBER Working Paper*.

Lamont, O. (1997), 'Cash-Flow and Investment: Evidence from Internal Capital Markets', *Journal of Finance*, vol. 413, no. 52, pp. 83–109.

Lang, L.H.P and R. Stulz (1994) 'Tobin's Q Corporate Diversification and Firm Performance, *Journal of Political Economy*, vol. 102, pp. 1248–80.

Lieberman, M. (1991) 'Determinants of Vertical Integration: An Empirical Test', *Journal of Industrial Economics*, vol. 39.

Marafin, S., F. Martinelli, M. Nicolazzi and C. Pozzi (2006) 'Alpha, Beta and Beyond', in G. Fusai and A. Roncoroni (eds), *Implementing Models in Quantitative Finance: Methods and Cases* (Berlin: Springer-Verlag).

Morck, R., A. Schleifer and R. Vishny (1990) 'Do Managerial Objectives Drive Bad Acquisitions?', *Journal of Finance*, vol. 45.

Ordover, J., S. Salop and G. Saloner (1990) 'Equilibrium Vertical Foreclosure', *American Economic Review*, vol. 80.

Perry, M. (1978) 'Price Discrimination and Vertical Integration', *Bell Journal of Economics*, vol. 9.

Scharfstein, D.S. and J.C. Stein (1997) 'The Dark Side of Internal Capital Markets: Divisionnal Rent-Seeking and Inefficient Investment', *NBER Working Paper*.

Scharfstein, D.S. (1998) 'The Dark Side of Internal Capital Markets II', *NBER Working Paper*.

Shumway, T. (1997) 'The Delisting Bias in CRSP Data', *Journal of Finance*, vol. 52.

Stigler, G. (1951) 'The Division of Labor Is Limited by the Extent of the Market', *Journal of Political Economy*, vol. 59.

Tirole, J. (1988) *The Theory of Industrial Organization* (Cambridge, MA: MIT Press).

Walker, G. and D. Weber (1984) 'A Transactions Cost Approach to Make or Buy Decisions', *Administrative Science Quarterly*, vol. 29.

Williamson, O. (1971) 'The Vertical Integration of Production: Market Failure Considerations', *American Economic Review*, vol. 61.

Williamson, O. (1975) *Markets and Hierarchies: Analysis and Antitrust Implications* (New York: Free Press).

Zingales, L., H. Servaes and R. Rajan (2000) 'The Cost of Diversity: The Diversification Discount and Inefficient Investment', *Journal of Finance*, vol. 55, pp. 35–80.

Index

accounting 1–2
  derived energy 6
  partial substitution 6
  primary equivalence 6
  regional accounts 4
  sectorial accounts 4
Adams, F.G. 9, 100, 101
Adelman, M.A. 9, 170
adjustment
  dynamic 27–8, 37–47
  models 30, 31–6, 46–7
  process 27–47
  speed of 42
  stock 35–6
AEEI (autonomous energy efficiency improvements) 123, 124, 125–6
agency cost 228
aggregates 7–12
  economic-energy aggregates 8–12
aggregation 3–6
Aghion, P. 227
AIDS (Almost Ideal Demand System) 38
Allais, 35
Allen, C. 37–8
Ambapour, S. 82
Anderson, G. 37
Andrews, W.K. 212
Ang, B.W. 20, 24, 98, 99, 100, 101
apparent energy 2
ARCH (Auto Regressive Conditional Heteroskedasticity) models 65, 66–8
ARDL (autoregressive distributed lag model) 35
ARIMA (Autoregressive Integrated Moving Average) model 63
ARMA (Auto Regressive Moving Average) model 54, 63, 67, 68–71, 192–3
  forward-spot prices 197–200, 201–2
Asafu-Adjaye, J. 78, 82
Asche, F. 171, 172
Augmented Dickey-Fuller text 58–9, 60, 129–31, 177–8, 213–14
automobile fuel efficiency 128–9
Azar, C. 123

Baade, P. 162
backwardation 133
Bacon, R.W. 14
Bain, J. 226
Balestra, P. 36
Baltagi, B.H. 102
Banerjee, A. 212
Baniak, A. 66
Barz, G. 64–5
Baughman, M.L. 151
Bayesian methods 234
behaviour optimization 38
Belgium 178–80, 182
Berger, P.G. 228
Berkhout, P.H.G. 31, 38
Berndt, E. 125, 150, 157
Bessec, M. 121–42
Binswanger, M. 125, 126
biomass 109
Birol, F. 77, 94
Bjorner, T.B. 31, 151, 161
Black, F. 66
blackouts 190
BLUE (Best Linear Unbiased Estimator) 103
Blundell, R. 37
Bohi, D.R. 32, 38, 42, 75
Bollerslev, T. 65, 68
Bolton, P. 227
Bosseboeuf, D. 24
Botterud, A. 189
Bourbonnais, R. 51–73, 78, 168–83
Box, G. 63
Box and Jenkins methodology 63
Boyd, G.A. 15, 20
Brännlund, R. 31, 151, 161
Brennan, M. 189
Brent 13
Breusch–Godfrey LM test 197
Brookes, L. 102, 125, 126

btu-aggregation 6
Bunn, D. 65, 66
Burniaux, J.-M. 126
Bystrom, H. 66

calorific value 5, 109
Carlton, D. 227
causality
  Granger 78–80, 81–3, 84, 87–8, 89–90, 129, 136–7, 141
  tests of 75; developing countries 83; oil price, intensity and fuel rate 136–41
chain indices 22, 23
Chang, C. 81
Chardon, S. 207–23
Cheng, B.S. 78–9, 83
Chevalier, J.-M. xiii–xxv
China: energy–GDP relationship 83, 88, 89, 91, 93–4
Chow, G. 213
Chow test 211, 212, 213, 214
Christensen, L.R. 38, 147, 150
Christiano, L.J. 212
Clark, C. 99
Cleveland, C.J. 9
climate change 121
CO_2 emissions 76, 103, 122, 126, 146, 165
  intensity 20
coal 109
  markets 171–2
  portfolio returns 229–30
  price-elasticity 158–9, 161
  spot markets 13
  units of measurement 5
  vertical integration 240–1
Coase, R.H. 226
Cobb–Douglas index 10, 150
cointegration 77–8, 84, 91–2, 183
  analysis 168–9
  as evidence of market integration 168
cointegration tests 80–1
  gas market integration 178–80
  Johansen 91, 122
  Johansen–Juselius 131, 134, 135–6
  oil price, intensity and fuel rate 131, 134–6
Colletaz, G. 108
commodity balances 4
Considine, T.J. 38, 147, 151, 154–7, 161
consumers 2
consumption
  and accounting procedures 4
  and balance sheet 7
  dynamic modelling 27–8
  and economic growth 75–95
  energy–GDP relationship 84–95, 121–42
  forecasting 45–6
  France 1978–2004 11
  and Human Development Index (HDI) 95
  and income 79, 81, 94
  and measures of energy intensity 19
  modelling 27–30, 31–5
  surges 192
  see also demand
contango 188
Contreras, J. 63
convenience yield 187, 189
cost
  agency 228
  energy shares 153
  function 15, 16–17, 148–9, 153

Dahl, C. 38, 75
Dargay, J. 164
Darmstadter, J. 100
Data Generating Process (DGP) 212
Davidson, R. 130
De Vany, A.S. 171, 172
Deaton, A. 38, 189
decomposition
  energy intensity 17, 18–24
  schema 21
demand
  captive 29–30
  conditional 29
  derived 29
  desired 34, 46
  and income 100–4
  long-run 29–30, 38
  long-run/short-run dynamics 39
  modelling 27–30
  real 46
  rigidity of 33

demand – *continued*
seasonal 53–5
short-run 29–30, 38
substitutable 29–30
see also consumption
Deng, S. 64, 66
deregulation of markets 51–2, 63, 66, 163–4, 168
and power exchanges 204
derived energy 2
accounting method 6
Desbrosses, N. 1–25
Destais, G. 98–119
developing countries 141–2
energy data sources 83–4
GDP–energy relationship 75–95
key energy indicators 76
oil dependence 141
results from causality tests 83
selection for study 76–7
testing for non-stationarity 86–7
DG Energy inquiry 181
Dickey, D. 58–9, 129
Dickey–Fuller test 58–9, 60, 80
Diewert, W.E. 15, 16, 150
Difference-Stationary processes 57, 58, 61, 63
distributed lag models 32–5
diversification *see* horizontal; vertical
Divisia index 10, 12, 15–17, 18
Dowlatabadi, E. 123
downstream activities 228, 238, 239, 240
Dubai 13
Durbin–Watson statistic 41, 90, 91, 197, 199, 202, 209, 222

Eckhaus, R. 121
ECM (Error Correction Model) 37–8, 78, 80–1, 84–5, 90, 91–3
and market integration 170, 171–2; gas 183
economic development and energy intensity 98–119
economic growth
effect of energy price 30
and energy consumption 75–95
EEX (European Energy Exchange) 186, 188, 193–4
EGARCH (exponential GARCH 201–3
elasticities 42–5, 151
Allen partial substitution of 149, 150, 154
arc 43
of consumption 40
cross price 44, 45, 149
of demand 43–4, 84, 85, 156
function 43
GDP and consumption 84, 85
income 43, 103, 106, 107–8; panel data models 111, 113–14, 115–18, 119
long-term 44–5
long-run price 42, 154, 156–7
own price 43
of production functions 45
short-term 44–5
short-run price 42
of substitution 45
Elder, J. 86
electricity 42, 109
and balance sheet 7, 8
inelastic demand 53
long-run price elasticity 159, 160, 161, 163
markets 171, 186–204
prices 52–3; characteristics 53, 68; spot and forward 186–204
spot markets 13
units of measurement 3
see also developing countries; energy
Elspot market 51, 53, 68, 69–72
Enerdata 109
energy
classification of sources 2–3
content 5
derived 2
operations and accounting 4
energy balance 2, 4
balance sheet 6–7, 28; aggregates 7–8
energy consumption 124
forecasting 45–6
and technology 121, 140–1
energy data 1–2
aggregation 3–6; first reconstitution 3–4; second reconstitution 5–6
data bases 4

energy efficiency 99, 121–2, 123
effect on consumption 124
rebound effect 123–4, 125, 126–7
energy flows 2
accounting 6–7
charts 4
commodity 4
decomposition of 6
and economic-energy aggregates 9
recording data 3–6
steps 1–2, 3
energy index *see* index
energy intensity
country disparities 100
country evolution 99–100
decomposition 17, 18–24; intensity effect 21, 22; methods of 19–24; structural effect 21, 22
decomposition analysis 1, 100
definition and measurement 19
and economic development 98–119
efficiency improvements 19–20
indicators 19
and prices 121–42
energy prices
and innovation 125
and substitution 163–4
energy system
aggregates 7–8
downstream 2
policy interventions 31
security of supply 121
upstream 2
energy taxes 122, 124, 141, 146–7, 165
Engle, R.F. 65, 67, 75, 78, 80–1, 129, 169–70
error correction model *see* ECM
Escribano, A. 64, 66
estimation methods
GMM 193, 200
heterogeneity/homogeneity 103
OLS (Ordinary Least Squares) 59, 77, 79–80, 81, 85, 88, 91, 157, 196–7
two stage least squares (TSLS) 193
two-step iterative 155–6
estimator: iterative Zellner 157, 158
Europe
1991–2005 biannual evolution of gas price 176
gas imports 173, 182
gas market integration 168, 172–83; Directive 173–4, 182
gas network 173
gas transit pipelines 174

Fama, E. 189
Fama–French method 231–3, 239, 240, 244
FEM (fixed effect model 115–18
filter
Hodrick–Prescott 208, 209–11
Kalman 211, 219–22, 223
Fisher, F.M. 29, 35, 47
Fisher, I. 15, 16, 18, 21, 22, 23
forecasting 45–6
prices 207; oil 220–3
fossil fuels 3, 8, 71
Fouquau, J. 98–119
France
energy cost shares 153
energy diversification 141
four-fuel price elasticities 159, 161
gas market 178–81, 182
interfuel substitution study 151–65
market shares of fuels 152
modelling energy consumption 39–46
three-fuel price elasticities 160
French, K.R. 189
Frisch, R. 35
fuel rate 128, 129, 131
Fuller, W. 58–9, 129
function
Barnett and McFadden 150
compensated demand 44, 45
cost 15, 16–17, 148–9, 153
demand 43–4
Fourier 150–1
generalized Box–Cox 150
Hick's demand 44
indicator 106
logit demand 38
price 43–4
production 45, 148, 150
transition 106–7, 108–9; PSTR models 111–12, 114
translog 38, 150, 151
utility 44
futures 171, 187, 194–5

Gallant, A.R. 150
Galli, R. 104, 115, 116
GARCH (Generalized Auto Regressive Conditional Heteroskedasticity) models 54, 65–8, 72, 186, 193, 200–3
  portfolio returns 234
Garcia–Cerrutti, L.M. 102
gas *see* natural gas
Gately, D. 14, 39, 42, 164
Gaussian white noise 56–7, 71, 180
Geary–Khamis ppp 110
Geoffron, P. 168–83
Geman, H. 212, 218
Germany
  gas market 172, 178–81, 182
  power market 188
  power prices and power load 193–203
Girod, J. 1–25, 27–48
Gjolberg, O. 189
Glasure, Y. 122
GMM (generalized method of moments) 193, 200, 201, 203
Goldemberg, J. 28
Golub, G.H. 150
Gonzales, A. 105, 108, 109, 118
Goto, M. 67
Gottron, F. 126
Gouriéroux, C. 42
Granger, C.W.J. 75, 78, 79, 80–1, 105, 129, 134, 169–70
Greene, D. 124
greenhouse gas emissions 76, 121, 122
  reducing 125, 126, 141
Greening, L. 124, 125, 126
Grepperud, S. 127
Griffin, J.M. 102, 151
Grubb, M. 124, 126, 127
Gülen, S.G. 171

Haas, R. 39
Haldrup, N. 171
Hall, V.B. 151
Hamilton, J.D. 221
Hansen, B.E. 104, 106, 110
Hansen test 211
Hart, O. 227
Hassett, K.A. 164
Haugland, T. 127
Hausman, J.A. 103
Hendry, D.F. 80–1
Henly, L. 125
Henry Hub 235
Herbert, J. 172
Herring, H. 125
Hessian matrix 149
heterogeneity/homogeneity 103
  panel model 103–4
heteroskedasticity 192, 197, 199
  errors 59
Hodrick, R.J. 210
Hodrick–Prescott Filter 93
Hogan, W.W. 38, 47
Holdren, J. 125
Holtedahl, P. 39, 78
homoskedasticity 67
  variables 56
Hondroyiannis, G. 122
horizontal diversification 225–6, 227–50
  oil with natural gas 241–4
  rolling regressions 247
  value performance 241–9
  see also portfolio returns
Horowitz, M.J. 39
Hotelling, H. 208, 212, 217
Howarth, R. 122, 125
Hsiao, C. 102, 103
Human Development Index (HDI) 95
Hunt, S. 226
Huntington, H.G. 14, 39, 42
Hurlin, C. 98–119
hydropower 72, 147, 189

implicit reserves 188, 189–91, 195, 196–7
income
  and demand 100–4
  and energy consumption 79, 81, 94
index
  Arithmetic–Mean Divisia 21, 22, 23
  chained 22, 23
  Cobb–Douglas 10, 150
  Divisia 10, 12, 15–17, 18; and intensity decomposition 21, 22, 23
  Edgeworth 15

index – *continued*
Fisher's ideal 15, 17
Jevons 15
Laspeyre 15, 17, 18, 21, 22, 23
Log–Mean Divisia 21, 22, 23
Marshall 15
Paasche 15, 17, 18, 21, 22, 23
price 15–17
quantity 15–17, 18
Tornqvist 10, 12, 15–17, 18; and intensity decomposition 21, 22, 23
Walsh 15
Index of Decomposition Analysis (IDA) 20
India: energy–GDP relationship 83, 88–90, 93–4
information criteria
Akaike 60, 112, 130, 180, 209
Schwarz 112, 130, 178, 180, 209
innovation and energy prices 125
interfuel substitution study 151–65
internal supply 7
Intriligator, M.D. 42
Italy 178–80

Jarque–Bera test 71, 93, 199, 200, 203
Jemelkova, B. 99
Jenkins, G. 63
Jensen, H.H. 151, 161
Jensen, M. 227
Johansen, S. 78, 80, 122, 129, 131, 134, 135–6, 175, 178–80
Johnsen, T. 189
Johnson, B. 55, 64–5
Jones, C.T. 151, 152, 161, 162, 163
Jorgenson, D. 38, 147, 150
Joskow, P. 52, 151
Joutz, F.L. 39, 78
Judson, R.A. 101, 115, 118
Jumbe, C. 122
jump-diffusion models 55, 64–5, 66
Juselius, K. 80–1, 129, 131, 134, 178–80

Kaldor, D. 187
Kalman filter 211, 219–22, 223
Kaminski, V. 64
Karakatsani, N. 65, 66
Karolyi, G. 67
Kaufmann, R.K. 9, 164
Kaysen, C. 35, 47
Keenan, J. 37
Kennedy, P. 86
Keppler, J.H. 75–96
Khaled, M.S. 150
Khazzoom, J. 29, 125, 126
Knittel, C. 55, 66
knotspline 118
Koyck adjustment 32, 35, 147
kurtosis 203
Kuznets, S. 99
Kwiatkowski, D. 55, 60, 62

Lagrange multiplier 60, 211
Lang, L.H.P. 228
Lanza, A. 171
Laroque, G. 189
Lau, L. 38, 147, 150
Law of One Price 168, 172
Lee, C. 81, 82, 83
Leontieff function 150
Lesourne, J. 75
linearity texts 103, 110, 118
Liu, C. 121
Liu, X.Q. 20
Ljung–Box Q-statistic 197
LNG 183
transport 172
see also natural gas
logarithmic mean weights (LMD1) 21
Longstaff, F. 66
Lovins, A. 125
LPRIX process 60, 61–2, 70
Lumsdaine, R.L. 212
Lundgren, T. 31, 151, 161

Maddison, A. 109–10
Malinvaud, E. 41
Manne, A. 126
Manning, N.D. 38, 47
markets 67
backward 188
bids and offers 186–7
coal 171–2
delineation of boundaries 168–83
EEX (Germany) 193–4
electricity 171, 186–204

markets – *continued*
  Elspot 51, 53, 68, 69–72
  gas 172–83
  integration of 169, 170, 172–83
  Nord Pool 68, 69–72, 186
  oil 170–1
  PJM (Pennsylvania–New Jersey–Maryland) 51, 53–4, 68–72, 186
  Powernext 186
Markov process 35
Martin, J.-M. 99, 100, 109
Masih, A.M.M. 78, 82, 84, 94
Masih, R. 78, 82, 84, 94
Massamba, C. 82
Matsukawa, I. 31
McFadden, D.A. 151
McKinlay, C. 203
McKinnon, J.G. 80, 130
Meadows, D.H. 28
mean reversion models 54–5, 64, 65, 66–7, 72
measurement units 3, 4, 5, 109, 127
Meckling, W. 227
Medlock, K.B. 101, 103
Méritet, S. 51–73, 94, 121–42
Merton, R. 64
Metcalf, G.E. 164
midstream activities 228
Miovic, P. 9
modelling
  substitution 146–65
  time series 53–4
models
  adaptive expectations 34–5
  adjustment 30, 46–7
  ARMA 54
  autoregressive 32–3, 41, 59
  cross-section 100–1
  distributed lag 32–4
  dynamic 27–8, 29–30, 31–4, 36–47; pioneering 35–6
  ECM (Error Correction Model) 37–8, 78, 80–1, 84–5, 90, 91–3, 170
  fixed effect (FEM) 102–3, 115–18
  flow adjustment 36
  GARCH 54
  heterogeneous panel model 103–4
  Hotelling 211, 217, 223
  individual effects 102–3, 106
  jump-diffusion 55, 64–5, 66
  linear logit 147, 151, 155–7
  linear state space 219, 220–1
  log-log 101–2
  logit 114, 151, 154–7, 158–62
  mean reversion 54–5, 64, 65, 66–7
  multinomial logit 151
  Ornstein–Uhlenbeck 212, 218
  Panel Smooth Threshold Regression (PSTR) 105–9, 111–15, 116–18
  Panel Threshold Regression (PTR) 104–5, 106, 114
  partial adjustment 33–4, 35, 39, 44; application 39–46
  and prices 14–17
  probit 114
  random walk 58
  STAR 105
  stochastic 215, 218–21
  stock adjustment 35–6
  translog 151, 153–4, 157–61, 162
  trend 29
  trivariate 122
Monfort, A. 42
Moody, C.E. 151
Morck, R. 228
motor vehicle fuel consumption 128, 129
Mount, T.D. 147, 151, 155, 156, 161
Mugele, C. 66
Müllbauer, J. 38
Müller–Furstenberger, G. 99

Nadiri, M.I. 37, 147
Narayan, P.K. 78
natural gas 42, 109, 147
  Europe 172–4
  horizontal diversification 241–4
  long-run price elasticity 159, 160, 163
  portfolio returns 229–30, 245, 246
  prices 13
  2030 global consumption 183
  vertical integration 239, 249
natural gas market 172–4
  integration 172–83
natural monopoly 52
Nelson, C.R. 57, 212
Nerlove, M. 36
Newbery, D.M. 52

Newbold, P. 129
Newell, R. 125
Ng, V. 189
Nguyen, V.N. 212
Nielsen, M.Ø. 171
Nobay, A.R. 9
Nogales, F. 54
non-stationarity 57, 58, 60, 62, 77–8
  and cointegration 77–8
  testing for 78–9, 80, 86–7
Nord Pool 51, 53, 67, 68, 69–72, 186
nuclear energy 3, 71, 109, 147

ODEX-indicators 24
ODYSEE data 24
OECD countries
  impact of oil shocks 168
  oil consumption 122
  technology and intensity 122, 127–42
Ofek, E. 228
oil
  Chinese consumption 94
  Indian consumption 94
  intensity 128, 130; and prices 130–42
  long-run price elasticity 159, 160, 161, 162–3
  portfolio returns 229–30
  units of measurement 3, 5, 109
  see also developing countries; energy
oil industry
  horizontal diversification 241–4
  portfolio returns 245, 246
  vertical integration 238
oil market
  crude and refined prices 171
  as great pool 170
oil prices 12–13, 122, 208
  143-year period 207–23
  1973 rise 30–1, 39, 125, 128, 130, 146
  1981 rise 30–1
  forecasting 220–3
  intensity and fuel rate: causality tests 136–41; cointegration tests 131, 134–6; unit root tests 129–31, 132–4
  mean-reversion 207–8, 210–11, 215, 216–17
  and oil efficiency 140–1
  and oil intensity 130–42
  stochastic modelling 218–21
  and technology 140–1
  time series analysis 208–23
oil shocks 121, 208, 223
  impact in OECD countries 168
  policies following 164
  second 12
OLS 85, 88, 91
  forward-spot prices 196–7
  long-term movements of time series 209
  portfolio returns 234, 235, 237, 238
OPEC oil prices 12, 217
Ordover, J. 227
Osterwald-Lenum, M. 134, 136

panel data analysis
  heterogeneity/homogeneity 103, 118
  income and energy demand 100–4
  macro-panels 102
  micro-panels 102
  nonlinearity tests 111–12
  parameter heterogeneity 102–4
  threshold approach 104–8, 110–11, 116–17, 119
  threshold variable 104–5, 106, 107–8, 110–112, 114, 118
Panel Smooth Threshold Regression (PSTR) model 105–9, 111–15, 116–18
Panel Threshold Regression (PTR) model 104–5, 106, 114
partial adjustment model 39, 44
  application to French consumption 39–46
  autocorrelation of residuals 40–1
Percebois, J. 99
Perron, P. 59, 61, 129, 130, 211–12, 213, 214–16
Perry, M. 226
petroleum products 42, 109
  markets 13
  see also oil
Phillips, P. 59, 61, 62, 137
Pindyck, R.S. 38, 64, 151, 162, 189, 211, 212, 217, 223
Pirrong, C. 189

PJM (Pennsylvania–New Jersey–Maryland) 51, 53, 54, 68–72, 186
  non-stationary prices 63
Plosser, C.I. 57, 212
Poisson processes 55
policy
  consumption and GDP 75
  following oil shocks 164
  and interfuel substitution 146
  interventions 31
  issues 124, 165
  and price forecasts 207
Popp, D. 125
portfolio
  high-minus-low 231, 232
  small-minus-large 231, 232
portfolio returns 225, 226
  analysis of 229–50
  cycles 248–9
  data sources 234–5
  Fama–French method 231–3, 239, 240, 244
  horizontal diversification 228
  market and fuel risks 244–9
  multi-factor approach 233–4
  natural gas industry 245, 246
  positioning and value 236
  pure player 228, 229
  results 235–49
  risk-adjusted 230–1, 233–4, 237, 238, 241, 248
  rolling regressions 232–3, 234, 244, 246–7
  value-weighted 230
  vertical integration 229
power implicit reserves 188, 189–91, 195, 196–7
power industry
  horizontal diversification 241–4
  portfolio returns 245, 246
  reserve capacity 190
  vertical integration 239–41
Powernext 186
Pozzi, C. 186–205, 225–52
Prescott, E.C. 210
price discrimination 226
prices
  and adjustment 42
  cash-and-carry rationale 188
  and deregulation 51, 52
  in econometric models 14–17
  and economic growth 30
  electricity 52–3; characteristics of 68
  evolution of 47
  final consumption 13–14
  forward 188–9
  forward-spot and residual capacity 203
  indices 15–17, 18
  law of one price 168
  leverage effect 66
  oil 12–13
  of primary resources 12–13
  seasonality 71–2
  shocks 63, 65, 72
  spikes 54–5, 63, 64, 190, 192, 193; oil 216–17
  spot: electricity 52–3; forecasting 54–63, 65–72
  spot and forward 186–204; and inventory levels 189, 191; and residual production capacity 189–90, 191–2
  volatility 53, 54, 65–7
primary energy 1, 2, 5, 7
primary equivalence accounting 6
PSTR (Panel Smooth Threshold Regression) model 105–9, 111–15, 116–18
PTR (Panel Threshold Regression) model 104–5, 106, 114
purchasing power parities 83, 110
Putnam, P.C. 98

Ramaswamy, K. 203
random walk 58, 219
rebound effect 123–4, 125, 126–7
regional accounts 4
renewable energies 7, 8
Renou-Maissant, P. 146–65
reserve capacity 190
Richels, R. 126
Ripple, R.D. 171
risk
  diversification 241, 248
  portfolio returns 230–1, 232, 233–4, 244–9

road transport: oil consumption 128
Roberts, M. 55, 66
Robinson, T. 64, 66
Roop, J.M. 15, 20
Rosen, S. 37, 147
Rotemberg, J. 38
Rowe, D.A. 35
Roy's identity 44

Saloner, G. 227
Salop, S. 227
Sari, R. 122
Sauer, D.G. 170–1
Savin, N.E. 157
scale economies 227
Schäfer, A. 100
Schipper, L. 39, 124, 126, 127
Schleifer, A. 228
Schmalensee, R. 101, 115, 118
Schmidt, P. 62
Schurr, S. 125
seasonal patterns of demand 53, 54, 55
secondary energy 2, 5
sectorial accounts 4
Security Market Line (SML) 236–7, 239, 241–2
Serletis, A. 171, 172
shareholder value 228, 249, 250
  and horizontal diversification 227–8
  see also portfolio returns
Shepard's lemma 44, 45, 149
Shin, Y. 62
Shrestha, R.M. 100, 101, 110
Siliverstovs, B. 172
Smyth, R. 78
SO_2 emissions 146, 165
Soligo, R. 101, 103
Soytas, U. 122
Spain 178–80, 182
spline function 211
spot markets 12–13, 171
  electricity 68–72
  gas 173
  and price formation 52–3
stationarity 54, 55–63, 71, 72, 169
  Difference Stationary 57, 58, 61, 63, 72, 177, 178
  trend regression 63
  Trend Stationary 57, 58, 63, 177
Sterner, T. 38
Stigler, G. 227
stochastic processes 33, 34, 40, 56–7, 63
  oil prices 207–8, 211, 218–21
  variables 56, 177
  volatility 66
stock
  accumulation 36
  of equipment 35–6
Stock, J.H. 212
Stoker, T.M. 101, 115, 118
Stoft, S. 65
Stone, J.R. 29, 35
storage theory 187, 188–9, 203
Storchmann, K. 39
Stulz, R. 228
substitution 9, 31, 33
  between energy sources 42, 47
  demand 29–30
  and energy prices 163
  inter-energy 99, 100
  interfuel 146–65
  modelling 146–65
Swamy, P.A. 104

Taheri, A.A. 151, 163
tce (tonne of coal equivalent) 5
technology
  effect of energy price 124–7
  effects on energy consumption 121
  endogenous progress 123
  and energy consumption 140–1
  and oil prices 140–1
Teräsvirta, T. 105, 108, 109
tests
  Augmented Dickey–Fuller 58–9, 60, 129–31, 177–8, 213–14
  of causality 75
  cointegration 80–1, 92; Johansen 91, 175, 178–80; Johansen–Juselius 131, 134
  Dickey–Fuller 58–9, 60, 80, 177
  Elliott–Rothenberg DF-GLS 213
  Jarque–Bera 71, 93, 199, 200, 203
  KPSS 60, 62, 213

tests – *continued*
  non-stationarity 78–9, 80, 86–7
  Perron 214–16
  Phillips–Perron 59, 61–2, 86, 87, 129, 177–8
  unit root 55–63, 64, 80, 129–31; and structural breaks 212–16
  see also causality
thermodynamic laws 5
time series analysis 53–72, 77–9
  forward-spot prices 191–2, 194–5
  oil prices 208–23
  quadratic trend 209
  STAR models 105
  structural breaks 211, 212
Tinbergen, J. 35
Tirole, J. 226, 227
Toda, H.Y. 137
toe (tonne of oil equivalent) 5, 109
toe-aggregates 6, 9, 10–12
Toman, M.A. 99
Tornqvist index 10, 12, 15–17, 18
  and intensity decomposition 21, 22, 23
transformation operations 2, 4, 7, 8
  cost of 13
Treadway, A.B. 37
trend-stationary processes 57, 58, 63
Turvey, R. 9
Type I and Type II error 169

unit root tests 54, 63, 64
  oil intensity and prices 129–31, 132–4
  oil prices 210–12
  and structural breaks 212–16
United Kingdom
  energy cost shares 153
  four-fuel price elasticities 159, 161
  gas market 178–80
  interfuel substitution study 151–65
  market shares of fuels 152
  three-fuel price elasticities 160
United States
  BTU tax 146
  oil market 171
  see also portfolio returns
units of measurement 3, 4, 5, 109, 127
upstream activities 228, 239, 240
Urga, G. 37–8, 151, 161, 163

Value Marginal Products (VMP) 9
Van Dijk, D. 105, 108, 109
VAR (Vector Autoregressive Representation) 39, 80, 129, 136, 137, 139–40
  lags 180
variables
  instrumental 193, 199
  lagged 32–3, 34, 35, 37, 91
Vasicek, O. 218
Vassilopoulos, P. 225–52
VECM (Vector Error-Correction Model) 122, 129, 134, 136–9, 170–1
  market integration 172; gas 174–81, 182
vertical integration 225–7, 228–50
  coal industry 240–1
  natural gas 239, 249
  oil industry 238
  power industry 239–41
  value performance 238–41
  see also portfolio returns
Vishny, R. 228
Vollebergh, H.R.J. 103

Wald test 211, 213
Wales, T.J. 150
Walker, I.O. 164
Walls, W.D. 171, 172
Walters, C. 38, 151, 161, 163
Wang, A. 66
Wårell, L. 171
Watkins, G.C. 9
Waverman, L. 162
Weiner, R. 170–1
Weiss, E. 63
West Texas Intermediate (WTI) 13, 235
white noise 56–7, 59, 70, 71, 180
Wilamoski, P. 171
Williamson, O. 227
wind energy 109
Wing, I. 121
Wirl, F. 126, 164
woods, units of measurement 3
Working, H. 187
Worthington, A. 66

Yang, H. 81, 83

Zarnikau, J. 9, 10
Zellner, A. 157–8
Zhang, F.Q. 20
Zilberfarb, B.Z. 100, 101
Zimmerman, M.B. 32, 38, 42, 75
Zivot, E. 212

GPSR Compliance
The European Union's (EU) General Product Safety Regulation (GPSR) is a set of rules that requires consumer products to be safe and our obligations to ensure this.

If you have any concerns about our products, you can contact us on

ProductSafety@springernature.com

In case Publisher is established outside the EU, the EU authorized representative is:

Springer Nature Customer Service Center GmbH
Europaplatz 3
69115 Heidelberg, Germany

www.ingramcontent.com/pod-product-compliance
Lightning Source LLC
Chambersburg PA
CBHW021016221025
34251CB00034B/5
* 9 7 8 1 4 0 3 9 8 7 4 8 8 *

PJM (Pennsylvania–New Jersey–Maryland) 51, 53, 54, 68–72, 186
  non-stationary prices 63
Plosser, C.I. 57, 212
Poisson processes 55
policy
  consumption and GDP 75
  following oil shocks 164
  and interfuel substitution 146
  interventions 31
  issues 124, 165
  and price forecasts 207
Popp, D. 125
portfolio
  high-minus-low 231, 232
  small-minus-large 231, 232
portfolio returns 225, 226
  analysis of 229–50
  cycles 248–9
  data sources 234–5
  Fama–French method 231–3, 239, 240, 244
  horizontal diversification 228
  market and fuel risks 244–9
  multi-factor approach 233–4
  natural gas industry 245, 246
  positioning and value 236
  pure player 228, 229
  results 235–49
  risk-adjusted 230–1, 233–4, 237, 238, 241, 248
  rolling regressions 232–3, 234, 244, 246–7
  value-weighted 230
  vertical integration 229
power implicit reserves 188, 189–91, 195, 196–7
power industry
  horizontal diversification 241–4
  portfolio returns 245, 246
  reserve capacity 190
  vertical integration 239–41
Powernext 186
Pozzi, C. 186–205, 225–52
Prescott, E.C. 210
price discrimination 226
prices
  and adjustment 42
  cash-and-carry rationale 188
  and deregulation 51, 52
  in econometric models 14–17
  and economic growth 30
  electricity 52–3; characteristics of 68
  evolution of 47
  final consumption 13–14
  forward 188–9
  forward-spot and residual capacity 203
  indices 15–17, 18
  law of one price 168
  leverage effect 66
  oil 12–13
  of primary resources 12–13
  seasonality 71–2
  shocks 63, 65, 72
  spikes 54–5, 63, 64, 190, 192, 193; oil 216–17
  spot: electricity 52–3; forecasting 54–63, 65–72
  spot and forward 186–204; and inventory levels 189, 191; and residual production capacity 189–90, 191–2
  volatility 53, 54, 65–7
primary energy 1, 2, 5, 7
primary equivalence accounting 6
PSTR (Panel Smooth Threshold Regression) model 105–9, 111–15, 116–18
PTR (Panel Threshold Regression) model 104–5, 106, 114
purchasing power parities 83, 110
Putnam, P.C. 98

Ramaswamy, K. 203
random walk 58, 219
rebound effect 123–4, 125, 126–7
regional accounts 4
renewable energies 7, 8
Renou-Maissant, P. 146–65
reserve capacity 190
Richels, R. 126
Ripple, R.D. 171
risk
  diversification 241, 248
  portfolio returns 230–1, 232, 233–4, 244–9

road transport: oil consumption 128
Roberts, M. 55, 66
Robinson, T. 64, 66
Roop, J.M. 15, 20
Rosen, S. 37, 147
Rotemberg, J. 38
Rowe, D.A. 35
Roy's identity 44

Saloner, G. 227
Salop, S. 227
Sari, R. 122
Sauer, D.G. 170–1
Savin, N.E. 157
scale economies 227
Schäfer, A. 100
Schipper, L. 39, 124, 126, 127
Schleifer, A. 228
Schmalensee, R. 101, 115, 118
Schmidt, P. 62
Schurr, S. 125
seasonal patterns of demand 53, 54, 55
secondary energy 2, 5
sectorial accounts 4
Security Market Line (SML) 236–7, 239, 241–2
Serletis, A. 171, 172
shareholder value 228, 249, 250
  and horizontal diversification 227–8
  see also portfolio returns
Shepard's lemma 44, 45, 149
Shin, Y. 62
Shrestha, R.M. 100, 101, 110
Siliverstovs, B. 172
Smyth, R. 78
SO_2 emissions 146, 165
Soligo, R. 101, 103
Soytas, U. 122
Spain 178–80, 182
spline function 211
spot markets 12–13, 171
  electricity 68–72
  gas 173
  and price formation 52–3
stationarity 54, 55–63, 71, 72, 169
  Difference Stationary 57, 58, 61, 63, 72, 177, 178
  trend regression 63
  Trend Stationary 57, 58, 63, 177
Sterner, T. 38
Stigler, G. 227
stochastic processes 33, 34, 40, 56–7, 63
  oil prices 207–8, 211, 218–21
  variables 56, 177
  volatility 66
stock
  accumulation 36
  of equipment 35–6
Stock, J.H. 212
Stoker, T.M. 101, 115, 118
Stoft, S. 65
Stone, J.R. 29, 35
storage theory 187, 188–9, 203
Storchmann, K. 39
Stulz, R. 228
substitution 9, 31, 33
  between energy sources 42, 47
  demand 29–30
  and energy prices 163
  inter-energy 99, 100
  interfuel 146–65
  modelling 146–65
Swamy, P.A. 104

Taheri, A.A. 151, 163
tce (tonne of coal equivalent) 5
technology
  effect of energy price 124–7
  effects on energy consumption 121
  endogenous progress 123
  and energy consumption 140–1
  and oil prices 140–1
Teräsvirta, T. 105, 108, 109
tests
  Augmented Dickey–Fuller 58–9, 60, 129–31, 177–8, 213–14
  of causality 75
  cointegration 80–1, 92; Johansen 91, 175, 178–80; Johansen–Juselius 131, 134
  Dickey–Fuller 58–9, 60, 80, 177
  Elliott–Rothenberg DF-GLS 213
  Jarque–Bera 71, 93, 199, 200, 203
  KPSS 60, 62, 213